A History of the Life of Edward the Black Prince: And of Various Events Connected Therwith, Which Occurred During the Reign of Edward Iii, King of England, Volume 1

George Payne Rainsford James

HISTORY

OF

EDWARD THE BLACK PRINCE

VOL. I.

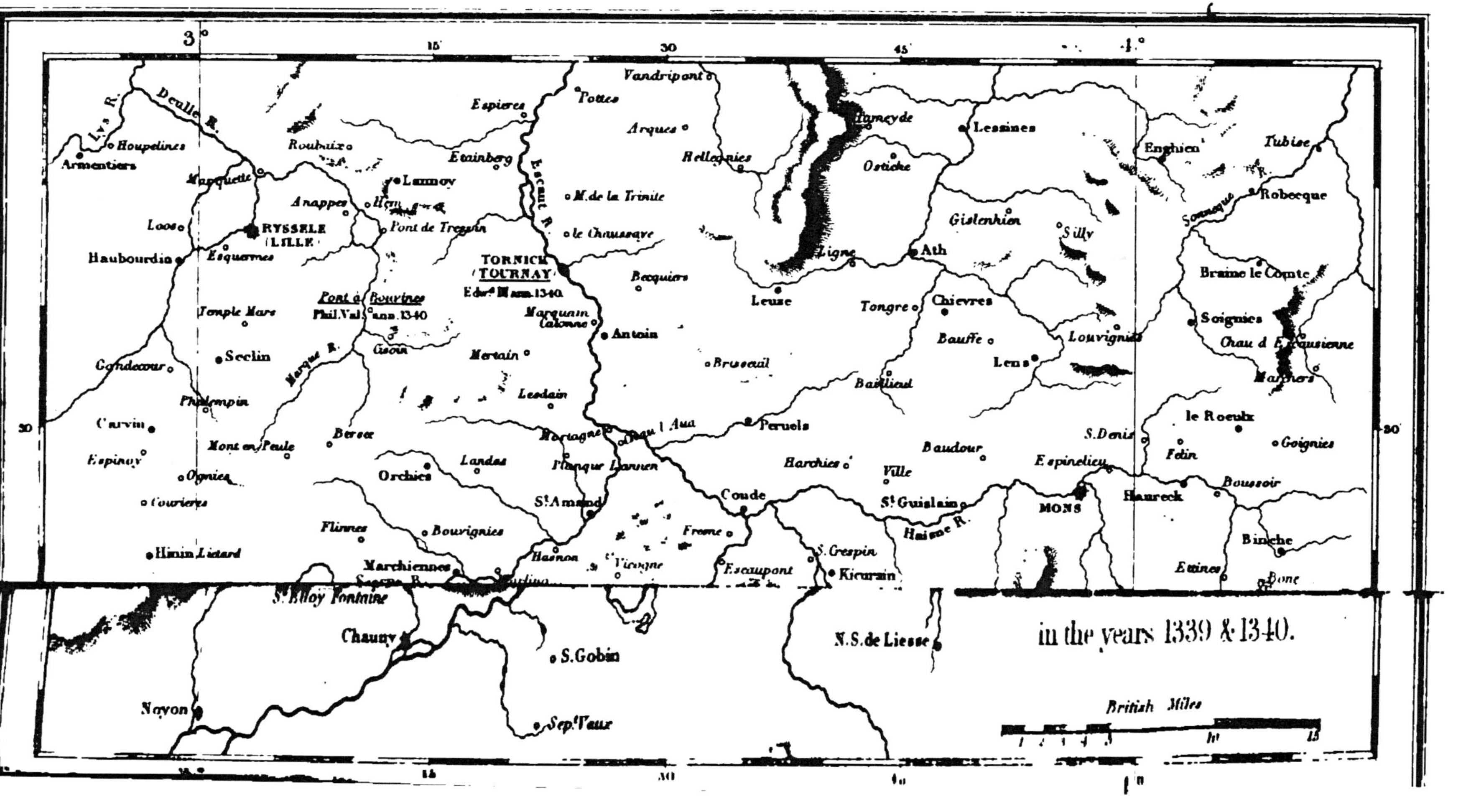

in the years 1339 & 1340.
British Miles
Lys R.
Deulle R.
Houpelines
Armentiers
Marquette
Roubaix
Loos
RYSSELE (LILLE)
Esquermes
Hauboudin
Anappes
Lannoy
Pont de Tressin
Espieres
Etainberg
Escaut R.
TORNICK (TOURNAY)
Edwd III ann. 1340.
Pont à Bouvines
Phil. Val. ann. 1340
Temple Mars
Seclin
Marque R.
Gondecour
Phalempin
Carvin
Espinoy
Mont en Peule
Ognies
Courieres
Hinin Lietard
Bersee
Orchies
Flinnes
Bourignies
Marchiennes
Scarpe R.
St. Amand
Landas
Mortagne
Flinque Lannen
Hasnon
Vicogne
Marquain
Calonne
Antoin
Mertain
Lesdain
Vandripont
Pottes
Arques
Hellegnies
M. de la Trinite
le Chaussaye
Becquiers
Leuze
Brusseuil
Peruels
Coude
Frome
Escaupont
S. Grespin
Kieurain
Ligne
Ostiche
Lessines
Ath
Gislenhien
Silly
Tongre
Chievres
Bauffe
Lens
Bailliul
Baudour
Harchies
Ville
St. Guislain
Haisne R.
MONS
Espinelieu
S. Denis
Louvignies
Enghien
Tubise
Robecque
Braine le Comte
Soignies
Chau d'Ecausienne
le Roeulx
Goignies
Fetin
Haureck
Boussoir
Binche
Ettines
Bone
St. Eloy Fontaine
Chauny
S. Gobin
Noyon
Sep. Vaux
N.S. de Liesse

A

HISTORY

OF

THE LIFE

OF

EDWARD THE BLACK PRINCE

AND OF

VARIOUS EVENTS CONNECTED THEREWITH,

WHICH OCCURRED DURING THE REIGN OF EDWARD III.

KING OF ENGLAND.

BY G. P. R. JAMES, ESQ.

IN TWO VOLUMES.

VOL. I.

LONDON:

PRINTED FOR

LONGMAN, REES, ORME, BROWN, GREEN, & LONGMAN,

PATERNOSTER-ROW.

1836.

TO

HER ROYAL HIGHNESS

THE PRINCESS VICTORIA;

THIS HISTORY

OF

A GREAT AND AMIABLE PRINCE,

WHO,

WHILE BY HIS PRIVATE VIRTUES HE ADORNED OUR COMMON NATURE,
BY HIS PUBLIC SERVICES AND NOBLE QUALITIES
RAISED TO THE HIGHEST POINT THE GLORY OF HIS COUNTRY,
AND ILLUSTRATED AN ILLUSTRIOUS RACE,

IS,

BY HER PERMISSION,

DEDICATED,

WITH EVERY ASPIRATION FOR HER HAPPINESS,
AND EVERY FEELING OF RESPECT,
BY HER ROYAL HIGHNESS'S
MOST OBEDIENT AND DEVOTED SERVANT,

G. P. R. JAMES.

PREFACE.

In submitting to the public what will probably be my last work of History, I may be permitted to say a few words in regard to the plan I have pursued in writing it; and to notice some omissions, which might reasonably be considered as the effect of carelessness, if the causes which induced me to make them were not explained. The struggle between France and England, which began with the unjust pretensions of Edward III. to the crown of the former country, naturally divides itself into four great acts. The first comprises the Gallic conquests of Edward and his son; the second, the cunning and gradual, but bold and masterly, recovery of his alienated territory, by Charles V. of France; the third, the re-conquest of nearly the whole of the disputed country by Henry V. of England; and the fourth, the expulsion of the invaders by Charles VII. It was my wish to give a sketch of the first of these epochs, which began and concluded in the space of time embraced by the life of Edward the Black

Prince. In pursuit of this object, it was open to me, either to notice particularly the affairs of Scotland and Ireland, or to pass over the latter country entirely, and only to refer to those events in the history of the former, which affected the immediate subject of my labours. I determined on the latter course, as I found that the work, with all the critical inquiries into particular facts which it behoved me to institute, might extend to a size likely to try the patience of the public, without the admission of any extraneous matter.

In the course of investigation, a number of errors in the former histories of this epoch were, as may well be supposed, rendered apparent: but the fact of having detected numerous faults in other writers upon the same subject, has inspired me with any thing but great confidence in my own work. I have, it is true, spared no pains, I have spared no reasonable expense, to discover and obtain correct sources of information; and during five years, which the manuscript has lain by me since it was first written, I have made many alterations, and, I trust, some improvements. I have put forth nothing without much consideration; and I have not suffered any peculiar fondness for particular theories to prevent me from sacrificing my opinions, whenever I have had good reasons for believing them to be erroneous. Nevertheless, I well know that, till the great mass of public documents which have long been withheld from general inspection, and which are even now only scantily available, shall be completely and judiciously thrown open to the nation, to whom they belong, nothing like an accurate history of the country can be written, and that every separate portion must appear with great defects. Still farther,—were those storehouses of important information open to me at will, with the best catalogues for facilitating my researches, I am but too conscious that my own imperfections of judgment and application would communicate themselves to the work, and would render it very different from that which I could wish to lay before the public. Many, indeed the greater part, of the defects which will be found in this book, are, of course, to be attributed to myself: nevertheless, various difficulties lie in the way of the historian who considers it his duty to ascertain facts ere he ventures to reason upon them; and these difficulties not only require great labour, but very considerable expense to remove. As an illustration of this truth, I may mention, that in regard to several points of Flemish history, intimately connected with the life of Edward the Black Prince, I entertained serious doubts, in order to solve which I made a journey to the town of Ghent. Monsieur Wallez, the Belgian Secretary of Legation at the British court, a gentleman as much distinguished for his acquirements as for his urbanity, had accidentally pointed out to me, without, I believe, knowing my pursuits, several sources of information in his native country; but, after spending some time in Ghent, I quitted it, disappointed, and as ignorant as I went. The book then proceeded on the authorities I had before possessed, and was partly printed, when a lingering hope of better success, together with doubts that I could not shake off regarding the accuracy of various details, led me to revisit that city, where, by the kind attention of Monsieur Voisin and the celebrated Cornelissen, I at length obtained information that led me to cancel several sheets, which had unfortunately gone through the press. The same has been the case in other parts of the work; and I have not the slightest doubt that, could I arrive at the original documents, by which the facts of history can alone be clearly established, I should still find much that would require alteration.

In regard to the more modern histories relating to the period of which I have treated, I have read almost every thing, I believe, that has been written; and in many instances it will be found that I have entirely differed from authors of very good repute. In some cases, where the point was of importance, I have stated my reasons, and referred to what has been said on the other side of the question. I have almost always given my authorities upon matters in regard to which there could be any doubt, and have sometimes entered into discussions respecting the credibility of various chronicles, pointing out the process by which my mind had arrived at the conclusion which I have ultimately adopted. But to have done this in all instances, even where I differed with very respectable writers, would have overloaded the book with notes, which are, perhaps, too abundant already; and I was obliged to refrain, though from no want of respect for the gentlemen from whose views I presumed to dissent. Various points in the course of the history of Edward the Black Prince, though mentioned by all the contemporary writers, have still appeared to me uncertain; and wherever I have entertained a suspicion of any asserted fact, although I have felt myself bound to give it admission, I have endeavoured to mark it by some expression of doubt.

Having said thus much, nothing, I believe, remains for me, but to offer my sincere thanks,—first, to the public, for long-continued favour; and, next, to the various gentlemen who, with the true liberality of spirit which should always distinguish literary men, have given me the kindest assistance in my laborious task. To Professor Napier, to the Reverend Doctor Lamb, to Sir Harris Nicolas, to Monsieur Cornelissen and Monsieur Voisin, to Professor Bähr, and to Monsieur Zacharia, junior, with a number of other gentlemen, who have aided me materially, by pointing out to me, and obtaining for me, valuable sources of information, I feel myself deeply indebted, and am proud to acknowledge it in this place. To Lord Polwarth, Lord Strangford, and many other gentlemen, especially those in whose hands the archives of the city of London are deposited, I have also to return my thanks for much kindness in the course of my labours upon this history. Though for those labours I anticipate no very great success, yet I am well pleased that they have been undertaken and completed; and only trust that they may not be found altogether unworthy of the kindness of those who have watched their progress with interest.

CONTENTS

OF

THE FIRST VOLUME.

INTRODUCTION.

Page

General Sketch of the relative State of England, France, and the Empire, in the early Part of the Fourteenth Century. - - - - - 1

CHAPTER I.

The Deposition of Edward II. — Isabella and Mortimer.— Marriage of Edward III. to Philippa of Hainault.— Death of Charles Le Bel. — Contest for the Regency of France. — Accession of Philip of Valois. — His Expedition against the Flemings. — He demands Homage of Edward III. for Acquitaine, &c.—Edward does Homage. — Birth of Edward the Black Prince. - - 18

CHAP. II.

The Execution of the Earl of Kent. —The Arrest and Execution of Mortimer.—Feuds on the Confines of Guyenne. — Capture of Sainctes and subsequent Negotiations. — Edward's Secret Visit to Philip of Valois. — The Effect of his Confidence on the French King. — Tournaments and chivalrous Exercises of the English Court.—Those Sports the Cause of political Advantages to England. — Invasion of Scotland by Edward Baliol. — Doubtful Conduct of Edward III. on that occasion. — Negotiations

Page

with France regarding the Marriage of Prince Edward. — War with Scotland. — Infancy of Edward the Black Prince. - - - - - - 44

CHAP. III.

The first Inducements which led Edward III. to invade France. — The Character and Life of Robert of Artois. — He aids Philip of Valois to ascend the Throne. — Renews his Claim to the County of Artois. — Is banished and persecuted by the King. — Takes Refuge in England. — His honourable Reception by Edward III., then engaged in the Scottish War. — The Conduct of Baliol. — Philip of Valois privately supports the Scots. — A New Crusade preached by Pope Benedict XII. — Philip visits Avignon, takes the Cross, and makes Preparations for a Holy War. — His Motives examined. — He sends an Embassy to Edward demanding his Co-operation. — Edward's Reply and subsequent Proposals. — Philip refuses to bind himself to give no Assistance to the Scots during Edward's Absence. — War determined on. — Robert of Artois seizes the Moment to urge an Invasion of France. — Edward resolves to follow his Suggestion. — Preparation for Confederation against Philip. — Edward the Black Prince created Duke of Cornwall. - - - - - - 67

CHAP. IV.

Preparations for War. — Constitution of Parliaments. — Parliamentary Grants to the King. — Other Means employed by Edward III. to raise Money. — Great Scarcity of Specie. — Defensive Preparations. — Constitution of the English Army. — Negotiations on the Continent. — State of Flanders. — Jacob Van Artevelde. — Death of the Count of Hainault. — Negotiations with the Emperor. — Interference of the Pope. - - 91

CHAP. V.

Page

Attempt to seize the English Ambassadors in Belgium.— The Ambuscade at Cadsand.— Battle of Cadsand and Defeat of the Flemings.— Negotiations for the Preservation of Peace.—Edward sails for Belgium.— Tedious Negotiations with his Allies.—Duplicity of the Duke of Brabant.— Conference between Edward III. and the Emperor.—The King of England created Vicar of the Empire.— Holds an Assembly of the Barons at Herck.— Is joined by Philippa.— Farther Negotiations and Preparations. - - - - - - 120

CHAP. VI.

Delays of Edward's German Allies.—Formal Declaration of War.— Attack of Mortagne.—Capture of Thun L'Evêque.—The King of England begins his March alone.—Confers with the Duke of Brabant at Brussels. —Is joined by a Part of his Allies.—Undertakes the Siege of Cambray.—The Duke of Brabant joins the Allies.— Siege of Cambray.—Philip's Preparations.— His Fleets ravage the English Coast.—He collects an Army to relieve Cambray.— Edward marches to meet him.— Passes the Scheld.— The Line of March.— Preparations for a Battle.—Philip's Reasons for avoiding a general Engagement.— The Two Armies separate. - 140

CHAP. VII.

Difficulties of Edward III. at the End of the War. —Views and Conduct of Artevelde.— Negotiations with the Duke of Brabant.— Congress at Brussels.— The Flemings propose that Edward should assume the Title of King of France.—Their Motives.—He accedes.—The Flemings acknowledge him as King of France.— He sails for England.—Proceedings of his Parliament.—Philip permits his Troops to ravage Hainault.— Indignation and Preparations of the Count.— He declares War against Philip.

Page
—Aubenton taken.—The Thierasche ravaged.—Alliances of the Count of Hainault.—Siege of Thun L'Evêque.—The Count of Hainault marches to its Relief.—Escape of the Garrison. - - - - 171

CHAP. VIII.

The French prepare to intercept Edward on his Return to Flanders — Edward sets Sail.— Battle of Sluys, and total Defeat of the French.—Oration of Jacob Van Artevelde.— Parliament of Villevorde, and Federal Union of the Netherlands.— The Pope and the King of Sicily endeavour to effect a Peace.— Edward and his Allies besiege Tournay.—The Flemings besiege St. Omer.—Edward challenges the King of France to single Combat.— Philip of Valois declines.— The Flemings defeated before St. Omer.— Siege of Tournay.— Of Mortagne.— Siege and Destruction of St. Amand.— Alleged Perfidy of the Duke of Brabant.—Joan of Valois carries on the Negotiations for Peace.— Edward's Difficulties.— Progress of the French in Aquitaine.— Of the Scots in Scotland and the North of England.— Peculations in the English Exchequer.— A Truce concluded.— Edward waits for Supplies to discharge his Debts on the Continent.— Sets out privately for England.—Finds Negligence and Confusion. - - 202

CHAP. IX.

Proceedings of Edward III. against Defaulters, &c.—Insolent Resistance and Humiliation of the Archbishop of Canterbury.— Exactions of the Parliament.— Edward grants the Statute required.— Annuls it after the Sessions.— Advantages gained by Philip during the Truce.— The Death of John Duke of Britanny, and its Consequences.— The Truce renewed.— Return of David Bruce to Scotland.— War renewed in the North of Britain.— Edward invades Scotland.— Story regarding the Countess of Salisbury examined. - - 247

CHAP. X.

Page

The State of France. — Death of John III. Duke of Britanny. — Claimants of the Duchy. — Their Claims considered. — Not affected by the Salic Law. — Measures of John III. to secure the Duchy uncontested to his Niece, Joan of Penthièvre. — The Count de Montford assumes the Title of Duke, and gains the Citizens of Nantes. — Takes Possession of the Treasures of Limoges. — Attacks and takes the Towns of Brest and Rennes. — Hennebon taken by Stratagem. — Vannes, Auray, and Guy la Foret, Surrender. — La Roche Periou makes good its Resistance. — Carhaix on the Sea surrendered by the Bishop of Quimper. — De Montford's Apprehensions. — Visits England in secret, and does Homage to Edward III. as King of France. — Returns to France, and attends the Court of Peers. — Finds his Cause prejudged, and his Visit to England known. — Makes his Escape from Paris by Stratagem, and retires to Nantes. — Charles of Blois takes the Field with great Force. — Nantes besieged. — The Burghers and Garrison betray De Montford. — Nantes surrendered. — De Montford made Prisoner. - - - - 266

CHAP. XI.

Heroic Conduct of the Countess de Montford. — She sends to implore Aid from the King of England. — Edward despatches Sir Walter de Mauny to her Assistance. — Siege of Rennes. — The Inhabitants rise against their Governor, and deliver the City to Charles of Blois. — Siege of Hennebon. — Exploits of the Countess de Montford. — The City straitened. — Treachery of the Bishop of Quimper. — The Garrison treat for a Surrender. — The English Fleet arrives. — Confidence restored. — Destruction of the French battering Engine. — Exploits of Sir Walter de Mauny. — The Siege raised. - - 289

CHAP. XII.

Page

Don Louis of Spain ravages Britanny.—Is pursued and defeated near Quimperlé by Sir Walter de Mauny.—Unsuccessful Attempts of the British Forces against La Rocheperiou and Faouet.—Auray and Vannes taken by Charles of Blois.—Affairs of Spain.—Second Siege of Hennebon.—Cruelty of Don Louis of Spain towards two Prisoners.—Exploits of Almeric De Clisson and Walter De Mauny.—The Prisoners rescued.—The Earl of Northampton and Robert of Artois sail in Aid of Joan de Montford.—Naval Engagement off Guernsey.—Vannes retaken by the English.—Left without sufficient Defence.—Retaken by the French.—Death of Robert of Artois. - - - - - - 309

CHAP. XIII.

Edward III. sails for Britanny in Person.—Takes Ploermel, Malestroit, Redon, &c., and besieges Vannes.—The Lords of Clisson, Loheac, Machecoul, and Retz, come over to the Party of de Montford.—The Pope sends Legates to treat concerning Peace.—The Earls of Norfolk and Warwick attack Nantes.—Raise the Siege, and retire on the Approach of the Duke of Normandy.—The English straitened in their Camp.—The Legates obtain a Truce.—The Treaty of Malestroit.—Violated by Philip, who puts to Death Fifteen Breton Nobles.—Indignation of the King of England and of the French Nobility.—Several of the Nobles of Normandy put to Death by Philip.—Godfrey of Harcourt makes his Escape, and ultimately takes Refuge in England. - -

CHAP. XIV.

Edward III. resists the Pretensions of the Ho[illegible]
Fruitless Negotiations before the Pope conce[illegible]
Peace.—Edward courts the Flemings.-
with the Duke of Brabant concerning [illegible]

Page

the Black Prince. — Negotiations with the King of Castille. — With the Kings of Portugal and Arragon. — A brief Account of the State of Society in the Fourteenth Century. - - - - 355

CHAP. XV.

Entrance of Edward the Black Prince into active Life. — He is created Prince of Wales. — A Feast of the Round Table proclaimed. — Death of the Earl of Norfolk. — Jealousy of Philip of Valois. — Violation of the Truce of Malestroit. — The British Parliament supports the King. — Edward's Remonstrances and Threats. — The Earl of Northampton commanded to declare War against Philip. — Edward's Manifesto. — De Montford escapes from Imprisonment. — Does Homage publicly to Edward for the Dukedom of Britanny. — Godfrey de Harcourt arrives at the Court of England. — Does Homage for his Lands in France. — The Earl of Northampton sails for Britanny, together with De Montford. — The Earl of Derby sails for Aquitaine. — Secret Expedition of the King and the Black Prince. - - - - 388

CHAP. XVI.

Motives and Proceedings of Jacob Van Artevelde. — Edward III. arrives at Sluys. — Conference with the Flemish Councils on board the King's Ship. — Artevelde proposes to raise Flanders to a Dukedom, and give the Coronet to Edward the Black Prince. — Difficulties of the Burghers. Conduct of Artevelde. — He gains Bruges and Ipres. — Neglects Ghent. — Machinations against him in that City. — He returns to Ghent. — Is besieged in his House. — His Death and Character. — Edward sails for England. 409

CHAP. XVII.

Page

Edward the Black Prince prepares to accompany his Father to France.—His Want of Economy.—Delays of the Expedition.—It sails for Normandy.—Proceedings at La Hogue.—The Black Prince knighted.—Valognes, Carenton, and St. Lo taken.—Storming of Caen.—Louviers and the Pont de l'Arche sacked.—March towards Paris.—Philip's Preparations.—Edward's ineffectual Efforts to pass the Seine.—The Passage effected.—Philip in force follows the British Army.—Edward attempts to pass the Somme.—Critical Situation of the King of England.—Passage of the Somme, and Battle of Blanche Tache. 428

CHAP. XVIII.

The Battle of Cressy. - - - - - - 464

CHAP. XIX.

Dispersed Parties of French defeated.—Number of Slain.—Edward undertakes the Siege of Calais.—Preparations for the Siege.—Philip of Valois makes new Efforts.—Determines to recall his Troops from Aquitaine and Britanny.—Negotiates with the Flemings—And with David King of Scotland. - - - - - 491

CHAP. XX.

Affairs of Guyenne.—The Earl of Lancaster arrives in Gascony.—Takes the Field against the Count de Lille.—Takes Bergerac by Storm.—Marches on Perigord.—Bold Exploit of the French Garrison of Perigueux.—Convention with the Count of Perigord.—Auberoche taken.—The Duke of Normandy arrives to defend Aqui-

Page

taine. — The French besiege Auberoche. — The Earl of Lancaster marches to its Relief. — Total Defeat of the French. — S. Baseille, Rochemeillon, Montsegur, and Aiguillon taken. — Siege and Capture of La Reole. — Farther Successes. — The Duke of Normandy takes the Field. — Angoulême reduced. — The Seneschal of Beaucaire takes St. Jéan d'Angely. — Siege of Aiguillon. — The French repulsed at all Points. — The Siege raised. — The Duke of Normandy retreats from Guyenne. — Farther Successes of the Earl of Lancaster. — He sails for England. - - - - - - - 507

THE

HISTORY

OF

EDWARD THE BLACK PRINCE.

INTRODUCTION.

GENERAL SKETCH OF THE RELATIVE STATE OF ENGLAND, FRANCE, AND THE EMPIRE, IN THE EARLY PART OF THE FOURTEENTH CENTURY.

THAT great men make opportunities, is one of the most common aphorisms of human vanity; but the history of every age and of every country affords sufficient proof, that the circumstances under which each individual is placed have as much influence upon his fate and conduct as the qualities of his mind and heart. Events, indeed, are seldom so adverse, that a man of real genius or pre-eminent virtue cannot, at some period of his life, find occasion to break through the petty crowd, and take his station amongst the great; but the annals of the world evince that few, if any, of those who have climbed to the highest pinnacles of fame, have not, at some point in their career, been peculiarly favoured by opportunity. True it is, that the most hopeful means afford, to the fool, the coward, or the sluggard, but opportunity of displaying defects; yet still, without some happy opening, energy can never clear the way through all impediments, and genius, with all his wings, can never soar above the prison walls of circumstance. The events which take place around us, and the mind which is within, act and react upon each other; and these two causes, sometimes opposing, sometimes facilitating one another, according to the all-wise will of Him who alone sees the ultimate result, work out the destiny of each intelligent creature.

There can be no doubt that, born at any epoch, or placed in any situation, Edward the Black Prince would have displayed the talents that command respect, and the virtues that endear the possessor; but they might have been restricted to the decoration of private life, had they not received a more splendid developement from his proximity to a throne. Nor were the circumstances of his birth or of his rank the only concurrents which placed within his grasp an immortal reputation; but the circumstances, also, of his times, his nation, and his family, were precisely those best calculated to call forth the qualities with which God had endowed him as an individual. His history, therefore, may be said to commence before his birth, and the actions of others must not be considered irrelevant, when they prepared the way for his own. At the same time, the state of society in which he lived, and the condition of the countries in which his principal actions were performed, are not unworthy of consideration, as the peculiarities of each materially affected his own fate. I shall, accordingly, pause for a moment, to make a few preliminary observations upon the political and religious system of Europe at that period; and shall endeavour, by noticing several of the differences which existed in the circumstances of France, Germany, and England, to point out some of the causes which contributed to produce the great military advantages that the latter country obtained during the reign of Edward III.

About the period in which Edward the Black Prince flourished, there existed that degree of restlessness and agitation in the minds of men, which is generally a prognostic of some great change in the state of society. Various efforts were made by persons of the most opposite classes and characters, and by the most opposite means and directions, to shake many old institutions, and to tear up many deeply rooted prejudices, although the result proved that the human mind — the soil in which such institutions and prejudices were founded and planted — was by no means prepared for their destruction.

It is evident that before a complete, though beneficial, alteration can ever be effected in any of the great establishments of society, it must be called for most strongly by an equal change in the circumstances of man. He must have become infinitely better, wiser, nobler, increased in numbers, or elevated in powers, since those establishments were framed; he must, in short, have undergone some of the immense variations which are continually occurring in his situation and attributes, before any permanent amelioration can be effected in his institutions. Nevertheless, it generally happens that, long before the progress of the human race will bear the change which it ultimately works out for itself, there start up spirits who forestal the age, and endeavour to hurry forward mankind to the object towards which they see it tending. Not a few of such spirits arose in the course of the fourteenth century, and it is not at all improbable that their efforts shook the fabric which they were not able to overthrow; but it will be evident to any one who fixes his eyes upon the picture that historians, satirists, and moralists have left of the human mind at this epoch, that though many persons of superior intellect existed both in the higher and the lower ranks of life, society in general was not at all prepared to yield at once the abuses of the feudal system, or to cast away the superstitions which had crept into the Roman church.

In almost every country in Europe, the feudal system was already on the decline. In England it had suffered most, and in Germany, perhaps, least; but in every land its own inherent defects, and the vices of the nobles, supplied a plentiful germ of decay; while the admission of the free communes showed an anomaly in its constitution, and a step towards its fall. Nevertheless, it had still to support it habit, possession, military skill, and the spirit of chivalry; while the paucity and the smallness of the cities, and the brutal ignorance of the commons in every country, with the exception of England, evinced that the lower classes themselves were as yet incapable either of effecting with power, or employing with moderation, a change in their institutions.

In regard to the Roman church, though the thunders of the Apostolic See were not quite so tremendous as they once had been *, and though several recorded instances of successful resistance formed precedents for future opposition, yet the immortal policy of the Ecclesiastical State was so much more refined than that of any other European court, that prudence, supported by the ignorance of opponents, still supplied, in an extraordinary degree, the want of real power. Nor was society prepared for a change in ecclesiastical affairs; for if we but look to the trials of the Templars, the massacres of the Jews and lepers †, and the barbarous executions which not un-

* The clear and judicious Mosheim traces the decline of the papal power to the period of the bold though barbarous resistance of Philip the Fair to the arrogant pretensions of Boniface VIII. A severe blow, however, had been given to the authority of the Popes by the bitter contempt with which they had been treated by the Emperor Frederic.

† We find recorded by the continuators of William of Nangis the fact of two or three unhappy wretches having been burnt alive, in the year 1322, for burying a black cat in a box; and a little earlier, the following horrible details are given concerning the massacres of the lepers and the Jews: —

"In the year of our Lord 1321, the King of France visited carefully the parts of Poitou, which he held of his father by hereditary right, and he had resolved, they say, to remain there long, when, towards the festival of St. John the Baptist, the public report reached his ears, that throughout all Aquitaine the springs and the wells either were, or soon would be, infected with poison by a great number of lepers. Many of these lepers, acknowledging their crime, had been already condemned to death and burnt in Upper Aquitaine. Their design was, as they avowed in the midst of the flames, in spreading poison every where, to destroy all the Christians, or at least to render them lepers like themselves; and they sought to spread so great an evil over all France and

frequently followed the frivolities of scholastic dis-

Germany. Various different causes were assigned for these things by various people; but the best founded, and most commonly adopted, was this which follows. The King of Grenada, afflicted at having been so frequently defeated by the Christians, and especially by the uncle of the King of Castile, of whom we have spoken before, and not being able to avenge himself by force of arms, sought to accomplish his purpose by villany. For this reason, it is said, he held a meeting with the Jews, to endeavour by their means to destroy the whole of Christendom by some charm, and offered them innumerable sums of money. They promised him to invent a charm, saying that they could by no means execute it themselves, because the Christians suspected them; but that the lepers, who were in continual communication with the Christians, could very easily accomplish the charm, by casting the poison into all the springs and wells. On this account, the Jews having called together the principal lepers, these last, by the intervention of the devil, were so seduced by their deceitful suggestions that, after having abjured the catholic faith, and, horrible to hear, pounded and mixed the body of Christ in these mortal poisons, as many of the lepers ultimately confessed, consented to execute the charm. The principal lepers, having met together from all parts of Christendom, established four general assemblies; and there was not a noble lazar house, as some of the lepers have since acknowledged, from which some one was not present at these assemblies, to inform the rest what was done there, with the exception of the two lazar houses in England. By the persuasion of the devil, served by the Jews in these assemblies of lepers, the principal amongst them said to the others, that, as their leprosy made them appear to the Christians vile, abject, and unworthy of any consideration, it was perfectly justifiable in them to cause the Christians to die or become covered with leprosy like themselves, so that, when all were lepers, none would be despised. . . . . .
An edict of the king on the subject of the lepers declared that the guilty should be given to the flames, and the rest confined for ever in the lazar houses; and that, if any leprous woman was found with child, she should be preserved till she was delivered, and then burned. The Jews also were burned in some countries, especially in Aquitaine. In the bailiwick of Tours, at a castle called Chinon, an immense pit was dug, and a great fire having been lighted in it, there were burned in a single day one hundred and sixty Jews of both sexes. Many of them, both men and women, sung as if invited to a wedding, and sprang of themselves into the pit; and many widows threw their own children

putation *, we shall find that priest and lawyer, noble and commoner alike, were still imbued with the same dark and gloomy superstition; and that those who dreamed of purer systems, or of better things, were only the few whose minds outstripped the age.

Real power, however, was beginning to make itself felt, occasionally, in opposition to the ideal authority of the church; and while the spiritual dogmas of the Roman See were treated with reverence and received as law, its judicial rule and temporal dominion had, from time to time, to encounter many a potent adversary amongst the crowned heads of Europe. In order to maintain themselves against these enemies, the popes were under the necessity of having recourse to the friendship of other princes; and, amongst the incessant contentions of a warlike age, powerful support was always to be found when required by the pontiffs. At the same time it is clear, that the allies and supporters of the Roman church learned the secret of its weakness by its frequent applications for assistance, and were taught to despise its threats when they found it convenient to resist its authority.

---

into the fire, for fear they should be torn from them, and baptized by the Christians and nobles present at the execution."

Such was the dreadful state of superstition and barbarism in which Europe was plunged at the beginning of the fourteenth century.

* A number of persons were burnt as heretics about this time, for the crime of declaring that our Saviour had been, in this world, possessed of property. The particulars of the dispute are too indecent and sacrilegious, to bear recapitulation with either pleasure or advantage to any one.

One of the most formidable opponents which the bishops of Rome had as yet encountered was Louis of Bavaria, who occupied the Imperial throne at the accession of Edward III. to the crown of England. Elected Emperor in 1314, by a majority of the electors, he soon saw himself opposed in arms by the unsuccessful candidate, Frederic, Duke of Austria; but, after a severe struggle, succeeded in making his title good with the sword. All his first acts, however, showed a determination to check the encroaching spirit of the Apostolic See: he proceeded to exercise the authority of emperor without the papal approbation; denied the right of the pontiffs to interfere in the Imperial election; invaded Italy, created an Anti-pope, and scoffed at the anathemas of Avignon.

Although the most considerable portion of Europe remained docile to the injunctions of the Holy See, and the Pope rested secure upon the bosom of France, at that time the favourite child of the church; yet the spectacle of one of the greatest monarchs of the age — whether considered in regard to dominion or talent — ruling powerfully in absolute contempt of the ecclesiastical authority, was, of course, not lost upon contemporary sovereigns. Its effect upon other countries does not require to be noticed here more particularly; and the consequences which followed, in regard to England, both from the fact of the Emperor's enmity towards the church, and from the precedent of resistance which his conduct afforded, will be traced at large hereafter. Such, however, at the accession of Edward III., was the situation of the empire in its relations with the Roman See. It was governed by a talented, courageous, contumacious, and excommunicated monarch; many of whose vassals would willingly have made his quarrel with the Pope an excuse for rebellion, had they not already suffered from the power of chastisement afforded him by his great military abilities.

In comparing the sources of power which at that time existed in Germany, France, and England, it must be remembered that, in geographical position and territorial extent, the empire, in the fourteenth century, occupied a space very different from that which it filled in Europe at the time of its overthrow by the Emperor Napoleon. The frontier provinces of almost all feudal states were portioned out amongst a number of great vassals, whose dependence upon their sovereign was very limited in itself, and very insecure in its duration. Such was more particularly the case with the empire, from various peculiarities in its constitution as a state; and, scattered in an irregular line along the boundaries of the great neighbouring kingdom of France, lay the fiefs of many powerful feudatories, whose subjection to the Emperor was more nominal than real. The greater part of Lorraine and Alsace, and the whole of Belgium, were divided into dukedoms, counties, and marquisates, over each of which either the Emperor or the King of France claimed the right of sovereignty: although the frontiers were seldom well defined, the right was very often doubtful, and the vassal was frequently arrayed in arms against his lord.

In this last respect, indeed, the law of feudal government was very loose. The right of armed resistance to the sovereign was recognised in many cases; but, as the express circumstances in which the appeal to force against the highest authority in the state was justifiable in the vassal, cannot be clearly established, it would seem that, in this, as in many other instances, the power to render the opposition successful, legalised the fact.

In Germany, however, the diets of the empire, and in France the King's Court of Peers, might have afforded a competent tribunal for the decision of all difficult points of feudal jurisprudence; and it would seem, at first sight, that judges who were the equals of the vassal would be naturally disposed to guard his privileges, inasmuch as they participated in the rights which they defended. But, in a dark state of society, future interests, even of great importance, are seldom suffered to counterbalance immediate advantages; and we find continued evidence to prove that the influence of the sovereigns who presided in the German diet and the French court of Peers — the fear of their power or the desire of their favour, — frequently outweighed, in the minds of the members composing those assemblies, the care of remote rights, or the apprehension of contingent dangers.

An elective empire, though, perhaps, more calculated for durability, can seldom be so actively powerful as a hereditary monarchy. There must be discrepant interests in its various parts, tending to divert its energies from external exertion towards intestine strife; and a sovereign can seldom be elected, without having to waste much of the time, and wisdom, and power, which are but scantily allotted to any man, in crushing the factions to which his nomination has given rise, and repressing the adherents of less successful candidates. Thus the immense natural power of Germany has been constantly shackled by the complication of its constitution, and the difficulty of producing rapid union in its various parts.

Not so France: united under one monarch, who, in general, succeeded unopposed to the throne, to the power, and to the resources of his predecessor, with a number of vassals who might be called into the field at a very short notice, and with no cause of discord permanently existing among them, she appeared free to pursue resolutely any continuous train of policy, and to act with the vigour of her whole people in whatever manner occasion might require. This capability of rapid exertion, however, was more apparent than real; and the prudence or policy, the vigour or the ambition, of her monarchs, could effect but little externally, unless supported by the will of her great nobles.

We must not forget, while considering the situation of France, that in the fourteenth century that country did not possess the territorial extent which her boundaries comprise at this day; and that the king, in common with all feudal monarchs, held but a very limited jurisdiction even over a great part of that portion of Europe which acknowledged his dominion. In the south, the kingdom of Aragon, however nearly allied to the neighbouring peninsula, stretched beyond its natural frontier of the Pyrenees, and encroached severely upon France itself; while in the north, the German empire reached and comprehended the city of Cambray. In the south-west lay the duchy of Aquitaine, one of the richest provinces of Gaul, claimed as a whole, and possessed in greater part, by the Plantagenet monarchs of England. Flanders and Hainault, though doing homage to the French crown, were but nominally its subjects; and Burgundy and Champagne appeared on all occasions more as allies than vassals. Britany, too, possessed a prince, whose obedience was always doubtful; and Auvergne, with a wide range of territory, was subject to its own Dauphin.

In the enumeration of those provinces which were thus loosely attached to the true realm of France, the city and small adjacent domain of Avignon would not deserve notice, had it not been at that time the seat of the Roman pontiffs. It did not, however, become absolutely the property of the popes till the year 1348 *, before which period it formed a

* Much obscurity hangs over the transaction which conveyed the city of Avignon to the Holy See. It was certainly sold to the popes by Joan, Countess of Provence; but many writers contend, first, that the money was never paid, and, secondly, that Joan, then a minor, and strictly prohibited by the will of her grandfather, in right of which she

part of the county of Provence, another great fief of the French crown.

Such were some of the peculiarities of situation affecting the two great continental powers in the beginning of the fourteenth century; and from the foregoing facts it will appear, that though France was decidedly more capable of general and rapid military exertions than the empire, yet each was encumbered with its particular difficulties, incident to the nature of its government and its constitution as a state.

The situation of England was very different, and the great advantages which its institutions gave it over both France and Germany, may be traced continually in the events about to be related. Various circumstances combined to render the feudal system, as established in this island, a much more manageable machine in the hands of an English monarch than it ever appeared on the Continent. In France that system had originated, had extended, and had arrived at maturity amongst a people by whom it was adopted almost universally. There, all its involutions, from the monarch, through a number of inferior grades, down to the serf attached to the glebe he ploughed, were complete and unbroken by any discrepancy but the existence of the communes, and a few rare instances of lands held by free tenure.

---

claimed the territory, from alienating any part of it, could not legally effect such a sale. The popes, however, remained in possession to a very late period.

The republican form of municipal government which existed in this city during the middle ages, offering a strange anomaly in the feudal system, is worthy the attention of antiquaries.

In Germany, too, the feudal system had been early introduced; but modified in some degree, and deprived of many of the good points which rendered it the best institution that could be adapted to chivalrous times, it still continued to act throughout the empire with great and mischievous vigour. To England, on the contrary, it was carried by the Normans, — men to whose own manners it was naturally extraneous*, and who, in conquering a nation certainly not less civilised than themselves, gradually adopted many of the establishments, and retained a considerable portion of the laws, they found in existence. Normandy became a dependence upon England, not England upon Normandy; and the conquerors received rather than destroyed the institutions of the conquered. Thus, in England, the feudal system did not grow up by degrees, but was fixed as a graft upon another tree; and while all the establishments with which it was now mingled, tended to modify and to soften it, the very suddenness of its introduction at the Conquest did not admit of its introduction as a whole. The general division of the territory acquired by William amongst his followers, though it created a powerful body of feudal nobility, cut off that higher class of princely

* I take it for granted, that even those who believe the institutions of chivalry to have been derived from the Danes and Normans, will not contend that the feudal system, which had its regular developement amongst the Franks, from its germ in their early tribes, before the fall of Rome, to the period when the first spots of decay appeared upon its full perfection in the times of Philip Augustus, is also to be traced to the same source.

feudatories who, in France and Germany, opposed and often governed their sovereign; and the great mass of the nation also — consisting of the Saxon the Danish and the British population, and comprising the yeoman, the franklin *, and the burgess — offered classes of people, who, with the exception of the burghers, were totally unknown upon the Continent, and whose numbers, industry, corporeal vigour, and aggregate wealth rendered their influence considerable, and their will of weight.

Time also had contributed to give this class importance; for long before the accession of Edward III., the Norman power in England had lost much of its predominance, and the Saxon had risen from its depression. A great amalgamation, too, of the nations had taken place, and national hatred was forgotten. The Norman barons, in wringing Magna Charta from the hands of a weak and vicious king, had done more for the ultimate liberties of the Saxon people than for their own peculiar privileges. With wealth following industry, the power of the commons had been constantly increasing, and in their influence a prudent monarch might always obtain a sure support.

We find, therefore, that in England, nothing like an unmixed system of feudal government existed; and the Norman aristocracy, though often turbulent and unruly in the time of peace, though ever ob-

* The yeomanry Bacon defines "the middle people between the gentlemen and the cottagers;" and the word franklin I believe to signify a person possessing freehold property under the value of a knight's fee: but I speak with doubt.

noxious to a tyrannical, and unsparing to a weak sovereign, were both more ready, at their monarch's call, to take the field, and more ready to obey him in it, than the vassals of any other crown in Christendom.

Nor was this all: besides his feudal followers, the King of England could always call forth a body of men unparalleled in military capabilities; namely, the English peasantry, who, combining, in an extraordinary degree, intelligence with subordination, active energy with unconquerable courage, have continually supplied a force more disposable and more serviceable than any other of which history has preserved the record.

Amongst other advantages possessed by England, her insular position is never to be forgotten; but, unfortunately for the views of some of our greatest monarchs, the presence of an internal enemy in the kingdom of Scotland neutralised, during many centuries, all the benefits of geographical situation. Of this weak point in the circumstances of the English king, the monarchs of France were actively aware; and through the course of the long rivalry between the two countries, from the days of Richard Cœur de Lion to the accession of James I., they may be said to have fought the sovereigns of England as much with the troops of Scotland as with those of France. Taking all these facts into consideration, and remembering that in territorial extent and numerical force England was ver far inferior to either France or the empire, we shall have a general idea of the relative capabilities of each, and may perceive by what means the kings of England, when aided by talent and courage, were enabled to wield less resources with greater success than attended the efforts of neighbouring monarchs.

CHAPTER I.

THE DEPOSITION OF EDWARD II. — ISABELLA AND MORTIMER. — MARRIAGE OF EDWARD III. TO PHILIPPA OF HAINAULT. — DEATH OF CHARLES LE BEL. — CONTEST FOR THE REGENCY OF FRANCE. — ACCESSION OF PHILIP OF VALOIS. — HIS EXPEDITION AGAINST THE FLEMINGS. — HE DEMANDS HOMAGE OF EDWARD III. FOR ACQUITAINE, ETC. — EDWARD DOES HOMAGE. — BIRTH OF EDWARD THE BLACK PRINCE.

HAVING said thus much upon the state of Europe in general at the birth of Edward the Black Prince, I shall now turn to notice more particularly the situation of England at that time, as the various occurrences which took place immediately previous to his entrance into life, added new peculiarities to the circumstances of the country, and laid the foundation of those wars which called forth some of the most shining qualities in his nature.

A few words, however, will be sufficient to give some idea of the events that preceded the marriage of Edward III. with Philippa of Hainault; from which union, as its first fruits, sprang Edward Prince of Wales, commonly denominated the Black Prince. The indolent weakness of the favourite-governed Edward II.; the turbulent idleness of the English barons, and the vicious ambition of the Queen, Isabella of France, shook the English throne, and cast the country into confusion. At length, choosing well her opportunity, Isabella set out for her native land, under pretences of negotiating a treaty of peace with her brother the King of France, and returned supported by an army from Hainault, in order to dethrone her husband. Landing in England, accompanied by her eldest son, who had followed her to the Continent, she succeeded after a short struggle in snatching the crown from the head of Edward II.; and on the first of February 1327, Edward III. was crowned King of England; thus, at the early age of fifteen, usurping the throne of his father.

The real power, however, as well as the real crime, remained with his mother. Twelve persons were appointed as a council of regency, to advise, or rather to control, the young monarch; and Isabella, in whom the presidency was vested, reposed all her authority in the hands of her favourite Mortimer. A series of acts of weakness and oppression succeeded, which rendered the Queen and her minion hateful to the nobility; and the employment of foreign troops, the murder of the deposed King, together with weak and unsuccessful wars upon the Scottish frontier, augmented from day to day the general contempt and detestation. The popular indignation, however, was confined to the just object, and the young King did not encounter any portion of that hatred which was universally directed against his mother. The common feeling of tenderness towards the young, indeed, affects the crowd as well as the individual; and a youthful monarch generally has the multitude on his side, rejoicing in his joy, and deploring his calamities with far more deep-felt sympathy than popular bodies evince upon other occasions. The young King had already displayed a warlike disposition, and his people's partiality saw therein the presage of warlike abilities. All other kingly qualities still remained to be tried; but expectation, which generally outdoes fulfilment, only rendered justice to Edward III. in anticipating future greatness.

Between France and England, as much harmony subsisted, as had existed for many years, although disputes productive of no important result were taking place continually between the subjects of the two countries upon the frontiers of Acquitaine. Charles le Bel, the uncle of the English monarch, still sat upon the throne of France; and though the want of lineage by either of his first wives had for some time opened a prospect of future dissensions in France, towards the end of the year 1327, the announcement that Joan of Evreux, his last queen, had become pregnant, silenced the hopes of contingent claimants to the French crown, and removed the apprehensions of the people.

Such was the state of England and France when ambassadors were sent from Edward III. to demand the hand of one of the daughters of William the Good, Count of Hainault. Whether a prior arrangement to that effect had been entered into at the time of the visit of Edward and Isabella to the court of Valenciennes, in the year 1326, is not clearly ascertained; but the demand of the English monarch was received as an honour, and acceded to immediately, by the lord of a small territory in Belgium. The English people received the announcement of the approaching marriage of their young monarch to the daughter of the Count of Hainault, with joyful acclamations, although they had shown the most inveterate hatred to the Hainaulters, who had been brought over by Isabella to serve with the English forces, and although the alliance itself had been planned and carried into execution by a woman they contemned and abhorred. So far, indeed, from extending their detestation of Isabella to her son, it seems probable that they regarded him as in some degree sharing the same oppression under which they themselves suffered; and at all events, it is very evident that popular affection and support were ready as a basis for his power, whenever Edward chose to shake off the trammels of his mother and her paramour. Each step towards manhood gave a nearer prospect of such a result; and his approaching marriage afforded the best hope that he would soon wrest the government from the hands of an upstart minion and a vicious though talented woman.

The year 1327 had nearly reached its conclusion, when Philippa of Hainault, one of the most amiable women that ever filled a throne, set out from her native land, at the tender age of fourteen, to become the wife of a great king, and the queen of a powerful nation. Beautiful in person, as well as amiable in mind, she might well calculate upon being received with tenderness and admiration, but various instances of unworthy caprice had made the minor princes of Europe cautious in bestowing their daughters upon more powerful sovereigns, without some better security for their reception at a distant court than princely courtesy and good faith. It had thus, probably, become a custom, when one prince demanded the daughter of another, to render the alliance inviolable by celebrating the marriage ceremony between a sufficient proxy on the part of the future bridegroom, and the bride in person, ere she was permitted to set out for the dominions of her husband. All * these precautions had been taken by the relations of the young Queen; and to guard against ecclesiastical interference or censure, all objections which might arise from some distant relationship between the parties, were nullified by a dispensation from the Pope.† The society of friends and relations consoled and supported the princess in her first separation from her parents ‡, and in her first acquaintance with new scenes and new duties; and the honest joy and thundering acclamations of her husband's subjects cheered her reception and welcomed her to their shores.

* Barnes. Froissart, cap. 46.

† Rymer.

‡ The silence of Froissart, and all contemporary historians, makes it doubtful whether Philippa was accompanied by her father or not. That he was expected to visit England on the occasion of his daughter's marriage is evident, from the fact of a safe conduct having been granted to him for the purpose, the copy of which is preserved by Rymer; and from a patent of Edward III. directed to William Clynton, Earl of Huntingdon, and Bartholomew de Burghersh, Constable of Dover Castle, commanding them to aid in the conveyance of the Count of Hainault and his daughter.

Her uncle, the famous John of Hainault, who commanded the small force sent with her to England as her escort, was already familiar with the people and the country; and under his guidance she proceeded from Dover towards London, met and honoured in every place by the nobles, and cheered by the populace. Her progress was a long and a joyful triumph; the magistrates of the capital * went forth in state to receive her; and all the quaint but splendid and costly pageantry in which the age delighted, was lavishly displayed at her approach.

From London the young Queen had still to proceed to York, at which place the court was then assembled. There, however, she was met in a different manner, by the love of a young and noble husband, and the chivalrous display of a military court.

Her coronation took place immediately after her remarriage † to the monarch in person; and at the end of three weeks of rejoicing and festivity, her uncle and his followers left her, while she remained, with a scanty train of her own countrymen, separated for ever from her own country, bidding adieu to the calm and quiet days of girlhood; and, by the short transition of her marriage pomp, passing to cares, anxieties, and alarms, the heavy duties of womanhood, and the sleepless watchfulness of a royal station. Philippa, however, was well calculated to encounter the fate to which she was called. She possessed in the strongest degree those qualities which

* Knighton, p. 2552.

† 24 January, A. D. 1328.

are woman's characteristic virtues and firmest supporters through life — gentleness, and fortitude. Nor could her fate, though perhaps not that which calm consideration would select, be looked upon as an evil destiny; for though she knew but little peace, she enjoyed much happiness, and possessed the noble privilege of doing good, — a privilege which it is her best encomium to declare that she appreciated to the utmost.

The only attendant, distinguished by contemporary writers from the rest of those whom John of Hainault left to attend upon the young Queen of England, was one whose after fame and great exploits rendered the particulars of his youth worthy of more investigation than was generally bestowed in that age upon the obscure years of any one. This was the famous Walter de Mauny, lord of the little town of Mauny, in the diocese of Cambray, whom the early death of his father, assassinated in Gascony, had cast upon the care of the Count of Hainault. Of a noble family, and connected with a sovereign prince, the Count of Namur, Walter de Mauny, was, nevertheless, subjected to that gradation of service in the palace of his patron, which all aspirants to the honours of chivalry underwent. He had, accordingly, spent several years as page in the palace at Valenciennes; and, being promoted to the rank of Esquire on the marriage of the Count's daughter to the English King, was left behind at the court of Edward, as an honour and advancement, in quality of Ecuyer tranchant, or carver at the table of the young Queen.

The fact, that not even the name of any other Hainaulter remaining to attend upon Philippa is mentioned by contemporary historians, would alone justify the supposition that but few of her compatriots were permitted to continue near her person, even were we not positively informed that the number of her countrymen left with her was extremely small.* Little doubt, indeed, can exist that Isabella, the Queen-mother, proposed to render her influence permanent with her son by the insecure policy of governing his young wife; a scheme which almost all women in her circumstances have attempted, but which has almost always failed, from the difficulty of persuading a mind that can rule, to rule for others rather than for itself. The gradual developement, however, of the young monarch's talents, the growing sense of powers of command and energy of action within his own bosom, and the acquisition of the most estimable boon of time — experience — were all silently working the downfall of Isabella's power, without the instrumentality of Philippa, who was, probably, yet too young to mark or to struggle against the chains with which her mother-in-law was striving to enthral her.

Had the moral conduct of Isabella been irreproachable, and her public acts been directed by great and noble views, it is not too much to suppose that her authority would only have ended with her life; for Edward himself, in his early years, repaid his mother's affection and care with grateful deference

* Froissart, cap. 46.

and affection, and showed none of that avidity of rule which would have led him to snatch the rod of power from a hand that used it well and wisely. But various circumstances, by calling upon Edward to act for himself, taught him his power of doing so; and others, by bringing him in near and private communication with his nobles, opened his eyes in regard to the conduct of his mother and her paramour, and dissolved the magic influence of habitual deference by the potent countercharm of contempt.

The first event of any great importance which followed the marriage of Edward III. of England with Isabella of Hainault, was the death of Charles, surnamed *le Bel*, King of France, who, after an illness of several weeks, expired at Vincennes, on the 1st of February, 1328*, leaving his Queen, Joan of Evreux, in a state of pregnancy. It cannot be doubted that intelligence of his probable dissolution had reached England prior to that of the event itself, and that ambassadors had been immediately sent over, in the name of the English king, to claim the regency of the realm of France, during the interregnum which was likely to ensue, on the actual decease of the dying monarch.

Another candidate for the government of the kingdom, however, appeared at the same time in the person of Philip Count of Valois; and although, previous to the delivery of the Queen, the contest between these two rivals could only openly refer to the regency, the award of the French peers was not only

* William of Nangis, Continuat. Froissart, cap. 49. 1st February, 1328.

greatly affected, but ultimately decided, by the latent claims of the two competitors to the crown. It was not, indeed, absolutely necessary that the decision should be founded on such a basis; for the Salique law, by which females were excluded from the throne of France, did not at all exclude them from the government of the kingdom as a delegate during the minority or incapacity of the male heir. But it was so evident that, in case the Queen should produce a daughter, the regent would possess immense advantages over his antagonist in the probable struggle for dominion, that it could hardly be doubted by any one that the nomination to the regency would, in fact, confer the throne itself if it proved vacant.

Both Philip of Valois and Edward III. were descended* in a direct line from Philip, the eldest son of St. Louis; Edward in the third, and Philip in the second, degree: but the young English monarch claimed the regency, and ultimately the crown, as next

* I subjoin the pedigree of Philip and Edward, as I find it drawn out in Barnes.

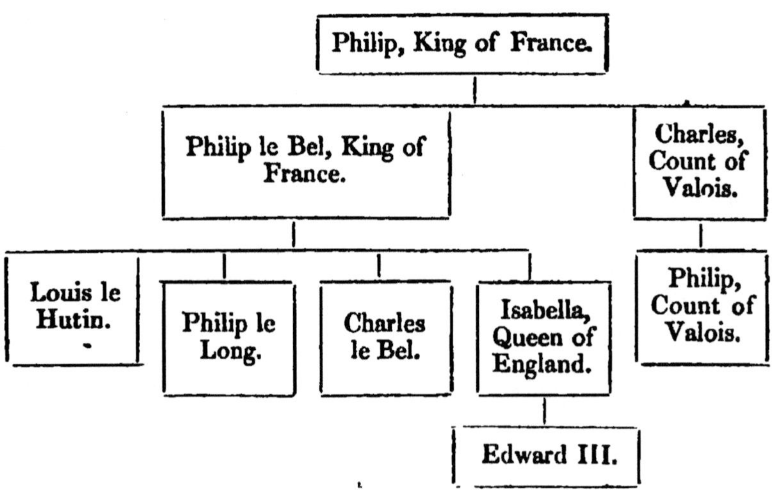

of kin male to the last King, Charles le Bel, being his nephew by the mother's side. The Count of Valois was obliged to ascend farther up to establish his title, being nephew, not to the last monarch, but to the last monarch's father. The line, however, in his case was unbroken from male to male; while in the case of Edward, his mother, still alive, was undoubtedly excluded from the throne by her sex. The question thus became — and a most important question it was — whether a female could transmit to her male issue a right from which she was barred by her sex alone.*

A court of Peers was held as soon as the tomb had closed over the royal dust of the last monarch of the direct Capetian line; and we find that keen and lengthened discussion took place in regard to the regency of the realm during the interregnum which must necessarily occur ere the vacancy or occupation of the throne could be known.† It appears, indeed, that the investigation of the claims of the two candidates was not confined, even in appearance, to the immediate question; but that, on the contrary, with somewhat rude, though perhaps necessary, foresight, the probability that the Queen would give birth to a daughter, and the consequences to ensue, were argued at length.

"The only question before the Peers," says one of the most perspicuous of contemporary writers‡, "was,

* This right was technically called the right of representation, and was in full force in many parts of France by the customary law of the province. The question, however, had never yet been decided in regard to the crown.

† William of Nangis, Continuat.

‡ Continuator of William of Nangis.

to whom they should confide the government of the kingdom, as the nearest relative of the late King; women in the kingdom of France being incompetent to ascend the throne in person. The English asserted that the government of the realm, and the throne itself, if the Queen did not give birth to a male child, would belong to the young Edward, King of England, as the nearest relation of the last monarch — he being son to the daughter of Philip le Bel, and consequently nephew of the late King Charles — rather than to Philip Count of Valois, who was only cousin-german to the late King Charles. A great many persons learned in equity and the canon law were of this opinion. They affirmed that Isabella, Queen of England, daughter of Philip le Bel, and sister of the late Charles, was, indeed, incompetent to ascend the throne or undertake the government of the kingdom, not, that by birth she was not the next of kin to the late King, but on account of her sex. As soon, however, as one can be produced who is the nearest relative by birth, and who is competent by sex to reign — that is to say, who is male — to him falls the throne and the government. On the other hand, those of the kingdom of France, indisposed to submit willingly to the sovereignty of the English, declared, that if the said son of Isabella possessed any rights to the throne, he could but derive them from his mother; and therefore, the mother herself having no rights, it followed that her son could not have any either. This opinion being received and approved by the barons as the best, the government of the kingdom was intrusted to Philip Count of Valois, who was called regent of the realm."

It would be tedious here to inquire what part hatred to the English bore in the decision of the French Peers. Few people will doubt, in the present day, that that decision was substantially just, and was the simple and straightforward interpretation of the law of France which excluded females from the throne. At that time, however, when scholastic subtleties pervaded both law and religion, many doubts seem to have existed on the point amongst the civilians both of France and England; and there appears great reason to suppose that the whole influence of one or two of the most powerful peers, accompanied by all the arts of intrigue and faction, was necessary to fix Philip of Valois firmly in the government. Amongst the most prominent of his partisans was his brother-in-law, Robert of Artois, Count of Beaumont le Roger, a noble of great possessions and renown, who spared no means to facilitate the advancement of his relation to the regency.*

All parties, of course, looked with great anxiety to the termination of the Queen's pregnancy, on which such important interests depended. At length, on the 1st of April, exactly two months after the death of her husband, Joan of Evreux was delivered of a daughter, named afterwards Blanche; and the Peers of France, without giving any farther attention

* Froissart, cap. 54.

to the claims of Edward, declared Philip Count of Valois to be of right King of France.*

The news of the birth of a princess immediately renewed in England the consideration of Edward's claim to the French throne; and in a parliament held at Northampton †, his right was publicly discussed, and means were taken to assert his title by words and documents, though the country was not in a state to enforce it by arms. The Bishops of Worcester and of Coventry were immediately despatched to Paris, to protest against the validity of Philip's nomination, and to oppose his coronation. The latter ceremony, however, was probably concluded before their arrival; for we find that the parliament of Northampton was held late in the month of May, and Philip of Valois was solemnly crowned at Rheims on Trinity Sunday, which fell on the 29th of that month.

Seated on the throne of France by the voice of her Peers, Philip of Valois had little cause to fear the opposition of the disappointed competitor; and at once to sanctify his authority by a just exercise of his power, he determined to perform, as the first deed of his reign, an act which had been neglected by the preceding King, though it was called for by the absolute duties of a feudal monarch.

St. Louis had strictly laid down that no serf, vassal, or subject of any feudal lord, could refuse to perform military service when demanded by his su-

* If we are to believe Froissart, Charles le Bel had by will appointed Philip of Valois regent of the kingdom, and, in case the queen should give birth to a male child, guardian to the infant monarch; but in other respects had left the question of succession open.

† May, 1328. . Barnes.

perior, even though he were required to act in open rebellion to the King himself; but, nevertheless, we find that the monarch might be called upon by his feudatories, to aid in compelling their vassals to subjection in case of revolt. The people of Flanders, always noted for turbulence and discontent, had for some years been more or less in a state of rebellion against their Count, one of the feudatories of the French crown*; and, in the present instance, their discontent was not without cause. Louis of Crecy, Count of Flanders, a young and weak prince, suffered himself to be governed by a favourite, named the Abbot of Vezelai, between whom and the Flemings existed a long and hereditary enmity. The citizens of Cassel, Ypres, and Bruges, raised the standard of revolt upon the subject of some unjust and burthensome taxes, placed at their head a man of rude but powerful mind, named Nicholas Zonekins, expelled the Count, and bade defiance even to the power of France.†

The Count of Flanders had wearied the French monarchs with entreaties, and the first act of Philip of Valois, in conformity with his duties as a feudal sovereign, was to march against the revolted subjects of his vassal. In this expedition his character appears in a fairer light than, perhaps, in any other event of his reign. On the eve of St. Bartholomew he gave battle to the rebels, who had entrenched themselves in the neighbourhood of Cassel; and, after a long and sanguinary struggle, in which Zonekins was slain, while performing feats of valour worthy of the most

* Contin. de Nangis.

† Annales de Flandres.

chivalrous education, he completely defeated the Flemings, and leaving 16,000 dead upon the field of battle, reduced the country to obedience.* Cassel, we are told, was given up to fire and sword; but the moderation of Philip's conduct throughout the expedition, and his speech to the Count of Flanders, would seem to imply that such excesses were not sanctioned by his authority.

"Fair cousin," he said, on leaving Louis of Crecy once more in possession of his territories, "I was brought hither by the prayers you have made me. It may be, nevertheless, that you have yourself given cause of revolt, by neglecting to render the justice that you owe to your people; a matter which I shall not examine at present. Such an expedition as that which I have accomplished must put me to great expense, and I might well claim to be reimbursed by you. But I hold you free of all; and I yield you your territories reduced and pacified. Take care, however, how you bring me a second time on the same errand. If your bad administration forces me to return, it will be less for your interests than for my own." †

Such an exhibition of vigour and energy as Philip displayed in the expedition to Flanders, was as politic by its collateral as by its direct effects. Had the Count of Flanders profited by the warning he received, and remained in command of his native do-

* All the Flemish historians assert that the attack was made by Zonekins, who nearly obtained possession of the king's person by surprise.

† Annales de Flandre.

minions, a steady and grateful ally was secure to France upon her weakest frontier; but at all events, on the great vassals of the crown, this proof of the will to protect them while they remained obedient, and the power to punish them if they proved rebellious, could not be lost. Nor could such demonstrations of activity and preparation be without their consequences, in deterring the disappointed claimant of the French crown from attempting to wrest it hastily from the head on which it had been placed; and Philip of Valois lost no time, after he had thus exercised his new power, ere he attempted to wring from Edward of England an act of acquiescence in the judgment of the Peers. This could only be done by summoning the young King to do homage, according to custom, for the territories which the English monarchs held in France.

It cannot be doubted, that Philip, in demanding this act, had fully calculated all the difficulties and obstructions which opposed themselves to any movements on the part of the English King in prosecution of his claim to the throne of France; or, in other words, that his youth, his inexperience, the weakness and passions of his mother, the instability of her government, and its embarrassments with the Scots, the disaffection of the English barons, and the exhausted state of England's pecuniary resources, had all been considered and counted upon by the King of France and his counsellors. At the same time it must be remarked that Philip was in some degree compelled to enforce the demand which he now urged upon Edward III. He could not well, without bringing his own title into doubt, avoid summoning the King of England to do homage for Aquitaine, Ponthieu, and Montreuil, fiefs held absolutely of the crown of France. His expedition, therefore, came happily to prove his capability of maintaining his right at a time when the assertion thereof could not be avoided; and as soon as the insurrection in Flanders was suppressed, he despatched the Lord of Aubigny* and the Lord of Beausault, together with two famous civilians, Peter of Massieres and Simon of Orleans, to claim the homage of the young King of England, and to persuade him to acquiesce in the demand.†

Although such a proceeding must have been anticipated by the English court, Edward and his council seem to have been greatly embarrassed by the first formal summons; as, in case of refusal, the whole of the possessions of the crown in France might be declared forfeited and seized while England was in no condition to defend them; and in case of acquiescence, the fact of doing homage to Philip of Valois might well be construed as a recognition of his right to the throne he had assumed. What result bold counsels might have produced at that moment, cannot be told; but the rule of Mortimer and Isabella over the mind of the young King was yet unshaken, and

* Some manuscripts of Froissart write Ancenis.

† It is evident that Philip sent two distinct embassies to claim homage for Aquitaine. His first ambassador was Peter Roger, Abbot of Fescamp, and afterwards Pope under the name of Clement VI.; but at what time that prelate visited England I cannot discover, and therefore confine myself to the subsequent mission, though the result of Philip's previous embassy might in some degree influence his display of power in the expedition against the Flemings.

the timid and unworthy expedient was adopted of consenting to the homage as a public act, while Edward at the same time, by a private reservation, made and kept in the secrecy of his council chamber, took exception to the right of Philip, and declared that he in no degree yielded his own claim by the deed he was going to perform.*

This childish piece of dissimulation having been perpetrated in form, the ambassadors from Philip were satisfied by a promise that Edward would visit France as soon as the affairs of England would permit, and do homage for the territories which he held of the French crown. The spot appointed for the ceremony to take place, was the town of Amiens; and the King of France, rejoicing in the hope of all dispute being done away in regard to his title to the throne, summoned the nobility of his realm to increase the splendour of the solemnity, and witness so important an event. The heart of Edward, however, seems to have burned from the first, at the indignity to which he was about to submit; and his train and equipage were rendered the more splendid, in order to veil the degradation under a show of pomp. Three bishops and twelve Peers were called upon to accompany the King to France; and the names of Beauchamp, Bohun, and Plantagenet, Montague, Cobham, Percy, Nevil, and Mowbray— names deathless in the annals of war and policy—gave lustre of a higher kind than rank, or wealth, or station. Besides

* I am afraid there can be no doubt of this fact. Barnes brings forward too strong proof of the pitiful evasion he describes, to leave the matter with any dubiety.

these, appeared the young Walter de Mauny; and with forty knights, and 1000 men at arms, the monarch, having left his brother, John of Eltham, in England, as custos regni, put to sea for that land which he was so often to enter as a conqueror.

The journeys of that day were usually performed on horseback, except when ill health offered an excuse for the softer conveyance of a litter; and Edward, whose fleet contained the necessary number of horses, disembarked his train at Whitesand, and rode forward to Boulogne. In that city he was met and welcomed by the Constable of France, and proceeded in his company to Amiens, where Philip awaited him, surrounded by a brilliant court, in which appeared, besides the Dukes of Burgundy, Lorraine, and Bourbon, the Kings of Bohemia, Navarre, and Majorca.

It may be doubted whether the splendour of the court, and the number of persons assembled, were very gratifying to the young King of England; but during the space that intervened between his arrival and the ceremony of the homage, no caress or honour was spared, which could render the unsavoury act he was about to perform more palatable to the monarch.

At length the appointed day arrived, and Edward and Philip appeared together in the cathedral church of Amiens; the one to render, and the other to receive, the homage. Some difficulties, however, now occurred as to the nature and extent of the act, which were at length removed by Edward acknowledging that his homage was to be considered as full and complete as that of his predecessors. Nevertheless, before he admitted any clear definition of those general terms, he demanded time to consult the documents preserved in England on the subject.* In the mean time, a paper was drawn up by the notaries, and signed by the witnesses present, containing an account of what had passed, with the acknowledgment of the English monarch that the homage he rendered was to be considered the same as that of his ancestors; after which Edward's† hands being placed in

* Rymer, t. ii. part iii. p. 27.

† All the particulars of this homage have been matter of historical dispute, although it would seem that the parties concerned did every thing in their power to transmit it clearly to posterity. Froissart, probably, wrongly informed by his English friends at a time that they were endeavouring to do away with all precise record of the event, asserts that Edward did not place his hands in those of the King of France, and render the act formally complete. But Rymer has preserved the formula written down at the time, and signed by names which could not be attached to a falsehood. It is to the following effect, and sets the question entirely at rest:—

"In the name of God, Amen.

"Know all men, by the tenor of this public instrument, that, present we notaries public and scriveners, and the witnesses here below named, came into the presence of the very high and excellent Prince, our dear Lord Philip, by the grace of God, King of France, and appeared personally the high and noble Prince, my Lord Edward, King of England, and with him the reverend Father the Bishop of Lincoln, and many other persons and counsellors, to do his homage for the duchy of Guyenne and peerage of France, to the said King of France.

"And then the noble Lord, my Lord Mille de Noyers, who was by the side of the said King of France, said, on the part of the King of France, to the said King of England, in this manner.

"'Sir, the King does not propose to receive you thus, as he has said to your council, for the things that he holds and ought to hold in Gascony and the Agenois, the which were held and ought to have been held by the late King Charles, and in regard to which the late King protested that he did not propose to receive you.'

"And the said Bishop of Lincoln said and protested for the said King of England, that by any thing which the King of England, or any

those of the King of France, Philip kissed him on the lips, receiving him as Duke of Guyenne, Lord of Ponthieu and Montreuil, and Peer of France.

---

one on his part, said or did, he did not intend to renounce any right that he possessed or ought to possess in the duchy of Guyenne and its appurtenances; or that thereby any new rights were acquired by the said King of France.

"And having thus protested, the said Bishop gave to the nobleman, the Viscount de Melun, Chamberlain of France, a schedule concerning the said homage, the tenor of which is here under written.

"And then said the said Chamberlain to the King of England thus: 'Sire, You become the man of the King of France, my Lord, for the duchy of Guyenne and its appurtenances, which you acknowledge to hold from him, as Duke of Guyenne and Peer of France, according to the form of peace made between his predecessors, Kings of France, and yours, according to that which you and your ancestors, Kings of England and Dukes of Guyenne, have done for the same duchy to his predecessors, Kings of France.'

"And then the King said, *Yes*.

"And the said Chamberlain said afterwards thus:—'And the King of France, our Lord, receives you with the protestations and reserves above mentioned.'

"And the King of France said, *Yes*.

"And then, the hands of the said King of England placed in the hands of the said King of France, kissed on the mouth the said King of England."

The tenor of the schedule, which the said Bishop gave for the King of England, follows here:—

"'I become your man for the Duchy of Guyenne and its appurtenances, which I admit to hold from you as Duke of Guyenne and Peer of France, according to the form of peace made between your predecessors and ours, according to that which our ancestors, Kings of England and Dukes of Guyenne, have done for the same duchy to your predecessors, Kings of France.'

"Done at Amiens, in the choir of the great church, in the year of Grace one thousand three hundred and twenty-nine, the sixth day of June, the twelfth Indiction, thirteenth of the government of our most Holy Father Pope John XXII., present, and to this appealed witnesses, the reverend Fathers in God, the Bishops of Beauvais, Laon, and Senlis; and the high Prince Charles Count of Alençon, my Lord Eudes Duke of Burgundy, my Lord Louis Duke of Bourbon, my Lord Louis Count

D 4

The whole conduct of Philip through this unpleasant scene, appears to have been dignified and yet gentle; and it is not unworthy of remark, that while supported and counselled by his brother-in-law, Robert of Artois, the first monarch of the line of Valois, seems to have acted with a calm propriety of demeanour, which he often forgot in the latter years of his reign. It has been asserted, indeed, but apparently without reason, that Philip proposed to seize the person of the young King after the ceremony*, and was only prevented from doing so by Edward's private departure. The fullest of contemporary historians †, in a work presented not many years after to the Queen Philippa, declares that the Kings of France and England passed some time together subsequent to the homage in festivity and recreation, and parted openly with mutual friendship and good will; and a journey which Edward made to France in 1331, accompanied by only fifteen persons, clearly shows that he entertained no doubt of the courtesy and good faith of his brother King.

After the return of the monarch to England, the

---

of Flanders, my Lord Robert of Artois Count of Beaumont, and the Count of Armagnac; the Abbots of Cluny and of Corbie, the Lord of Beaujeu, and Bernard Lord of Albret; Math. de Trye and Robert Bertrand, Marshals of France: Item, the reverend Father Bishop St. Davids, Henry Lord Percy, Robert Ufford, Robert de Wasteville, Robert de Mesville, William de Montague, Gilbert Talbot, John Maltravers, Seneschal of the King of England, Geoffrey de Stropt, and many other witnesses, to this appealed and required."

* Knighton, col. 2555. n. 10. † Froissart, cap. 52.

matter of the homage was pursued; and probably the unwillingness which Edward evinced to complete it distinctly by the examination of the records, and the issuing his letters patent, induced Philip to press more urgently for an explicit acknowledgment of the terms in full. Nearly a year and a half was passed in embassies on the one part, and delays and investigations on the other *; but in the end, as we shall notice hereafter, Edward sealed the patent demanded, expressly stating the full mode of homage done and to be done in future for the dukedom of Guyenne.

Before the whole of this business was concluded, Philippa of Hainault, after having been more than two years married to the King of England without giving promise of an heir to the throne, was at length delivered of a son at Woodstock, on the 15th of June, 1330.† The strength and beauty of

* Froissart, cap. 53. Rymer, vol. ii. part iii.

† It seems to be somewhat doubtful in what year Edward was born. Although, in general, correct in point of facts, Barnes, the historian of Edward III., is the most incorrect of writers in regard to dates; and consequently, as he continually makes one event depend upon another, which, instead of preceding, really followed it, he is almost invariably wrong where he attempts to trace cause and effect. Thus, he places Edward's second expedition to France in the year 1330, when we find, by the original documents preserved in Rymer, that it took place in 1331; and he deduces events which occurred in the former year from causes that followed in the latter. A tournament, also, which he declares was given in 1330, to exhibit the prowess of the English nation to the ambassadors sent to demand the homage of Edward, took place late in 1331, after the last act of the homage was completed, and the ambassadors gone. Nevertheless I am inclined to believe, that, in regard to the birth of Edward the Black Prince, he was right in placing that event in 1330. I find, indeed, beyond all doubt,

the child increased the happiness of the parents, and the expectations of the nation; and by many marks of royal munificence, the young father signalised his gratification at the event. High rewards, as was then customary, were bestowed on the messenger who brought the news to the King, on the nurse who attended the child, and on the *bersatrix* who rocked the cradle of the infant hero. The new æra which was to follow, and the splendid change which was to take place in the situation of the country, seemed anticipated by the people, the details of whose unusual rejoicings fill many a contemporary page. The name of Edward was bestowed upon the young prince, and his baptism was celebrated with unequalled festivity and joy. It appeared as if all the magnificent actions which that infant hand was afterwards to perform, were spread out in glorious array before the eyes of his father's subjects. Every one throughout that land known of old by the endearing

---

that the mother of Philippa was in England in 1331, by the patents directing the Earl of Huntingdon to provide ships for her return; and it has been supposed, on the one hand, that the Countess of Hainault's visit to England in 1331 was either to attend her daughter during her first confinement, or to be present at the baptism of the child; while on the other, it has been contended, that Hemingford, Walsingham, John of Tinemouth, and almost all the older writers, place the event in 1329; yet all agree that the day was Friday, and the 15th of June, which coincidence happened only in 1330, and in neither of the other years. I have also carefully examined the dates of all the state papers of the three years; and though in neither 1329 nor 1331 I find any one dated from Woodstock, where the Prince was born, in 1330 Edward must certainly have spent the summer months at that place, as all his patents bear that date.

name of merry England, rejoiced — the peasant, the noble, and the King; and popular enthusiasm, with prophetic gladness, welcomed the coming of the gentlest of heroes, and the noblest of conquerors.

CHAP. II.

THE EXECUTION OF THE EARL OF KENT. — THE ARREST AND EXECUTION OF MORTIMER. — FEUDS ON THE CONFINES OF GUYENNE. — CAPTURE OF SAINCTES AND SUBSEQUENT NEGOTIATIONS. — EDWARD'S SECRET VISIT TO PHILIP OF VALOIS. — THE EFFECT OF HIS CONFIDENCE ON THE FRENCH KING. — TOURNAMENTS AND CHIVALROUS EXERCISES OF THE ENGLISH COURT. — THOSE SPORTS THE CAUSE OF POLITICAL ADVANTAGES TO ENGLAND. — INVASION OF SCOTLAND BY EDWARD BALIOL. — DOUBTFUL CONDUCT OF EDWARD III. ON THAT OCCASION. — NEGOTIATIONS WITH FRANCE REGARDING THE MARRIAGE OF PRINCE EDWARD. — WAR WITH SCOTLAND. — INFANCY OF EDWARD THE BLACK PRINCE.

THE year 1330 was fertile in great events to England. Although there can be little doubt that while Edward III. remained in France, the nobles by whom he was surrounded took advantage of the absence of Mortimer and Isabella to assail the influence of his mother and her paramour in the mind of the young King, it is clear that their power, though shaken, was by no means overthrown; and the first open demonstration of resistance made by the barons, was followed by the arrest and execution of the Earl of Kent, the monarch's uncle.* It is not necessary here to investigate the evidences of treason brought against that unhappy prince. Although he had ever

* At Winchester, 19th of March, 1330. Knighton, col. 2555.

evinced a turbulent and rebellious disposition, it is probable that, in the present instance, he was the victim of an artful scheme to strengthen the waning authority of Isabella; and it would seem that his condemnation was obtained, and his execution hurried, by the intrigues of Mortimer himself.

Such a tremendous example of severity did not succeed in overawing the English nobles, or silencing the murmurs, complaints, and rumours of the people. A report was industriously circulated, that the Dowager Queen was pregnant by Mortimer; and good care was taken that the scandal should reach the ears of the young monarch. It would appear that Edward at length complained to some of his Peers of the dishonour brought upon his house, of Mortimer's insolence, exactions, and usurped authority. The barons pointed out an easy remedy; and undertook to carry it into effect upon condition of the King's co-operation. A promise to that effect was willingly given by a prince weary of the domination of others, and eager to reign and conquer for himself; and in a consultation held in October with the most faithful and resolute of the English barons, it was determined to seize on the person of Isabella's minion at the parliament then sitting at Nottingham.

This, however, was not to be easily effected; for, by the power he possessed, Mortimer had rendered himself more powerful. By the accumulation of immense wealth, and the long disposal of the royal revenue, he had obtained the means of buying adherents, and had attached many to himself by interest, who could not have been won by regard. At the parliament of Nottingham he appeared with more than royal splendour; and lodging, as was his custom, in the same dwelling with Isabella, he took up his abode in the castle, while the King, and other members of the royal family, were obliged to content themselves with an inferior place of residence.

Although pride was one of the sins which more than any other worked out the minion's overthrow, yet it is probable that fear had a greater share than ostentation in leading him to take possession of the strong and guarded fortress of Nottingham; in proof of which we find that, when the castle gates were locked at night, the keys were always brought by the constable, and delivered to the Queen herself. Holding in his pay nearly 200 knights, and a large body of men at arms, a part of which followed him continually, no opportunity of arresting Mortimer during the daytime could be found, without the chance of desperate resistance; and the fortress, to which he retired at night, afforded him still greater means of defence against any open attack. It was determined, under these circumstances, to apply to Sir William Eland, constable of the castle, a gallant and royal gentleman, between whom and Mortimer existed no particular tie of interest or affection. Upon him the King's commands were laid to assist the barons charged to arrest the favourite; and he agreed at once to do so, though he pointed out the difficulty arising from the fact of the keys being demanded at his hands each day at sunset.

A subterranean communication, however, existed (since called Mortimer's hole) between the inner works of the castle, and the country without the walls. It had been constructed in former years, by some of the early possessors of the fortress, as a means of escape in time of need, and perhaps, also, as a sally port. Originally framed with a view to concealment, it had been long neglected, and was nearly forgotten; and by this inlet, on the night of the 19th of October, 1330, nine resolute noblemen—the Lords Montague, Suffolk, Stafford, Molins, and Clinton, with three brothers of the race of Bohun, and Sir John Nevil—led by Sir William Eland, prepared to penetrate into the strong-hold of the guilty Queen and her ambitious favourite. Leaving the town before nightfall, the Lords appeared about to absent themselves on some distant expedition either of pleasure or business; but returning towards Nottingham at midnight, they made their way into a cavern which served as a mouth to the subterranean passage, and proceeding along it for some way, entered the rocky base on which the castle was founded, and through which a staircase led upwards to the Keep. Directing their steps at once towards the suite of apartments which Mortimer was known to inhabit, they found him not yet in bed, and conversing with the Bishop of Lincoln.* A number of his friends were in the room; and at the very first appearance of the Lords Montague and Clinton, his known enemies,

* Knighton, col. 2556.

swords were drawn, and vigorous resistance was menaced. The barons were not backward to oppose force to force; and in a moment Sir Hugh Turpleton and Richard Monmouth* were slain fighting on the part of the Queen's paramour, who was himself overpowered with little difficulty; while the voice of Isabella was heard from a neighbouring chamber, exclaiming, "Beau fils, beau fils! ayez pitié du gentil Mortimer!" †

The rest of the favourite's friends and followers, who were within the castle, do not seem to have offered any farther resistance; and possession of the fortress being secured, the gates were guarded to prevent the exit of any one who might communicate the events which had taken place to Mortimer's adherents without. His altered fortunes, therefore, remained unknown till the following day, when several more arrests were made; and the parliament having been adjourned to London, the object of popular hatred was arraigned, tried, and condemned for many acts of felony and treason, of which the principal was the murder of Edward II.

No doubt can exist that the sentence was substan-

* Rymer, tom. iv. p. 475.

† This exclamation, or something tantamount, which is generally reported by historians, would seem to prove that Edward was there in person, which other circumstances render doubtful. It being now clearly established, however, that Mortimer was not in the Queen's bedchamber, as has been frequently asserted without foundation, and that Isabella, hearing the clashing of swords, and instantly divining the cause, made this appeal in behalf of her favourite, without seeing who was present, she might very well conjecture that the King himself was at the head of the assailants.

tially just; but one of the great ends of the formal part of judicial inquiry is, to guard against the operation of prejudice and popular hatred; and in this respect two fearful errors were committed in the trial of Mortimer. The judgment against him is expressly stated to be founded on public notoriety — the most dangerous, questionable, and iniquitous of testimonies, — under which every sort of injustice might be practised, every sort of tyranny might be committed; and, in the second place, we are told that his whole trial was ex parte, and his condemnation pronounced without any defence being permitted, — a precedent of injustice which would be fearful were it not for its enormity. He himself, it is true, had directed the same proceeding towards others; but the very fact of its having once taken place, should have been the strongest argument against its repetition. He was hanged* at Elmes†, without mercy or delay; and after having been exposed for two days on the gibbet, his body was granted to the Gray Friars of London, who performed in charity the last human offices towards the clay of the favourite Mortimer.

Several other executions followed; but filial piety interfered to save the greatest criminal amongst so many, and Queen Isabella was doomed to strict confinement in Castle Risings, where she lingered

* Robert of Avesbury, p. 9. Hemingford.

† It would appear that he was tried, condemned, and executed on the same day, the 26th of November, 1330; for on that day the parliament had been summoned to meet; and he was buried in the Gray Friars on the 29th, after having hung two whole days and a half on the gibbet. See Dugdale and Walter Hemingford.

through the greater part of eight and twenty years which yet remained of a misspent existence.*

The affairs of France now seem to have divided the attention of the young King, with the rejoicings which followed his assumption of authority, and his punishment of those who had restricted the royal power, and abused their own. A great alteration, however, took place in the policy of England towards the neighbouring country as soon as Isabella had been removed from the government. We may well suppose that the Queen-dowager had been pained to see a kingdom, so long the patrimony of her ancestors, pass away to a distant race. Nor is it improbable that her natural reluctance to acknowledge the sway of another over the land of her birth and the dominions of her father, had contributed to produce those delays and evasions in regard to the homage, which continued during the whole term of her power.

It is true that Edward long afterwards revived his claims to the throne of France, and, as opportunity presented itself and ambition extended with years and capabilities, pursued his pretensions with vigour and pertinacity. But it is no less true, that immediately after the removal of his mother from authority,

* The account universally given by historians, implies that she never after this quitted Castle Risings; and that Isabella only once more, during her life, mingled in public affairs is probable. It is nevertheless clear that she did not always remain at Risings, as I find, in the year 1341, a paper witnessed by her "in hospitio Episcopi Wyntoniensis apud Suthwerk," Rymer, tom. ii. part iv. p. 115.; and she was afterwards appointed to negotiate a peace between France and England.

a complete change became apparent in his demeanour towards the French monarch; the completion of the homage*, as before noticed, was almost instantly accomplished; and all his letters and commissions in the most unequivocal terms admit the title of Philip of Valois to the throne of France.†

Various circumstances, however, over which Edward had no control, had nearly caused a breach between England and France towards the end of the year 1330; and had not a frank policy and sincere wish for peace existed on both parts, extensive hostilities must have taken place. Former wars, and the ambiguous treaties by which they were in general

* 30th of March, A. D. 1331.—In regard to this date, a double error in the month and year has been committed by most of the historians of Edward III., who place the declaration of liege homage, which completed the transaction, in May 1330. The original document, however, is preserved in Rymer, with the correct date, 30th of March, 1331, and the mistakes are easily accounted for. The substitution of *Mai* for *Mars* is to be found in almost all the printed copies of Froissart, at the point where he mentions these circumstances; and he also places the event in 1330, because, in common with many, or rather most, writers of the middle ages, he began the year at Easter; and thus, that festival falling on the 31st of March, 1331, the year had not yet commenced, according to his computation, on the 30th of that month.

Let me here remark, that, from not attending particularly to the precise day on which various nations began their year, historians have fallen into innumerable faults, not alone in chronology, which would be venial, but in regard to the dependence of one fact upon another, and the reasonings upon cause and effect, which form one of the noblest attributes of history. At the period of which I speak, the court of England commenced the year on the 25th of March, and the French historians at Easter; and many modern writers have attributed effects produced in the end of 1330 to causes which really took place in January and February 1331, because those months were included by contemporaries in the former year.

† See Rymer's Fœdera, ann. 1331, the letters to the Pope, &c.

terminated, had left the limits of English Aquitaine, and the property of British subjects in Guyenne, very vague and undefined; and a system of border feuds and mutual robberies, not at all unlike those of the Scottish frontier, had been the consequence. From time to time these proceedings assumed a more important character; and national animosity, excited by reciprocal wrongs, produced formidable military movements on both parts. In all hostile attempts upon the French territory, the city of Sainctes, and the garrison of its strong castle, were foremost; and the incursions and depredations of plunderers from that place became so frequent and audacious, that Charles of Valois, Count of Alençon, the French monarch's brother, marched in force against the town, took it after a severe struggle, and began the total demolition of the English fortress. Instant remonstrance was made on the part of Edward; and it would appear that, even prior to the receipt of that monarch's letter on the subject*, Philip, being informed of his brother's expedition, had despatched a messenger to stay any aggression upon the territory of the English King. The destruction of the town, however, was by this time nearly complete; and the Count of Alençon, though he put a stop to further operations, continued to hold the part of Aquitaine he had subdued.

Negotiations ensued, and a treaty was entered into between Philip and ambassadors on behalf of Edward, which appears never to have been ratified;

* See a letter patent of Philip, preserved in Rymer, vol. ii. part iii. p. 64.

and, indeed, the many humiliating and disadvantageous conditions imposed upon England, were not likely to receive willing sanction from a monarch whose power and inclination to defend his rights were now every day increasing. According to this convention, various strong places in Aquitaine were to be destroyed; several sums of money were to be paid by the English sovereign; and the seneschals of France received power to search for and apprehend culprits and fugitives even within the English pale.

It would appear that, finding new difficulties arising at every step, while the negociations with the King of France were carried on by deputy, Edward, with the bold confidence of youth, talent, and energy, determined upon one of those steps of generous vigour which have seldom been without effect.

Philip was at that time residing at St. Christofle, in the forest of Halate*, between Pont St. Mayence and Senlis; and after having despatched the formal patent of homage on the 30th of March, Edward†, accompanied only by fifteen persons disguised as merchants, set out from Dover on the 4th of April‡, to

* Rymer, p. 65. 13th of April.

† Walsingham, p. 112. Knighton, col. 2555.

‡ This date has been stated wrongly by almost all writers, being usually referred to the 8th or 12th of April; and a doubt has been raised as to whether Edward undertook this journey for the purpose of conferring with Philip, or that of fulfilling a vow to visit some shrine in France. The date and the object, however, are both ascertained by two state papers preserved in Rymer. The first is a *memorandum de transfretatione regis*, dated 4th of April, 1331, which shows that, though the excuse was a vow, other purposes were to be obtained.

The words are, " Dominus Rex, quasi hora prima possuit se in mari in portu Dovorriæ, in quadam Navi, et transfretavit versus partes

confer with the French King in person. His journey was as rapid as possible; and his stay with Philip must have been short; for at that period journeys on land were performed on horseback, over roads both circuitous and uneasy; and yet we find that, by the 20th of the same month, Edward had concluded the negotiation, and returned to the port of Dover.

Nevertheless, much was obtained by this brief expedition. On the one hand, the manner in which he was received, and the effects which his generous reliance on Philip produced, must have been highly gratifying to the young King of England. On the other, the impression which his sudden and confiding coming into France, with no guard but the honour of the French nation, no security but the character of the French King, made upon that monarch, may be judged by four decrees which must have been issued by Philip of Valois while Edward was still with him. By the first of these, the territory of Sainctes was not only ordered to be restored, but 30,000 livres tournois were promised as indemnifications. By the second, the castles marked by the treaty for demolition were conceded to Edward in the state in which they then stood, and

Franciæ, pro implendo quodam voto, quod in quodam periculo constitutus emiserat, et pro quibusdam aliis negotiis suam et regni sui utilitatem tangentibus." Rymer, vol. ii. part iii. p. 62.

The second is a letter patent of Philip, dated the 13th of April, 1331, in which he refers to his personal conference with the English monarch, and recals certain exiles from banishment, " à la prière et supplication de notre ame et feal cousin le Roy d'Engleterre et Duc de Guvenne fait à nous en sa personne."

without any condition in regard to their destruction. By the third, all penalties incurred by Edward, as Duke of Aquitaine, for neglecting homage, and sheltering rebels in his dukedom, were remitted: and by the fourth, a number of persons banished from France, were recalled at the solicitation of the King of England.*

Having been thus received with courtesy, treated with the same confidence he had himself evinced, and allowed to depart with honour, Edward returned to his native land; and for some time the happy effects of mutual reliance and mutual good faith were seen in uninterrupted harmony and peace. By a voluntary act, immediately following his arrival in England, Edward resigned some ancient pecuniary claims on France; and all the state papers of the time tend to prove that nothing was less desired or contemplated by either party, than any renewal of hostility between the two nations.

While these public events occupied the more serious moments of the young monarch, his domestic life, after the removal of his mother from authority, seems to have passed on for some time in one smooth current of even tranquillity. The keen and comprehensive intellect, which afterwards founded on a sure base the commerce of Great Britain, and which first called forth and directed that manufactural industry whose efforts stand unrivalled through history and amongst nations, then slumbered unconscious of

* Rymer's Fœdera, tom. ii. part iii. pp. 63, 64, 65.

its powers, or only ran, with the tottering steps of a child, in the course it was afterwards to tread as a giant. Those hours of comparative leisure, which were not allotted to the perilous intricacies of foreign policy, or to providing for the immediate expenses and necessities of the state, were about this time given either to the suppression of many fierce and unruly bands of men *, which the unsettled state of the previous years had encouraged to assemble for the purposes of plunder and outrage, or to the society of his queen and child, and the rude but splendid pageants of the day.

Edward's taste for military sports and spectacles developed itself early; and his court speedily became celebrated throughout the whole world for its magnificence and its chivalrous spirit. No sooner had he returned from France, than he held a tournament at Dartford †; and shortly after, another was appointed in West Cheape, between the Cross and Soper's Lane. ‡ Fifteen knights, of whom the King is supposed to have been one §, challenged all comers, and for three consecutive days, in the sight of the ladies and the court, maintained the field against an immense number of strangers, who came from all parts of Europe to exhibit their prowess at the court of the English King. The part of the street marked off for the spectacle, was thickly strewed with sand,

* Walsingham, p. 113. Knighton, col. 2559.

† Walter Hemingford.

‡ Stow's London, p. 280. 21st of September, 1331.

§ Holinshead, p. 893.

to prevent the feet of the horses from slipping on the pavement, and a large gallery of wood was erected for the Queen and her attendants to view the pageant. Besides the curious picture which it affords of the state of the great capital at that period, this tournament is worthy of notice, as the first occasion on which the Queen, Philippa, displayed that generous clemency which renders her name beautiful in history. The scaffold from which she beheld the feats of arms, had been left insecure by some culpable negligence on the part of the master workman, and gave way in the midst of the sports. The Queen and her attendants, precipitated from a considerable height, were placed in extreme peril by the accident, and a number of persons were severely injured. Whether Philippa herself was hurt is not known; but it appears that her petition, offered on her knees to her husband, was barely sufficient to prevent Edward from inflicting an instant and somewhat despotic punishment on those through whose carelessness the evil had arisen.*

Although the passion for military spectacles was the natural consequence of a chivalrous spirit, acting, in a barbarous age, on an ambitious mind; and though it is more than probable that Edward, in first encouraging such pastimes at his court, was only animated by the same inclination which led others to frequent them; yet various great political objects were obtained by the renown which the English court rapidly acquired amongst the knighthood of Europe. Every

* Stow's Survey.

age has its predominant passion, by which men may be governed more easily than by any other; and, according to the state of society at the period, it is the rage of superstition, of barbarism, of chivalry, of fanaticism, of interest, of vanity, or of change, that leads the human herd for the time. The differences of national character, of course, affect the peculiar spirit of the times, and modify it in each different country; but no one who reads the most uncommented book of chronology, can lay it down, without perceiving that a distinct and generally pervading tendency characterises each particular age in the world's history. He who, with energy, marks the spirit of his day, and has the art to make his personal desires, however different in reality, assume the same garb and appearance, will deceive and rule the great bulk of mankind; and this has been the means almost universally employed by successful tyrants, hypocrites, and usurpers. It is reserved for the Mighty Few alone to change or govern the spirit of the age.*

In the time of Edward III., the enthusiasm of chivalry was the prevailing passion of the day. The great encouragement it received from the young monarch of the English, and the great celebrity which his court acquired, gave him means of conquest, and opened roads to ambition, which would otherwise have been shut against him. His name became formidable,

* One of the best tests of human greatness might, perhaps, be to inquire how far each individual, to whom we are inclined to assign that distinction, did change or govern the spirit of his age. Were this test adopted, we should find the great men lamentably few.

even before it had been elevated by any great exploits. To him the wronged and the oppressed of other countries fled for support and protection; to him came the chivalry of other lands, eager to distinguish themselves in his sight, and willing to serve under so famous a prince. His own subjects, too, trained to every military exercise, and constantly excited by martial display, were ever ready to support their king in war, and always prepared to take the field. The multitude of petty sovereigns also, who, scattered over Europe, only existed by the chivalrous and feudal systems, gladly courted his alliance; and we find that many of them were but pensioned retainers of the English monarch.*

These of course were great advantages; but amongst his own vassals, the military spirit of the age was excited to such a degree as not always to prove very manageable; and in many of the wars in which Edward engaged, though his own ambition had doubtless a large share, yet the necessity of occupying a brave and restless baronage, may not have been without its part also. Thus, not long after the monarch's return from France, some hostile movements took place against Scotland, which were probably hurried on by the warlike enthusiasm of the English nobility, though the subsequent conduct of Edward led him to be suspected of contriving the whole device.

As the wars with Scotland but little affect the history of the Black Prince, it is not my purpose to enter upon them in detail; but it may be necessary

* Rymer, tom. ii. part iii. passim.

to take some notice of their commencement, inasmuch as assistance yielded to the Scots was used as a pretence, if it did not form a motive, in a more deadly struggle which soon after began between France and England.

The determination, courage, conduct, and wisdom of Robert Bruce, and the re-awakened energy of the Scottish nation, had expelled Baliol from the throne, and driven the English from the land. The struggle had been faintly prolonged during the declining years of a weak monarch, Edward II., and during the regency of a vicious woman; but in March of the year 1328, a truce for four years, was concluded between the two countries; and the Lady Joan, sister of Edward III., was given in marriage to David King of Scotland, son to Robert, better known under the title of the Bruce. Various clauses, somewhat degrading to the English sovereign, and unpalatable to his subjects, had entered into the treaty concluded on this occasion by Mortimer and Isabella; and, after their fall had been wrought, it became probable that the expiration of the truce would be welcomed by both the King and his people as the signal for a renewal of the war.

Whatever were his views in this respect, Edward, either from politic consideration or moral principle, seems to have been unwilling to call upon himself the odium of breaking the truce before its natural termination; but the military spirit and restless ambition of his nobles would not wait the regular course of events. Many of them, by marriage or by grant, held claims upon lands in Scotland, from which they had been ejected, and to which, by the treaty of 1328, they were to be restored. Edward, as well as the parties concerned, had pressed the fulfilment of that stipulation*; but every application had been met by evasion, and the English monarch was not at all unwilling that his subjects should do themselves justice by any means that presented. At the same time, Edward Baliol, the son of the famous rival of Robert Bruce, driven forth from France, in which his father had taken refuge, ruined in fortunes, but ardent, ambitious, and brave, now resided in England, and courted every idle and restless spirit to aid in asserting once more the claims of his family to the Scottish throne. A number of the English nobles leagued themselves with the young exile; some bands of German free companions were engaged in his support†; and it is apparent that Edward himself did little to discourage him in his proposed attempt to recover the long contested crown; an attempt, indeed, which formed a good experimental prelude to that monarch's subsequent expedition, but which it might have been more for his honour to have left uncountenanced. He forbade, it is true, the absolute march of Baliol's troops through England; but he permitted the levies to be made, and the stores to be prepared for an incursion, which was but precursory to that which, beyond all doubt, he already meditated himself.

Accompanied by a force which by some is said to

* Rymer. Henry, book iv. p. 192.

† Walsingham, Hist. p. 112. Knighton, col. 2560.

have numbered 2500 men *, but, by no account, exceeded 6000, Edward Baliol set sail from Ravenspur in Yorkshire, and landed shortly after at Kinghorn. The wildest dream of hope could not have anticipated brighter success than attended the first efforts of the young adventurer's arms. Two superior forces of Scots, sent to oppose him, were, by mismanagement on their part, and activity on his, completely defeated; many of the discontented nobles flocked to his standard; a number of English followed to share in his exploits; and at the end of a few weeks, he was crowned at Scone, as King of Scotland.† Success after success followed for some time; and if the object of Edward in permitting Baliol to invade Scotland was to sow dissension throughout the nation, and prepare the way for the greater efforts he himself intended to make, his scheme was perfectly successful. At length, however, lulled into security by various artifices, Baliol dismissed a part of his forces, was attacked while off his guard, suffered a complete defeat, and fled almost unattended to Carlisle.‡

It would appear that the Scots, in the exultation of victory, committed various aggressions upon the English border §, in revenge for the countenance which Edward had given to the invader of their land; and though not unjustifiable, their conduct in this respect was certainly unwise. Had they refrained, Edward ||,

* Walsingham, p. 131. Walter Hemingford, p. 273.

† Robert of Avesbury, p. 22.

‡ Walsingham, p. 132. Knighton, col. 2561.

§ Rymer, tom. ii. part iii.

|| Finding infinite contradictions in our historians regarding the commencement of this war, I have taken my view of it almost entirely from

who was then preparing for a voyage to Ireland, might have remained satisfied with the experiment which had been made, and abandoned the execution of his own schemes against Scotland. Fraternal affection, however little weight the relations of domestic life may have when balanced against policy, might perhaps have brought him to spare his sister's husband, when difficulties and hazards were cast in the scale against ambition alone. But the Scots gave him a new motive, and a fair excuse; and Edward was not tardy in avenging his insulted frontier. The conquest of Scotland was a favourite dream of his race, and little was required to persuade him to undertake the enterprise, or to carry it on with energy; but at the same time it was necessary to guard against assault from without, while he endeavoured to subdue the people who shared the island with himself. This ne-

---

the Fœdera of Rymer; and, indeed, throughout the work, I have placed small reliance on the uncertain statements of even contemporary writers, in those instances where I could obtain the surer guide of state papers. Amongst a multitude of documents relating to the Scottish war, there are several to be found in the third part of the second volume of Rymer, which prove, beyond a doubt, that Edward not only contemplated an expedition to Ireland, instead of to Scotland, but that he had entered into considerable expense, and undertaken considerable labour, in preparations which proved useless. Nor was he without difficulty prevailed upon to abandon his purpose against Ireland. It is equally certain, however, that he threw no stronger impediment in the way of Baliol's invasion, than by forcing him to convey his forces by sea rather than land; that he received from him an act of homage for the kingdom of Scotland, and the formal cession of Berwick upon Tweed. See Rymer, vol. ii. part iii. pp. 83, 84, &c. It is therefore probable that though he had determined upon an after expedition to Scotland, as one of the remote visions of young ambition, yet that the actual commencement of the war was hurried on much more rapidly than he desired by the actions of others.

cessity became the more urgent, from the flight of David Bruce and his queen to the realms of Philip of Valois; and Edward, while he hastened his preparations for beginning the war in the north, left no means untried to secure the neutrality of the French monarch. The measure most constantly debated between the two crowns, was the marriage of one of the daughters of Philip to the infant son of the King of England. Nor is the fact that the first proposal of such an alliance was made by Edward at the time that Baliol was setting out on his expedition against Scotland, without some significance in judging of the monarch's motives.* During the three years which followed, though various petty jealousies and insignificant disputes arose, prophetic of more serious misunderstandings to come, every ambassador from France to England, or from England to France, was instructed to treat of the marriage between Edward, eldest son of the English King, and Johanna, daughter of Philip of Valois.†

While these proceedings were taking place; and while Edward III., willingly counselled to hostilities by his parliament, was carrying on an active and successful warfare against Scotland, his son, the subject of so many treaties, was increasing in that bodily vigour which was so essential to a warrior of those days. Nursed at the bosom of his mother, he received health and strength from the same pure blood that had given him existence; and the gentle impress of her own sweet mind fixed upon her child, during his

* Rymer, tom. ii. part iii. July 15th, 1331.
† Rymer, tom. ii. part iii. 2d of October, 1332.

early education, those kindly virtues which tempered in his nature the fierceness of his father's courage. Never, perhaps, in the world's history, do we find so strong an example of the qualities possessed by both parents being blended in the child, as in the case of the Black Prince, in whose heart the generous and feeling nature of Philippa elevated rather than depressed the indomitable valour and keen sagacity of Edward III.

That every advantage might be given to a prince for whom fate appeared to have in store the great but difficult task of ruling a mighty nation, Philippa herself seems to have selected a person as his tutor, of whose talents and virtues she had possessed the opportunity of judging.* This was Walter Burleigh, a well known scholar of Oxford, who had been appointed almoner to the Queen on her arrival in England, and had remained from that time attached to her household. Although in that age, as in every other that the world has yet seen, or perhaps ever will see, favour and friendship had a great share in the disposal of posts and occupations; yet, in the instance of the appointment of Dr. Burleigh, we have every reason to believe that judgment went hand in hand with regard. True it is, that we do not know what system of education he pursued with his pupil; but the result is sufficient to stamp its excellence and do honour to his name.

About this time, also, the infant prince received the first title by which he is distinguished in history; his

* Holinshead, Chronicle, 1002.

father granting to him, at the age of three years, the rank of Earl of Chester, together with all the revenues and privileges of that county. The next dignity conferred on him was that of a dukedom — the first ever created in England. On the death of his uncle John of Eltham, Earl of Cornwall, that county was raised into a duchy, and the ducal wreath was bestowed upon the heir apparent to the throne, then in his seventh year. But as many occurrences of great political importance preceded that event, it may be necessary to notice briefly the circumstances which either remotely or immediately tended to bring about the long and bitter war that ere long commenced between England and France.

CHAP. III.

THE FIRST INDUCEMENTS WHICH LED EDWARD III. TO INVADE FRANCE. — THE CHARACTER AND LIFE OF ROBERT OF ARTOIS. — HE AIDS PHILIP OF VALOIS TO ASCEND THE THRONE. — RENEWS HIS CLAIM TO THE COUNTY OF ARTOIS. — IS BANISHED AND PERSECUTED BY THE KING. — TAKES REFUGE IN ENGLAND. — HIS HONOURABLE RECEPTION BY EDWARD III., THEN ENGAGED IN THE SCOTTISH WAR. — THE CONDUCT OF BALIOL. — PHILIP OF VALOIS PRIVATELY SUPPORTS THE SCOTS. — A NEW CRUSADE PREACHED BY POPE BENEDICT XII. — PHILIP VISITS AVIGNON, TAKES THE CROSS, AND MAKES GREAT PREPARATIONS FOR A HOLY WAR. — HIS MOTIVES EXAMINED. — HE SENDS AN EMBASSY TO EDWARD DEMANDING HIS CO-OPERATION. — EDWARD'S REPLY AND SUBSEQUENT PROPOSALS. — PHILIP REFUSES TO BIND HIMSELF TO GIVE NO ASSISTANCE TO THE SCOTS DURING EDWARD'S ABSENCE. — WAR DETERMINED ON. — ROBERT OF ARTOIS SEIZES THE MOMENT TO URGE AN INVASION OF FRANCE. — EDWARD RESOLVES TO FOLLOW HIS SUGGESTION. — PREPARATION FOR CONFEDERATION AGAINST PHILIP. — EDWARD THE BLACK PRINCE CREATED DUKE OF CORNWALL.

Perhaps no period in the range of history affords a more striking example of what infinite evils may follow many nations, through many centuries, from the follies or vices of a single private individual, than the space comprised in the reigns of Philip of Valois and Edward III.

Desolation and bloodshed were now about to spread over the face of the world; and though it is more than probable, that a war of a minor extent between England and France would soon have ensued from other causes, yet there can be no doubt that the persecution of one of his subjects by the King of France hurried the commencement of hostilities, and gave them a peculiar, an extensive, and a pertinacious character.

The man, whose suggestions, more than any other motive, tended to incite Edward III. to his first invasion of France, and whose misfortunes and errors, with their consequences, thus involved Europe in a century of strife, was Robert of Artois, Count of Beaumont le Roger, a man possessing rank, power, and wealth, talents, generosity, and many high qualities, who was once foremost in the esteem of his countrymen, and whom we have seen enjoying the highest place in his sovereign's favour at the meeting of Philip and Edward at Amiens. To understand how he fell from honour and his high estate, requires some insight into his previous history, which shall be given as briefly as possible.

Robert II. Count of Artois, a prince of the blood royal of France, became the father of two children; Philip, his apparent heir, and Mahaut, a daughter. Philip married, and died before his father, leaving a child, his heir, Robert of Artois, of whom I now speak.* Mahaut also married; and her two daughters were united to the two sons of the then reigning monarch, Philip le Bel †, each of whom afterwards became in turn King of France. At the death of the old Count of Artois, his daughter Mahaut claimed the territory, to the prejudice of the young Robert her nephew; alleging that such was the custom of the

* Lancelot, in the Mém. de l'Acad. des Inscript. vol. viii. Mezeray P. de Valois.

county; and that, in Artois, the nearest survivor, whether male or female, succeeded to the feof of the last vassal. A protest against this doctrine was taken on the part of Robert, then a minor; but Mahaut was put in possession of the feof, leaving the young Count's claim to be urged when he attained his majority. What was really the customary law of Artois, I have not been able to discover; but it is evident that, when Robert, under the race of Philip le Bel, urged his claim before the peers of France, the chief of the court in which his cause was tried was a party strongly interested.

After various efforts, both in the field and before the tribunal, Robert acquiesced in the decision of the Peers against him; and, till the accession of Philip of Valois, ceased to contend for the inheritance of his grandfather. As his influence, however, had greatly aided* in securing the crown to the new monarch, Robert of Artois hoped for impartiality at least, and perhaps for favour, in a fresh endeavour to obtain the lands he had lost; and he determined once more to bring his cause before the court of Peers.

At the same time it would appear that he was principally instigated to these new efforts by a bad and disappointed woman, named, by the annalists of that day, the Demoiselle de Divion, who had long held an illicit connection with Thiery d'Irichon, a bishop, the minister and favourite of the Countess Mahaut.† At the death of the bishop, the Countess had been

* Froissart, cap. liv.

† Lancelot, Mém. de l'Acad. des Inscript. vol. x.

appointed the executor of his will. In this will, or by some previous deed, great wealth was conveyed by the dead priest to his concubine; and Mahaut, instead of fulfilling his intention, drove his paramour from her territories with virtuous and politic indignation. The Demoiselle de Divion instantly applied to Robert of Artois, and produced a letter apparently in the hand-writing of Thiery d'Irichon, in which the writer, using the name of that prelate, acknowledged having made away with various papers necessary to the establishment of Robert's claim upon Artois.* Although this letter was afterwards declared to be a forgery, thus far Robert of Artois does not seem to have been implicated in any malpractices. He afterwards, however, claimed to have his cause re-argued; produced a number of witnesses and a number of documents; and endeavoured to bear down opposition by a torrent of evidence. His witnesses were objected to, examined, menaced with the torture, and at length many of them were brought to confess that they had been suborned, that the papers produced were factitious, and that bribery or intimidation had been used to pervert the course of justice. Mahaut died shortly after the commencement of the trial; and her eldest daughter Joan soon shared the same fate as her mother. According to the custom of the time, the death of each was attributed to poison, and the storm of popular clamour began to fall upon the head of Robert of Artois. That nobleman boldly maintained his innocence, and offered to do battle with his accusers; a

* Lancelot, ubi suprà.

proof of his courage, but certainly no refutation of the charges against him. The witnesses adhered to their last declarations, and some of them sealed their guilt with their death, though on which side they lied most deeply has never yet been discovered. The Demoiselle de Divion expired in the flames; and Robert, finding not only his reputation lost, but his life in danger, fled from the court of France. His Peers had already declared the papers he brought forward to be forged, and the witnesses he had called to be suborned; and shortly after his flight, Philip pronounced a sentence of perpetual banishment against him.*

So far, perhaps, that monarch was justified; but Robert of Artois, in the madness of disappointment, had uttered some words of idle wrath against his sovereign; and Philip, forgetting kingly dignity and the grand quality of justice—calmness—proceeded to persecute him whom he had already judged. To give an appearance of equity to these proceedings, we find a thousand charges recorded against Robert of Artois during his exile at the court of Brabant, which, by their absurdity, cast great suspicion† upon the

* 8th of April, 1332.

† The chief accusation against Robert of Artois, after his quitting France, consists in his having formed a waxen image to represent Philip of Valois, and having, by pricking it to the heart, endeavoured to destroy the King. Such a charge needs no comment, as it shows how great a prejudice must have existed against the man, before any one would have dared to urge it against him. M. Lancelot, whom I have cited for the whole of this case, although he has by no means proved what he wished—that Philip acted with temper, moderation, or justice—deserves great credit for the diligence and research with which

more probable accusations urged against him, whilst the high and chivalrous character which he previously bore, and the honour and distinction with which he was afterwards received by princes of unspotted reputation, leave the whole proceedings in doubt and uncertainty.

However obscure may have been the conduct of Robert of Artois, that of the French monarch admits of no question. Philip, in banishing his brother-in-law*, his friend and favourite, might be supposed to do violence to his own feelings, and to sacrifice private regard to a sense of public justice. But when he arrested the exile's unaccused wife, and doomed two of his unoffending children to perpetual imprisonment†, the judge became the oppressor—the monarch was changed into the vindictive persecutor.

Nor was this all: the unhappy Count de Beaumont had scarcely taken refuge at the court of the Duke of Brabant, when Philip, by his ambassadors, demanded his instant expulsion from the territories of

---

he has brought forward a great deal of obscure information. He would have done better, however, had he pointed out that the Chronique de Flandre, from which he borrows much, is a very inaccurate document, and was composed under the eyes of Robert d'Artois's enemies; that the witnesses against that unhappy prince varied greatly in their statements, and were by their own confession unworthy of credit on either side; and that the paper called the Procès de Robert d'Artois was an ex-parte statement, compiled by those who persecuted him. M. Lancelot himself is obliged to acknowledge that, in every circumstance but this unhappy trial, Robert of Artois had proved himself a prince of the highest qualities.

* Robert of Artois married Joan of Valois, sister of Philip.

† Histoire Généal. de la Maison de France, vol. i. p. 387.

that prince. The Duke, allied by blood to the exile, hesitated to obey; but his frontier was violated by the allies and vassals of the French King, led by the Constable of France, and the pillage and destruction inflicted on his subjects, forced him to drive forth his cousin upon the world.* The same means compelled the unhappy Count to quit his next asylum in the county of Namur; and with imprecations on his lips, and vengeance in his heart, he gave himself to the seas, and set his foot upon the shores of England.

It is proverbially dangerous to tread upon a worm. Robert of Artois, ruined, degraded, banished, troubled the existence of his persecutor, and shook the throne of France.† He found the English monarch lately returned from Scotland‡, and full of victory and success. Between the beginning of May and the end of July, 1333, Edward had invaded Scotland, defeated the Scottish army at the memorable field of Halidon Hill, captured Berwick, and restored the dominion of the Caledonian portion of Great Britain to Edward Baliol. A young, brave, ambitious king, he had tasted the cup of conquest; and it is not natural to suppose that he would set it down till he had drained it to the dregs. Nevertheless, although ambition may be like an eagle, it is not on the first

* Froissart, cap. liv.

† Lancelot, Mém. de l'Académie des Inscript. tom. x.

‡ Froissart places the arrival of Robert of Artois in England before the siege of Berwick, and the Scottish expedition, in which he has been followed by Barnes; but Lancelot, in his dissertation, shows that he was ill at Namur in the end of the year 1333.

trial of her wings that she dares to stretch them in their fullest flight. The conquest of France, though it might have been one of the brightest day-dreams of Edward's kindling youth, required some one to sanction and confirm it, before it became more than a mere speculation. Thus it is probable, that when Robert of Artois arrived in England, the young monarch looked upon the conquest of his mother's native land, less as a thing that was ever really to be, than as an enterprise which might have been glorious and hopeful, had the extent of his own territories been less confined, and the resources of his kingdom more extended.*

The honour and distinction with which he treated the fugitive may have had its origin, perhaps, in a spirit of retaliation. David Bruce had been received, supported, and encouraged at the court of France; and the King of England might not find it ungrateful to welcome an enemy of the French monarch. Nor were the claims of kindred wanting, either as an inducement to receive the unhappy Count de Beaumont, or an excuse for giving him asylum at the

* We find, in confirmation of this surmise, that all Edward's communications with the King of France about this time, though breathing a firm and independent spirit, are calculated to preserve peace at any sacrifice which did not involve the true dignity of the English crown. Thus, in 1332, we find letters in Rymer complaining of the occupation of lands in France by Philip contrary to treaty; and in a letter to the citizens of London, Edward complains of many grievances inflicted by the French King. Yet we find, also, continual negociations towards a stricter alliance going on; and in 1333, Edward condescends to justify himself in the eyes of Philip with regard to the Scottish war, and prays that monarch not to credit any evil reports against him.

British court. He was a descended in a direct line from Henry III. of England, by that monarch's daughter Beatrice; and therefore bore a nearer relationship to Edward than he did to the king of France.* His reception, then, was as favourable as his best hopes could have anticipated; and after being forced to quit Namur under the humble disguise of a merchant, and to seek the shores of Britain by the most obscure and covert track, he was welcomed at the court of his young cousin with respect and honour, and instantly emerged again into splendour and command.

It seems allowed on all hands, that the instigations of Robert of Artois, the counsels which his knowledge of France afforded, and the pictures, which resentment and revenge taught him to colour too highly, of the disunited state of the French monarchy, first gave a tangible form to the ambitious dreams of the young monarch of England. But at the time of his arrival, Edward's honour and reputation were too deeply engaged in seating Baliol on the throne of Scotland, to admit of his undertaking a distant and perilous enterprise against any other country. The means, however, which that adventurous prince took to secure to himself the support of the English king, seemed devised for the purpose of alienating the affection of his Scottish subjects. He dismembered his country, to gratify the prince who had aided him to regain it; he divided a large part of his lands

* Barnes, chap. vi.

amongst the English nobles, and he rendered the crown of Scotland itself a feof of the crown of England. Hatred and indignation gave new vigour to his enemies, and encouragement from France was not wanting to prompt their resistance. During the three years which followed, Edward was again and again obliged to enter Scotland in support of Baliol; and though he strode through the land as a conqueror, finding none to oppose him in the ruined fields and deserted cities, yet no sooner were his steps turned to the south, than the patriots poured from the fastnesses of their mountains, and strove to efface the marks of his progress, and destroy the remnants of his power.

Various truces, it is true, intervened between the Scots of the party attached to David Bruce, and the English monarch; and we find that more than one embassy was sent by the French King and by the Pope for the ostensible purpose of negociating a peace. These missions, however, proved of no effect; and though Edward suffered the ambassadors from France to proceed to Scotland through his dominions, it would appear that they occasionally used the privilege to encourage and assist the opponents of the English King. From secret aid, the French monarch gradually proceeded to afford more open countenance to the Scots *, and Edward began to take measures

* Various papers referring to these events are to be found in Rymer, and, better than any other source of information, afford the true motives and circumstances of the time. On the 28th of June, 1335, we find a letter commanding William Clynton, Constable of Dover Castle, to ex-

against the armaments which were now extensively preparing on the coast of France.* The activity, energy, and shrewdness of the young monarch, displayed themselves most strikingly in all the manifold dangers that now began to surround him ; and whether in watching the conduct of Philip, remonstrating against the encouragement given by that monarch to his enemies, or thanking those sovereigns who had proved their friendly feelings towards himself, we find a mind expanding under the experience of its own powers, and ready to grasp even greater and more magnificent designs.

While Philip was thus playing a double and somewhat unworthy game, by giving partial and underhand encouragement to the Scots, without affording that bold and efficient aid which would have rendered a just cause successful, events were taking place, which at a previous epoch might have dispersed the clouds that hung above Europe, and removed the storm of war and desolation to the East.

---

amine whether there be not ships prepared in the port of Calais and other places for the injury of English subjects. On the 2d of July of the same year, Edward complains of injuries done to his people by Frenchmen, on pretence of the Scottish war, and of countenance shown to the malefactors by higher authority. On the 26th of August, a press of vessels is ordered to guard the seas against the Scots leagued with foreigners; and in September, 1336, we find a letter to the authorities of Bayonne, then an English possession, commanding them to prepare vessels of war, and to send them with all speed to the British channel, the King being certainly informed of large armaments assembling on the Norman and other French coasts, for the purpose of aiding the Scots, and otherwise injuring England.

* Rymer, tom. ii. part iii. pp. 129. 134. 151.

The events of which I speak were the predication of a new crusade by the reigning Pope in person, and the acceptance of the cross by several of the most distinguished personages in Europe. The immense progress made by the Mohammedan arms in Asia, and the almost total annihilation of the Christian sects which had once peopled the northern parts of that continent, affected the pure and noble mind of Benedict XII., who, by this time, had succeeded to the corrupt John XXII., with a touch of that fire which had animated many of the elder prelates of the Roman church.* Personally moderate and disinterested, yet encumbered by the superstitions of his age, the energy and enthusiasm of the Pope found no channel for action, except in one of those wild but grand expeditions which had been made from time to time for the purpose of freeing Syria from the yoke of the Moslem, and which had been feebly recommended by his predecessor. Scarcely, therefore, had the tiara bound his brow, when he called the princes of Europe to lay aside their unbrotherly feuds, and draw the sword for the deliverance of the Holy Land. It was a call that the principles of their religion and their knighthood did not allow them absolutely to refuse; but the two monarchs, whose co-operation was the most necessary to the success of the expedition, were impeded by jealousies and doubts of each other.

As early as the commencement of the year 1332,

* Mosheim, Cent. xiv. part ii. cap. ii.

at which time John still filled the apostolic seat, negociations had been entered into between Edward III. and Philip of Valois * in regard to a general crusade, preparatory to which a personal interview was proposed between the two kings. Each expressed his willingness; yet the meeting did not take place, and the expedition was delayed. At length, in October of the following year †, Philip solemnly assumed the cross, and ordered the crusade to be preached throughout his dominions. New negociations succeeded with the English monarch, but were as fruitless as those which had preceded them; and while the conference which was to produce concord, and the enterprise for which concord was absolutely necessary, were equally delayed, new causes of disunion were daily springing up, and frequent acts of aggression were rendering co-operation every hour more unlikely. ‡ Nevertheless, while such was the state of affairs in Europe, and when his own palpable encouragement of the Scots had rendered the preservation of peace at least improbable §, Philip

* Rymer, tom. ii. part iii. p. 79.

† Chron. de France, cap. 12. G. de Nangis contin.

‡ Rymer, vol. ii. part iii. and iv.

§ Many historians have placed this expedition of Philip in the preceding year, and have thereby lost sight entirely of the true state of Europe and the views of the French monarch, as well as of the very legitimate cause, that Edward of England had to doubt the object of Philip's great preparations. Any one, who will take the trouble of casting their eyes over the third part of the second volume of Rymer, will see, that during the course of 1335, Philip afforded continual aid and countenance to the Scots; that he delayed the fulfilment of various conventions concerning Aquitaine; and that his encouragement of Edward's enemies, was, during that year, far more decided than it had ever

of Valois made a pompous progress to Avignon *; listened devoutly to the preaching of the Pope, now Benedict XII.; and in company with John King of Bohemia, Peter King of Arragon, Philip King of Navarre, James King of Majorca, four cardinals, several bishops, and a number of sovereign princes, he once more received the cross, and solemnly dedicated himself to the deliverance of the holy city.

What were the motives which influenced the King of France in this proceeding may be difficult to determine. Some suppose that he hoped, under the badge of the crusade, to shelter himself from the animosity to which his support of the Scots on the one hand, and his intrigues in regard to Cambray on the other,

---

yet been. The mistake, therefore, by which his visit to Avignon and his vast preparations are placed in the beginning of the year 1335, instead of 1336, is of vital importance to the true history of the period; for at the latter epoch Philip had become Edward's enemy, when before he had been his friend; and while, in the first half of 1335, we have many letters of the English King, speaking in the most amicable terms of his brother of France, and apparently unwilling to believe the acts of aggression committed by his subjects to be countenanced by himself, before the end of September, 1336, he boldly states some of the preparations made for the holy war to be mere contrivances against England, and thanks the princes who have destroyed them, as if the fact were a matter of common notoriety. That Philip's expedition took place in 1336, is proved by the continuators of William of Nangis and the Chronicles of France, which leave the matter beyond all doubt; nor, indeed, can there be much question that Philip, at the time, was well aware that peace could not be preserved with England. At the same time it must be granted, that the recovery of the Holy Land was an object he often affected to have greatly at heart. "L'impresa di Terra Santa, che Filippo Re di Francia fingeva di voler fare, per divorar intanto le decime del clero," says Moreri ad ann. 1334.

* A.D. 1336.

had given rise in the north of Europe; but it is more probable that, determined to support the cause of David Bruce, he designed, under the plea of an Asiatic expedition, to obtain the means and to conceal the object of extensive operations against England. At all events, it is certain that he succeeded in gaining from the Pope considerable pecuniary aid; that he levied immense forces, constructed fleets, and laid up stores, at a time when he could hardly entertain a reasonable hope of effecting the apparent object of such preparations.* Nor is it at all doubtful that, at the time, Edward of England regarded this activity as the forerunner of hostility towards himself; and that, by a public letter, he returned thanks to the King of Sicily and the States of Genoa, for impeding and destroying the stores and munitions collected in Provence and Italy for the real purpose of attacking England, though covered by the pretence of a holy war.†

The most charitable construction to be put upon the conduct of the French monarch, and one which it would be unjust to suppress, seems to be, that, believing the crusade would prove a motive as strong with the King of England, as it had been with himself, he hoped to withdraw Edward from the prosecution of the Scottish war, by engaging him to spend the energies of his young ambition in the deliverance of Palestine. It is, however, certain that he despatched the Count

* Froissart, cap. lxi.

† Rymer, vol. ii. part iii. p. 151. 2d of October, 1336.

d'Eu as ambassador to the English court, declaring his purpose of marching for the Holy Land, and soliciting the presence and co-operation of the King of England.* Edward, in his reply, stated his belief that the preparations of the King of France were intended to act in Europe rather than in Asia, but at the same time promised to send envoys in return, charged to propose the only conditions on which he could embrace the crusade.† This embassy was faithfully sent, and consisted of two prelates and two celebrated barons. The terms demanded were neither severe nor unjust; and, indeed, without their concession, Edward would have been little better than insane, to have quitted his dominions for a distant and perilous expedition; he proposed, then, a firm league of amity between the two countries, extending to every one of their dependencies: he demanded that all castles and towns in Aquitaine, taken by Charles of Valois, should be immediately restored, according to a promise frequently made but never executed; and he farther required that the King of France should bind himself by oath to give no assistance, either direct or indirect, to the Scots, in the struggle which was then taking place between Scotland and England.

To the first two proposals Philip was willing to

* Fabian, p. 199. Gaguin, 133. — N. B. In regard to these two references I have relied upon Barnes, whose correctness in regard to citations I have ascertained in many other instances.

† Pantaleon, l. iv. p. 100.

accede; but, in regard to the third, he positively declined treating till David Bruce should be restored to the throne of his father. Had he made this declaration of his intention to support the dethroned monarch at an earlier period, and pursued it with more vigour, his conduct would have been noble and generous; but it lost much of its lustre from the moment and the circumstances in which his purpose was announced. These demonstrations on the part of the French King, his neglect of Edward's repeated application for justice respecting the lands withheld in Aquitaine *, and the long and irritating hostilities which had been carried on by bodies of Frenchmen under colour of the Scottish war, rendered an ultimate rupture between England and France inevitable. The only questions seemed to be, when the strife was to commence, who should first begin it, and where the scene of contention should be laid.

Such a moment was too favourable to the schemes of Robert of Artois, the disgraced, the banished, the trampled kinsman of the French monarch, not to be seized with avidity. The cup of long-treasured vengeance was now ready to cool the burning lip of hate, and eagerly he hastened to snatch and drain it to the dregs. An ancient French poem †, written on the subject, represents the un-

* Rymer, tom. ii. part iii. p. 146.

† Le Voeu du Heron is, beyond doubt, one of the most extraordinary and interesting poems of the age of chivalry, not alone in its historical details, but in its structure and its dissection of character. Finding that the notes on these volumes are somewhat too long already, I am

happy exile as choosing the moment when the English King and his warlike nobles were assembled at a high festival, in order to direct the animosity they already felt against France, towards the most complete gratification. He enters the banquet-hall, preceded by two noble maidens carrying a heron, which had that day been struck by his hawks; and, on this bird — reckoned, in those days, the most pusillanimous of fowls — he calls upon the knights present to swear each some vow of chivalrous daring. He first presents it to Edward himself, giving him to understand, in no very indistinct terms, that he looks upon him as but little braver than the heron, for resigning, without dint of sword, the fair inheritance of France, which was his own by right. Edward, blushing at the reproach, rises, and vows to enter France in arms; to wait one month in order to give Philip of Valois time to offer him battle; and, on his so doing, not to refuse the combat, even should he bring numbers as ten to one. Each knight follows the example of the King; the ladies, also, of the royal court make such vows as are most likely to encourage their lovers and husbands to high deeds; and, before the heron is removed, Robert of Artois sees the whole chivalry of England solemnly pledged to the invasion of France.

---

obliged to abandon my first purpose, which was to subjoin a translation; but any one who takes an interest either in tracing the manners of old times, or the rise of poetry in Europe, will find themselves well repaid for their trouble in reading the Vow of the Heron.

So strange and fantastic were many of the proceedings of those days, that it is perfectly impossible to say that some device, similar to that related in the Vow of the Heron, was not really employed by Robert of Artois to stimulate the King of England and his nobles to the enterprise he wished them to attempt. However, whether he had recourse to any such bold and dangerous step, or trusted rather to the influence of secret but repeated efforts to effect his design, the common voice of history attributes to his instigations the great but hazardous measure on which Edward now determined, of forestalling the purposes which Philip had tacitly avowed in favour of Scotland, by attacking the French monarch in his own dominions.

Listening to the suggestions of Robert of Artois, no sooner did war become inevitable, than Edward resolved that the scene thereof should be the territories of his adversary rather than his own; but whether, from the first, he did or did not intend to claim the title of King of France, is somewhat more doubtful. He had acknowledged Philip on so many occasions as King of France, that he had no straightforward way of sheltering himself from the consequences of the fact. He might have owned that he had done so from necessity; and he might have declared that, as his rights were inherent, no concessions on his part could do away his hereditary title. This, though certainly no excuse, was the only plain way of meeting the difficulty; but Edward did not seem at all inclined to encounter it at once, and his assertion of a right to the throne of France was made step by step, the style and title not having been added to those of England till long after he had been fighting for the reality.

The first great public measure taken by the King of England, in the prosecution of his design, was an embassy sent to consult with his father-in-law *, William the Good, Count of Hainault, concerning the best means of carrying on the war; and it is probable that the whole intentions of the English King, as they then existed, were communicated to that prince.† It was evident that Edward could not, unaided, support an offensive war against the united power of France, especially at a time when Philip was in a state of active preparation, which was at present the case. The announcement of a crusade, though it was now publicly postponed, had not only afforded a means of raising money, and a pretence for collecting armies, but it had bound a multitude of petty princes to Philip as allies in the same cause; and though the object was altered, it was not difficult to maintain the confederation.

All these circumstances were to be considered by the English King; and, while he revolved at home the measures necessary to secure full supplies, he applied to his nearest connection and wisest ally on the

* The ambassadors sent to the Count of Hainault were Henry Burwash, Bishop of Lincoln; William Montague, Earl of Salisbury; and William Clynton, Earl of Huntingdon.

† Froissart, cap. lxii. Walsingham, p. 108. Rymer, tom. ii. part iii. pp. 166. 168.

Continent for information concerning the situation and disposition of the minor states of the North. The Count of Hainault pointed out to the ambassadors of his son-in-law, a number of nobles, who, scattered upon the German frontier, with small territories and revenues, differed little, in fact, from the leaders of armed bands, except in the title of sovereign princes. Several of these nobles had been already employed by the King of England; and the Marquis of Juliers, the Duke of Gueldres, and the Count of Namur, had, at various times, received subsidies from the English King, and rendered that limited homage which referred alone to military service.* Of those who had already borne arms in his favour, Edward felt secure; and the Count of Hainault gave him reason to believe that almost all the leaders of the German Netherlands would join him as soon as he raised his standard against France. Besides these prospects of alliance and support, the ambassadors whom he had sent to Hainault, were particularly instructed to inform the English monarch, on their return, that his father-in-law regarded the enterprise he proposed as rational and hopeful, if undertaken with caution, and carried on with vigour.

Such encouragement gave energy to his determination, and Edward resolved to lose no time in cementing the general alliance he proposed against France, by his personal exertions in Belgium. So early as the month of December, in the year 1336 †, his firm purpose seems to have been formed of setting

* Rymer, tom. ii. part iii.

† Ibid. p. 155.

out on his expedition without delay*; and no effort was wanting on the part of the English King to rouse in the bosoms of his subjects that martial enthusiasm which could alone give success to the mighty enterprise on which he was about to stake his fortunes and reputation. Foreign lances might, indeed, fill up the void places in the English army, and foreign helmets might add to the number and magnify the array of the English troops; but it is on the swords and hearts of his own subjects, however few they be, that a monarch must ever rely, and alien succour can only be useful to follow where native energy leads the way. The stake was cast down by the King of England, and Edward was too wise to doubt that the men of England would be those who struck most boldly to win it for their monarch, however chivalrous might be the others who fought upon his side. At the same time, however, he might contemplate with pleasure the state and spirit of his kingdom at that moment. Four years of constant and harassing warfare with the Scots had given his troops that veteran firmness, and that practical skill, that familiarity with danger, and that habit of endurance, which leaves every energy free room and ample means to act in all times and circumstances. It is true, that though his soldiers might be steeled to fresh blows by long service, the nation in general might be wearied by protracted hostilities; but the

* This is proved by a paper De Commissariis ad interessendum tractatui pro defensione regni in absentia regis.

people of England have derived from both their Saxon and their Norman ancestors, a spirit of warlike enterprise, which may slumber for a time, but is easily roused; and Edward, while he applied himself to raise the means of carrying on his projected expedition, took the surest methods of exciting the military fire of his subjects.

In a full parliament, held at Westminster, on the 17th of March, A. D. 1337, Edward, the monarch's eldest son, was brought into the presence of his father, who, giving him the patent we have already mentioned, granting to him the name, title, and dignity of Duke of Cornwall, girded him with a sword, and saluted him the first English Duke.* The prince immediately, though but seven years of age, in exercise of his new dignity, dubbed twenty † knights ‡ from amongst the most distinguished aspirants to chivalry attached to his father's court; and we may well believe that the knighthood then bestowed was a matter of no small pride in after years, when that infant hand had become the conqueror of kings, and the victor of innumerable fields.

* Selden's Titles of Honour. Knighton, 2568.

† Stow, p. 233. Holinshead, p. 900.

‡ This is a striking example of the fact that princes, often before receiving knighthood themselves, conferred it upon others, for the girding the prince with the sword must only be considered as a symbol of investiture, and not of knighthood. It is true the heirs of sovereign houses sometimes received the order of chivalry even at the baptismal font, and also that it was sometimes bestowed more than once on the same person; but it would appear that Edward the Black Prince was not dubbed previous to the first military expedition in which he accompanied his father.

It was not on his son alone that Edward III. bestowed those distinctions which, in that day, laid the strongest obligation upon those who received them, to do some speedy deed of chivalry in behalf of their native land. Six of the nobles * who had gained high renown in the wars with Scotland, were created Earls; and a variety of royal grants and donations evinced the monarch's gratitude for services already performed, and, perhaps, marked his expectations of exploits to follow. Nor did he, in this instance, deviate from the ordinary practice of the day, though he somewhat extended its scope. It was at that time a common custom, previous to any general battle, to create a number of knights, in the generous hope that the dignity they had just received would incite them to actions honourable to the rank they held. Edward III. gave a magnificent extension to the same fine principle; and by frequently elevating several of his nobles, previous to any great undertaking, showed that he conceived a high station to be as much an obligation to brilliant actions as a reward for past services; nor did he ever find that he had deceived himself in his expectations, or had miscalculated the spirit of the English nobility.

* Dugdale's Bar.

CHAP. IV.

PREPARATIONS FOR WAR. — CONSTITUTION OF PARLIAMENTS. — PARLIAMENTARY GRANTS TO THE KING. — OTHER MEANS EMPLOYED BY EDWARD III. TO RAISE MONEY. — GREAT SCARCITY OF SPECIE. — DEFENSIVE PREPARATIONS. — CONSTITUTION OF THE ENGLISH ARMY. — NEGOCIATIONS ON THE CONTINENT. — STATE OF FLANDERS. — JACOB VAN ARTEVELDE. — DEATH OF THE COUNT OF HAINAULT. — NEGOCIATIONS WITH THE EMPEROR. — INTERFERENCE OF THE POPE.

The magnitude of the enterprise which Edward was about to undertake, required the most energetic exertion of a powerful mind; and though the young King necessarily wanted the experience which age alone can bestow, yet that deficiency was, perhaps, more than compensated by the ardour and activity of youth. The extent, the rapidity, and the variety of his preparations give a grander idea of the monarch's intellectual vigour, than is afforded by any of his mere military exploits; and no point in regard to which foresight could be available, was left unguarded, nor any advantage which could be secured by exertion, suffered to rest on chance. His preparatory measures divide themselves naturally into two classes; those which took place in England itself, and those which were executed on the Continent.

In regard to his proceedings at home, as large supplies both of men and money were necessary to success, Edward laboured by every means to render the expedition he contemplated popular in the eyes of the people; and he succeeded to an extent unprecedented in English history. His first recourse for pecuniary support was, of course, to parliaments, which by this time had received a form and consistency that already rendered them the source of all substantial power in England. It would be out of place here to trace the origin of these assemblies; but it is no less absolutely necessary to point out their precise state at the period of which I write. The general scheme of parliament, at this time, was formed upon that plan which had obtained the name of Leicester's parliament, from having been introduced by the Earl of Leicester during a former reign. It comprised all the great barons, or immediate vassals of the crown, whether lay or clerical, who were called individually by writ; and of all orders of the commons, whether clergy, freeholders, or citizens, appearing by their representatives. A great variety of changes took place, during the reign of Edward III., in the minor forms and customs of this assembly; and even the very important point, of the number of representatives summoned to meet, appears to have been left entirely to the will of the monarch, who sometimes demanded that one, sometimes that two members should be elected from each county and borough. The number of boroughs in each county, also, which returned a member, was very uncertain; and the will of the sheriff, we have reason to believe, was the chief guide in determining this point. One great cause of irregularity in this respect appears to have been, that the people in general, being obliged to pay their representatives, were very unwilling to be represented at all.

The parliament, properly so called, met almost uniformly in one chamber, whatever were the various ranks of which it was composed. On many occasions, however, and especially on questions of taxation, they separated into more than one body, the precise distinction differing at different times till about the year 1343, when the admirable division of lords and commons took place for the first time, which, with occasional interruptions, has remained in use to our own days.

At the period when Edward was preparing for his first war with France, another form of separation was customary, when it was found necessary for the various classes to discuss apart any point which was submitted to the consideration of the assembly. The prelates, about that time, retired to a chamber with the proctors of the inferior clergy, the barons and knights of the shires consulted by themselves, and the citizens and burgesses held their own conference together. Each order in the state determined what proportion of their annual revenues they could yield to supply the expenses of the government; and, meeting again together, they declared, in general assembly, the result of their separate deliberations.

How far the military enthusiasm of the King had extended to all classes, may be judged by the immense supplies which were voted in the parliaments of Nottingham *, Westminster †, and Northampton ‡; the second of which granted him one half of the wool to be shorn in the summer following, a part of which alone was sold, on the Continent, for 400,000*l.*§ This sum, itself, was enormous, according to the comparative value of money and the limited revenue of those days; but this, as I have said, was the produce of only a part of the wool given by the parliament; besides which, a variety of other taxes had been granted, as well as an increase of customs and duties, which raised the funds placed at the disposal of the crown to an amount never before known in this country.

Although these burdens weighed heavily upon the people, yet they were, beyond all doubt, sanctioned by the representatives of those who were to bear them, upon a clear and honest statement of the uses to which they were to be applied; and they were, therefore, fairly obtained by the monarch who levied them.

Edward, however, did not content himself with this just and honourable manner of swelling the funds required for his approaching enterprise. The parliament also granted, and the King accepted, all the money which had been collected in the churches under the pretence of a holy war; but this also, though certainly a misapplication of such a deposit, was comparatively justifiable when set beside his confiscation of all the goods and money of the Lombard mer-

* A. D. 1336. † A. D. 1337. ‡ A. D. 1338.

§ Knighton, col. 2570.

chants — men at that time the bankers and goldsmiths of Europe.* Yet so little were the laws of nations, and the rights of individuals, understood in that age, that this notorious infraction of the first principles of justice passed unopposed, and is recorded without censure. A number of severe and inquisitorial edicts also were renewed, to squeeze gold from the corrupt and the timorous; and the clergy, who, denied the means of defence permitted to other men, are, in general, the first prey of every tyranny, whether of the one or of the many, were railed at for their wealth and possessions, and were forced to yield their property to support a war which their principles should have taught them to condemn. Not contented with the immense supplies which the ecclesiastics had granted him in parliament, under various pretences, the King seized on large quantities of plate and goods belonging to many abbeys and priories throughout England, and exacted sums from all in a manner which was only not robbery, because it was not resisted.†

Another means to which Edward had recourse for raising the immense funds which he foresaw would be needful, was the appropriation of all revenues belonging to foreign priories throughout his dominions, — an act which had at least precedent in its favour. These revenues continued to be applied to the King's use for more than twenty years; and as the priories in England alone, dependent upon foreign monasteries, amounted to 110, the sums

* Dugdale, Baron. tom. ii. p. 146. † Knighton, col. 2571.

thus obtained must have been very considerable.* No measure, however, was neglected, which could increase his treasure, however extraordinary and undignified. When all the supplies which he could ask had been given by the general assembly of his people, he demanded of each county provisions of bacon, wheat, and oats; he borrowed † wherever he could find any one to lend; and pawned his jewels, and his crown itself, for gold to hire soldiers and to bribe allies. So completely did he drain the land of its specie, that money changed its relative value in England, and became enormously increased in price. Immediately previous to the expedition, an ox was commonly sold in London for 6*s.* 8*d.*, a fat sheep for 8*d.*, a goose for 2*d.*, and six pigeons for 1*d.*‡ We might suppose that some other accidental circumstance had affected these articles; but that commodity, which, from its universal necessity, has been judged, in general, the best measure of val[illegible] or, in other words, the best representative of labour—corn—bore nearly the same relative proportion to the other goods named, which it does at present; the current price of the quarter of wheat was reduced to 2*s.*, which clearly proves the excessive scarcity of money which had been then produced. § Having now noticed some of the financial measures taken by the King of England to give effect to his designs, it

* Barnes, p. 113.

† Walsingham, p. 146. Knighton, col. 2571.

‡ Fabian, p. 203. Knighton, col. 2569.

§ The price of wheat appears to have varied on ordinary occasions between 4*s.* and 6*s.* per quarter, during part of the thirteenth and the beginning of the fourteenth century.

may be as well to speak of the military preparations which he personally made, while his ambassadors were endeavouring to ensure abundance of subsidiary forces on the Continent.

The protection of his own territories was not forgotten by Edward, while preparing to attack those of his adversary; and we find extant a number of proclamations and precepts, commanding various classes of men to take measures for guarding those parts of the sea-coast of England with which they were connected. The defence of the mouths of great rivers on the shores opposite to France was carefully provided for; and the isles of Sheppey and Thanet, from their proximity to the capital and to the entrance of the Thames, were especially noticed in the monarch's preparations. The Isle of Thanet, indeed, was intrusted to the care of a body of men, which in the present day we should not judge well calculated to protect it *; the monks, who held numerous possessions in that part of Kent, being compelled by the king to defend the portion of the country from which they derived their revenues. This office was, of course, performed by deputy, as the feudal service of the church generally was in other instances; but that circumstance did not at all prevent the military duties of the clergy from being fully and efficiently executed; and it was generally remarked, that no troops in the army fought with more sturdy courage than the forces levied by the abbeys and priories.

While such means were taken by land to oppose

* Rymer, tom. ii. part iii. p. 182.

any hostile descents from France, great naval preparations were made by the King of England, to clear the narrow seas of inimical armaments. Repeated orders were issued for collecting and arming ships; and a number of admirals were appointed to distinct stations upon the coast *, amongst whom we find the same Walter de Mauny, who about ten years before had first arrived in Britain, as carver at the table of the young Queen of England. Various brilliant actions performed in the Scottish war had by this time rendered his name famous, and placed his skill and courage beyond a doubt; and the honour of knighthood, which had been conferred on him with great ceremony some years earlier †, was a prelude to the offices of high trust and distinction which he was now about to fill.

Such were some of the active preparations instituted by Edward III. for the defence of the realm, during the expedition he was about to make into France; but at the same time it must not be forgotten, that at that period the materials for active opposition to any sudden attack were never wanting in the English nation. Every male adult of free birth, within the limits of the land, on any occasion either of foreign invasion, rebellion, or tumult, might be called upon at once, by the local authorities, to take arms against whatever enemy presented himself at the moment. Nor was the *posse comitatûs* thus formed an undisciplined and unexperienced mass, the members of which were igno-

* Rymer, ubi supra.

† Dugdale, tom. ii. p. 148.

rant of the use of the weapons put into their hands. Each man liable to serve therein was bound to appear with the particular arms assigned to him by law, in good order and repair; and particular periods of the year were appointed for inspecting and training this local force, which could not, however, be obliged to pass the bounds of the county.

On the other hand, the movable military force of England, with which Edward was now preparing to act offensively in the war with France, was levied and organised in a very different manner; and it may be as well to notice its constitution here, that the events which follow may proceed without interruption. At the Norman conquest the land had been generally divided, and its population and capabilities had been ascertained at the time of the compilation of the famous Doomsday Book, from which period but little change took place in the military levies of the English kings, till the feudal system itself fell into desuetude. As the allotment of the territory conquered had been made in every different proportion that favour or merit could indicate, it was found necessary to ascertain, by some fixed rule, the quota of men-at-arms which each baron might be called upon to bring into the field according to the extent of land that he possessed. The various estates, therefore, underwent an imaginary subdivision into portions called knights' fees, one of which, in the reign of Henry II., was supposed to produce *20l.* per annum, bearing a relative value of nearly *300l.* of our present money, considering the difference of prices in those days and the present. Each knight's fee was bound to furnish a man-at-arms with his horse, fully accoutred, and prepared to serve the king either at home or abroad for the space of forty days *; and according to the number of knights' fees comprised in an estate, the lord thereof was obliged to supply his contingent to the royal army. The body of cavalry thus constituted, when fully called out, amounted to about 60,000 men; but, from various causes, which it is not necessary to investigate in this place, it seldom happened that so large a force of men-at-arms ever took the field with an English monarch. Besides these men-at-arms, the army was accompanied by a lighter sort of cavalry soldiers, called Hobelers, few in number, and principally serviceable in reconnoitring an enemy, or harassing him on a march.

The infantry of the English armies of that day was of a very mixed kind, and was chiefly raised amongst the tenants † and retainers of the great

* This was the general feudal time of service, and a longer attendance on the monarch could not be enforced; but the rigid term was rarely adhered to, and a popular monarch seldom found his troops disposed to leave him before his expedition was finished.

† By what authority, or under what form of law, the English infantry was raised, I have not yet been able to ascertain precisely. I find, both previous to the Scotch and the French war, letters from Edward, addressed to various barons, desiring them to raise within their district a certain number of the light cavalry, termed *Hobelarii aketonis bacinettis et ceroticis ferreis ac equitaturis, et prædicti Sagitarii, prout ad ipsos pertinet bene ac sufficienter muniti;* but no law is cited, nor any mode prescribed, for raising either one or the other.—Rymer, tom. ii. part iii. A curious letter is also to be found in Rymer, tom. ii. part iii. p. 186., concerning the levying and clothing 1000 men in Wales, which proves that the custom of clothing, at least, a part of the British troops, is of much older date than has been generally supposed. Se-

barons; a bold, hardy, and resolute race, alike fearless of danger, and skilful in the use of their various weapons. The chief of these weapons, the most tremendous, the most serviceable, and that to which England owed more than half her victories, was the bow; the simplest of all offensive arms, but one of the most fatal. The archer of England, who for four centuries formed the strength of the British infantry, relied chiefly on this weapon and the four-and-twenty arrows with which it was accompanied. He was not, however, without other arms, both offensive and defensive; and when he first stood in the ranks ready for service, before fatigue or accident had caused him to abandon any part of his accoutrements, he was furnished with a steel cap, a brigandine or leathern coat plated with iron, a short sword, and a dagger. Sometimes a pike was added, and a leaden-

---

veral of the barons, indeed, were bound by tenure to furnish men on foot; and it would appear from the various statutes, that in his early wars Edward employed the commissions of array — the original purpose of which was to call out the local force of a county in case of invasion (1 Edw. III. stat. 2. cap. 5.) — as a means of raising the infantry force required in his invasion of France. Against such abuses of the royal prerogative, Selden clearly shows (Hist. and Polit. Discourse, part ii. p. 59.) that the Parliament made many vigorous efforts, and that Edward himself, though often obliged to have recourse to extraordinary means of raising men, did not oppose the establishment of a more legal and regular mode of levy. The summary of the various acts of parliament on this subject, during the reign of Edward, seems to me to have amounted to a general declaration, that, if the King enter upon a war with the consent of Parliament, the Parliament grants him the forces, regulating the numbers from each county and borough; but that, if the King undertake a war without its approbation expressed, all his men but those bound by tenure must be volunteers.

headed mallet; and, on all occasions of approaching strife, the archer bore a long pointed stake, which, being planted firmly in the ground, with the point protruding outwards, formed an excellent chevaux-de-frise when the bowmen were charged by men-at-arms. Bill-bearers and pikemen, together with an irregular body armed with heavy malls, and other less formidable weapons, made up the rest of the infantry force; but the men-at-arms and the archers were the true strength of the English armies.

Although each baron commanded the troops he brought into the field, a regular scheme of subordination was not wanting. The cavalry was divided into bodies consisting of thirty-five men, headed by their constable, and of one hundred and fifty commanded by a knight banneret*, while a long grada-

* It has been stated that the men-at-arms were at that time formed into squadrons, or solid squares. I find no proof of it myself; and it is certain that they fought in a single line. The authority of the famous La Noue seems to establish that the use of the squadron was unknown in modern Europe till the time of the Emperor Charles V.; and St. Palaye, the surest guide in regard to every chivalrous custom, states positively that the cavalry of the more ancient armies fought alone in wing or hedge, as it was then called. His description of a conflict between two bodies of cavalry in those days, is as follows: — " Lorsqu'une fois les chevaliers étoient montés sur leurs grands chevaux, et qu'ils en venoient aux mains, chaque écuyer, rangé derrière son maître, à qui il avoit remis l'épée, demeuroit en quelque façon spectateur oisif du combat; et cet usage pouvoit aisément s'accommoder à la façon dont les troupes de cavalerie se rangoient en bataille sur une ligne, suivie de celle des écuyers, l'une et l'autre étant rangées *en haie*, selon la manière de parler usitée alors; car à peine commencions nous, dans le siècle des capitaines la Noue et Montluc, à combattre en escadron, ou, comme on s'exprimait alors, *en host*. Pendant ce tems là l'écuyer, spectateur oisif dans un sens, ne l'étoit point dans un autre; et ce spectacle, utile à la conservation du maître, ne l'étoit pas moins à l'instruction du serviteur. Dans le choc terrible des deux

tion of superior officers ascended step by step to the commander-in-chief for the time being. The infantry was likewise portioned into small bodies of twenty, led by a vingtener, five of whom were placed under the command of the centenary, or chief of one hundred. The strict amount, however, was very seldom closely adhered to, and, by a comparison between the numbers of soldiers and of officers reported on various occasions, we find that the vingtener sometimes had under him at least fifty men, and the banneret very often could not muster above seventy.

Such were the elements of the army that Edward employed his utmost energies in collecting and disciplining, during the time which intervened between the taking of his resolution and the execution of his purpose. His letters were directed to every barony and every county, calling out the local force for the defence of the territory, and commanding the raising

---

haies de chevalier, qui fondoient les uns sur les autres les lances baissées, les uns blessés ou renversés se relevoient, saisissoient leurs épées, leurs haches, leurs masses, ou ce qu'on appeloit leurs plommées ou plombées, pour se défendre ou se venger; les autres cherchoient à profiter de leur avantage sur des ennemis abattus. Chaque écuyer étoit attentif à tous les mouvements de son maître, pour lui donner, en cas d'accident, de nouvelles armes, parer les coups qu'on lui portoit, le relever et lui donner un cheval frais, tandis que l'écuyer de celui qui avoit le dessus secondait son maître par tous les moyens, que lui suggéroit son adresse sa valeur, et son zèle, en se tenant toujours dans les bornes étroites de la défensive."—*Lacurne de St. Palaye, Mém. sur l'Ancienne Chevalerie*, partie i. p. 19. Victor Cayet, a contemporary, implies that Henry IV. first introduced into France the practice of forming the cavalry into squadrons at the battle of Ivry. See *Chron. Novenaire*, page 328. vol. i.

and training all those who were willing from zeal, or obliged by duty, to accompany the monarch beyond the seas; and officers, called apparators, were sent down to the spots where these levies were carried on, in order to enforce the commands of the king, and inspect the state of the recruits. Immense and increasing exertions were made in every quarter of the kingdom; and from sea to sea the whole of England rang with the din of arms and the bustle of preparation.

At the same time the energy, the rapidity, and the foresight of Edward's measures on the Continent, were, if possible, more extraordinary than his efforts to call forth the military strength and financial resources of his own kingdom. Nothing which the most skilful diplomacy could effect was left undone, to bind old allies more firmly to the English nation, and to gain new friends against the moment of action and difficulty. Numerous letters to the Kings of Castille and Aragon, and to the maritime states of Italy, bespoke their friendship or their neutrality; and every independent prince in the neighbourhood of Aquitaine, from the leader of a hundred spears to the sovereign of a hundred baronies, was hired or solicited to defend or spare that exposed outpost of the English territories.* Aquitaine itself, also, was put in a strong and commanding posture: forts were built and repaired; soldiers were levied and trained; and fresh forces with experienced commanders were

* Rymer, tom. ii. part iii. passim, ad ann. 1337–8.

sent from England, to support and direct the natives of the land.*

But it was towards the north of Europe that the King of England looked most anxiously for assistance; and thither his chief endeavours were directed. The advice of the good Count of Hainault was followed to the letter, and a commission to treat with the other princes of Belgium, in the name of the King of England, was sent over to him immediately.† At the same time, however, the Bishop of Lincoln, and the Earls of Salisbury and Huntingdon, were despatched as ambassadors extraordinary to the Low Countries‡; and no accessary of splendour or expense was spared to dazzle or to win the petty sovereigns with whom they were about to negotiate. Forty knights, and a large body of attendants of minor consequence, followed them from the English shores; and the most unbounded profusion and magnificence accompanied their progress. Such pomp and display — never without some effect, even in the most calculating age — was far from impolitic, at a time when external splendour passed current with a rude people for real greatness. But, besides this direct influence, it gave the needy lords of the German frontier a proof that England possessed that wealth, which was the chief object of their desire, and that power of affording them sufficient protection, which was, of course, a principal consideration in the alliances they formed. Nor was the number of renowned knights attached

* Rymer, vol. ii. part iii. pp. 173, 174.

† Froissart, chap. lxiii. ‡ 19th April, 1337.

to the embassy, unlikely to attract a chivalrous population to the party of the King of England; while a particular circumstance in their appearance, which must not be passed over in silence, was well calculated to excite that curiosity, which soon becomes interest, and which proceeds by the steps of rumour and noise to excitement and enthusiasm.

I have before noticed the poem of the Vow of the Heron, and a custom practised by knights in that day, of engaging themselves in the most solemn manner to the performance of the wildest feats of valour. Although the poem cannot properly be considered as an historical document, yet we find that one of the vows mentioned in its course was really taken by a body of the English knights.* The courtiers and fair dames of Valenciennes were surprised to remark that a number of the gay youths of England, who followed the ambassadors to Hainault, were apparently blind of one eye, which was covered with a piece of scarlet cloth.† Although they refused to state the facts themselves, the rumour soon spread abroad, that this strange guise was assumed in consequence of a vow, never to open that eye till they had accomplished some great deed of arms within the pale of France. The very secrecy which they imposed upon themselves, of course caused the fact to be more widely told; and we

* Although many very learned antiquaries have judged the Vow of the Heron to deserve the place of an historical fragment, yet there are so many inaccuracies in the details, that it is impossible to receive it as an authority for any thing farther than the customs and manners of the times.

† Froissart, chap. lxiii. Barnes, chap. x. p. 109.

may well suppose, that the example of their vow was not without its effect upon the chivalry of the country in which they now showed themselves. That such engagements were productive of the most extraordinary efforts on the part of those who took them, is never more clearly established than in the present instance, as the persons whom we find named on this occasion, have left deeds on record, in accomplishment of their oath, which can never be wiped out as long as the history of England exists.

The negotiations at Valenciennes were soon concluded; and the ambassadors proceeded to the court of the Duke of Brabant, who, notwithstanding his connection with the King of France, suffered himself to be won by the words, or bribed by the money, of Edward's ambassadors; and entered into an engagement to supply 1000 men-at-arms, for the service of the King of England, upon the receipt of various sums which were actually paid. This contract, however, was limited, on his part, by a proviso, that the other vassals of the empire should join in the alliance; a condition which afterwards afforded an excuse for much tergiversation and evasion.

The Count of Hainault had already treated with various other princes in the neighbourhood; and, as he was still confined to his bed by sickness, the ambassadors, after concluding their arrangements with the Duke of Brabant, returned to Valenciennes, and invited those leaders to a personal conference in that city. The Duke of Gueldres and the Marquis of Juliers,. Archbishop of Cologne, empowered to treat also in behalf of his brother Waleran*, and, lastly, the Lord of Fauquemont, immediately obeyed the summons of the English ambassadors, and speedily entered into the terms proposed.† Each agreed to furnish a body of men-at-arms on his own part, and each also undertook to engage a number of other chieftains from the farther bank of the Rhine, to aid the King of England, as soon as he should appear in arms on the French frontiers.

Of those nobles who thus appeared at Valenciennes treating with the crown of England, the first two were sovereign princes, possessing considerable territories of their own, though held as great fiefs of the German empire: the last, however, the Lord of Fauquemont, was one of those captains of adventurers whose whole patrimony was their sword, whose whole territories the battle-field. In those days a distinguished name and a reckless courage soon gathered together, for a leader, a band of men as brave, as remorseless, though perhaps not so talented, as himself. With these he sold himself for the time to any prince who required the aid of mercenary troops, pillaged, ravaged, and slaughtered wherever he came, and amassing during war the sums necessary to support himself and his followers during the idle and piping time of peace, passed the days of his vigour

* The obscure words of Froissart have led many writers to suppose that the archbishop was present, but such was not the case. The name of the Archbishop of Cologne was at this time Waleran, or Walram of Juliers; and even in Messrs. Dacier and Buchon's excellent edition of Froissart a mistake is made in two instances regarding that prelate and his brother.

† 24th, 27th May, and 1st June, 1337. Rymer. Froissart, chap. lxiv.

and his passions in debauchery and bloodshed, and then attempted to expiate a life of crime by an expedition to the Holy Land. Such was in those days the life of a leader of adventurers, and such we have reason to believe was the existence of the Lord of Fauquemont.* Nevertheless, it is evident, from his being always placed on a par with the princes of the empire, in all contemporary writings, that the original station which this adventurous leader held in society was one of high rank; for, though necessity often compelled the monarchs of those times to employ partisans of a very inferior grade, and the courage and fidelity of these free companions themselves obtained for them in general great consideration, kings were scrupulous in keeping their chiefs in their just place, and a proud and fearless nobility took care that that place should be distinctly marked.

An instance, however, of the English barons having laid aside this haughty adherence to the distinction of ranks appears about this very time, and took place in the course of the next negotiation upon which the ambassadors of Edward III. were called to enter, in pursuit of their master's interest. The rich county of Flanders, with its great manufacturing towns, was, of course, not to be neglected in the efforts made on the part of the English monarch to secure a general alliance in his favour amongst the small states on the north-western frontier of France. Although, as I have before pointed out, the unhappy sovereign of that country had begun his reign over his turbulent subjects with unpopularity and injustice,

* St. Palaye, tom. ii. p. 86.

and though, after he had been restored to his territories by the King of France, the same conduct continued on his part, and the same resistance was renewed on the part of his people; yet it was to him, however little real power he might possess, that Edward first applied for free passage through Flanders, and for military aid in his proposed undertaking.*

The Count, though weak and incapable in his general conduct, adhered nobly to the cause of his benefactor, refused constantly to accede to the alliance against Philip of Valois, and exerted his whole authority to impede the measures and frustrate the views of that monarch's enemies.

Edward, finding solicitation in that quarter vain, now commanded his ambassadors to address themselves to those in whom resided the true power of the state; and the envoys, consequently, opened a negotiation with the towns of Ghent, Bruges, and Ypres, which, to use the terms of the Flemish annalist, then governed the country at their pleasure.† The chief of these powerful cities, Ghent, exercised a considerable influence over the others, and it again was, at this time, entirely under the domination of one man, whose character and fortunes were so curious, that I shall relate them as nearly in the words of those who lived at the time as possible, taking care to correct some errors as I proceed.

Jacob Van Artevelde was born a citizen of Ghent, and obtained at an early age, though by what means is unknown, a post in the household of the Count

* Rymer, tom. ii. part iii. passim.

† D'Oudegherst, Ann. de Flandres, tom. ii. p. 429.

of Valois, whose son became, as we have seen, King of France. The young Fleming accompanied his lord in an expedition to the Isle of Rhodes, and seems to have conducted himself well; for he was advanced, after his return, to the household of Louis, who shortly after ascended the French throne and acquired the name of Hutin. Before the accession of Philip of Valois, however, he had quitted the service of the King and returned to his native town of Ghent, with great natural talents improved by experience and knowledge of the world.* Both his name and the station which he occupied in the household of a royal personage would prove that his birth was noble†; but his circumstances seem to have been poor; and shortly after his arrival he is said to have married the widow of a brewer of mead, and is generally supposed to have continued the trade in which he found her employed, In this business he prospered, and obtained so much the grace of all the Flemings, that, in the words of Froissart, "every thing was done, and well done, which he devised or commanded, throughout the whole of Flanders, from one side to the other. No one, however great he might be, dared to disobey his commands or contradict them." The chronicler then goes on to relate, with no slight appear-

* Chron. de Fland., pp. 142, 143.

† It would appear that his mother was either a sister or a daughter of the famous Zegher of Courtray, a noble of high family, probably descended from the old Chatelains of Ghent. See Diericx, Mémoires sur la Ville de Gand, t. iv. p. 45. Cornelissen believes that Artevelde's name was merely enrolled in one of the trades as a matter of form, as were the names of the nobles of Florence amongst the trades of that city. See Cornelissen, Mém. sur les Chambres de Rhétorique.

ance of partiality, how the satellites who attended Artevelde would at his signal put any person to death without delay, "however great or noble he might be, without waiting for another word. Thus it happened often, and thus he caused many of the *grand masters* to be slain. On this account he was so much dreaded, that no one dared speak against whatsoever he chose to do, nor scarcely even think of contradicting him. And as soon as these sixty varlets had brought him back to his hotel, each went to dine in his own house, and immediately after dinner they returned to his hotel, and waited in the street till it pleased him to come out to play and amuse himself in the town, and thus they conducted him till supper. And you must know, also, that each of these mercenaries had every day four Flemish groats, or *compagnons*, for his wages and expenses, and he took care to pay them well from week to week."

"Thus, also, he had through all the towns and castles of Flanders, serjeants and soldiers in his pay, to do his bidding, and to spy if any one were disobedient to his orders, or did or said any thing against his will; and no sooner did he discover such in any town, than he ceased not till he had either caused them to be slain or banished. By this means, all the most powerful men, knights, squires, or burgesses, whom he suspected of being favourable to the Count, he drove forth from the country, appropriated the one half of their revenues, and left the rest for the provision of their wives and children."*

* Froissart, chap. lxv.

Such is the account given by Froissart of this extraordinary demagogue, whose vices were accompanied by splendid talents, and whose selfishness wielded the sword as well as wore the cloak of patriotism. The mal-administration of the Count of Flanders had afforded the first step in his ascent to power, and it would seem that Artevelde had distinguished himself by opposition to a weak prince *, not only in the council but in the field. Instead of attempting to win back the alienated affections of his people, Louis of Cressy had lately given them new cause of hatred, by the decapitation of a Knight Banneret of Courtray, called Zegher, whose great exploits had gained him general renown, and whose universal courtesy had obtained the enthusiastic love of the people. The real offence which this unhappy gentleman had committed, consisted in having shown hospitality to Sir Bernard Brett †, the first ambassador from the English King, and having advocated in an Assembly of the States, called by the Count himself, the policy of allying Flanders to England, rather than to France. The pretence for his execution was but a suspicion that he had received a bribe from England, but this suspicion was never proved to be correct; and his decapitation was certainly impolitic and apparently unjust.

The people of Flanders heard of his death with hatred and horror, and adopted the principles for which they believed he had suffered, with obstinacy and enthusiasm. His friends became their friends,

* Fabian, p. 205. † Ibid., 204.

his enemies theirs; and while they received with pleasure the new ambassadors from the English King, their ancient enmity towards Philip of Valois, who had certainly counselled the death of the Knight of Courtray, was increased in a tenfold degree.*

Such was the state of affairs in Flanders when the English ambassadors, dividing themselves into three bodies, in order to negotiate more rapidly with the great cities, arrived at Ghent, Bruges, and Ypres. Selected from the English nobles, for the qualities most likely to win the people to whom they were sent, they appeared amongst the Flemish citizens with unknown splendour, and dispensed their wealth with a studied profusion; so that all was magnificence around them. Under such circumstances the Flemings were easily induced to yield themselves to the wishes of the English King, and the proud barons of England did not disdain, for the service of their master, to treat personally with the brewer of Ghent.† One unforeseen obstacle, however, opposed itself to the complete success of the negotiation, the Flemings having bound themselves to the Pope, by a bond of two millions of golden florins, never again to take arms against the King of France; and, consequently, though they promised free entrance, passage, egress, and regress to the armies of the English monarch, and such hospitality and assistance as did not imply the infraction of their covenant, they could afford no military aid in the war on which he was at present intent.

* Froissart, chap. lxvi. † Ibid.

The subsidiary forces for which the ambassadors had already stipulated with other states, if fully brought into the field, would have produced, when joined to the troops of England, an army sufficiently large to undertake and accomplish all the purposes for which it was assembled. Contented, therefore, with the good wishes of the Flemings, and the promise of a free passage through their country, the Bishop of Lincoln and his companions returned to Valenciennes. That city was by this time in mourning for the death of William, called the Good, Count of Hainault* and father of the Queen of England. His death, however, produced no disadvantageous effects at the time; and his son, who succeeded, embraced the cause of the English monarch, with perhaps less of the prudence of years, but far more of the vigour and energy of youth.

In the mean time a different and far more difficult series of negotiations had been carried on with the Imperial Court. Various causes of enmity existed between Louis of Bavaria, the reigning Emperor, and the monarch of the French, which strongly disposed the head of the Germanic body to espouse the interests of the King of England. In his quarrels with the Pope, France had always been the stumbling-block in the way of the Emperor's vengeance, the supporter of the papal power, and, it has been surmised, the instigator of the inexorable rigour displayed by the Holy See †, even when governed by wiser and milder

* 7th June, 1337.

† Mosheim, cent. xiv. part ii. chap. ii.

prelates than the pontiff whose ambitious pretensions first kindled the flame of strife.

Even so far back as the time of his election, the whole influence of France had been exerted against Louis; and his opponent, John of Luxemburgh, King of Bohemia, retiring to the French court, remained the bosom friend and ally of Philip of Valois, while he ceased not to be the implacable enemy of the house of Bavaria.

Nevertheless, various circumstances opposed the alliance of the Emperor with the King of England. On the one hand, Benedict XII., who had succeeded John XXII. in the papal chair, had shown a more lenient and less ambitious disposition; and Louis was not without hopes, that by moderation on his own part, if unopposed by France, he might remove the excommunication which hung upon him as a burthen, more galling from its continuance than its weight. On the other side, Edward did not forget that the censure of the church not only extended to the Emperor but to all who allied themselves with him; and therefore, as a preliminary, he made use of every effort to raise at least that part of the sentence of excommunication.* We find, also, that he left no means untried to bend the more placable mood of Benedict XII. to a complete reconciliation with the Emperor. But the Pope was a Frenchman; and though his prejudice in favour of his own country, and his dependence upon the King of France, never led

* Rymer, tom. ii. part iii. p. 185, &c.

him to commit any gross act of injustice, yet such motives could not but bias his judgment in regard to the demands of the English monarch. Thus, in the case of the Emperor, he returned a steady refusal to requests which would undoubtedly have been granted, had they been offered by the King of France, and nothing could induce him to alter the terms of the excommunication pronounced by his predecessor.*

There is very little doubt, indeed, that Edward's intercession and its evident motive were unfavourable to the cause of Louis of Bavaria in the eyes of a French Pope, and that Louis, had his disposition inclined him to tergiversate, might have easily obtained absolution, by making it the condition of his amity or even neutrality towards the monarch of France at the opening of the war. The Emperor, however, was of a bold and fearless, rather than an artful and intriguing character. He scorned to treat with his enemies, and boldly seconded the views of the young King of England.

Though in the judicial character which the church assumed, Benedict had suffered himself to be influenced by prejudices that, however natural, the impression of his sacred function should have removed; nevertheless, by profession a peacemaker as well as by inclination, he left nothing undone to avert the bloody scourge with which Europe was

* Oderic. Rainald contin. Baron, ad an. 1337.

menaced. Both by letters and by embassies he endeavoured to bring about a reconciliation between the monarchs of France and England, and late in the year 1337 *, two cardinals were despatched as legates to the English court, for the purpose of negotiating a peace. Their reception by the King was as favourable as they could expect, and every honour that could be shown to the missives of the church was displayed upon their public entry into London. A number of the superior clergy and the lay magistrature met the legates on Shooter's Hill: Edward the young Duke of Cornwall received them a mile from the city gates, and the King himself descended to the door of his palace to give them welcome; but the effect of their mission was less than might have been anticipated.† Edward, indeed, agreed at once to a truce of some months with the French king; but he neither banished Robert of Artois from his councils, which was strongly recommended by the Pope, nor ceased his preparations for war. At the same time he published manifesto after manifesto, stating the various efforts which he had made as the basis of a secure peace, and declared boldly that they had been rejected by Philip.‡ These offers appear in many instances to have been such, that if they had been made and met in a sincere spirit, peace must naturally have ensued; but still Edward's preparations for war were incessant, and Philip himself, beyond all doubt, afforded the fairest

* Rymer, tom. ii. part iii.

† Barnes, p. 119.

‡ Rymer, tom. ii. part iii. p. 187.

pretexts for war, by suffering his subjects, and even his troops, to commit continual aggressions upon the territories of Aquitaine and the coasts of England.

Little doubt, indeed, can exist that both sovereigns, warlike by nature, rivals in ambition, thirsty for renown and well prepared for war, had determined upon it already in their own bosoms; and that the attention they seemed to pay to the pacific remonstrances of the Pope proceeded but from a sense of decency, and a desire of throwing the odium of aggression upon their adversary.

CHAP. V.

ATTEMPT TO SEIZE THE ENGLISH AMBASSADORS IN BELGIUM. — THE AMBUSCADE AT CADSAND. — BATTLE OF CADSAND AND DEFEAT OF THE FLEMINGS. — NEGOTIATIONS FOR THE PRESERVATION OF PEACE. — EDWARD SAILS FOR BELGIUM. — TEDIOUS NEGOTIATIONS WITH HIS ALLIES. — DUPLICITY OF THE DUKE OF BRABANT. — CONFERENCE BETWEEN EDWARD III. AND THE EMPEROR. — THE KING OF ENGLAND CREATED VICAR OF THE EMPIRE. — HOLDS AN ASSEMBLY OF THE BARONS AT HERCK. — IS JOINED BY PHILIPPA. — FARTHER NEGOTIATIONS AND PREPARATIONS.

SUCH important negotiations as those which Edward III. was carrying on, could not of course escape the attention of Philip of Valois; and he not only took every measure necessary to strengthen himself both by levies and alliances, but he also endeavoured to impede and harass the proceedings of his enemies in the Low Countries. His faithful friend and vassal, Louis Count of Flanders, though possessing little or no real power in his own dominions, still held various small cities and portions of territory which acknowledged his sway; and though he might be said to reside entirely in France, he visited Belgium about the time of Edward's negotiations. Through his instrumentality, Philip determined to seize the persons of the English ambassadors; and a large body of Flemings attached to the Count were stationed on the small island of Cadsand, by which it was supposed the envoys would return to England.

News, however, of this formidable ambuscade was communicated to the Bishop of Lincoln and his companions; and taking a circuitous route by Holland, they embarked at Dort, to which port Edward despatched several vessels for their conveyance and escort.* The voyage to England passed without any incident of greater import, than the capture of two vessels in the act of conveying armed succour from the King of France to Edward's enemies in Scotland†; and their arrival at Sandwich was the signal for fitting out an expedition against the force collected at Cadsand.

This was the first open act of hostility committed by the King of England against either the vassals or the territories of the French monarch; and its results afforded a type if not an augury of the event of the wars which followed. Henry Plantagenet Earl of Derby‡, and Sir Walter de Mauny, appear to have possessed the chief command of this armament. Both had highly distinguished themselves in the preceding wars with Scotland, and neither lost the fame in after years which they had already acquired; but whatever might be their military rank, the birth of the Earl of Derby immediately connected with the royal family of England, of course gave him a degree of precedence over his comrade in command.

To these two officers was joined Reginald Lord

* Ashmole, p. 647. † Barnes, p. 116.
‡ Froissart.

Cobham; and a considerable number of knights and gentlemen were allowed to volunteer their services. The force sent, however, was by no means too great for the occasion, consisting only of five hundred men-at-arms and two thousand archers, while the garrison of the town against which they proceeded was computed at five thousand men at the least, the principal part being men-at-arms.* The English navy bearing the expedition towards the Belgian coast, set sail from the Thames late in the year 1337; but the weather proving favourable, and the wind fair, the passage was easily effected; and about mid-day on the 9th of November, they arrived in sight of Cadsand. Immediate preparations were made for attack on the part of the English captains; but as their arrival had been perceived, and their purpose divined by the garrison, ample time to oppose their landing was obtained by their enemies, and no exertion had been spared to insure their repulse.

Five thousand men, all eager to try their strength with the chivalry of England, were drawn up under the command of Guy, the bastard brother of the Count of Flanders, upon the dikes and on the sands of the sea-shore. According to the general practice before a battle, sixteen new knights had been made on the spot; and arrayed under their several banners, the Flemings waited the approach of their adversaries, well knowing that the eyes of all Europe

* Froissart, chap. lxix.

watched anxiously the first efforts about to be made in the opening warfare of France and England.

No parley took place, the English drew onwards towards the shore, and the Flemings saluted them alone with their battle cry; but then, as the distance lessened into nothing, the terrible arrow flight of the archers of England swept along the enemy's ranks, and the famed and fearful cloth-yard shafts falling like hail amidst the Flemings drove them back from the beach, while the men-at-arms sprang out of the boats upon the land. Each rushed forward as he touched the shore; but the soldiers of Flanders, recovering from their momentary terror, closed in upon the invaders. The fight became hand to hand, superior numbers began to tell against the English knights, many were not yet disembarked, some had ceased to strike for ever, and at last the Earl of Derby himself went down in the midst of a host of enemies. Sir Walter de Mauny had just reached the land when he beheld the Earl fall; but instantly raising the battle cry of his friend's house to call his followers to his aid, he rushed forward, shouting, "Lancaster to the Earl of Derby*," dashed all that opposed him to earth with his battle-axe; and clearing the space around, raised his fallen comrade from the ground.

Such instances of individual exertion in that day often won a battle. The Flemings gave way before De Mauny and his companions; the Earl of Derby was but slightly hurt, the strife was renewed with

* Froissart, chaps. lxix. lxx.

more vigour than ever; and after a long and severe struggle, in which four thousand men were slain, the Flemings were totally defeated. Cadsand fell into the hands of the English, and underwent the extreme rigour of military law, or rather of warlike want of law. The town was pillaged and burnt, and it is said that a number of the inhabitants perished in one of the churches.* The English did not return to their native country till they had effaced every trace of a place, which might be considered as the first outpost of their enemy; and the number of prisoners, and quantity of spoil which they brought back, were worth a much more extensive victory, on account of the earnest of success which they afforded, and the encouragement which they held out to greater endeavours.

The commander of the Flemish forces, who had fought with the most determined valour as long as resistance could be available, was now amongst the prisoners, and was received by Edward with the chivalrous courtesy of the day. All that was demanded was his parole: he was suffered to remain at large in the brilliant court of England; and before a year had passed, Guy of Flanders had done homage to Edward, and taken service in the English army.† The other prisoners were not only numerous, but must also have been of high rank; for we find that those which surrendered to Walter de Mauny alone, were bought by King Edward shortly

* Walsingham, Hist. p. 132.

† Froissart, chap. lxx.

after, for the large sum of eight thousand pounds *; from which circumstance we may naturally conclude that the ransom demanded from each was that of a person belonging to the most elevated classes of society.

In the meanwhile, although war had not been formally declared, the negotiations, as well as the acts of the monarchs of France and England, began daily to assume a more hostile character. On some occasions Philip refused to admit the English ambassadors to his presence †, and Edward, in addressing him, began to lay aside the form he had formerly used, and to style him alone Philip of Valois, and Our cousin of France.‡ The English monarch, however, had not yet openly arrogated to himself the title of King of France, which he refused to Philip, though we find that on one occasion he so calls himself in a commission addressed to the Duke of Brabant in 1337 §: but this assumption was for the time laid aside again, and it is not unworthy of remark, that while Edward was asserting in arms his right to the French crown, he hesitated long to take the title which he claimed. So much importance is often attached to a mere word.

Still embassies and negotiations, conducted under the mediation of the holy see, continued to occupy the chanceries of France and England, with the vain view of concluding peace, and various truces were granted and renewed, while the two monarchs mu-

* Holinshed. † Barnes.

‡ 21st June. Rotul. Aleman. 12 Ed. 3. p. 1. m. 5.

§ Ashmole, p. 647. ex Rot. Aleman. 11 Ed. 3.

tually declared their sincere desire for the tranquillity of Europe, and in the mean time prepared diligently for the inevitable war.

The news of the English victory at Cadsand spread rapidly through the states of Edward's allies, and none seem to have felt more pleasure at the defeat of the Flemings attached to the Count's party, than their countrymen, the citizens of the good towns.* As the leader of those seditious cities, Jacob Van Artevelde wrote to congratulate the English king, and at the same time strongly recommended an immediate journey to Flanders, which he declared would no less gratify the Flemings than promote the King's views, by affording him a clearer insight into the affairs of the Continent. On this step, Edward had determined long before; but the church was making its last effort to preserve peace between the two crowns, and the Archbishop of Canterbury, with several other prelates and noblemen, were still in France upon that pacific errand. For their return Edward perhaps delayed a short time; but by the end of June his preparations were complete, the chance of peace hopeless, and on the 12th of July, 1338, he put to sea, and shortly after landed in safety at Antwerp.†

Of the force which actually accompanied the English monarch, we have no clear account, but there is every reason to believe that it was considerable. Five hundred sail were employed in transporting it from England to Flanders; and the number of the great

* Froissart, cap. lxxi.

† Rymer, tom. ii. part iv. p. 28.

barons and their retainers who are enumerated by the best authorities*, seem to prove that an important part, though not the whole, of the feudal array of the kingdom, escorted the monarch on his foreign expedition. Although Queen Philippa remained behind in England, yet in order either that she might speedily follow her husband, or that the Prince might be early initiated into affairs of state, Edward, the young Duke of Cornwall, was named custos of the realm during his father's absence. A council was appointed to aid him, of whom the Archbishop of Canterbury was one, that prelate being recalled† from his embassy to France immediately after the landing of Edward at Antwerp.‡

Hitherto every thing had smiled upon the enterprise of the English monarch; nothing had crossed his purpose, nothing had obstructed its execution, but henceforth Edward was destined to encounter all the pains and perplexities of an intricate diplomacy, with several lukewarm and mercenary allies, whose sole tie was interest, whose whole object was gain. Though perhaps a minister may find in a tortuous negotiation, carried on with all the calmness of a third person, the degree of pleasure derived from one of those games in which skill and hazard may nicely balance each other; yet to a young and ardent sovereign, with not only his own interests but his own happiness engaged, the delays, evasions, and cavils of

* Dugdale, Baronage.

† The letters of revocation issued the 22d July, 1338.

‡ Rymer, tom. ii. part iv.

personal diplomacy must have been a wearisome load indeed.

The splendour of the monarch's court and retinue drew multitudes to gaze upon him on his first arrival at Antwerp; but the allies whom he had subsidised were slack in paying him even the courtesy of a visit, and it was not till he summoned them to his presence that they appeared.

At length the Duke of Brabant, the Duke of Gueldres, the Marquis of Juliers, John of Hainault Lord of Beaumont, and the Lord of Fauquemont, presented themselves, and were called to a general conference by the English king. Edward set forth, in the address with which he opened the business before them, the great expense he had incurred in coming thither upon the promises they had made to aid him with certain bodies of men; he also represented the increased expenditure to which every day's delay must put him, while maintaining so large a force in a foreign country; and he begged them to consult together in regard to the first steps to be taken, and to let him know what would be the earliest period at which they could each join him with the contingent they had agreed to furnish.

After much discussion, the only reply made by the barons was, that they had come thither merely to show their respect to the King of England, but were unprepared at the moment to satisfy him on the points he propounded. With his leave they further proposed to separate for a time, and after consulting with their friends and followers to meet again and yield a definitive answer.

Edward was obliged to comply; but, at the time fixed for the second meeting, he received messengers from the barons, commanded to state that they were all prepared and ready to march, but that they would not join him till the Duke of Brabant, who was the nearest to the spot but appeared the most tardy in his efforts, should have put his troops in motion. To the Duke of Brabant the English monarch now addressed the most pressing entreaties to hasten his movements; but that prince, whose cold countenance had cast a damp and hesitation over the council held at Antwerp, instead of taking any measures to give effectual aid to his cousin the King of England, had passed his time in despatching envoys to Philip of Valois, beseeching him not to give credit to any of the evil reports against him, and, in short, endeavouring, by the basest dissimulation, to temporise with both the rival monarchs, till he saw clearly where he should find the greatest advantage. He now replied to the urgent messages of Edward, that he would prepare without delay, but that in the first place he must confer with the other barons.

" The King of England, seeing that he could gain nothing further by putting himself into wrath," says the quaint old chronicle, consented to what his cousin demanded; and a general meeting of the confederates was appointed at Halle, upon the confines of Hainault and Brabant. Edward was again present, but the result of the meeting was less satisfactory than ever; and, after long deliberations, the German barons replied to the demands of the King of England, that they could not appear in arms against France, unless their own sovereign, the Emperor, authorised them so to do, by personally defying the French monarch. So pitiful a subterfuge discomposed, for a moment, the calmness of the English king; but, though he plainly saw that the Duke of Brabant was the fabricator of this new obstacle, the same motives for smothering his anger against that prince, which had before affected him, still existed; and he dismissed his tardy and unwilling allies for the time, in order to negotiate with the Emperor respecting the difficulty which had been thus thrown in his way.

His parting address to the Belgian lords seems to have been temperate, but firm; and, before concluding, he declared his intention of remaining on the Continent till they were prepared to act, and pointed out to them the disgrace which would attend him for ever, if he retired to his own country, after such great military preparations, without having struck a blow, adding, "Aid me then, nobles, with your best advice, for your honour's sake and for mine; for be you sure that, if in this affair I meet with shame, your own reputation will not remain unstained."

This appeal was not without its effect on several of the German feudatories. They explained to Edward that the Emperor had many sufficient motives for countenancing the war against Philip of Valois, who had appropriated a great part of the county of Cambresis, although it was, in fact, a high fief of the empire. The Marquis of Juliers agreed to accompany the ambassadors which Edward proposed to send to the German monarch, and the Duke of Gueldres offered to despatch envoys at the same time to support the request of his ally.

Edward's preceding negotiations with Louis of Bavaria, and his exertions in favour of that monarch, had so far prepared the way for his own views, in the present instance, that the Emperor appears to have met his wishes without a moment's delay; and a personal interview between the two sovereigns was instantly determined upon. In the latter end of August, 1338, Edward set out for Coblentz, with the purpose of meeting Louis of Bavaria in that city; and, having been received by him with honour and distinction, was created Vicar of the Empire. The ceremony of his installation was performed with great pomp and splendour in the market-place, in which, we are told, 17,000 knights and squires were assembled on the occasion. At the same time the Emperor, in his own name, publicly defied (as the act of declaring war was then termed) the King of France; and gave into the hands of Edward III. the whole power which he himself possessed in the lower circles of Germany from the Rhine to the sea.*

* The account given by Barnes, and that in the Chronicle of Flanders, afford a much more graphic narrative of these events than that to which I have found it necessary to confine myself. But Barnes has followed Knighton and Walsingham, who place the meeting of the sovereigns at Cologne; while the Chronicle of Flanders lays the whole

The real power transmitted was not very great, but the military nature of the authority which the Vicariate conveyed was precisely that which Edward desired. He accordingly lost no time in proceeding to exercise his new functions; and, returning to Antwerp * as soon as decency permitted him to terminate his visit to the Emperor, he once more issued a summons to the German nobles. The place appointed for their meeting was the small town of Herck, on the frontiers of Brabant; and the multitude of barons, knights, and squires who now flocked thither was so great that space could scarcely be found for their accommodation.† What induced the monarch to choose so insignificant and incommodious a spot does not appear; but, besides the smallness of the town itself relatively to the numbers by which it was now crowded, it offered the additional inconvenience of possessing no public building of sufficient size and dignity for the conference of the King and his

---

scene at Frankfort. M. Dacier, however, in his notes on Froissart, clearly establishes, from papers which leave no doubt of his accuracy, that the conference of Louis and Edward took place at Coblentz; and I have, consequently, been obliged to reject the more picturesque narrative, as I could not suppose those authors to have been well acquainted with the details who were ignorant of the principal facts. I have searched diligently amongst the German writers for some further elucidation upon this point; but, notwithstanding that ruggedness of style, and tone of authority, which so often pass for erudition, I have found less accuracy than I could have expected. Pfeffinger, for instance, in his Corpus Juris, places the meeting in "*Villa Rens super Rhenum*," with the date 1336; during the whole course of which year Edward never quitted Great Britain.

* September, 1338. Rymer, tom. ii. part iv.

† Froissart, chap. lxxvi.

allies. The only place which could contain the assembly was the hall in which the common markets were held; and the hasty attempts to give it splendour for this occasion added ridicule to discomfort.* The whole building was hung with fine cloth; and the throne of the English monarch, raised five feet above any of the other seats, owed its elevation to a butcher's block, on which at other times meat was cut up and sold.

On this strange and ominous platform Edward sat crowned in state † to receive the barons; and, after some preparation, his commission as Vicar of the Empire ‡ was read aloud before the people. A cause being then called on and argued, Edward proceeded to pronounce judgment as the first act of his new authority, and then turned to consider the means of forwarding his views against France.

Although all excuse for neglecting to fulfil their engagements to the King of England was now taken away from the German barons, for that year at least the time of action had past by, as before their whole forces could have been brought into the

* Froissart, chap. lxxvi.

† 12th October, 1338. Ed. Dinterus, cited by Dacier.

‡ The powers conferred upon Edward are thus stated by Froissart; and, as far as I have been able to discover, he is sufficiently accurate on this point:—"Là endroit par devant tout le peuple qui là étoit et par devant tout les seigneurs, furent lues les lettres de l'Empereur, par lesquelles il constituoit le Roi Edouard d'Angleterre son vicaire et son lieutenant pour lui, et lui donnoit pouvoir de faire droit et loi à chacun du nom de lui, et de faire monnoie d'or et d'argent aussi au nom de lui; et commandoit par ses lettres à tous les princes de son empire et à tous autres à lui sujets qu'ils obéïssent à son vicaire comme à lui même et fissent féauté et hommage comme au Vicaire de l'Empire."

field, winter would have arrived to stay their operations. They now, however, gave promise of greater activity, binding themselves by oath to be completely ready within three weeks after St. John's day of the following year *; and Edward, foreseeing that his absence might again deprive the confederates of that energy which his presence alone had inspired, resolved to pass the winter on the Continent. The large body of troops which he had brought with him from England became unnecessary in his present situation, while their want was much felt on the Scottish frontier, where insecure truces, granted and broken every day, were the only safeguards to tranquillity. Determined not to quit the spot, he desired his Queen, Philippa, to join him at Antwerp; but, after the conference at Herck, he sent over the greater part of his forces to guard the northern marches during the winter: for though no regular campaigns were undertaken at that season, yet the French were endeavouring to effect a diversion from their own country by strenuously aiding the Scots in their efforts against the English.

Philippa, obeying at once her husband's mandate †, arrived ‡ at Antwerp in the autumn, accompanied by a splendid train; and the winter passed over, on the part of Edward, in various endeavours to extend

* Froissart, chap. lxxvi. † Walsingham, Hist., p. 132.

‡ It is not unlikely that Edward foresaw, long before, the course that events would take, for Philippa, who arrived in Antwerp some time in October, was probably summoned to join her husband prior to the parliament of Herck, and, perhaps, even before the meeting of her husband with the Emperor. She was at this time pregnant of Lionel of Antwerp, afterwards Duke of Clarence.

his alliances, and to increase the activity and zeal of the allies he possessed, both by courting their affections and displaying his wealth. To meet his expenses, a parliament, held at Northampton by the young Prince his son *, granted fresh supplies to a large amount; and donations from the clergy, as well as tithes of their revenues for two years, added considerably to the sums already at his disposal.

In the meanwhile, the double-dealing Duke of Brabant found that the prolonged stay of the King of England might prove destructive to the course of policy he was pursuing towards France. Nevertheless, knowing well the force of reiteration, against which the power of demonstration itself is not always available in the human mind, he despatched one of his most attached friends, Louis Lord of Cranehen, to repeat to Philip of Valois the same false assurances of good faith and friendship with which he had hitherto deceived him: His protestations were not only successful with the King of France, but the consummate art of the Duke was sufficient to deceive even his own ambassador, notwithstanding all that passed before him previous to his departure for Paris. Cranehen remained at the court to which he was sent, fully persuaded that his lord was sincere in maintaining neutrality between the French and English monarchs: for every new and suspicious circumstance, which betrayed his master's real intentions to the court of France, he was furnished by that wily

* July, 1338. Barnes, p. 125.

prince with some specious excuse; and, deceived himself as well as deceiving others, he continued to the last maintaining strongly and successfully the purity of the Duke's intentions. At length, however, the mask was thrown off: the Duke of Brabant appeared in arms as a partisan of the King of England; and Cranehen, struck with shame, astonishment, and despair, at having been made the tool of such base duplicity, fell sick and died at the court of France, proving by his grief and death the honesty of his own belief.*

Though deceived in regard to the Duke of Brabant, Philip of Valois was not at all ignorant of the designs or measures of the King of England; and, while he laboured to compel his enemy's return to his island-dwelling by fomenting the hostilities on the Scottish frontier, and suffered the Pope to make a thousand ineffectual efforts to turn Edward from his purpose in a more pacific manner, he neglected no exertion in order to repel force by force, and retaliate war for war, though, as it proved, the defensive preparations of his menaced frontier were most unwisely forgotten in vague schemes of offence.

With this view, while the chivalry of his own realm were held ready to take the field at a moment's notice, he received into his pay various large armaments, equipped in the ports of the maritime states of Italy: Spain also contributed a considerable number of naval adventurers; and, besides these, Philip

* Froissart, chap. lxxvii. lxxxiii.

increased his fleet by squadrons fitted out by his vassals on the sea coasts of Normandy, Britany, and Picardy. Far more zealously than any of his other subjects, the Normans entered into the interest of the French monarch; and, with an absurd and ignorant vanity, the inhabitants of that duchy voluntarily proposed to undertake the conquest of England.*

Philip of Valois was neither so weak, nor so ill-informed, as to think that 4000 Norman men-at-arms, and 20,000 archers, could subdue a land which was changed in every respect since the fall of Harold; but he, nevertheless, eagerly accepted the offer of his subjects, believing that even the rumour of such a transaction, and far more the attempt of such an enterprise, might divert the English forces from his northern frontier.

Not relying entirely upon this probability, however, he took care to draw some more certain benefit from the ready zeal of the Normans, and inserted in the covenant established between him and them, that, in case of France being invaded, the 24,000 volunteers prepared against England should serve in his army to repel the invaders. Upon this condition he willingly suffered the Normans to divide as they liked, upon paper, the island they proposed to conquer, and to provide for all sorts of contingencies, which were never to occur.

As the spring of 1339 opened upon the world, the preparations for a general war were completed on

* Du Tillet, Recueil des Traités, pp. 216. 232. Robert de Avesbury, p. 131.

both sides. Before the day appointed for the meeting of the allies, Edward had recalled his forces from England, and had concluded treaties with several other German princes. The very extent of the armaments on each part rendered an amicable adjustment of their dispute improbable; but negotiations for peace were still carried on, and conferences were held, both at Compiègne and Arras, between the prelates of Canterbury, Durham, and Lincoln, in behalf of Edward and the bishops of Rouen, Langres, and Beauvais, as the representatives of Philip of Valois.*

Nothing, however, ensued to stay the approaching war; and, indeed, it is more than probable that each monarch consented to these transactions more with a view of screening himself from reproach, than from either the desire or expectation of peace. A fair reputation is not to be despised even by states; though states, in general, as bodies of men, possess a mass of accumulated selfishness far greater than that of any single person, without the better qualities and more generous feelings which more or less influence every individual. But at that time the responsibility attached to all national movements rested chiefly with the king; and the war was decidedly far more between Philip of Valois and Edward III. than between France and England. Edward felt, therefore, that he must leave no means unemployed to justify the steps he was taking, and neglect no pacific show which might conceal his desire for war. He

* Barnes, p. 126.

listened to every overture of peace, and negotiated as often as it was proposed; and, when all the conferences had terminated, he did not think it unnecessary to address an exculpatory epistle to the Pope, setting forth the rights he claimed, and the grounds on which he claimed them.

The letter is long and elaborate, filled with false and subtle reasoning, and displaying a great deal of that almost blasphemous familiarity with sacred things which was in that day looked upon as pious. The Pope replied in the same style, but, certainly, more as a partisan of the French king, than as a mediator between him and his enemy; and Edward, summoning his forces to the field, proceeded to carry his long-projected schemes into execution.

CHAP. VI.

DELAYS OF EDWARD'S GERMAN ALLIES. — FORMAL DECLARATION OF WAR. — ATTACK OF MORTAGNE. — CAPTURE OF THUN L'ÉVÊQUE. — THE KING OF ENGLAND BEGINS HIS MARCH ALONE. — CONFERS WITH THE DUKE OF BRABANT AT BRUSSELS. — IS JOINED BY A PART OF HIS ALLIES. — UNDERTAKES THE SIEGE OF CAMBRAY. — THE DUKE OF BRABANT JOINS THE ALLIES. — SIEGE OF CAMBRAY. — PHILIP'S PREPARATIONS. — HIS FLEETS RAVAGE THE ENGLISH COAST. — HE COLLECTS AN ARMY TO RELIEVE CAMBRAY. — EDWARD MARCHES TO MEET HIM. — PASSES THE SCHELD. — THE LINE OF MARCH. — PREPARATIONS FOR A BATTLE. — PHILIP'S REASONS FOR AVOIDING A GENERAL ENGAGEMENT. — THE TWO ARMIES SEPARATE.

Before St. John's day, Edward had assembled the whole of his own forces at the small town of Vilvorde, between Brussels and Mechlin, and for some time he waited there impatiently the coming of his allies. But new delays took place. The Duke of Brabant showed no sign of readiness; and, though the other leaders were prepared, they would not take any decided step till that prince led the way. Thus passed the time till the beginning of September; when, losing patience, Edward, whose expenses for the maintenance of 1600 men-at-arms and 10,000 archers had already been considerable, issued his peremptory summons for the barons to meet him at Mechlin ere the expiration of a fortnight, and marched in person to that city. On the day appointed the leaders presented themselves, but they were without troops; and though it would have appeared that the time for all discussion was at an end, and that action was alone suited to the moment, yet long and wordy disputes were again entered into, in regard to the measures to be pursued and the conduct of the proposed expedition. At length Edward induced them to take, at least, one irrevocable step; and, while they promised once more to meet him in arms within fifteen days, each despatched to Paris a declaration of war against the French king. From the number of these, however, must be excepted the Duke of Brabant, who appeared still determined to temporise till such time as the allied army should by its advance cover his frontier from the French. The letters of defiance from all the rest were, of course, entrusted to messengers, whose functions secured them immunity in their dangerous errand. For this purpose the Bishop of Lincoln and the Windsor herald, then the principal English officer of arms, were selected; and, having reached the French court, the Bishop delivered the warlike epistles with which he was charged, and the herald, according to established form, solemnly defied Philip of Valois in the name of the King of England and his allies. The hostile messengers were received and dismissed with courtesy by the French monarch; and, with scrupulous care, Edward and his partisans abstained from any act of hostility, till they were certain that their adversary had received their defiance.

No sooner was that fact ascertained, than the war began with one of those chivalrous exploits which gave a strange adventurous charm to the hostilities of those days. Before the week was at an end which saw the declaration of war delivered in Paris, Sir Walter de Mauny chose forty lances from amongst his best companions, and, praying them to accompany him upon an adventure, set out from Brabant. Such was the wild and enterprising spirit of the time, that the greater part of those who followed him were ignorant whither he intended to lead them, and what was the purpose of his movements. At length, in the wood of Blaton, on the very frontier of France, Mauny informed his friends that, in accordance with a vow which he had made in England in the presence of knights and ladies, to be the first to take some town or castle in France and to do some deed of arms in the war, he had conducted them thither for the purpose of endeavouring to surprise the small city of Mortagne, almost under the walls of Tournay. This news was communicated while the party halted in the wood; but such a proposal instantly gave new spirit to the knights, and, again mounting their horses, they paused not till they came within sight of Mortagne, which was descried a little before sunrise the next morning. Advancing as quietly as possible, they reached the gate unperceived; and, to their surprise, found the wicket open. Dismounting first himself, Sir Walter de Mauny entered the gate; and, finding the street clear, he left some of his companions to secure his retreat, while with the rest he rode on towards the large tower which served as a citadel to the place, hoping to find it as negligently guarded as the city. In this expectation, however, he was deceived. The gate was firmly closed; and, the approach of enemies being instantly perceived by the warder, the garrison was soon roused by the sound of his horn, and the shout of "Trahis! trahis!" by which he announced the presence of a foe.

With but forty lances De Mauny could not hope to force the tower to surrender; and the inhabitants of Mortagne, as well as the garrison, being by this time alarmed, he applied himself to make good his retreat before he was overwhelmed by numbers. To leave indelible traces of his attempt, however, as well as to occupy those who might have impeded him in his progress through the narrow streets, he set fire to the houses in the neighbourhood of the tower; and, under cover of the conflagration, drew his men off with ease and safety.

He then directed his march across the country; and, proceeding with a degree of rapidity scarcely conceivable, when we remember the weight of armour in those days, he approached Cambray; and turning towards the strong castle of Thun l'Evêque, made himself master of it by surprise, before those placed to defend it even knew that an enemy was near. Having secured his conquest, by leaving a sufficient garrison to maintain the fortress for the time, and placed it under the command of his brother, Sir Giles de Mauny, who had accompanied him, Walter returned with all speed to the King of England, whom he found still at Mechlin, waiting the arrival of his tardy allies. Under such circumstances the news he brought was matter of no small rejoicing; for, independent of the advantage derived from the first stroke of the war being successful — a point of considerable importance in all ages — high deeds of chivalry, done in favour of the one side or the other, had, in those days, a separate and intrinsic value, which we can hardly estimate fully in the present times.

About the same period a similar incursion was made into the territory of Liège by the Earl of Salisbury; but that nobleman contented himself with spoiling the country, and gathering what tidings he could of the French preparations for defence. These, indeed, had been hitherto so greatly neglected on the frontier likely to be attacked, that, by the report of his officers, new motives were added to those which already urged Edward to avoid all further delay.

At length, then, indignant at the remissness which had already wasted so much valuable time, the King of England began his march with his own forces only, declaring loudly that he would not turn back till he had pitched his tent on French ground, and unfurled his standard to the winds of France, and calling down shame upon those false allies who should not follow him to the field. At Brussels, as he marched on, he conferred with the Duke of Brabant, and extorted from him an oath that he would join him as soon as his forces sat down before Cambray, which Edward had by this time determined on besieging. At Brussels, also, the English monarch had, at length, the satisfaction of being joined by the greater part of his German allies, to the amount of 20,000 men-at-arms*; and with these he marched on by Nivelle and Mons to Valenciennes, where he was splendidly entertained by the young Count of Hainault, his brother-in-law, who was straining every nerve to render his co-operation both energetic and serviceable.

From Valenciennes, Edward once more set out on the 20th of September†; and it now appeared that nothing but the movement of any one had been wanting to excite the other confederates to activity. Fresh reinforcements continued to arrive from every side, as the English monarch marched on; and at length he sat down before Cambray, with forces fully sufficient to render his enterprise hopeful.

Almost immediately after the investment of the city, the Count of Hainault, and his more famous uncle, John Lord of Beaumont, joined the besiegers with large forces; and on the sixth day of the siege the Duke of Brabant also appeared, followed by 900 knights‡ and a large body of inferior soldiers. With his usual selfish prudence, that prince encamped

* This reinforcement was led by the Duke of Gueldres, the Marquis of Juliers, the Marquis of Brandenburg, the Marquis of Misnia and Osterland, the Count of Berghen, the Count of Salms, the Lord of Fauquemont, and several others of less note.

† Robert de Avesbury.

‡ I have here used the term knight, because I can put no other interpretation upon the words of Froissart, who makes a strong distinction in this place between lances, as he calls them, and other men-at-arms. His expression is:—"Vint le Duc de Brabant en l'ost, moult étoffément et en grand arroy, et avoit bien neuf cent lances, sans les autres armures de fer, dont il y avoit grand foison."

his men distinct from the rest of the allied forces, taking care, however, for his own security, to throw a bridge across the Scheld, which river separated him from the main army.* At the same time he sent his defiance to the King of France; and, all parties being now fairly engaged in hostilities, Edward had a right to hope that his title to the crown of France would be decided by the fortune of his arms.

The siege of Cambray, however, gave no very certain promise of success; for, though Philip had most unaccountably neglected, during the whole of the preceding year, to provide for the general defence of the very frontier so long threatened with attack; yet, as soon as he had received the defiance of the King of England, he despatched a reinforcement of 200 lances to Cambray, under Stephen de la Baume †, grand master of the crossbow-men of France, who immediately took the command of the garrison, and defended the city with the most determined courage.‡

* As far as it is possible to judge, Edward, beginning his march from Valenciennes, had followed the Scheld from that city, and had attacked Cambray from the right-hand bank; while the Duke of Brabant, setting out from Brussels, kept on the left side of the river after having once crossed it. Otherwise Edward and the Duke must have changed places afterwards, which was not at all likely. It appears from the accompanying map that the village of Marcoing extended to both sides of the Scheld.

† Froissart, note de M. Dacier.

‡ A paper preserved in Rymer, tom. ii. part 4. p. 52., and dated from Marcoing on the 4th October, 1339, seems to show that the French monarch began a negotiation for peace through the mediation of the Duke of Brabant, even while the siege of Cambray was going on. Probably the purpose of Philip was merely to gain time for further preparation, or to deceive his enemy; for although, by the patent men-

At the same time, Philip strained his means to the utmost, both to increase the forces he had prepared for the repulse of the invaders, and to retaliate upon England the evils which Edward's coming had inflicted upon France. The united French and Genoese fleets, under the command of Hugues Quieret, admiral of France, Nicolas Behuchet, and Egidio Bocanegra the Genoese admiral, swept the English Channel, made various descents upon the coast, and at last, landing at Southampton *, plundered and set fire to the town, committing more than the ordinary excesses attending a successful assault. The town itself had made no resistance, being unfortified, and its inhabitants at church when the descent took place: but the next morning, a large body of the French, who had foolishly remained on shore too long after their companions had embarked, were surprised by Sir John Arundel and some troops which he had collected in haste, and were put to death almost to a man.†

News of the continual ravages committed on his coasts reached the King of England, together with the tidings that a general rendezvous of the French chivalry had been appointed at Péronne, for the purpose of raising the siege of Cambray. He con-

---

tioned, Edward permits the Duke of Brabant to bring envoys to treat of peace within three or four leagues of the camp, yet we hear nothing more of the transaction.

* 5th October, 1339.

† Barnes, p. 186. The French obtained a number of other successes, which are related in the eloquent work upon the "Naval History of England" lately published in Lardner's Cabinet Cyclopædia.

sequently increased all his efforts to hasten the capture of that city before any considerable army could be brought to its aid; and his various allies lost no opportunity of signalising both their courage and their zeal in his cause. The young Count of Hainault, amongst others, endeavoured to force one of the gates of the city, called the gate of St. Quentin; while his uncle, with Walter de Mauny and the Lord of Fauquemont, attacked another. The besieged, however, were prepared to receive their enemies at all points, and offered vigorous and successful resistance. Before the gates of a city themselves could be assailed, it was necessary to win the strong palisades by which they were usually defended, and in fighting for these barriers some of the most brilliant exploits of chivalrous warfare generally occurred. At the palisades before the gate of St. Quentin, the Count of Hainault and his companions fought the whole day, till at length a young English squire, who afterwards immortalised the name of Chandos, leaped over the barriers, and cast himself a lance's length amidst the crowd that defended them. He was instantly opposed by one of the young French aspirants to chivalry, called John of St. Dizier, and between the two many gallant feats of arms were performed in the sight of both armies. In the mean time the Hainaulters, following up their comrade, won the palisade, and pressed their adversaries towards the gate. No further advantage, however, was to be obtained; and the Count and his followers retired as night approached, tired out with the heat, and the length of their exertions.

Cambray was still as far from its fall as ever, and nothing, probably, would have compelled it to a speedy surrender, but the employment of cannon, which, though by that time well known *, do not appear to have been used in this siege. Neither do such mighty engines † seem to have been brought to batter the walls of the city, as we find mentioned on other occasions. Probably the difficulty of conveying such immense machines from England had prevented Edward from attempting in this siege to make use of any of those which had been employed both by himself and his ancestors in the Scottish wars; and it was, of course, unlikely, that the petty princes with whom he had allied himself should be provided with implements which are represented as of immense

* Gunpowder had now been invented some time; and Barbour, in his Bruce, declares that Edward III. employed cannon against the Scots in 1327. Of this fact, however, as that author was not an eye-witness, I have some doubt; no public record of the circumstance existing that I can discover. But Ducange (Glossary, voce *Bombarda*) shows, that, in 1338, cannon had been used by the French at the siege of Puy Guillaume. We find, also, that the Scots employed cannon at the siege of Stirling in 1339; and in the Parliament held by Edward at Westminster, A. D. 1340, we find mention made of thirty-two tons of powder, which was to have been furnished by one Thomas Brookhall.

† The various engines used in battering the walls of castles and cities were too numerous to be cited here. The mangonel, the catapult, and the martinet, however, were the principal; and the extraordinary force with which they acted may be conceived from the facts, that many of them threw stone balls of three hundred pounds weight (Walter Hemingford, Ed. I.); and that some of these balls were known to penetrate through the two outward walls of Stirling Castle. (Matthew West., lib. ii. p. 448.) In regard to the weight and bulk of these engines, we find from Rymer, that, in 1342, when Edward had carried them to the seaside for the invasion of France, he found, on examining his fleet, that he must either leave behind him his army or his military engines; and, of course, chose to send back the latter.

value. The means of blockade and of frequent assaults seem to have been those alone employed by the besiegers, though the garrison were plentifully furnished with every sort of machine then used in the defence of fortified places, and consequently possessed advantages which rendered the speedy capture of the town improbable. By the care of the bishop, also, Cambray had been abundantly supplied with provisions; while the besieging army, with the usual improvidence of feudal hosts, had furnished itself scantily with the necessary stores, and had left no measure unemployed to ravage and desolate the country round about. At the same time, day after day brought fresh tidings of immense preparations made by the King of France; and it now became necessary to consider whether policy demanded that the King of England should march forward to meet his adversary before the whole levies of the hostile army were complete, or still continue before a town which promised a long, if not a successful, resistance.*

This question was accordingly discussed in the King's council; and Edward seems to have been influenced chiefly by the advice of Robert of Artois,

* It is an extraordinary fact, that Edward himself, in the letter wherein he gives an account of this campaign, never alludes in any shape to the siege of Cambray. Indeed, from this extraordinary silence, I might have been inclined to doubt the fact of its ever having taken place, had not every other authority unanimously stated the fact. Mezeray declares, that John Duke of Normandy, Philip's son, had assumed the command of the garrison of Cambray; but I find no confirmation of the assertion.

in his determination to raise the siege, and march forward to meet the King of France in the field. It must be noticed particularly here, however, that Cambray, though now doing homage to the French crown, and adhering strongly to the party of Philip, was originally a feof of the German empire, and was, in consequence, regarded by no party as absolutely a part of France, although the monarch of that country actually held it under very specious claims. These facts greatly affected the English king in two ways. In the first place, he had declared that he would enter the French territory in arms in pursuit of his right, which as yet he had not done, though such a declaration, once made, was in those days, and to a man of Edward's character, the strongest inducement to exertion, and even to temerity, in the fulfilment of his boast. On the other hand, several of his allies—especially the Count of Hainault *—holding a great part of their lands in feof from the crown of France, were willing to aid Edward with all their power so long as his warfare was waged without the absolute boundaries of the neighbouring kingdom; but were obliged by every principle of feudal law to withdraw from his army as soon as he took one step in arms beyond the French frontier.

The many considerations, however, which urged the young King of England to give battle to the French monarch, outweighed the probable loss of part of his forces; and on the 10th of October, 1339, he raised the siege of Cambray, and advanced into the

* Froissart.

territories of his adversary; following, as he did so, the cruel custom of the times, by ravaging and desolating the country through which he passed, to the distance of six or seven miles on each side of his line of march.* Leaving the little village of Marcoing, at which his head-quarters seem to have been fixed since the 25th of September, the King of England directed his course towards the abbey of Mount St. Martin, situated on the opposite bank of the Scheld, and near that place began the passage of the stream unopposed.† I have not been able to ascertain what were the exact boundaries of the Cambresis in those days; but it is evident that the Scheld, in this spot, marked the frontier line of the French kingdom, for on the banks of that river the young Count of Hainault withdrew his troops from the army of his brother-in-law, urging his duty to the King of France, and boldly declaring to Edward that, as a faithful feudatory, he was called upon to aid the French monarch, now that his territories were actually invaded.‡

So powerful was the respect still existing for feudal institutions, that the King of England offered no opposition to this determination, but parted from the Count in perfect amity. In the meanwhile his marshals, the Earls of Northampton, Gloucester, and Suffolk, superintended the passage of the troops, and at length the monarch himself crossed the Scheld, and for the first time set his foot upon French ground as an enemy. To signalise this event, he conferred the honour of knighthood upon a young Flemish

* Robert of Avesbury, p. 46. † Knighton, col. 2574.
‡ Froissart, chap. lxxxv.

squire, called Henry of Flanders, of whose previous history little is positively known *; and shortly after, during a halt of two days at the abbey of St. Martin, he bestowed on Lawrence Hastings, a descendant of the well known Aumory de Valence, the earldom of Pembroke.† Various other acts were performed to perpetuate the memory of Edward's first inroad into France; and, during his halt at St. Martin's ‡, several

* He has been confounded with Guy of Flanders, taken at the battle of Cadsand; but, if the difference of name were not sufficient to show that the two were totally distinct persons, the very fact of the knighthood would prove them to have been such. Guy of Flanders must have been already a knight at the battle of Cadsand, as he was there found commanding knights, while it is expressly stated that Henry was an esquire till dubbed by Edward on the present occasion.

† Selden's Titles of Honour, p. 644. Fœdera, tom. ii. part iv. p. 54.

‡ I have had very great difficulty in tracing the march of Edward III. correctly, especially as I found that many errors had been committed in regard to this point in English history. The account of Froissart had been doubted, and the names of many towns and villages which he mentioned had been changed by his editors and commentators, who, meeting with no such places now in existence, had fancied the manuscripts erroneous. At first I found but two sources of certain information for the rectification of former mistakes and for my own guidance, namely, the state papers of the time, and a letter from Edward himself to his son; but I have since obtained full confirmation of the opinion I then formed, by a map, of a very early date, in the valuable library of Hugh Scott, Esquire, of Harden, to whose courtesy and kindness I am also indebted for various sources of information, which I could procure no where else. The map to which I allude points out the positions of a number of hamlets, abbeys, and monasteries, which have long ceased to exist, and perfectly reconciles the account given by Froissart with the letter of Edward III. and the state papers in Rymer. The exact line of march pursued by the English monarch is thus clearly established. On the 20th of September Edward left Valenciennes, according to his own letter, which again states that he reached Marcoing near Cambray on the 25th. The public acts preserved in Rymer also show that he was at that place on the 26th. On the 13th of October other papers in the Fœdera prove that he was in the abbey of Mount St. Martin, on the frontiers of Picardy, confirming the account of Froissart, who says, that on decamping from before Cambray he passed the Scheld, and remained two days at the abbey of that name. The Duke of Brabant

detachments from the royal army spread themselves over the country, and endeavoured to gain some town or castle by surprise, as the first-fruits of the invasion.

---

at the same time, still keeping on the left of the Scheld, advanced as far as the abbey of Vaucelles, or Vauchelles. On the 16th, Edward states in his letter that he crossed the Oise, of which Froissart makes no direct mention. He virtually, however, says the same; for he declares that, after advancing towards St. Quentin, and finding it prepared for defence, Edward, followed by the Duke of Brabant, turned to the east, and, taking the way towards l'Eschelle, or l'Esquielle, passed a whole day at the abbey of Behoury; to reach which, I find, from the map I have mentioned, the King must have crossed the right branch of the Oise. On the 18th, Edward received notice that the King of France would give him battle, and the next five days were spent in ravaging the country, and waiting the attack of Philip near Flamengerie, a village about a mile and three quarters from La Chapelle, in the direction of Avesnes. In the meanwhile, Philip advanced from Noyon as far as Buironfosse, about three miles to the south-west of La Chapelle, but, as will appear hereafter, wisely avoided a battle with the King of England and his allies.

It is necessary here to notice some of the great mistakes which have been made in regard to this march by authors of well-deserved reputation. Rapin, taking the word Marcoing for Marchiennes, has carried Edward nearly forty miles too far to the north; and M. Dacier, whose labours on Froissart are invaluable, generally speaking, has, in this instance, erroneously changed the name Honnecourt, or Honnencourt — which is in every MS. of Froissart that I have been able to meet with — to Hainecourt, a place then within the territories of the Count of Hainault. The consequence is, that, in the new edition of Froissart, the troops of Edward are represented as attacking a friendly town, nearly thirty miles to the north of Cambray, while he was marching to the south. M. Dacier has also placed the abbey of Vaucelles on the right, instead of the left, bank of the Scheld; so that the Duke of Brabant appears, by his version of Froissart, to have crossed the river after the siege of Cambray, which was not the case. Either through an error of the same kind, or a mistake of the chronicler himself, the English King is said by Froissart to have encamped for some time on Mount St. Quentin, and yet to have been within sight of all that passed at the gates of the town of that name. A similar error is committed in regard to Edward's march upon la Flamengerie, to reach which place he passed l'Echelles instead of the reverse, as we find generally stated.

Henry of Flanders especially, in hopes of doing honour to his new rank in arms, joined himself to a number of other knights, and directed his course towards Honnecourt, a small but strong town, in which the people of the country had collected all their wealth as in a place of security. It is not at all improbable that the proposed expedition, spoken of too generally amongst the idlers of the camp, attracted many more adventurers than he by whom it was first designed either expected or desired. At all events, it is certain that, besides Henry of Flanders himself, and several other young men of promise, there were present upon this occasion the celebrated John of Hainault, the adventurous Lord of Fauquemont, and at least 500 other knights.

The town, however, had received notice of an enemy's proximity by an attack made upon it during the preceding day by a small body of rovers from the English camp; and the abbot of the monastery of Honnecourt, wisely judging that a stronger force might follow, had taken vigorous measures to put the place in a defensible state. He was, we are told, bold and valiant as a man-at-arms, and it is not at all improbable that, before assuming the frock, he had borne the shirt of mail. At all events, his preparations argued some skill in war; and, causing a strong palisade to be constructed in haste before the principal gate, he armed his followers and the people of the town with quicklime, large stones, and every sort of missile which might drive back an attacking enemy; and, placing a number of persons to watch the approach of any hostile force, he himself remained with the rest of the burghers to defend the barriers he had constructed.

The expected enemies were not long in appearing; and coming down in a close body, they advanced directly to the palisade. The state in which they now saw the town was undoubtedly very different from that in which they had hoped to find it; but still their numbers gave them every probability of success, and, dismounting from their horses, they instantly began the attack.

The courage they brought to the assault was not greater than that with which the defence was conducted. With the gates of the town wide open behind them, and the townsmen on the battlements ready to shower down masses of stone, trunks of trees and pots of quicklime on the assailants, the abbot and his soldiers were planted along their palisade, the stakes of which, fully half a foot apart, left space for blows to be given and received.

During several hours this barrier was attacked and defended with the most determined valour, Henry of Flanders and the abbot rivalling each other in deeds of prowess. At length the young knight made a lunge at his opponent with his lance* through one of

* No word has suffered a more general wrong translation than the word *glaive*, which is used by Froissart in narrating this fact. It has more than once been rendered *a sword;* and from that circumstance an immense number of errors and contradictions have occurred. It is only necessary, however, to read Froissart attentively, to see that it meant a lance, though, in some instances, he applies the term to a sort of weapon, formed partly like a lance, but slightly differing

the apertures, and the abbot, watching his moment, seized the weapon of his adversary, and dragged him so strongly towards the palisade that first his hand and then his arm up to the shoulder was drawn through the bars. The knight, as a point of honour, held firm his lance, and the pugnacious churchman would certainly have pulled him into the town, had the space between the bars been large enough to admit the passage of his body. "I can tell you," says the quaint Froissart, "that the said Sir Henry was not at his ease while the abbot held him; for he was strong and sturdy, and dragged without sparing."

At length, the young knight was delivered from the gripe of his adversary by the aid of his companions, but not without the loss of the lance, which the abbot kept as an honourable trophy of military deeds, and which the monks showed with veneration long after their superior's death. From noon till

---

from it in the form of the iron head. In the combat between Albert of Cologne and the Lord of Potelles, chap. cxiii., we find it used as a lance:—

"Si retourna franchement et baissa son glaive, et férit cheval des éperons, et s'addressa sur le seigneur de Potelles, et le chevalier sur lui, tellement qu'il le férit sur la targe un si grand horion que le glaive vola en pièces; et l'Allemand le consuivit par telle manière de son glaive roide et enfumé que oncque ne brisa ni ploya, mais perça la targe, les plates, et l'hocqueton, et lui entra dedans le corps et le poignit au cœur, et l'abattit jus de dessus son cheval."

At the assault of Mortagne, however, he describes a glaive of a different construction, somewhat similar to the pikes with hooks used in the Irish rebellion. With this the Lord of Beaujeu, on the walls, contrived to draw a great number of the assailants out of their boats, and drowned them in the river. See Froissart, chap. cxxxv. See also chapters xcix. liv. i. xliii. liv. ii.; but especially in chap. lxxx. of the second book, where the indentity of the glaive and the lance is placed beyond doubt, as well as the distinction between that weapon and the sword.

vespers the assault continued; but the defenders yielded not a step, the palisade stood firm, the loss of the assailants was becoming severe; and, finding that they could obtain nothing but shame and hard blows, they gathered up their dead and wounded and withdrew; while the abbot retired to his monastery with the satisfaction of knowing that by his skill and energy he had saved the town.

A number of similar expeditions were made by the various commanders who had joined the English monarch; and it is not surprising that, in almost all instances, these enterprises in an open and unprotected country proved successful. An immense number of small towns and villages were burned; and ruin, destruction, fire and bloodshed, marked the advance of the invading force. Those places in which he lodged himself, as he marched on, Edward took care to secure from pillage; but the parties detached from his army on every side appear to have had his express commands to desolate the land through which they passed.* On these scenes of cruelty and rapine it is unnecessary to pause, though, in one point of view, the facts are not uninteresting, as illustrative of the barbarism which was so strangely and intimately mingled with the chivalrous courtesy and scrupulous honour of the age.†

* See his own letter.

† Amongst other places attacked by troops under the command of the English monarch was the town of Guise, and the forces by which it was captured were those of John of Hainault, to whose son-in-law Louis, Count of Blois, the town and its dependencies belonged. The daughter of the old warrior was in the Castle of Guise at the time, and,

The march of the royal army was directed in the first instance towards St. Quentin; but, after having appeared in battle array before that town, which was found prepared for defence, Edward turned to the east, and advanced by slow marches, ravaging the country, then called the Thierasche, towards La Chapelle and Avesnes. At length a scarcity of provisions began to be felt in the allied army, and deliberations were held as to whether it would not be necessary to retreat upon Hainault. In fact, Edward seems to have made some movements to that effect; but the news which now quickly reached him, that the King of France had left Péronne with an army of a hundred thousand men, and was marching in search of him, changed his purpose.* On the ensuing Monday, the 18th of October, letters from the grand master of the cross-bowmen of France were received in the English camp, announcing to Edward, through one of his officers, that, if he would choose an open field, undefended by wood, water, or morass, the French king would give him battle on the Thursday following.†

Edward still moved on, however; either because he

---

terrified at the fire which she saw spreading around her, she sent to remonstrate with her father, begging him, for her sake, to desist, and spare at least the territories of his own children. The thoroughgoing partisan, however, was deaf to all her entreaties, and did not pause in the work assigned to him till he had reduced the town to a heap of ashes.

* Robert of Avesbury, p. 46.

† Epist. Edwardi, apud Robert of Avesbury.

was aware that Philip had not yet passed St. Quentin, or because he could not look upon the communication he had received as official * ; but on the Wednesday following certain intelligence was received that the French monarch had arrived at Buironfosse, a small village resting on the great forest of Nouvion, between L'Echelle and La Chapelle.† In the meanwhile the English army had reached the latter of those towns; and Edward, finding himself within two leagues of his adversary, sent a herald to demand whether Philip held his intention of giving him battle. Although the messenger was, as usual, received with great honour and rewarded with magnificent presents, and though the prospect of speedily deciding the war by a general engagement seemed to spread joy through the whole French army, yet Philip, from what cause does not appear, did not return an answer in his own name. The King of

* Edward had left Stephen de la Baume in Cambray.

† I have endeavoured, as far as possible, to reconcile the account given by Froissart with the letter of Edward himself, as preserved by Robert of Avesbury. Nor, indeed, is there any very great discrepancy. Froissart does not, it is true, mention the letters of the grand master of the French crossbow-men; and Edward abridges the whole detail as much as possible. I have, therefore, taken the minute particulars from Froissart, correcting a few errors in date and circumstance from the letter of the monarch. The principal facts contained in this letter do not admit of a doubt, especially as various heralds are expressly stated to have been the bearers of the different messages; and any one who knows aught of the customs of chivalrous warfare must be aware that one part of the herald's duty, which was strictly performed till a much later epoch, was to keep an exact register of all deeds in which they took any part, and not to suffer a false statement, to the honour of one knight or dishonour of another, to go forth uncontradicted, however high the rank of either party. Heralds in those days were bitter critics upon bulletins. The Chronicles of Monstrelet, who flourished long after this period, are full of examples of this kind.

Bohemia, however, and the Duke of Lorraine * sent back letters under their hands and seals, confirming the appointment made by the Grand Master Stephen de la Baume; and Edward the next morning drew out from La Chapelle, and approached La Flamengerie, a spot undefended by any natural bulwarks, where the two armies might find a fair field of combat.†

His forces, expecting every moment the attack of the enemy, now took up their position in three large divisions, and a reserve, having the baggage placed behind, and the horses in a little wood not far distant, which was guarded and fortified. The first body was led by the Duke of Gueldres, and comprised the great bulk of the German auxiliaries, and the free companions, who on such occasions were generally destined to receive the onset. Under his command, the Duke of Gueldres had thus 8000 men, ranged under twenty-two banners, and sixty knights' pennons; while the second division, commanded by the Duke of Brabant, offered scantier numbers, but a greater array of chivalry, displaying twenty-four banners and eighty pennons, with only 7000 combatants.‡

The main body was commanded by the King of England in person, and in it appeared twenty-eight banners and ninety pennons, leading on 6000 men at arms and 6000 archers. Besides these three divisions, the reserve, consisting of 4000 men at arms and 2000 archers, commanded by the Earls of

* Froissart, chap. xc.

† Robert of Avesbury, p. 46.

‡ Froissart, chap. xcii.

Warwick and Pembroke, the Lords of Berkeley and Milton, was stationed on one of the wings, to render aid wherever it might appear necessary.

The reserve remained upon horseback, all the rest of the men at arms having dismounted; and in this state the English army continued a part of the Thursday appointed, and on the Friday again took their position in the same order. On the morning of the second day, Edward, expecting to be speedily attacked, rode through the ranks, accompanied only by Lord Cobham, Walter de Mauny, and Robert of Artois, encouraging his soldiers, and exhorting them to remember that his honour and their own depended upon their exertions during the approaching strife.* As a farther incentive to valour, he made several new knights, amongst whom was the same John Chandos who had distinguished himself in the attack of Cambray.

No enemy, however, appeared; and the only tidings which Edward could obtain concerning his adversary's movements were given by the French spies, who, having fallen into the hands of the allies, assured them that Philip would give them battle the following day.†

A number of circumstances combined to deter the French monarch from risking a battle, which at first, it would appear, he had firmly determined to hazard. As he had advanced, it is true, his army had increased at every step; and at Buironfosse he had been joined

* Froissart, chap. xciii. † Robert of Avesbury, p. 48.

by the young Count of Hainault, who now came to do feudal service against those very invaders with whom he had continued to act as long as they did not infringe the French frontier. Philip, however, unwisely resented the aid he had formerly given the English, and probably trusted but little either to his affection or his faith.* It is not improbable, also, that many others in his host laboured under the same suspicion from other causes; and that the King's best friends, knowing his right to the crown to be questioned, foresaw that on the issue of a battle his throne itself would depend.

On the Friday, however, his troops were marshalled for the attack; and never did a more magnificent array give promise of an easy victory.† Two hundred and twenty-seven banners, and five hundred and sixty pennons, floated along the French lines; and under them were collected four kings, six dukes, thirty-six counts, and a hundred and five thousand men. Philip himself is represented as eager, under any circumstances, to lead them on to battle; but, a council being called, no unanimity could be obtained. The dispute was long and vehement; many of the King's wisest councillors showing that the stake between him and the King of England was by no means equal; as, if Edward were conquered, he lost but a battle, while, if Philip were defeated, he lost crown and kingdom. The other party urged strongly the disgrace which would fall upon them, after all their preparations,

* Froissart, chap. lxxxviii.

† Id. chap. xciii.

their gallant force, and their promise given, if they let the English army retire without battle. Neither would yield their opinion to their adversaries, and many hours were spent in discussion.

The superstitious dreams, however, of a clever but visionary prince are said to have at length decided what the counsel of the wisest men in France had not been able to determine. While the debate still continued, letters were brought to the French Sovereign from Robert of Provence, King of Sicily, who passed for the most skilful astrologer in Europe; and who, on the present occasion, sent expressly to warn Philip of Valois * that he had cast his horoscope on the first news of his contention with Edward of England, and had found that he would be defeated as often as he fought against the English monarch. He warned the King of France and his council, therefore, to avoid battle where Edward was present in person; and though Philip was still anxious to fight, the discouragement which these letters had spread amongst his chief nobility, the late hour to which the discussion had been prolonged, the scarcity of provisions and of water † under which his men were suffering, and the difficult nature of some part of the ground between his army and that of Edward, which was still a league and a half distant ‡, combined as motives with the other cogent reasons which had been before urged upon him. He determined at length not to

* Froissart, chap. xciii.

† Chroniques de France, chap. xvii.

‡ Robert of Avesbury.

fight; and no one who considers his situation can doubt that he had much to lose and very little to gain.*

* In giving the details of this day's events, I have followed principally Froissart, at least as far as regards the French army, for various reasons. In the first place, his lord the Count of Hainault was present; and, in the next place, Froissart declares (chap. xciii.) that he had his account from an eye-witness, probably meaning Jean le Bel, who furnished materials for the greater part of his first book. It is still further to be remarked, that he was contemporary, and that his work, which, even in his own day, was famous throughout Europe, though erroneous occasionally in minor circumstances, could not be well false in matters of great and vital import. For the rest of the facts I have taken as my authority the letter of Edward to his council and to his son, which, though it enters into no details, and states but the broad facts, was correct beyond all doubt in regard to those facts; as none but a madman would write a public account to his own country, which could be contradicted by every soldier and baron in his army, and was certain to be contradicted by every herald on the part of the enemy. Both Froissart and Edward declare that the English army waited for the attack of the French on the day appointed, and that Philip determined not to give battle as he had promised. The compiler of the Chronicles of Franee confirms this account in the chief point, inasmuch as he admits that Philip determined not to give battle, and assigns some of the reasons which I have adopted in the text, such as the want of food and water; adding one which I have not admitted — that Philip's army had marched five leagues that day; which we know to be false, as Philip had been at Buironfosse for some time. In opposition to this only two anonymous writers have been brought forward, of whom the one most worthy of credit is the continuator of William of Nangis, who declares that Edward retreated first. The other authority on that side is the Chronicle of Flanders, which states, that on the Saturday Philip crossed the difficult ground between his army and the English camp, took possession of the ground Edward had abandoned, and remained there two days. This, Monsieur Dacier insinuates, "may be very well reconciled with Edward's letter — allowing that the English prince strove throughout that epistle to dissemble the little desire he had to come to blows." How far it can be reconciled with Edward's letter will be best shown by translating part of it. "We, seeing these letters now the next day (Thursday), drew to La Flamengerie, where we remained Friday all the day. At vespers were taken three spies,

In the mean time his troops had remained under arms almost the whole day; and an event occurred

---

and were examined, each by himself, and agreed that the said Philip would give us battle on the Saturday, and that he was at a league and a half from us. The Saturday we were in the field a good quarter before the day, and took our position in a place convenient for him and us to fight. Early in the morning we took some of his scouts, who informed us that his avant guard was in array in the field, and coming towards us on one side. The news come to our host agreed that our allies would carry themselves forward very heavily; toward us, for a certainty, they were of such a good will, that never were folks so willing to fight. At the same time one of our scouts, a German knight, was taken, who had seen all our array, and told it in his peril to our enemy, so that now he caused his avant guard to retreat, and gave orders to encamp, and dug trenches round about them, and cut down large trees to impede the approach. We remained all day under arms on foot, till towards vespers it seemed to our allies that we had remained long enough; and at vespers we mounted our horses, and went near to Avesnes, at a league and a half from our said cousin, and gave him to know that we would await him there all the next day; and so we did. No other news had we of him, except that on the Saturday, at the time we mounted our horses to depart from our position, he supposed that we were coming towards him, and such haste was he in to take a stronger ground, that a thousand knights at once plunged into a morass, in his passage, so that one came tumbling over the other. The next day (Sunday) the Lord of Fagnoeles was taken by our people. The Monday morning we had news that the said Sir Philip and all his allies had disbanded and retreated in great haste." — *Robertus de Avesbury*, p. 46. &c.

Such is the account of Edward himself, in direct contradiction in every point to the Chronicle of Flanders; and it remains for any one to judge whether this narrative, given by a monarch who came on purpose to seek his adversary, and subject to contradiction, if false, by a thousand eye-witnesses, confirmed in every material point by Jean le Bel, a writer attached to a prince, who, before his work was written, had abandoned the English party, and also confirmed in the great point by the " Chroniques de France" themselves — it remains, I say, for any one to judge whether such a narrative, so supported, is not worth two anonymous chronicles, one of which, that of Flanders, is notoriously incorrect in regard even to circumstances where no

amongst the Hainaulters which was likely to render all the transactions of that morning peculiarly interesting to their vanity, and thus to perpetuate a tradition of the facts. While the soldiers were sitting in their ranks, waiting for the decision of their chiefs, a hare was by some accident started in the fields between the English and the French armies, and ran directly towards the French position.*

The first line of soldiers, when they beheld it, set up a loud halloo; and others, who very likely did not know the cause, joined in the cry, till the clamour became so great that the division behind, in which were stationed the troops of Hainault, believed that the enemy had advanced to the attack. Helmets were instantly caught up, and swords were drawn; and the

national prejudice existed, as in the present instance, to bias its account.

The attempt to prove that Philip did not decline the battle is absurd. He did so, and he did so wisely, well counselled, and judiciously; and he showed far more skill and strength of mind in restraining his impetuous nobles on this occasion, than in yielding them their will at Crecy. To prove that Philip did not decline the battle, is quite unnecessary to the military renown of the French nation, which stands upon the noblest foundation — that which they have done at all times in their history. That their King declined a battle, and that his troops acquiesced, when a battle was not only unnecessary, but would have been folly, was to the honour of all, and not to the discredit of any.

The story of Philip having fortified his camp with trees, and of a thousand knights having been plunged into a marsh, was, in all probability, amongst the wild rumours of the enemy's movements, which are always floating about a camp.

* Froissart, chap. xciii.

young Count of Hainault, in expectation of immediate battle, dubbed fourteen new knights, who, when the mistake was discovered, and the cause of the outcry ascertained, received the name of Knights of the Hare, which they continued to bear ever after.

Towards evening it became apparent to all that no battle would take place; and the Count of Hainault, not much delighted with his reception, quitted the French camp with his troops, and returned to Quesnoy.

In the mean while, the English army remained under arms during the whole of Friday and Saturday, within four miles of the French position; but, no enemy appearing at the hour of vespers on the latter day, Edward retired from the open field, and took the way to Avesnes. His provisions were exhausted, and his allies were anxious to retreat to their own territories, loaded, as they were, with the booty of which they had swept one of the richest districts of France. Nevertheless, Edward sent to inform his adversary that he would wait him the whole of the following day at Avesnes, which he accordingly did. The King of France, however, had already dismissed a great part of his army; and, with the rest, he retired to St. Quentin, to prepare his frontier towns for resisting any new efforts which the English monarch might make against them in the following year.

Edward remained upon the frontier of France till the Monday; and then, taking leave of the greater part of his allies, he suffered them to lead home their various forces, while he himself accompanied the Duke of Brabant to Brussels. Thus ended the first campaign of the English monarch against his rival, Philip of Valois; a campaign in which, though he injured his adversary, and desolated territories which he claimed as his own, he neither won honour or advantage equivalent in any degree to the expense he had incurred, or the preparations he had made. He had failed before Cambray; he had been deterred from attacking St. Quentin; he had conquered nothing which he could keep, and his expedition into France reduced itself to a plundering excursion.

Philip of Valois, on the contrary, would have won, as he merited, high credit, had not a claim been made for glory, on account of deeds which he never performed. Regarding, simply, what he did do, we find that he maintained all his frontier towns; that, by his maritime expeditions, he retaliated severely on his enemy the aggression committed on his own territory; and that, while he collected a large army to repel his incursions, and followed him closely till he was obliged to retire, he avoided a hazardous battle, which could have been productive of very little benefit if gained; and, if lost, might have involved the ruin of his kingdom, and the fall of his throne.

Thus would have stood the simple facts in history, had not some persons weakly attempted to prove, upon the authority of some of the most doubtful records in existence, that Philip sought and Edward avoided a battle. The mass of contemporary evidence, however, decidedly establishes the contrary;

and, in the details which it affords, displays Philip in a very inferior light to that which is cast upon him by the general results of the campaign.*

* Walsingham †, Knighton ‡, Robert of Avesbury §, Froissart, and above all, Edward's own letter, all show Philip as, in the first instance, declaring that Edward should not remain a day on French ground without a battle, then appointing the day on which it was to take place, and then suffering three distinct days to pass over without attempting to fight him. If it be asserted that these are all partial authorities, the reply is, that opposed to them there are only two authorities equally partial, notoriously incorrect, anonymous, and unsupported by any collateral circumstance to afford them even a shade of authenticity ‖; while it must be clear to any who considers the circumstances of Edward and Froissart, that neither of them dared to have stated a falsehood in any material point. Edward might have been wrong in the numbers of his adversary, or in the account of his own troops, or any other minor circumstance; but he dared not have stated that he and his allies remained all day during Friday and Saturday waiting, in vain, for the attack of Philip of Valois, if they had not done so. Nor would the "Chroniques de France" have distinctly admitted that Philip determined not to fight, if, as M. Dacier declares, that monarch actually marched out to take possession of the English camp.

In regard to the causes which induced Philip not to give battle, I have not the slightest doubt that his principal counsellors were moved greatly by the motives of expediency; but at the same time we must not suppose the age wiser than it was; and every record tends to prove that such a prognostication as that contained in the letters of the King of Sicily was calculated to have the most powerful effect both on the mind of the King and his soldiers. Not to have believed in judicial astrology in those days would have been looked upon as gross impiety.

---

† Hist. page 128. ‡ Col. 2575. &c. § Page 46.

‖ The Chron. of Fland., and the continuator of Nangis.

CHAP. VII.

DIFFICULTIES OF EDWARD III. AT THE END OF THE WAR.—VIEWS AND CONDUCT OF ARTEVELDE.—NEGOTIATIONS WITH THE DUKE OF BRABANT.—CONGRESS AT BRUSSELS.—THE FLEMINGS PROPOSE THAT EDWARD SHOULD ASSUME THE TITLE OF KING OF FRANCE.—THEIR MOTIVES.—HE ACCEDES.—THE FLEMINGS ACKNOWLEDGE HIM AS KING OF FRANCE.—HE SAILS FOR ENGLAND.—PROCEEDINGS OF HIS PARLIAMENT.—PHILIP PERMITS HIS TROOPS TO RAVAGE HAINAULT.—INDIGNATION AND PREPARATIONS OF THE COUNT.—HE DECLARES WAR AGAINST PHILIP.—AUBENTON TAKEN.—THE THIERASCHE RAVAGED.—ALLIANCES OF THE COUNT OF HAINHAULT.—SIEGE OF THUN L'EVEQUE.—THE COUNT OF HAINAULT MARCHES TO ITS RELIEF.—ESCAPE OF THE GARRISON.

THE winter, which set in early, suspended all military operations; but the war of the cabinet, not less difficult than the war of the field, was now about to be renewed.* The first great inconvenience that Edward suffered, and that which brought about many others, was the want of money. All his allies, with very few exceptions, were merely bound to him by

* Edward's journey from Avesnes to Antwerp seems to have been as rapid as possible, and it is scarcely possible to suppose that he travelled with the encumbrance of an army. In all probability, as soon as he heard that the French force had dispersed, he left his own troops to be brought back by his marshals, and set out with a mere escort. He left Avesnes on the 25th of October. His letter in Avesbury is dated the 1st of November, at Brussels. A convention with Gaston of the Island, in Rymer, is dated on the 2d, at Ghent, and we find him in the midst of a thousand various negotiations at Antwerp on the 4th.

mercenary ties; and the alliance which he had formed with such labour, was, of course, likely to be dissolved as soon as the golden bonds which united its members to one another were cut by the hand of necessity. The chief in the league, by power, by influence, or by avarice, was the Duke of Brabant, who, aware of the importance of his friendship, sold his scanty assistance to his needy cousin with the most ungenerous avidity. Before he had consented, in the first instance, to expose himself to the wrath of Philip, by joining his arms to those of Edward's supporters, he had exacted from the King of England a gratuity of 60,000*l.*, and from time to time received a number of other subsidies.* He had also prevailed upon Edward to bind himself, by a public act under his hand and seal, not to quit the Low Countries till the war in which he engaged was fully terminated; and he endeavoured artfully and perseveringly to draw more deep and lasting advantages from the difficulties which opposed themselves to his cousin's ambition. But while Edward found himself compelled to yield to the cravings of the Duke, as far as mere pecuniary demands went, he displayed as much policy as that prince himself in other respects, and still held before his view the prospect of an union between the young Duke of Cornwall and Margaret of Brabant, the Duke's daughter. This, however, as well as a marriage between a son of the Duke of Austria and the Princess Isabella of England †, though treated of from

* Rymer, vol. ii. part iii. July 1. ann. 1337.

† Rymer, tom. ii. parts iii. and iv.

time to time, was artfully held in suspense to counterpoise, in some degree, the urgent claims of foreign confederates.*

Before the first campaign was concluded†, we find it stated by Edward's ministers in parliament, that he was already indebted to persons on the Continent in various sums to the amount of 300,000*l.*, for subsidies to his allies, and the necessary expenses of his own army. At the end of that campaign there can be no doubt that his debts were much larger; and at the same time it was evident that his forces would diminish in the exact proportion that his expenditure was lessened, unless some means could be found to engage less mercenary auxiliaries to swell his army in the campaign of the following summer. Besides these considerations, it was supposed that, without many more troops than he had hitherto brought into the field, he could never hope to obtain, by force, possession of the country to which he laid claim.

Three great objects, therefore, were before him on his return to the Low Countries: first, to insure the permanence of the alliances he had already formed; secondly, to add to the number as far as his circumstances permitted; and, thirdly, to obtain supplies in order to pay off the obligations he had contracted, and to carry on the war with renewed activity. To accomplish the first two of these designs,

* The negotiations with the Duke of Brabant were carried so far, that security was given by various of the King's ministers, that the Duke of Cornwall should marry his daughter; for which Edward afterwards agreed to bear them harmless. — *Barnes*, p. 178.

† Barnes, p. 150.

no sooner had he arrived at Brussels than he appointed a general meeting of all his allies to take place at Antwerp, on the *morrow after St. Martin* *; but afterwards, upon reflection, he determined upon changing both the place and time of assembly. Brussels was then named as the rendezvous to which, besides all the princes and leaders who had marched in alliance with Edward, Jacob von Artevelde, the demagogue of Ghent, was summoned, to consult with the English monarch and the princes of the empire.†

At the time appointed, Artevelde repaired to Brussels, well disposed to go all lengths in favour of the sovereign who so honoured him. Nor were political considerations, as well as gratified vanity, wanting, to bind him strongly to the cause of Edward. He existed as a ruler solely by the popularity which could be maintained by no other means than by agitating Flanders, and keeping it in a state of excitement and anxiety. A prolongation of the war between England and France offered the best opportunity of perpetuating his ascendancy, while its termination held out nothing but ruin in prospect. If Edward were at once successful, honour, protection, and fortune were before his friend and ally; if the war were pro-

* Epist. Edwardi, apud Robert de Avesbury.

† From the papers preserved in Rymer, we find that, throughout the whole of December, Edward was negotiating with the Flemings by different envoys; and although he, in fact and truth, transacted the whole affair with Artevelde, and the burghers of Ghent, Bruges, and Ypres, yet feudal customs required that the name of the Count of Flanders should be constantly used in conjunction with that of his good citizens.

longed, Artevelde had still at his command all those means of rule which he already possessed, increased by the confidence and support of a great king. On the other hand, if peace were re-established, he could but look to the decay of his own power, and to certain punishment if ever Philip of Valois found himself disengaged from his present difficulties, and free to re-establish the Count of Flanders in his rights. Every motive, therefore, which could induce a wise man, every prospect which could allure an ambitious man, and every hope that could seduce a vain man, combined to attach Artevelde to the cause of the English monarch; and, at the same time, policy required that he should engage Edward to the prolongation of the war, by some step more irrevocable than the common acts of aggression daily perpetrated by sovereign against sovereign.

Such were, probably, the feelings and calculations of Artevelde, when he set out for Brussels; and so great was his influence throughout Flanders, that — although there is every reason to believe that Philip of Valois and the papal legates had used strenuous means and promised extraordinary concessions in order to detach the Flemings from the English party — the municipal councils of the great cities accompanied their leader, in state, to the conference with the King of England, and showed themselves more devoted to the interest of that monarch than many who had taken arms in favour of his unjust pretensions.*

The situation of Edward, when he arrived at the place of conference, was by no means so prosperous as

* Rapin, p. 418.

it had been. The young Count of Hainault *, who had appeared in the field both for him and against him, now refused to take part in the measures agitating in his favour; the Scots had again infringed his northern frontier; the events of the war in Gascony, though carried on languidly by both parties, had been hitherto less propitious to England than to France; and the parliament, which had been held by his son on the 13th of October, 1339, had done any thing but satisfy his demands or supply his necessities. The nobles, indeed, had, with generous promptitude, granted the monarch a tithe of their chief revenues — the tenth lamb, the tenth fleece, and the tenth sheaf — without burdening their gift by any condition. The Commons, however, had hesitated, demanded a delay to consult with their constituents, and showed an evident determination to grant nothing without exacting a number of concessions from the exigencies of the monarch.†

While the necessity of counteracting these unpropitious circumstances at home called loudly for the monarch's presence in England, the Duke of Brabant, fearful of being left to his fate if Edward quitted the Low Countries, urged the tenour of the contract between them, which bound the King of England to remain upon the Continent till the war should be concluded. The difficulties of his cousin's situation,

* Froissart, chap. xcvii.

† Barnes, p. 150. The most extraordinary of the demands made on this occasion were, that free pardons should be granted for various felonies, that a number of commissioners, &c. should be arrested in default of immediate payment, and that the King should abandon several feudal dues called aids.

however, and, still more cogently, the prospect of losing the pecuniary supplies, of which he had already nearly exhausted the sources, induced him, at length, to allow the monarch to absent himself upon such conditions as insured his own safety and the King's speedy return.* Another covenant was accordingly drawn up and signed by the English King, by which he engaged to revisit Flanders on or before St. John's day of the following year; and, in the mean time, to give, as hostages for the execution of this promise, Henry Earl of Derby and William Earl of Salisbury, to whom were to be added, before the conclusion of Lent, the Earls of Northampton and Suffolk.† In addition to these, Edward, whose purpose of returning was perfectly sincere, determined to leave, at Ghent, his queen, then pregnant with the famous John of Gaunt, and his son Lionel, born the year before at Antwerp. Edward, also, his eldest son, arrived about the same time at Antwerp; and it is more than probable, that the expectation of speedily concluding the alliance between that prince and Margaret of Brabant might likewise move the Duke, and tend to relax the tenacity with which he had previously adhered to the terms of his former treaty.

Still the situation of the English King, when he

* Edward, on the 4th of December, 1339, granted permission to the Duke of Brabant to raise and keep up a body of 1000 men at arms of good family, at his expense, during the whole time of his absence; and also, in case of need, to raise 1000 more, to guard his territories of Brabant against the arms of the French King. — *Rymer*, tom. ii. part iv. p. 58.

† Rymer, tom. ii. part iv. pp. 57, 58. Date, 4th of December, 1339.

arrived at the parliament of Brussels, offered few advantageous points in the present, and few hopes for the future; but, as in almost every case where human foresight is brought to calculate dangers and obstacles at a distance, the apparent difficulties which surrounded him were removed by various accidental circumstances; while events, which had never entered into consideration, took place, and in the end overthrew all his greatest designs.

At Brussels, Artevelde appeared in almost royal pomp, and was received by all with almost royal distinction. His interests, however, and his vanity, in the present instance, walked hand in hand; and his influence with the people of Flanders was, of course, increased by the respect which he received from foreign princes. Besides the deputies from the good towns of Flanders, almost all the allies of the English King were present upon the occasion; and, called upon to treat amongst princes, the burghers of Ghent, and Ypres, and Bruges, could not but feel gratified at the circumstances in which Artevelde had placed them. The conference was opened with an urgent request on the part of the English monarch and his confederates that the worthy citizens of Flanders would lay aside their scruples, and embrace his cause with the same zeal and boldness which the other states of Belgium had displayed. As an inducement to take arms in his favour, Edward proposed the immediate siege of the frontier town of Tournay, the capture of which would open the way, at once, to the conquest of Lille, Douai, and Bethune, and, of all the country which had been put into the hands of France as a pledge for the obedience of Flanders.

Although the prospect held out was most grateful to the Flemings, they urged, in reply to Edward's demand, the same motives for neutrality which they had stated before; namely, their convention with the French King, and the bond of two millions of florins which they forfeited to the Pope if ever again they took arms against a King of France.

Edward was not in a condition to indemnify them for so great a sacrifice; but an expedient was now proposed by Artevelde, which removed all difficulties. The King of England, he said, had long contended that he had a right to the throne of France; he was in arms to assert that right, and the Flemings were convinced of the justice of his claim. Though bound by their obligations, they could not aid him either as King of England or Vicar of the Empire; yet, as soon as he assumed the style and title of King of France, and quartered the arms of that monarchy with those of England, the objection would be removed, and the people of Flanders, acknowledging him as their lawful sovereign, would instantly take arms in defence of his right.*

Though the proposal was in no degree extraordinary, and Edward had already called † himself King of France in more than one public document,

* The first state paper which mentions the proposal of the Flemings to recognise Edward as King of France, is dated 4th of January, 1340.

† In letters of procuration to the Duke of Brabant and other persons. See Hallam, Middle Ages, vol. i. p. 52.

it seems to have taken him by surprise; and he demanded time to consult with his council, as to whether he could call himself king of a country in which he did not possess one foot of ground. He was not without many precedents even in that age; and his determination was soon taken. The reasoning was conclusive that, if he were, by right, King of France, he was justified in calling himself so, whether he possessed the land or not. He entered into no abstruse speculations as to the true nature of rights; but, seeing much to be gained by the bold assumption of a name which was but the shadow of the reality he fought for, he agreed to the proposal of the Flemings, on the condition that they would immediately acknowledge him as sovereign of France. The Flemings who were present agreed to this stipulation at once; but, to give more solemnity to the whole proceeding, it was determined to call a general assembly of all the councils of Flanders, to be held at Ghent; at which the deputies undertook that a treaty should be signed to insure the King against all tergiversation; and it was understood that, immemediately afterwards, Edward should assume the name and arms of King of France.

By the whole of this proceeding Artevelde gained many great objects. He removed the objection of the Flemings to aid the King of England in arms, and thereby bound Edward to him by the strong ties of mutual interest. He created for himself a scene of action in which he hoped to distinguish himself, and to establish his power on a stronger basis than that on which it was at present founded; while, by the irrevocable act of assuming the name of King of France, he believed that Edward would pledge himself beyond recall to the unceasing prosecution of his claim. At the same time, by making the alliance with the King of England a public act of the whole Flemish people, that far-sighted politician removed from himself the responsibility; and, probably, anticipated, from the difficulties and schisms which might ensue, but an increase of fame and authority. To arrange the treaty with the burgher councils, Edward, in the first instance, despatched three ambassadors to Ghent, — the Earl of Salisbury, Henry Lord Ferrers, and Sir Geoffrey Scroop *; but, as soon as the preliminaries were arranged, he proceeded to that city † in person, accompanied by his queen; and, when the convention had been signed and sealed on all parts, solemnly took the style of King of France, and quartered the fleurs de lys with the leopards of England. ‡

Not contented with this act alone, he now dated all his letters from the first year of his reign in France; he notified to the Pope the change he had made in his title, justified his so doing by his rights

* Rymer, tom. ii. part iv. p. 62.

† What was the date of the assembly of Brussels I am not able to discover. An almost uninterrupted series of papers, signed with Edward's own hand, exist from the time of his arrival at Antwerp, on the 4th of November, till his journey to Ghent on the 25th of February, 1340 (Rymer, tom. ii. part iv. p. 63.); and it is not possible that he could have spent more than two whole days at Brussels during the intervening period. Perhaps the word Brussels in Froissart may have been erroneously substituted for Antwerp; at which place we know, from Edward's letter, that he had called a meeting of his allies on the morrow of St. Martin.

‡ 23d of January, 1340. Villani, lii. c. 108.

to the French throne; and, addressing a proclamation to the nobles and people of France, he called upon them to take example by the Flemings, and submit to his authority.*

The Pope replied at length †, advocating the cause of Philip fully as much as the cause of peace, and sharply rebuking the King of England for still continuing in alliance with Louis of Bavaria. The French people were, of course, silent; but did not look upon Edward as more really their King because he had taken the name, or regard the English less as their enemies because a prince, whom they did not

* Rymer, tom. ii. pp. 64—66. 8th of February, at Ghent.

† Edward's letters to the Pope were sent by one Nicolas de Flisco (probably a corruption of "Fiesco"), a man apparently of some eminence, and possessing in the highest degree the confidence and regard of the King of England. Little, indeed, is known concerning him; but many of Edward's public letters, preserved in Rymer, mention him in high terms of commendation and regard. While at Avignon, upon his present mission, some partisans of the King of France broke into his house during the night, and, carrying off the envoy, together with his son and a servant, kept him a strict prisoner for some time. The Pope, however, indignant at such an outrage offered to a person under the immediate protection and safeguard of the Holy See, thundered his anathema against all who were concerned in his abduction; executed summary justice upon some of his own dependents who had a share therein; and even, it would appear, put France in interdict till the King of England's envoy was set at liberty. Philip of Valois, on his part, protested loudly his innocence of any participation in the crime which had been committed; remonstrated against the extreme measures to which the Pontiff had had recourse; and caused the object of so much contest to be freed from durance, and conveyed to Avignon. It is not, however, to be supposed that Edward passed over in silence the insult offered to his messenger, or the wrong done to the sacred person of an ambassador; and we find amongst the state papers a letter to the Pope upon the subject, which contains many expressions calculated to leave a conviction that Edward regarded his envoy with feelings of greater respect and affection than his mere station implied.

acknowledge, claimed dominion over both. Edward, who, probably, had never anticipated any great effects, as far as regarded the French nation, from the assumption of his new title, rested satisfied with the homage of the Flemings, added the words *Dieu et mon droit* to the quartered arms of France and England, and caused a new great seal to be engraved, bearing the emblems of his assumed authority.

On the other hand, the Pope launched the thunders of the church at the Flemings, for supporting the enemy of the church's beneficent protector; and, in the name of God, placed the whole of Flanders in interdict. The clergy of that country, who were either French themselves, or attached to the French court, willingly proceeded to enforce the sentence of the Holy See, by depriving their flocks of all the religious offices they were appointed to celebrate *; but, while all parties thus impiously made use of the name of the Most High to sanctify their insect contentions, Providence was pursuing, uninterrupted, His inscrutable course, to the destruction of all the laboured schemes and intricate policies of man.

Before the interdict had reached Flanders, Edward had sailed for England †, and almost immediately after held a parliament at Westminster. The presence of the King had, of course, great effect upon the representatives of his people; and he induced them to grant him vast supplies for carrying on the war, shackled by

* Barnes, p. 160. Froissart, chap. cvi.

† He disembarked at Orwell on the 21st of February, 1340; and instantly proceeded to London, where he held the parliament.

no condition to which he could reasonably object.* The strictest inquisition, also, was instituted into the collection of the taxes formerly imposed, in which vast peculations had, undoubtedly, taken place; and Edward, relieved from his pecuniary embarrassments, proceeded, with immense activity, to provide for all the necessities of the state, and for the defence of both his Scottish frontier and his territories in Aquitaine.

His voyage to England had thus removed most of those difficulties which had attended him from the insufficiency of his supplies; and, during his stay in London, events took place in Belgium which tended to strengthen and consolidate his alliances on the

* The principal grants and enactments of this Parliament are stated by Barnes to have been as follows: —

The lords and commons granted to the King the ninth of their wool, the ninth lamb, the ninth sheep, and the ninth of all grain and moveables; at the same time giving power to take from foreign merchants, and others not living by agriculture, the nineteenth of their goods lawfully to their value.

In return for this grant, Edward declared, by statute, that it was to form no precedent for future times, and that no charge or claim for aid should thenceforward be made by the King, unless by the common consent of the prelates, earls, barons, and other great men, and commons of the realm; and still farther, that all profits arising from this supply, as well as from escheats, customs, marriages, wards, and other feudal sources of revenue, should be spent upon the maintenance and safe keeping of the kingdom of England, and the prosecution of the war in Gascony, France, and Scotland, while those wars continued, and on no other matter whatever.

In addition to the above aid, the clergy contributed a tenth; and means were taken to increase the revenues arising from the foreign priories in England; while Edward, anxious for the prosperity of his realm, as well as the more immediate gratification of his personal ambition, laboured with his subjects to promote the commerce with Flanders, and to increase the trade in wool and woollen cloths, which he had already striven assiduously to found; measures in which present policy and remote interests were equally considered.

Continent, and to afford a fair promise of greater unanimity and vigour than had hitherto been displayed by his confederates.

The first movements, however, which afterwards brought about these results, were any thing but favourable to the allies of the King of England. In dismissing his troops at Buironfosse, Philip of Valois had not neglected the wise precaution of strengthening his various frontier garrisons; and had filled the towns upon the Somme and Scheldt with large bodies of young and ardent warriors, whose greatest desire was to signalise themselves against the enemy.

Between these bodies and the troops of the neighbouring states, continual skirmishes were taking place, which, at first, extended only to the subjects of the French King, and to those of princes positively allied to his adversary; but they soon involved the Count of Hainault also, who had pointedly abstained from the renewed league against Philip of Valois, which had been consolidated by the Parliament of Brussels. In most of the sudden excursions which they made, the French were very successful; and their efforts seem especially to have been directed against the lands of the famous John of Hainault, who had given good subject for retaliation, by ravaging and desolating a great part of Picardy in the late invasion of France. The strong town of Chimay belonging to that nobleman was attacked, and the whole surrounding country laid waste. Nearly at the same time the Castle of

* Froissart, chap. xciv.

Ralengues, also belonging to John of Hainault, was besieged; and, the garrison having made their escape in the night, it was burned to the ground. In addition to these exploits, the garrison of Cambray and that of Thun l'Evêque waged incessant war against each other; and, at length, in an excursion made by Giles de Mauny, the commandant of Thun, his companions were defeated, and he himself was taken prisoner, mortally wounded, and carried into Cambray. This success did not deliver the inhabitants of that city from the enterprises of the garrison of Thun, as two brothers of the deceased captain, equally fearless and enterprising with himself, came immediately from Bouchain, to put themselves at the head of his companions, for the purpose of revenging his death.

Hitherto the war had respected the territories of the Count of Hainault; but, according to Froissart, the Bishop of Cambray, by representing to the French King the ravages which the Hainaulters had committed in Cambresis, while Edward had besieged the town, at length induced Philip of Valois to treat as an enemy a prince whom a little forbearance might have secured as a friend. The chief cities on the French frontier were, as I have said, strongly garrisoned; and as the reward of military service in those days was, principally, what each individual could gain by his strength, his courage, and his activity, — whether in plunder, which was not only permitted but commanded, or in prisoners, whose ransom was according to their wealth or distinction,

— the commanders of the various fortresses desired nothing so much as permission to seek riches and adventures in the rich country of Hainault. In Cambray still remained the Grand Master La Beaume, together with John de Levis, Mareschal de Merepoix, and several other distinguished knights. Hugh de la Roque, seneschal of Carcassonne, commanded in St. Amand; the famous Lord of Beaujeu in Mortagne; and in Tournay was that Godemar de Fay, whose firmness on one occasion and weakness on another proved afterwards the salvation and the ruin of France.

No sooner was it announced to these officers that the King allowed the garrisons of the Cambresis to push their excursions into Hainault itself, — for to Cambresis alone, which had suffered by the Hainaulters, the King's permission seems to have extended, — than a force was collected, somewhat larger, in all probability, than that territory itself could have afforded, consisting of 600 men at arms, which always implied treble the number of soldiers. Every thing was arranged as quietly as possible; and, setting out immediately after dusk, the adventurers directed their course towards Haspre, the first large town of Hainault, which lay in fancied security, totally unprepared for defence. The French entered at once through the unguarded gates; and, taking possession of the sleeping city, proceeded to plunder at their ease. Haspre was soon completely swept of its riches and its inhabitants. A large priory of Black Monks shared the same fate; and, when every thing had been collected which could be carried away, the invaders left the place, driving their living prey before them. They departed not, however, without setting fire to the town as they retired; and the unfortunate inhabitants, carried away captives at a moment that they fancied themselves in profound peace, saw their city, with all its sweet domestic memories, reduced to a heap of grey ruins before their eyes, their hearths covered with the ashes of their homes, and nothing left of their birthplace but the name.

The tidings of the French aggression reached Valenciennes that night; and the young Count was roused from his sleep to hear that one of his chief cities was assailed by the French. Starting from his bed, he instantly buckled on his armour; and, calling round him the few knights that his palace contained, issued forth into the market place, where he caused the alarm bell to be rung, from one of those belfries which all large towns possessed for the purpose of calling the neighbouring country to arms in case of attack. Without waiting, however, for the assembly of a larger force than that which was already prepared, he sprang upon horseback, and, spurring onward towards Haspre with all the eagerness of anger and indignation, left whatever troops might be collected after his departure to follow as fast as they could. But, before he had ridden far, he was met by news of the complete destruction of the town he went to aid; and was assured that the French had retired beyond reach of pursuit.

Amongst the first who received the tidings of the fall of Haspre was John of Hainault, Lord of

Beaumont, who had already suffered so greatly himself by the incursions of the French, and who was not sorry, perhaps, that his nephew had met with so ungrateful a return for the moderate and somewhat temporising course he had pursued towards the King of France. He nevertheless set off instantly for Valenciennes, to aid the Count by his presence and advice; and the conversation said to have taken place between the uncle and nephew on their first meeting is too characteristic of the manners of that age to be omitted.

"Fair uncle," said the Count as they met, "your war with France is greatly embellished."

"God be praised, Sir!" replied the Lord of Beaumont. "For your wrong and grief, I should be angry enough; but you have this for the love and service you have always borne the French. However, we must now ride against France. Look to what side it shall be upon."

"You say true," answered the Count; "and it shall be full shortly."

A meeting of all the vassals of Hainault was immediately called at Mons; and much debate ensued as to whether it would be necessary to give any warning to a monarch who had violated the peace without notification on his part, or whether it would not be expedient to follow his example, and attack his territories at once. It was, at length, determined to follow nobler rules, and defy the French King openly before his dominions were invaded. Thibalt, abbot of Crespy, was charged with the Count's defiance, which he delivered to Philip in form.

The King received it with contempt, merely replying that his nephew was an "outrageous fool, who took the best means to have his whole country consumed." But surely, if there was any outrage and folly committed through the whole transaction, the accusation thereof would appear to rest upon the man who cast away a friend while assailed by many enemies, and who violated the common and generous custom of the times, to commit a cruel aggression on his nephew's territories.

The more noble and open proceeding of the Count of Hainault did not prevent him from taking signal vengeance upon his adversary. No sooner was the defiance given, than, entering France with 10,000 men at arms, the Count and his uncle instantly proceeded to Aubenton — a town which expected their attack, and had been strongly reinforced and prepared to resist. The first day, after a long and severe contest, the barriers without the gates were won by the Hainaulters; and on the second day the gates themselves were forced. The battle, however, still continued within the walls; though the inferiority of numbers, of course, deprived the French of all chance of successful resistance. The Vidame of Chalons, who commanded, was taken, severely wounded; and his two sons, whom he had knighted at the gates in the morning, were found dead in the market-place. The Lord of Vervins, who had been a principal actor in the desolation of Chimay, saved himself by the swiftness of his horse; but few others escaped alive to bear the news of the storming of Aubenton.

From that city, the Count of Hainault directed his march through the Thierasche, burning and desolating a great part of the diocese of Rheims. Forty towns and villages, which had escaped at the time of the English invasion, were now levelled with the ground; and the wanton aggression which Philip had suffered his troops to commit was avenged, for the time, in the most signal manner. The Count of Hainault, however, was well aware that such an expedition would call down speedy retaliation; and he was no less conscious that, however brave and active were his soldiers, their numbers could not at all suffice to protect the country against the far superior force of France. Support became necessary to him; and as war now existed in its most implacable form between his dominions and France, his natural allies were, of course, the enemies of the French King.

To Edward, then, as the chief of those enemies, he now determined to apply, although, on a previous occasion, he had himself shown much indifference to the success of the English King; but their interests were now united, where they had before been distinct, and he calculated justly when he supposed that his brother-in-law would embrace his alliance with pleasure. The transaction, however, was one of such delicacy, and the necessity of his case so urgent, that he determined to conduct the negotiation in person; and, leaving his uncle governor of Hainault, Holland, and Zealand during his absence, he embarked at Dordrecht for England. His expectations in regard to the disposition of the King of England were in no degree disappointed; and in a very short space of time he had concluded an offensive and defensive alliance with that prince, and obtained the assurance of his prompt support and assistance. From London the Count directed his course, as rapidly as possible, to the court of the Emperor, and entered into a general league with all those German nobles who had before aided the King of England. In the mean time, events had occurred in Hainault, which rendered these alliances not only necessary to the security of his dominions, but to his very existence as a prince.

The invasion and desolation of a part of his territories by a petty prince of the Empire* had kindled the rage of Philip of Valois to a far greater degree than the more potent rivalry of the English King; and the consequence was the march of a large army for the destruction of Hainault. This force was commanded by the brave but unhappy John Duke of Normandy, afterwards King of France; and, assembling at St. Quentin before the conclusion of April, a body of 14,000 men approached the frontiers of Cambresis, and halted at the small town of Montay. Confiding in their numbers and their valour, the French took no precautions against surprise; and, during the first night of their invasion, they found that the activity and the daring of their adversaries might cause them more serious loss and danger than a much larger force commanded by less enterprising leaders. Werchin

* Parts of the Count of Hainault's territories were fiefs of the empire; parts were held of the crown of France.

Gerard, seneschal of Hainault, had kept a wary eye upon the enemy; and as soon as he learned the carelessness of the French dispositions, he conceived the daring project of carrying off the Duke of Normandy, their commander-in-chief.* In the dead of the night he made his way into Montay with only sixty companions, and proceeded boldly, in the midst of the French army, to attack the principal house of the town, in which he naturally concluded that the son of the King of France would make his temporary abode. In this, however, he was mistaken; and on breaking in the door, he found two of the principal French nobles, but not their leader. An immediate struggle ensued, in which the Lord of Bailleul was killed, and his companion, the Lord of Briançon, was

* This gallant exploit has a parallel in modern history which I cannot pass over in silence. In the early part of the American war General Lee, an officer of very considerable reputation and talents, joined the ranks of the republicans, and much was expected from his zeal and abilities. A report, however, having reached the British army under Sir W. Howe, that General Lee's corps was marching towards Alexandria for the purpose of crossing the Delaware, Lieutenant-Colonel Harcourt (afterwards Field Marshal Earl of Harcourt) volunteered to reconnoitre the enemy's movements, obtained exact information in regard to the head quarters of the general, and instantly formed the daring design of carrying him off from the midst of his army. With thirty men of the 16th light dragoons, he reached General Lee's quarters unperceived; and finding a house on either side of the road, he divided his men, and attacked both. Considerable resistance was made by the guard, and a ball fired from the window passed through Colonel Harcourt's helmet; but before any succour could arrive, General Lee was taken, placed on a horse before a dragoon, and was carried a prisoner to the British camp. The gallant nobleman by whom this bold deed was performed has not been many years dead, and there are some still living who can testify that in him all the better qualities of the chivalrous character continued to exist in an age which produced very little of the kind.

taken prisoner by the Hainaulters, together with ten or twelve more, all men of note; after which the assailants, finding that the alarm was given, and that the troops were getting under arms, retired with all speed, and, regaining their horses, rode back to Valenciennes with their prisoners. Many attempts of the same nature, were undertaken by the Hainaulters and their allies; nor were careful precautions against the enemy wanting on the part of John of Hainault, during his nephew's absence. Not having yet a sufficient force to keep the field against the army of the Duke of Normandy, he was of course obliged to abandon the open country, and the unfortified towns and villages, to be plundered by the foe; but in every city which afforded the possibility of resistance, he took care to place a sufficient garrison to maintain it against any thing but a regular siege; and at the same time he collected, in the towns of Valenciennes, Bouchain, Avesnes, Landrecy, Maubeuge, and Quesnoy, ample provisions, and large bodies of troops, headed by the most experienced commanders of the country.

The expedition of the Duke of Normandy, therefore, reduced itself to a mere devastating incursion. An immense multitude of villages and hamlets were destroyed; great booty was obtained; and the whole open country of Hainault was swept of all its produce. No fortified town or fortress of any import, however, was taken, or even besieged, by the French, with the exception of Escandeuvres on the Scheldt, which was surrendered to them after a short siege, by the treachery of its commander. He expiated his crime by an ignominious death shortly after at Mons; and the castle of Escandeuvres was rased to its foundations by the captors. After this small success, the Duke of Normandy retired to Cambray; and having made a brief halt, and reinforced some of the neighbouring garrisons, he directed his whole remaining force against the castle of Thun l'Evêque.

The renown of the gentlemen who held the fortress for the King of England, as well as the strength of the place itself, rendered greater preparations necessary than the size of the castle or the number of the garrison seemed to require.* Fresh levies were made by the French general; and several of those great engines which at that time were still generally used instead of cannon, were brought from Cambray and Douai, against the small fort of Thun l'Evêque. Six of these machines are mentioned as particularly powerful; and from these, day and night, immense masses of stone were continually hurled against the castle, beating down the battlements and the roofs, so that no shelter was left to the garrison but in the cellars and subterranean chambers, with which almost every fortress in that day was provided. Still, however, the bold counsels of Sir Richard Lamesi, and of two

* That no great force was ever employed in the defence of Thun l'Evêque, we may conclude from the account already given of its capture by Walter de Manny, who, at the time, had with him only forty lances, making in all a force of about 120 men. A part of these only were left by him to guard his conquest; and consequently, at the utmost calculation, the garrison could not consist of more than 100 men.

brothers of the house of Mauny, who seem to have been united in command of the place, maintained the courage of the defenders; and no probability of their surrender existed, when the Duke of Normandy had recourse to one of the most cruel and barbarous expedients which war ever produced. By means of the same engines which had battered down the roofs, he cast in upon the brave garrison every sort of putrid carrion that could be found; and the number of dead horses and cattle, which he thus accumulated within the small space of the castle, in a moist atmosphere, and at a sultry time of year, created within the place a pestilent stench, becoming more and more horrible every hour. Such a means of warfare was not to be resisted; and after suffering for some days the terrible scourge inflicted upon them, the garrison prayed a fortnight's truce, upon the promise of surrendering the fortress at the end of that time if still unrelieved.

The Duke of Normandy consented; and a squire was permitted to go forth for the purpose of informing John of Hainault of the situation of the garrison. The messenger found that prince at Mons; but he was himself less able than ever to collect sufficient forces to give battle to the Duke of Normandy. The garrisons of Lille, Douai, and Tournay were carrying on a continual though desultory warfare upon the frontiers of Flanders and Hainault; and though the Earl of Salisbury had effected some retaliation by the surprise and destruction of Armentieres *, that temporary success had

* Chron. de France, chap. xvii. Ann. de Fland., p. 240.

been more than compensated by the capture of that noble himself by the people of Lille, while endeavouring to pass by that city in company with the Earl of Suffolk, for the purpose of marching with Artevelde to the siege of Tournay.* Continual incursions, and the presence of a large French force upon the borders of the two countries, required that no part of the territory should be left unguarded; and no sufficient force could be collected to succour the besieged fort, without depriving many places of the garrisons necessary to their defence. The Regent, however, informed the messenger from the garrison of Thun, that he had received assurances of his nephew's immediate return; and that he hoped and believed, before the end of the truce, the Count would not only be present, but would also be enabled, by the alliances he had formed, to force the Duke of Normandy to raise the siege.

* Most of the English authors declare, that the two prisoners received the most unworthy treatment. The account given by Barnes is as follows: — "At last it was determined that these two illustrious captives, being fettered and shackled with iron, should be sent and presented to the French King as a lucky hansel of his future success. As they were conveyed to Paris, they were drawn in a cart through the midst of every town, village, and hamlet in their way, with great shouts and cries of the vulgar, and scoffs and railings of the rascal sort of people. Being at last brought into the King of France's presence, he most unworthily commanded they should be put to death; but to this the most noble King of Bohemia, John of Luxemburgh, opposed himself with words to this effect," &c.

A good deal of national prejudice is probably mixed up in this account, which is not confirmed by Froissart, who did not scruple to display many of the intemperate proceedings of Philip of Valois. It appears from the papers in Rymer (tom. ii. part iv. p. 107.), that the companion of Lord Salisbury was the Earl of Suffolk himself, and not his son, as Barnes supposes.

With these tidings the envoy returned to the castle; and a few anxious days still passed, while the arrival of the Count remained uncertain. At length that prince appeared at Valenciennes; and the effect of the alliances which he had formed was instantly felt. Conscious of being now able to bring immense forces into the field against his adversary, he delayed not one moment to act vigorously in his own defence. From every quarter he called the chivalry of Hainault to Valenciennes, and summoned his allies to meet him with all speed at Thun l'Evêque.

Activity and eager thirst for revenge spread through the country, as the means of gratification were presented; and setting off from his capital with a force already considerable, at every step the young Count found his power increasing. Before the termination of the truce, he arrived on the banks of the Scheldt, opposite to the besieged castle; the Count of Namur followed with no insignificant reinforcements; and shortly after, the Dukes of Brabant and Gueldres appeared with large and veteran forces. Last of all came Artevelde of Ghent, with an army of 60,000 Flemings; and more than 100,000 men appeared upon the banks of the Scheldt.

Such a display of power now showed Philip of Valois that it is wiser not even to tread upon a worm. The Duke of Normandy sent instant messengers to his father at Peronne, informing him of this immense host, which, like the fabled produce of the serpent's teeth, seemed to have risen all armed out of the earth; and Philip immediately despatched

1200 men at arms to reinforce his son's forces. The French monarch, it appears, had bound himself by oath not to lead an army across the frontiers of the empire; but the dangerous situation of his troops, who were only separated from the superior force of the Count of Hainault by the waters of the Scheldt *, induced him to forget the niceties of honour, and to join the army as a volunteer. The Duke of Normandy still remained nominally the commander-in-chief of the army, but Philip of Valois directed all its movements.

The various forces which Philip now called to his aid, soon restored a degree of equality to the two hosts; and the siege of Thun l'Evêque proceeded with renewed vigour. To have effectually relieved the castle, it would have been necessary to cross the Scheldt, and fight the besieging army; but although the Count desired nothing more than a battle, the passage of such a river in face of a powerful adversary was a step only to be taken by a bold, active, and skilful general, with forces over which he had the sole command. Such was not the situation of the young Count; and whatever might have been his own military abilities, there were quite enough commanders

* It is scarcely possible to divine how both Mezeray and Barnes could suffer themselves to be misled into placing the castle of Thun l'Evêque upon the river Sambre, where no such place ever existed; while Froissart, whom they both consulted, mentions its position on the Scheldt at least twenty times. A village, indeed, called Thuin, exists upon the Sambre; but Thun l'Evêque was placed upon the left bank of the Scheldt, half way between Cambray and Bouchain. The Count of Hainault, therefore, was on the right, the Duke of Normandy on the left, bank of the river.

in his camp to defeat the best schemes that ever were devised.

All that could be done, therefore, was to keep up a severe discharge of missiles across the river, in aid of the besieged garrison, who by this time were unable to hold out any longer. Under cover of constant flights of arrows and quarrels *, several boats were brought down the river to the castle; and the brave garrison, after enduring the most dreadful distress, set fire to the fortress, and escaped in safety to the opposite shore. The young Count was still desirous of fighting the enemy; but the Duke of Brabant overruled his opinion — declaring that, out of respect to the King of England, who was daily expected in Flanders, they could not fight a general battle without his presence, except under extraordinary circumstances, which did not exist.

It is by no means improbable, that the very circumstances which they held out as an inducement to the Count to refrain, and which were, in fact, merely excuses to themselves for retiring, were the strongest arguments in his mind for urging on a battle. The return of the King of England would, of course, deprive the Count of all the honour which in those days was to be gained by commanding in a general engagement; and it was very natural that a young and ardent prince, mistaking his own zeal for capability, and making his hopes the measure of probabilities, should feel certain of success in an enterprise where the attempt itself was honourable.

* The bolt or sort of arrow discharged from a cross-bow.

It appears that, under these circumstances, he sent twice, without consulting any one, to propose terms of battle to the Duke of Normandy, who, under the advice of his father, refused to accede to the proposed arrangements. After a council also, in which he found that the greater part of his allies were bent upon returning home, the Count still strove to force them to an engagement, by sending word to the adverse commander that, if the French would grant him a truce of but three days, he would build a bridge over the Scheldt, by which either they should pass over unmolested to fight him, or he would pass over to fight them, at their choice. The French general still declined, however, and couched his very prudent determination in terms of bravado and insult.* The Count still continued to linger on the opposite bank, and by much persuasion induced his confederates to keep the field also; but the tidings soon after arrived, that the King of England had returned; and rumours of a great naval engagement having taken place spread through the army. Such reports at once dissolved the only ties that kept the Count's force together; and all the various members of the confederation he had formed, hastened to meet and confer with the greater and more successful prince, whose arrival was now known.

* The reply sent to the Count of Hainault by Philip and his son is thus stated by Froissart: — "Sire de Maubuisson, vous direz, de par nous, à celui qui ci vous envoie, que en tel état comme nous avons tenu le Comte de Hainaut jusques à maintenant, nous le tiendrons en avant et lui ferons engager sa terre: ainsi sera-'t-il guerroyé de deux cotés; et quand bon nous semblera, nous entrerons en Hainaut si à point que nous parardrons tout son pays." — Chap. cxix.

CHAP. VIII.

THE FRENCH PREPARE TO INTERCEPT EDWARD ON HIS RETURN TO FLANDERS. — EDWARD SETS SAIL. — BATTLE OF SLUYS, AND TOTAL DEFEAT OF THE FRENCH. — ORATION OF JACOB VAN ARTEVELDE. — PARLIAMENT OF VILLEVORDE, AND FEDERAL UNION OF THE NETHERLANDS. — THE POPE AND THE KING OF SICILY ENDEAVOUR TO EFFECT A PEACE. — EDWARD AND HIS ALLIES BESIEGE TOURNAY. — THE FLEMINGS BESIEGE ST. OMER. — EDWARD CHALLENGES THE KING OF FRANCE TO SINGLE COMBAT. — PHILIP OF VALOIS DECLINES. — THE FLEMINGS DEFEATED BEFORE ST. OMER. — SIEGE OF TOURNAY. — OF MONTAGNE. — SIEGE AND DESTRUCTION OF ST. AMAND. — ALLEGED PERFIDY OF THE DUKE OF BRABANT. — JOAN OF VALOIS CARRIES ON THE NEGOCIATIONS FOR PEACE. — EDWARD'S DIFFICULTIES. — PROGRESS OF THE FRENCH IN AQUITAINE — OF SCOTS IN SCOTLAND AND THE NORTH OF ENGLAND. — PECULATIONS IN THE ENGLISH EXCHEQUER. — A TRUCE CONCLUDED. — EDWARD WAITS FOR SUPPLIES TO DISCHARGE HIS DEBTS ON THE CONTINENT. — SETS OUT PRIVATELY FOR ENGLAND. — FINDS NOTHING BUT NEGLIGENCE AND CONFUSION.

WHILE the contest between the Count of Hainault and the King of France, through Philip's own imprudence and misconduct, had prepared in the Low Countries a powerful confederacy, and a large and well appointed army ready for the return of the English monarch, Edward had been by no means negligent in his own dominions, in taking measures to give him power and authority amongst the princes with whom he was to act. He had secured supplies of money from his people, and had collected a formidable military force to augment that which he had left behind.

This being done, he hastened his return as much as possible; and leaving his son again guardian of the kingdom, with a council which he believed to be both wise and zealous, he proceeded to the sea-coast, and embarked at Orwell, in Suffolk, on the 22d of June. The promptness with which his general arrangements had been concluded would, perhaps, have enabled him to set out earlier; but news had been received both by himself and by various members of his council, which rendered a much more extensive naval force requisite than he had at first proposed to employ. The tidings which thus altered his plans, were given by his brother-in-law, Reginald Duke of Gueldres*, and imported that an immense fleet had been collected on the sea-coast of Flanders, to oppose his passage. Rumours of this kind had reached England some time before; but Edward had hitherto paid no attention to them. The letters of his brother-in-law, however, not only bore the stamp of authenticity, but entered into various particulars which proved the necessity of activity and precaution. Edward thus learned that the various fleets which had so long swept the channel, and which had not only ravaged his coasts, but had also taken many of his largest ships of war†, had now been collected into one large body, and augmented by immense efforts to the number of 400 ships, of which 140 were of the

* Walsingham, Hist. p. 134.

† Froissart, chap. cvi.

largest class.* These were manned by 40,000 fighting men accustomed to the sea, and commanded by three experienced admirals†, who for the last two years had been constantly employed in carrying on a naval war against England, in which they had met with infinite success. The orders which had been issued to this force, directed the leaders to guard the coast of Flanders; and the admirals Bocanegra, Behuchet, and Quieret had been warned by the French King, that if, by any default on their part, Edward was suffered to land on the Continent, their heads should answer for their negligence.‡ The English historians add, that the French commanders had sworn to present the King of England dead or alive in Paris, if he attempted the passage; and their experience, their preparations, and their force gave them every prospect of keeping their word.

Edward had already collected near 200 vessels for the transport of his troops and of his suite, which had been greatly increased by the presence of almost all the ladies of the English court, who were about to attend the Queen at Antwerp.§ It became ne-

* Froissart, chap. cxx.

† All that has been written in the French Chronicles, and copied by French historians, in regard to this battle, and to the misconduct of Behuchet having been the cause of its loss, proves nothing against the simple fact, that that officer had been chosen for his naval talents, and had been for two years constantly sweeping the British Channel with great and singular success. The words of Froissart particularly mark the great advantages possessed by the French in this respect. — "Et convint là les Anglois souffrir et endurer grande peine, car leurs ennemis étoient quatre contre un, et toutes gens de fait et de mer."

‡ Froissart, chap. cvi.

§ Walsingham, Hist. p. 134.

cessary now, however, to increase his naval force, and he waited as long as the terms of his convention with the Duke of Brabant permitted, endeavouring to collect a fleet equal to that which opposed his passage. Nevertheless, on the 22d of June*, but two days before St. John's day, on which he was bound to be in Flanders, the number of ships which he had obtained only amounted to 260; and with these he set forth, as before said, from Orwell, directing his course towards Sluys. The wind was fair; and the next day, towards evening, Edward came in sight of the coast of Flanders, near Blankenberg, a small town and fort midway between Ostend and Sluys. At the same time the French fleet was discovered lying across the mouth of the great sinus leading to the port of Sluys, and then called t' Zwyn. It was too late at that time for either party to seek an engagement; and Edward contented himself with sending Lord Cobham and Sir John Chandos, with some others, on shore, to reconnoitre the enemy from the land side.† This having been done, and the adverse force sufficiently ascertained, Edward ordered his own fleet to anchor, and waited for the morning to attack that of the foe.

Early on the following day he made his dispositions for battle, taking care at the same time to provide for the safety of the ladies‡ who accompanied the fleet. His largest vessels formed the van, and

* 1340. † Knighton, col. 2577.
‡ Froissart, chap. cxxi.

these were disposed alternately, one ship being manned with archers, and one with men at arms. A squadron also, containing archers alone, was held in reserve on the wing, for the purpose of counteracting any unexpected movement. In this order he beat up to windward a little, in order to place the sun, which at first shone directly in the eyes of his troops, in a different position, and then soon after mid-day bore down upon the enemy, who did not seem inclined to draw out from the haven.

On the part of the French, no such prudent arrangement seems to have been made; and more time was consumed in watching the manœuvres of the English, than in preparing their own fleet for the approaching engagement. At first, indeed, they appear to have made the extraordinary mistake of thinking Edward's movement to windward originated in a design to retreat; and the sight of the royal banner of England bearing down upon them, was the first thing that inspired them with any great activity. Their proceedings even then, however, showed no signs of union, or general design; and it would appear that dissension and misunderstanding reigned between the French and Genoese admirals.

Edward, however, sailed on into the mouth of the haven, and the whole forces on both sides were soon engaged.* A combat at sea was, of course, in those days, very different indeed from a naval engagement

* Knighton, col. 2578. Froissart, chap. cxxi.

at present; the only missiles used were arrows, quarrels, and masses of stone; and boarding was the principal manœuvre practised by either party. The English archers poured into the enemy's vessels, as they came up, that tremendous hail of arrows which the historian of every new battle, during the earlier ages of our history, records with expressions of wonder and dread. The crossbows of Genoa were silenced in a moment; and the Christopher, the great ship, as she was the first to advance, was the first to be captured from the enemy.* She was taken, we are told, solely by the bowmen of England; but by this time the two fleets were fully engaged. Running side by side, each ship grappled with its neighbour; and the two, united together by iron hooks and lashings, became a stage on which commenced a hand to hand fight, only different from a battle by land in the smallness of the space and the impossibility of escape. Each party fought with desperation; and for many hours—from mid-day far into the ensuing night—the combat was continued with lances, swords, battle-axes, and bows, till, notwithstanding their superior numbers, ship after ship was taken from the French; and Bocanegra, seeing the battle hopeless, and a prospect of escape open for himself, hoisted all sail, and with a small part of his division secured himself by flight.†

* Froissart, chaps. cxxi. cxxii.

† The account which I had originally given of this battle had been framed upon a comparison of the French historians on the one side,

No quarter seems to have been given on the occasion; and it is not impossible that the terrible

---

the English historians on the other, with Froissart, as the most impartial, between them. I had rejected, however, the greater part of the accounts given by the great Chronicles of France, and by the continuator of Nangis; not only because they are directly contradicted by Robert of Avesbury, Knighton, and Walsingham, but because they are both opposed to Froissart, and seemed to be utterly improbable. I have since been obliged to change my opinion on one of the most essential points, in consequence of the account given in a letter from the king himself, pointed out to me by Sir Harris Nicolas, to whom I am under great obligations for much valuable information.

The French historians assert, first, that Behuchet was incompetent to command; and that his total want of naval knowledge — he being treasurer of France, and not a naval man — caused the defeat of the French.

Secondly, they state that the French fleet, by his desire, remained in the haven; and that the battle was fought in the haven itself.

Thirdly, they declare that the engagement took place on the day after St. John's day; and, fourthly, descending to minor particulars, that Edward was wounded in the thigh, that Quieret was slain in cold blood after having yielded, and that Edward hanged Behuchet at the mast of his own vessel.

In reply to the first, it is to be observed, that though Behuchet certainly was treasurer, that circumstance, in those days, did not at all imply that he was not the most skilful officer in the realm. We have seen him also appointed two years before to the command of the French fleet, which could not have taken place without some presumption of skill; and — a much more important fact — we have seen him remarkably successful during those two years.

In regard to the second assertion, that the French fought in the haven, it seemed to me utterly improbable; for even if this statement had not been directly contradicted by Froissart, and by every English historian, would it be credible, I asked myself, that the French did keep the haven, when all was to be lost, and nothing gained, by doing so? The shore was guarded by the Flemings of Bruges, their most determined enemies; and the advantage of numbers must have been lost by such a confined position. At the same time, the very purpose of their enterprise was to fight the King of England, and either repel him

ravages which the French had committed on the English coast, rendered the one side implacable and the other desperate. At all events, it is known that an immense number of the French leaped into the sea and found a watery grave, either from the effects of terror or of hopelessness.* Of all the magnificent

---

from landing, or take him a prisoner to Paris; not to lie quietly in harbour, and let him sail whithersoever he pleased.

The letter of Edward, however, which will be found in the Appendix (No. II.), forces me to abandon this opinion, and to cancel the sheet in which it was promulgated. It has also produced several other important alterations, showing that the battle began after mid-day, instead of at day-break, and was continued during the ensuing night; that the number of large vessels in the French fleet were 190, and of armed men 35,000, and that 24 ships and 5000 men escaped, though some of these were afterwards taken.

We farther find that Edward positively fought on St. John's day; but in regard to the death of Behuchet and Quieret, it can only be said, that their being put to death after the battle depends solely upon the authority of the French historians; for there can be no doubt that Fabian copied his account, absurd as it is in several particulars, from the French; while Froissart, who was not likely to have passed over such an incident in silence, makes no mention of the fact. In regard to Edward's wound, also, the assertion would appear to be false; as, besides the certainty of his never having mentioned it in his own letter, we find that, with the interval of one day, he made a pilgrimage on foot to show thankfulness for his victory.

In concluding this note I cannot help expressing my sense of the courtesy and kindness with which the gentlemen intrusted with the archives of the city of London gave me access to those important repositories, and of the zeal and talent with which they aided me in my researches. Where I have found the sense of the letter of Edward not clear, I have, in the copy printed in the Appendix, inserted in italics the words which I think were really intended to be used by the writer; but it will be remembered that such words are not to be found in the MS. preserved in the city archives, whereof the letter as printed with the chronicle of London is a correct transcript.

* Walsingham, Hist.

fleet which had been collected to oppose the passage of the English monarch*, scarcely one eighth escaped; and about 30,000 French perished in the combat. The King of England himself led his navy against the enemy; and through the whole engagement he continued alternately to command as an admiral, and to fight as a knight, with a union of those splendid qualities of ardent courage and calm presence of mind which seldom fail from difficulties to win glory. The greater part of the enemy's ships were taken, and went to swell the English fleet. A few were sunk, perhaps by the engines for casting large masses of stone commonly used on such occasions. Those which escaped under the command of Bocanegra, were pursued by Sir John Crabbe, with thirty sail, but effected their flight in safety; and the James of Dieppe, which had captured an English vessel, and carried it off for some way, was afterwards retaken by her prisoners, and brought back on the following day.†

Edward after his victory passed some time on board the fleet, whence the sound of various musical bands, which we find on all occasions accompanied the English armies, wafted, during many hours, the rejoicings of the victors to the shore. The monarch, however, appears to have been far from arrogant in his success; and the letters by which he announced the battle and its event to his son and to the council of

* Knighton, col. 2577.

† Adam Muremouth. Fabian's account of this battle is not at all to be trusted.

England, breathe that excellent moderation in every line, which is at once the fruit, and the proof, of a firm and powerful mind.*

The tidings of this great battle, the most important which had ever been fought in those seas, and the only one in which an English king had commanded in person, spread, of course, like lightning through the whole of Flanders, and soon reached in a thousand forms the two camps before Thun l'Evêque.† To the French it came like an earthquake, overthrowing at once all the hopes of overrunning Hainault and destroying the Flemish league, which they had built up upon the great probability of Edward being defeated, and either captured or driven back by the immense armament with which the coast had been guarded. Philip, however, is said to have remained some time in ignorance of the events which had taken place — no one daring to tell that hasty and intemperate monarch the defeat which his fleet had sustained, till his jester one day ran into his presence exclaiming, "Oh, the English cowards! the dastards of England! the faint-hearted Englishmen!"

"Why call you them cowards, Sir Fool?" demanded the King.

"Because they dared not leap out of their ships into the sea so gallantly as our valiant men of France have done at Sluys," replied the jester.‡

Although it would have seemed the natural policy of the Count of Hainault and the confederates in-

* Rymer, tom. ii. part iv. † Froissart.
‡ Walsingham, p. 148.

stantly to attack the enemy, while the French were depressed by the news of recent defeat, and while their own troops were animated by new success, the very opposite course was pursued; and finding that the allied army could not be kept together, the Count returned to Valenciennes, accompanied by the Duke of Brabant, and many of the other barons of the empire. Jacob von Artevelde also followed the Lord of Hainault to his capital, and seems to have been treated in every respect on a par with the other great chiefs with whom circumstances had leagued him for the time.

In point of native talent, though not in point of military skill, the brewer of Ghent was superior to the greater part of his noble comrades. On the occasion of his visit to Valenciennes, he displayed, in a striking manner, those powers of popular oratory which he seems so greatly to have possessed; and in the public market-place harangued, for a length of time, the nobles who had accompanied him from Thun l'Evêque, as well as an immense concourse of people assembled to hear him. He chose for the subject of his discourse, the two themes which at that time agitated the whole country. First, with a plausible and engaging eloquence which won all his hearers, he advocated the claims of Edward Plantagenet to the throne of France; and then turning to a better subject and a juster cause, wherein sound policy and true wisdom gave the best basis for his oratory, he showed the immense advantages accruing to each and all by the intimate union of Flanders, Brabant, and Hainault. He pointed out the security it gave to either of those small states, while surrounded by larger and more powerful realms; he proved the consideration which they would all obtain in Europe by a league, which, leaving to each its individual form of government, afforded to all a strength which they did not individually possess. The advantages of mutual commerce, the increase of general prosperity, the vigour of united efforts, and the tranquillity insured by confederate power, were all displayed with perspicuity and force*; and on closing his oration, Artevelde left his hearers with the impression he desired,—a thorough conviction that his reasoning was just, and that he himself was worthy to exercise the power he had usurped.†

* Froissart, chap. cxxiii.

† Great difficulties exist in regard to the precise date of these events. Copies of a treaty, nearly to the same effect as that proposed by Artevelde, exist, bearing date 3d of December, 1339; and yet there are many reasons to believe that the definitive arrangements were not made till Edward's return from England, in 1340. However, whether the treaty was signed in the former or the latter year, the conception must be assigned to Artevelde, who, during both years, was almost absolute in Flanders, especially in Ghent, where the treaty received signature. I add the document of 1339 to the Appendix, where the reader will see that the great point of difference between its provisions and the proposals of Artevelde consists in the omission of Hainault, which country must have been included in an after treaty, as, in 1339, the Count of Hainault was at peace with France. This has probably caused the confusion of dates. The statement of Froissart is so completely borne out by ascertained facts that I do not doubt its substantial truth; nor that he has given (whether the date be 1339 or 40) a just summary of Artevelde's speech at Valenciennes, the capital of his own country.

This speech seems to have been the first sketch which Artevelde ventured to give of the grand and comprehensive plan afterwards proposed at the parliament of Villevorde, for the federal union of the Netherlands — a plan which, had it been duly carried into execution, would have raised up, in the north-west of Europe, a great commercial and manufacturing state, possessing advantages superior, in many respects, to any other

Such was exactly the preparation which the King of England could have desired; and no sooner had he arrived at Ghent, which was as shortly after his victory as possible, than all his confederates hastened to wait upon him, as a matter of ceremony; and at their meeting a general conference for the determination of their future proceedings was appointed to be held speedily at Villevorde.

The meeting, or, as it is called, the Parliament of Villevorde, however short was the duration of the compact there entered into, and however quickly the individual selfishness of one of the confederates rendered abortive the efforts there made, was one of the most singular and important steps in the progress of Europe towards the great changes which took place within two centuries afterwards. At that parliament was framed the model of the most extraordinary federal union on record, in which the principles of the feudal system were intimately blended with the rising power of the democratic body. The nobles of Hainault, Brabant, and Flanders, appeared there together, with the representatives of all the free communes in their dominions, not mutually to assert and resist real or imaginary rights on either part, as they had hitherto met; but, sacrificing prejudices and animosities for the general good, to bind themselves together in one great league—the people

---

country in Europe; which, by its striking contrast with many of the principal institutions of the day, would have tended greatly to change and improve the social system; and which, by drawing the preponderence of commerce and power in another direction, would have altered all the political relations of Europe throughout succeeding times.

supporting the nobles, and the nobles protecting the people.*

There was no discussion of rights, it is true, nor any parade on either side of making sacrifices. The policy which their situation required, as it had been explained by Artevelde at Valenciennes, seemed to have spread generally throughout the three countries as a matter of conviction; and the simple result was, that "all the good towns of Flanders, Brabant, and

* I am not aware that this view of the parliament of Villevorde (or of Villenorte, for it does not clearly appear which is the correct reading) has been taken by any one but myself. The more, however, I consider the particulars, the more extraordinary I am inclined to think the whole proceeding. We must remember that on the Continent the feudal system was established on quite a different basis from that which served it as a foundation in England. The Saxons, in the latter instance, formed the people; the Normans, the nobles; and the rights and laws of the Saxons, though trampled on in many instances, had not been swept away. But in Belgium the feudal system was the unmixed principle of society; and the communes which had arisen within the circle of feudal influence, had wrung their independence from their lords by long and bloody struggles, and maintained it by the same means alone. Time had in but a small degree wiped out the animosities and jealousies which these struggles had left behind; and the free towns, of that country especially, had hitherto looked upon the nobles as their natural enemies, while the barons regarded them but as insurgent subjects. The first efforts for the establishment of communes had been made subsequent to the year 1150, and had been, in almost all instances, crushed at first. Through the course of the following century, the communes had struggled on through fire and blood, till Philip Augustus, in the beginning of the thirteenth century, by making them the instrument of depressing the overgrown power of his vassals, gave them their first really great support, though they had been occasionally upheld by his two immediate predecessors. By so doing, however, he did not render them less hateful to the barons, whose power they served to counterbalance; and from the time of the first struggles of the communes of Laon and Vezelai in the middle of the twelfth century, to the accession of Philip of Valois, nothing but contention had reigned between the nobles and the free cities.

Hainault sent," to use the words of Froissart, "two or three worthy burghers of each, in the manner of council. These burghers debated and discussed the whole preliminaries, with the princes of the conference; and various acts and statutes were determined and drawn up by the consent of all. The conventions were then signed and sealed; and the King of England became the depository of the deed and the guarantee of its execution.

It is more than possible, that the general tenour of these statutes might be discovered correctly, though I have hitherto not been able to do so; nor, indeed, is it necessary in this place — Froissart supplying all that refers to the progress of the events immediately connected with England. According to his account, it was agreed by the three countries of Hainault, Brabant, and Flanders, that they should thenceforth aid and support each other at all times and in all affairs.* They farther bound themselves by agreement to defend each other in case of war, with whatsoever country it might arise; and if any difference should occur between any two of the states, the third was to act as arbitrator, while the voice of the King of England remained as the means of final decision. In confirmation of the friendship and union thus established, it was determined to coin peculiar pieces of money, to have currency generally through the three states, which pieces were called indifferently companions or allies.

* Froissart, chap. cxxv.

It is my firm belief, though unsupported by any stronger historical authority than general inference from the known facts, that the whole of the measures here pursued, — the union of the burghers and the nobles throughout the whole country, the compact between the states, and the first great fact of the meeting of the two distinct, and I might almost say hostile, classes in equal deliberation, — were devised by Artevelde beforehand, with those grand and general political views that dignify and ennoble his personal ambition, as much as his cruelty and avarice degrade his private character. Nor can I help pausing to call particular attention to the strange and important effect this Belgian confederacy might have had upon the affairs of Europe in general, and even upon the march of society itself, had some bond of union sufficiently strong to bind intimately the selfishness of each of its members to its preservation, been added to give it general consistence and durability.

In addition to this general league between the states of Belgium, the immediate prosecution of the war was determined upon; and Edward willingly agreed to lead his forces against Tournay, a town which the Flemings were most anxious to conquer. Great levies of men were accordingly prepared by all the princes, though by no one more zealously than by Artevelde; and towards the end of July, Edward marched upon Tournay, leaving his allies to follow as speedily as they could.*

* Froissart, chap. cxxvii.

In the meanwhile, though the greater part of Europe stood calm spectators of a contest which employed the energies, and gave food to the desires, of two ambitious monarchs, whose power and activity might have been dangerous to the rest of the world, had they not turned their arms against each other; one of the most polished if not the most humane of the sovereigns of that day was making exertions, which must not be passed over in silence, to stay the progress of the war and reconcile the rival princes. Robert the Good, King of Naples and Count of Provence, to whose predictions are attributed the resolution of Philip not to fight his antagonist at Buironfosse, now again hastened to interpose, and undertook a journey from Italy to Avignon, with a view of interesting the Pope in the same cause.* Robert himself was by no means without ambition: his title to the dominions he possessed is more than doubtful; and long the chief of the Guelfs of Italy, he had passed an anxious and disturbed life; embellished, however, by the culture of the arts and sciences — sweetened by the calm and happy pursuits of elegant literature, then almost extinct in Europe— and adorned by munificent protection of the poet, the historian, and the sage. In the present instance, he laboured indefatigably to bring about a peace between the monarchs of France and England. Whether the stars he judged by were a knowledge of human nature, and an insight into the characters of the

* Labbe, Chron. Tech. ad Ann. 1340. Froissart, chap. cxxiv.

two rivals; or whether he believed that the irritable and self-willed monarch of the French was more likely to be wrought upon by the wild visions of loss and disgrace, than by the calm reasonings of charity and friendship, does not appear: but it is certain, that he again warned Philip of Valois against warring with Edward in person, and predicted the continued ascendancy of the English king. The Pope, on his part, willingly entered into the views of the Neapolitan sovereign; and though Edward had lately added to the offence given to the Holy See by his league with the Emperor, the new affront of bringing over priests from England to celebrate the services of the church in the interdicted land of Flanders, Benedict consented once more to send two legates to negociate a peace, if possible, between France and England.

On the first news of the English King's arrival, Philiph of Valois, like the Count of Hainault, had retired from the neighbourhood of Thun l'Evêque; but it was with the purpose of strengthening by every means in his power the garrisons of his frontier towns, and collecting an army of reserve behind his frontier, to act in whatever direction circumstances might render necessary. Godemar du Fay, whom I have already mentioned, was now despatched to Tournay, which, since the Flemings had joined the English league, was likely to be one of the first objects of attack; and without loss of time he began to provide for a siege. Mortagne, Aire, St. Venant, and St. Omer, were strongly reinforced; and all the French cities on the Flemish frontier were garrisoned by the flower of the kingdom's chivalry.

The results of the parliament of Villevorde were soon known at the court which the French monarch held at Arras; and it then became certain that Tournay would be first attacked, rumour rendered it probable that a part of the large forces which the English king had now at command, would be despatched to besiege St. Omer. For the provision of those two fortresses, therefore, Philip strained every nerve; and fresh reinforcements were poured into Tournay, as well as immense supplies of food, ammunition, and artillery.

To St. Omer, the Duke of Burgundy and the Count of Armagnac were despatched, as well as the Dauphin * d'Auvergne. A force more than sufficient for the defence of the place was placed under their command †; and while the frontier towards Flanders was defended on every point, a large garrison was placed in Mortagne to keep in check Hainault. Nor did Philip's preparations confine themselves alone to the protection of his own country; considerable forces were sent to Scotland, in order to support the party of the exiled King, and call Edward's attention to the North; while an army under the Count de Lille, which had been lately assembled at Thoulouse, was ordered to effect a diversion in that quarter also.‡

* The title of Dauphin was at that time peculiar to the Princes of Auvergne and the Viennois, with the inheritance of which territories it became hereditary in the royal family of France.

† Chron. de France, chap. xx. Froissart, chap. cxli.

‡ Froissart, chap. cvi.

The monarch himself, having thus provided wisely for the safety of his dominions, and the punishment of their invader, remained at Arras to watch the movements of his enemies. Edward, in the mean time, set forth from Ghent, with 200 knights, 4000 men at arms, and 9000 archers, besides a body of irregular troops on foot. With this small army he marched direct for Tournay; and on the 23d of July sat down before that city, establishing his head quarters at the village of Chin lez Tournay.* Almost immediately, the English monarch was followed by the Duke of Brabant, with about 20,000 men at arms, besides the contingent of the communes armed on foot. This insidious prince, however, still kept himself apart; and encamped on the other side of the Scheldt, stretching his line from the Abbey of St. Nicholas to the Valenciennes gate of the city. The Count of Hainault followed next, with a great power; and then appeared Artevelde, with 60,000 men from the districts of Ghent and Bruges. Nor did this force alone, large as it was, form the whole of the levies which the zeal of the Flemings had induced them to make. Another numerous army had been raised by the territories of Cassel, Ypres, Berghe, and other places; and under the command of Robert of Artois and Henry of Flanders, it was directed to besiege St. Omer; so that two of the most important frontier fortresses of France were invested nearly at the same time.

* 1340. Hist de Tournay, p. 136.

The subsidised barons of the German empire did not fail to present themselves at the siege of Tournay: and the German eagles, still floating beside the English leopards in the camp of Edward as Vicar of the Empire, the Germans attached themselves more particularly to his host; and closing up between him and Hainault, rendered the blockade of Tournay complete.

Each member of the confederacy, except the Duke of Brabant, now strove to show his zeal in the cause which had here united them: the Flemings day after day harassed the city by assaults; the Count of Hainault swept the country and burned the small towns and villages round about by detachments from his army; the Germans pushed their incursions far into France; and Edward himself had recourse to a more chivalrous manner of displaying courage and enthusiasm.

On the third day of the siege, he despatched * a

* 26th July. — I subjoin a copy of the challenge and the reply, as two very curious historical documents; though the cramp Norman French in which Edward's epistle is written will render it, I am afraid, difficult of comprehension to the generality of readers: —

" Philip de Valeys, par lonc temps avoms pursui par devers vous, par messages, et toutes autres voyes, que nous savissioms resonables, au fyn que vous nous voulsissiez avoir rendu nostre droit heritage de Fraunce; lequel vous nous avez lonc témps détenu et à grand tort occupé. Et par ce que nous véoms bien que vous éstes en entent de persévérer en vostre injuriouse détenue, sans nous faire rayson de nostre demande, summs nous entrez en la terre de Flandres, come seigneur soverayn de ycele, et passé parmi le pays.

" Et vous signifions que, pris ovesque nous, le eyde de nostre Seigneur Jesu-Christ, et nostre droit, ovesque le poer du dit pays, et ovesque nos gentz et alliez, regardant le droit que nous avons à

herald to Arras, bearing his personal challenge to Philip of Valois, and calling him to decide their dif-

---

l'heritage, que nous détenez à vostre tort, nous nous treoms vers vous, por mettre droit fin sur nostre droitur chalaunge, si vous voillez approcher. Et pur ce que si grand poer de gentz assemblez, qui veignent de nostre part, et que bien quidoms que vous averriez de vostre part, ne se purront mie longement tenir ensemble, sans faire gref destruction au people et au pays, la quelle chose chascuns bons Christiens doit eschuer et especialement prince, et autres qui setignent gouverneurs des gentz; si desiroms mont, que brief point se prist pour eschuer mortalité des Christiens, ensi comme, la querelle est apparaunt à vous et à nous, que la discussion de nostre chalaunge se sist entre nos deux corps, à la quelle chose nous nous ofroms, par les causes dessus dites, coment que nous pensoms bien le graunt noblesse de vostre corps, de vostre sens, ausi et avisement.

"Et en cas que vous ne vourriez celle voye, que adonques fut mis nostre chalaunge, pour affiner ycele par bataille de corps de cent personnes des plus suffisaunts de vostre part, et nous autres taluns de nos gentz liges.

"Et si vous ne voillez l'une voye ne l'autre, que vous nous assignez certaine journé devant la cité de Tourney, pur combattre, poer contre poer, dedans ces dis jours proscheins après la date de ces lettres.

"Et nos offres dessus dites voloms par tout le mount est reconnues, ja que ce est nostre désyr, ne mye par orgul, ne sur quidance, mais par les causes dessus dites, au fyn que la volunté notre Seigneur Jesu-Christ montre entre nous, repos puisse estre de plus en plus entre Christiens, et que par ceo, les ennemis de Dieu fussent résistez, et Christienté en saufeté. Et la voye sur ce que eslire voilles des offres dessus dites, nous voillez signifier par le portour de ces dites lettres et par les vostres, en lui fesaunt hastive déliveraunce.

"Donée de souz nostre privée seal, à Chyn, sur les champs de leez Tourney, le 26de jour du mois de Juille, l'an de nostre règne de Fraunce primer, et d'Angleterre quatorze."

To this Philip replied almost immediately as follows: —

"Philip, par la grâce de Dieux, Roi de France, à Edouart Roi d'Angleterre.

"Nous avoms veu vos lettres apportées à nostre court de par vous à Phelip de Valeis, en quelles lettres estoient contenuts ascunes requestes, que vous feistes al dit Phelip de Valeis.

ferences by combat. In this curious epistle he set forth his claim to the kingdom of France; desired Philip to consider the great evils that must afflict his country in consequence of the continual presence and movement of large armies; represented that the quarrel was not between the nations, but between themselves personally; and, expressing a high opinion of his rival's courage and wisdom, demanded that the

---

"Et pur ceo que les ditez lettres ne venoient pas à nous, come et que les ditz requestes ne estoient pas faites à nous, apert cleirement par le tenor des lettres, nos ne vos feisons nul réponse, nient mye, pur ceo que nos avoms entenduz par les dits lettres, et autrement, que vos estes entrez en nostre roialme, et à nostre people, mes de volenté, sauntz nul rezon, et noun regardant ceo que homme lige doit garder à son seigneur, car vous estes entrez encontre vostre hommage lige, en nous reconnissant, si come rezon est, Roy de Fraunce, et promis obéissance fiel, come lon doit promettre à son seigneur lige, si com appert plus clerement par vos lettres patentz, seales de vostre graunt seale, lesqueles nos avoms de pardevers nos, et de queles vous devetz avoir à taunt devers vous. Nostre entent si est, quant bon nous sembler, de voz geter hors de nostre roialme, et en profit de nostre people, et à ceo faire avoms ferme esperaunce in Jhesu-Christ, dount tout puissance nous vient.

"Que par vostre entreprise, qu'este de volonté, et nom résonables, d'estre empeschez la saint voiage d'outre meer, et graunt quantité de gentz Christiens mis à mort, le service divine apetisez et sainte église en meindre reverence. Et du ceo qu'escript avoiez que vous entendez avoir l'ost des Flemings, nous quidoms estre certain que les boms gentz et les comunes du pays se porteront par tiel manere, par devers nostre cosin le Count de Flaundres lor seigneur sauntz meine, et nos, lor seigneur soveraign, qu'ils garderont lor honure et lor loialte.

"Et que ceo qu'ils ont mepris jusques à cy, ceo ad a est par malvais conseil des gents, que ne regardans par au profit commune, ne honure de pays, meas au profit de eaux taunt seulement.

"Donné sous les Campes, près de la priorie St. Andreu, soutz le seal de nostre secret en l'absence du Graunt, le 30 jour de Juyl, l'an de grace 1340."

arbitrement of their differences should rest between their own bodies, ventured in single combat.

In case of his declining this method of terminating the war, Edward proposed as alternatives, that the decision should take place by the combat of a hundred on each side, or that Philip should summon his army and risk all upon a general battle.

He ended by declaring that he made this appeal, not from pride or vanity, but solely that the will of God might be speedily fulfilled, Christendom restored to peace, and the enemies of the faith repressed without any farther delay.

There can be little doubt, from the character of Philip of Valois, that he would willingly, as far as he was personally concerned, have accepted the challenge of the English King; but either on his own judgment, or with the advice of wise counsellors, he rejected the proposal. He had to remember, that a king on the steps of his throne lays down for ever his individuality — that he becomes but a part of the state, and that his actions must always more or less affect the welfare of the whole. He had to consider also, that whichever monarch fell in such a combat as that proposed, or whichever party was unsuccessful in the contest of 200, neither nation was at all bound, nor, indeed, likely to abide by the decision; and that a more devastating war than ever would very probably ensue. As to a general battle between the two armies, the same motives were opposed to it, which had prevented its taking place at Buironfosse; and though, had all other means of saving his frontier towns failed, he would probably have been justified in risking an engagement for the purpose of preserving them, yet, as long as they held out firmly, no motive for incurring the hazard existed.

He replied to Edward's letter with more calm dignity than he usually displayed; and passing over the challenge as a thing which did not concern him — the letter of Edward merely being addressed to Philip of Valois, and not to the King of France — he proceeded to notice the entrance of the King of England into his territories. He animadverted strongly upon Edward's conduct in claiming the crown of France after having acknowledged his title by doing homage; and he assured him that, at the proper time, he would find means to cast him forth from the land he had invaded. In regard to the Flemings, Philip declared, that he doubted not they would in general yield obedience to their Count; and he expressed his conviction that those who had acted ill hitherto, had been misled by people who considered their own interests more than the public good.*

Thus ended the transactions upon Edward's challenge; but on the very day on which that challenge was written, an event occurred, which, though it had no effect upon the siege of Tournay, evinced strongly the wisdom of the course which Philip had pursued. The Flemish army, composed of the communes of Flanders, and commanded by

* Robert of Avesbury.

Robert of Artois, had already appeared before St. Omer, to the number of nearly 60,000 men. Badly disciplined, and but little used to the service of the field, the Flemings were ill calculated to produce any great effect against a well-fortified town and a large garrison. At that time, however, St. Omer was surrounded by large suburbs and villages attached to them, one of which was attacked on the first day of the siege by a considerable body of the besiegers, while Robert of Artois and his main army lay ready to yield support in case of need. After a slight struggle, the village was carried; and the Flemings, thinking their conquest secure, dispersed to plunder; when suddenly a large detachment from the garrison issued forth, under the command of the Duke of Burgundy in person, and with levelled lances charged the Flemings in the streets as they hastily attempted to reassemble. In confusion and disarray, the party which had been thrown forward against the village was driven back upon the main body, which was advancing to its succour; the disorder and the panic spread; the fugitives did more to defeat their friends, than the lances of the enemy; and, in a few minutes, the Flemish army was in full flight, leaving between 3000 and 4000 dead upon the field.

Whether any of the forces under the command of Robert of Artois escaped the general overthrow, and maintained their position till night, is very uncertain; but if they did, it is beyond doubt that a fresh panic fell upon them during the darkness, and that, before the morning of the 27th of July, not one of the besieging army was before the walls of St. Omer.*

Notwithstanding the bad tidings concerning his division of the army, which Robert of Artois brought

* In regard to this siege, Froissart and the other chroniclers give different accounts. In those particulars where his narrative was reconcileable with any of the others, I have combined the two; which forms the most probable account of the affair. In other respects, where he was directly contradicted by the other historians, I have in this instance adopted the version of those whom I generally look upon as less worthy of credit, and have done so for the following reasons: — In the first place, none of the Hainaulters, from whom Froissart derived his accounts of these wars, was present at the siege. In the next place, it was not likely that Robert of Artois, an experienced commander, would suffer a body of his troops, unsupported and uncommanded, as implied by Froissart, to assail one of the suburbs of a town he was besieging. In the next place, it is evident that the whole forces of Robert of Artois were struck with panic, and that the siege was raised by the events of this day; which requires something else to account for it than the mere defeat of a skirmishing party in the morning.

Nevertheless, I cannot believe, as the other Chronicles affirm, that the Duke of Burgundy, with merely the garrison of the town, intentionally gave battle to the whole force of the Flemings; and as, in general, truth lies between such conflicting accounts, I am inclined to suppose that the battle was brought on by the rout and pursuit of a body sent to attack one of the suburbs; and that their flight and terror, as often happens, carried confusion and panic into those ranks that were advancing to give them support. The account of Froissart, however, is in brief, that a party of 3000 light Flemings left their camp to skirmish with the garrison of St. Omer; entered the suburb which he calls Arques, and breaking open the houses, began to pillage. The noise they made alarmed the garrison, from which 800 men were sent forth, who attacked them, put them to flight, killed 1800, and carried 400 into St. Omer. In the following night, without any cause, a terrible panic seized the rest of the army, and packing up their baggage with all speed, they decamped, notwithstanding all that their leaders could do to stay them, and restore their courage. — *Froissart*, chaps. cxli. cxlii. D'Oudegherst speaks of these events as an ordinary battle between the French and the Flemings, in which the latter were totally defeated. — *Annales de Flandres*, chap. clix.

with the scattered remains of his forces to the camp before Tournay, the siege of that city was not for a moment relaxed. It was carried on, nevertheless, in a very different manner by the different nations of which Edward's host was composed. The Flemings, to whose territory the town was likely to be annexed if captured, exerted themselves with more energy and perseverance than any of the rest against the place itself; and the Count of Hainault, whose territories still reeked with the traces of the French invasion, directed almost all his efforts to carry back the bloody scourge with which France had afflicted his land, in baleful retribution, to her own bosom.

Artevelde, who well knew how much that frail thing, popularity, depends upon success, strained every nerve to distinguish himself at Tournay. As his forces stretched down to the Scheldt, he caused moveable towers called belfries to be erected on board some barks which he had collected in the river; and from these, as well as by land, he day after day urged the assault against those within the town, with the most unconquerable perseverance. Still, however, he was unsuccessful, and the courage and vigour of the garrison opposed invincible obstacles to all his endeavours. The most important assault made during the siege was one under his command, upon a postern of the town, which opened on the water and had been strongly fortified by barriers. Against these barriers, and the postern of the arch, as it is called, during one whole day, the Flemish efforts were directed. The vessels charged with the belfries ran close up to the town; and a number of other boats, which had been long in preparation for that express purpose, endeavoured to force the barriers; while the men-at-arms in the towers engaged the garrison. The defence, however, was conducted with the same determination; and after seeing one of the best vessels sunk before his eyes, and 120 persons drowned before they could be succoured, Artevelde drew off from the attempt and returned to his quarters.

In the mean time, though we do not find that the garrison attempted to disturb the besiegers by any sallies *, the French troops in the neighbouring towns took care to ravage the open country of Hainault and Flanders, which the draught of so many men as the siege of Tournay required, had left bare and undefended. Amongst others, the garrison of St. Amand made many a bold incursion into the lands of the Count of Hainault; and took by surprise the town and abbey of Hasnon, on the Scarpe, carried off all that it contained, and burned it to the ground. The abbey of Vicogne also was attacked, but was saved by the presence of mind of its abbot; who, fleeing at the first assault to Valenciennes, returned with powerful succour, as the French and Genoese were in the act of burning down the door. †

Nor was the garrison of Mortagne inactive; but swept the country of Hainault, and extended its excursions to the very gates of Bouchain. In some

* Monseur Lesbroussart says that the garrison did make sallies, but I find no confirmation of the assertion.

† Froissart.

instances, however, they had cause to repent their daring; and the war between the Hainaulters and the French continued to show alternate victory and defeat, advantage and injury on both sides.

One or two of those expeditions which the Count of Hainault himself made during the siege of Tournay, it may not be improper to mention here, as that siege itself was soon reduced to a mere blockade; and although it is not very certain at what precise period each of these events happened, it appears probable they occurred in the earlier part of the time which Edward spent before that fortress. The first attempt of any importance made by the Hainaulters, was the separate siege of Mortagne, at that time strongly fortified, and provided with every means of defence. As no hope existed of taking it by surprise, the Count made every preparation for assailing it with vigour; and commanded his capital, Valenciennes, to furnish him with the necessary machines for battering the walls, as well as a body of fresh troops to reinforce those which he could withdraw from before Tournay.*

The Count himself attacked the city on one side, the burghers of Valenciennes on two others; and from the moment of their first appearance before the walls, a continued shower of bolts from the crossbows, and immense stones from mangonels, continued to

* In regard to almost all the particulars of the siege of Tournay, I have followed the details given by Froissart; as I find that the earlier English historians, with the exception of Robert of Avesbury, borrowed their accounts from him, while the Flemish annalists confirm but abridge his narration.

pour upon the defenders. The Lord of Beaujeu, however, who commanded within the city, had provided every means of defence. The navigation of the Scheldt had been interrupted by immense piles driven into the bed of the river; and deep trenches, in attempting to pass which an enemy was necessarily exposed to the missiles of the garrison, guarded the town on the land side. Not contented with skilful preparations, when the assault had once commenced, the gallant commander acted the part of soldier as well as leader; and hastening to the gate of Mandé, where the fortifications were less strong, and the attack more violent, than on the other side, he passed the whole day in aiding to repel the continued efforts of the enemy. Armed with a lance, the back of which was furnished with a strong hook of steel, he caught such of the assailants as approached within his reach, by their brigantines or haubergeons, and, plunging them into the river, is said that day to have drowned twelve of the Hainaulters with his own hand. Foiled at this point, the next effort on the part of the besiegers was to draw the piles out of the river, and for that purpose they passed three days in constructing an engine fitted to accomplish such an undertaking. When it was complete, however, its effect was much less than had been anticipated, and the attempt was abandoned. Still one of the great machines of Valenciennes continued to annoy the garrison by the vast masses of stone which it cast into the town; but the chief engineer of the place undertook to destroy this source of danger, and speedily produced an engine of the same kind, which at the third discharge rendered the other useless. Its destruction seems to have decided the Count of Hainault to raise the siege of Mortagne; and at the end of the third day he returned to Tournay, not a little mortified with his repulse.

He had already, however, determined upon the siege of St. Amand; and ere leading his troops from Mortagne, he had appointed the burghers of Valenciennes to meet him on a certain day before the walls of the latter place, the garrison of which had already proved very destructive to Hainault. The seneschal of Carcassonne, who commanded in St. Amand, knowing the weakness of the place, as a fortress, had caused every thing valuable within it to be removed, and had sent away the monks from the abbey. He had also informed the people of the town and the garrison whom he had found there on his arrival, of the impossibility of maintaining the town against any considerable army. "Not," he said, "that he sought to quit it himself; but he warned them of the event, if they called an attack upon themselves by their excursions."

The garrison contemned his apprehensions; and when the burghers of Valenciennes appeared before the walls, to the number of 12,000 combatants, received them with the usual gallantry of French soldiers, and repelled them with great loss. This body of the communes had arrived on the day appointed by their lord; but some circumstances of which we are not aware, having detained the Count at the camp before Tournay, they began the assault without his presence, were repelled, and wondering at his delay, retreated to Valenciennes.* The next morning, the Count himself appeared; and finding his citizens gone, attacked the town with about 3000 men, which had accompanied him thither. The assault, however, of the men at arms was more effective than that of the communes, and the barriers of the gate towards Mortagne, were conquered after a severe struggle, in which both the Count and his uncle, John of Hainault, had nearly been killed by a mass of stone thrown from the walls. The gate itself was now found so strong, and the way so narrow, that the forcing it promised to be a work of danger and great loss; and it was determined that the attack should be turned against the abbey, which formed part of the wall of the town. Large piles were immediately procured; and being driven against the old masonry of the monastery, a sufficient breach was speedily effected to admit the whole of the Count's forces. The way was now open into the town; and the seneschal of Carcassonne, finding that the place could no longer be defended, displayed his banner in the market-place, and made his last stand for honour in his death. Two hundred men at arms supported him, and a number of Genoese crossbow-men; but over-

* Both the mercenary troops and the feudal military looked upon the burgher communes with great contempt; and on the present occasion, while the Valenciennois were retreating from the walls of St. Amand, the garrison saluted them with shouts of derision, exclaiming, "Allez boire votre *gout ale*,"—the Hainaulters being at that time celebrated for brewing a liquor called by them very nearly by the same name, which it has retained in England to the present day, *i. e.* good ale.

powered by the number of Hainaulters, who, in revenge for the injury the garrison had inflicted on their country, gave no quarter, they were driven from street to street, and house to house, and slain without mercy.

The seneschal himself fell beneath his banner in the market-place, with almost all the men at arms, and the rest were massacred in detail, fighting to the last. The Count of Hainault returned the same night to Tournay, and thus ended the bloody day of St. Amand. On the following morning, however, the people of Valenciennes returned, and setting fire to all the buildings, covered the traces of the massacre with the ashes of the city.

In the mean while, the siege, or rather the blockade, of Tournay continued; and, notwithstanding the efforts which had been made by the French to supply it plentifully with food, signs of scarcity soon began to manifest themselves in the town. The first circumstance which gave notice to the besiegers that their close investment had in some degree produced the effect they intended, was the fact of all the poor and needy classes being expelled from the town by the garrison. The cruel principles of warfare, as then practised, required that they should be driven back by the assailants; but the Duke of Brabant, to whom they immediately addressed themselves, gave them free passage through his part of the camp; an action which would have been noble, if it had originated in charity.

These signs of famine within Tournay, of course, gave as much pain and apprehension to Philip of Valois, who received the news at Arras, as they afforded pleasure and hope to Edward. The French monarch now found, that in order to save the city, he must resort to some more active means than he had hitherto employed for that purpose; and accordingly he used every exertion to collect a sufficient force, either to fight the English monarch under the walls of the city, or to allure him from the siege by the prospect of a battle, as he had done in the case of Cambray. The sound of war was never unwelcome to a Frenchman's ears, and the King had soon at his command one of the largest armies * that had been brought into the field for many years, with which he immediately marched forward to the banks of the small but deep river Marque, at a spot where marshes and difficult passes rendered an impregnable position very easy to be found. The bridge which existed at that time was, it appears, so narrow that only one person could pass at once; but of course another could have been constructed without difficulty where no opposing force was prepared to harass the workmen. Philip, however, was now within three leagues of Tournay: other means less hazardous than a battle were operating secretly to defeat the purpose, if not the army, of the King of England; and the French monarch resolved to wait encamped, and watch the event of many circumstances which were combining in his favour.

Though the French camp was now within so short

* Walsingham, Hist. page 135. Froissart, chap. cxxxiii. D'Oudegherst, chap. clix.

a distance, Edward was not to be led from the object he had in view; and he remained fixed before Tournay. A variety of skirmishes took place between parties detached from the two hosts; and, on the one side, the Lord of Montmorency was captured by the Germans; while a leader, called Waflart de la Croix, was taken by the French, and being shamefully given up by Philip to the citizens of Lille, with whom that unhappy gentleman had long been at enmity, was by them put to an ignominious death, after some months of imprisonment.* Eleven weeks had now passed since the commencement of the siege, and a considerable period had also elapsed since the assailants had learned, by the exclusion of the poor, that famine had decidedly begun to show itself within the walls, and yet no greater signs of scarcity manifested themselves; a fact scarcely to be reconciled with the close blockade in which the place was apparently held. Suspicion at the time turned upon the Duke of Brabant, whose tergiversation had so long delayed the commencement of the war; and it can hardly be doubted now, that Philip had found means to engage that prince in his cause, while Edward had weakened still farther the weak bonds between him and England, by delaying the final arrangement of the alliance which had been proposed between a daughter of the Duke and the heir of the English crown.† It has been boldly asserted by Villani, that the sovereign of Brabant had

* Froissart, chap. cxxxiv.

† See the state papers thereunto relating, Rymer, tom. ii. parts iii. iv.

received bribes from the King of France *, and that provisions were introduced into Tournay through the part of the allied camp held by that prince.† No absolute proof, indeed, has been offered; but the fact remains clear, that the besieged city held out much longer than its circumstances at a very early period of the siege had led Edward to expect.

At the same time, the persons who had undertaken the charitable office of restoring peace to Christendom, were indefatigable in their exertions; and a new and more powerful voice had been added to those which already advocated the cause of humanity. The Pope and the King of Sicily still used every effort to bring about a peace between the rival monarchs; and Joan of Valois, the Dowager Countess of Hainault, took upon herself the task of mediatrix.‡ Equally bound to both parties by the ties of kindred and affection, that amiable princess, although upon the death of her husband she had devoted herself to the cloister, could not be supposed to see, without pain, the armies of her son-in-law the King of England, joined with those of her son the Count of Hainault, ravage the territories and besiege the towns of her brother, the King of France. Nor, of course, could she anticipate, undismayed, the very probable result of a general battle, in which her brethren and her children would meet as enemies in deadly strife. Coming forth, then, from the seclusion of Fontenelle, and

* Villani, lib. ii. cap. iii.

† Mezeray has adopted the same opinion.

‡ Froissart, chap. cxliii.

passing continually from one army to the other, she strove by every means of persuasion and entreaty to move the two monarchs to peace. Although the great loss his forces daily sustained by the insalubrity of the situation he had chosen, must soon have compelled Philip either to risk an engagement or conclude a truce, it is more than probable that Edward, on the contrary, after his vast preparations, and with his large and vigorous army, would have listened to no reasonable terms, had not various other motives imperiously commanded him to accede to whatever proposals would give him a fair excuse for terminating the war.

These motives might be classed under three heads. First were the events which had taken place in Aquitaine, where the Count de Lille *, marching with an overwhelming force from Toulouse, had driven all Edward's partisans from the field, and had laid siege to Bordeaux.† The fortresses of Guyenne, indeed, still held out; but their fate was sealed if the capital were taken. Next were the circumstances of Scotland, where the reinforcements sent from France had raised up again the party of David Bruce. The Scottish nobles, defeated but not conquered, had come

* Bertrand Count of Lille Jourdain. The end of the 129th chapter of Froissart, which gives an account of this leader's expedition into Gascony, is omitted in almost all the printed copies of Froissart, though found in all the best manuscripts. Although I have compared various copies of Froissart, the one which I have cited in the margin is the edition of M. Buchon, throughout, except in one instance, relating to the march of Edward in his first expedition, where I consulted the copy in the well-known Marchmont library belonging to Hugh Scott, Esq., of Harden.

† Froissart, chaps. cvi. cxxix.

forth from the fastnesses of their country on the first prospect of success, had taken castle after castle, and city after city *; and, not confining their efforts to the recapture of towns in their own land, had pushed their excursions into England, and ravaged the counties of Northumberland and Durham. The last and greatest cause, however, of Edward's embarrassment, and that which shackled his personal exertions, while his distant territories and frontiers on both sides were suffering from an enemy, was the mingled perfidy and neglect of those whom he had left in England to supply him with the means of indemnifying distant losses by individual victory and conquest. The parliament † voted him immense subsidies ‡; the people, elated with his

* Froissart, chaps. cxxx. cxxxi.

† The parliament met at Westminster shortly after the King's return to the Continent, 7th of July, 1340, and again voted him the ninth of the corn, wool, and lambs of the Lords and Commons. The clergy at the same time undertook to raise 20,000 sacks of wool of different qualities; the best to answer the King 6*l.* per sack, the second 5*l.*, and the worst 4 marks; neither did this grant affect his custom of 40*s.* for every sack, which had been conceded long before. All these grants were to be raised immediately, and various individuals undertook to supply in a desultory and separate manner the money required on the security of the parliamentary votes. It would be difficult, and perhaps frivolous, to inquire here how these grants were rendered almost void by the avidity of those employed in the collection, and who were the real culprits. Certain it is, however, that but a very small part of the liberal grants of parliament ever reached the coffers of the monarch, and equally certain that the Archbishop of Canterbury, to whom the government of the kingdom, under the name of Prince Edward, was in reality confided, by no means exerted himself as he ought to have done in behalf of the absent monarch. Edward himself attributed the deficiences entirely to the wilful inactivity of that prelate, and bestowed upon him openly the name of traitor, which is explained by the suspicion of historians that he was corrupted either by bribes from France, or by honours and promises from the Holy See.

‡ Rymer, Fœdera, date 7th of July, 1340.

naval victory, were willing to yield him every aid to win more, but, by the peculation and delays of his officers the money never reached the King; and after being obliged to incur debt after debt, at usurious interest, Edward found his finances exhausted, and no prospect of obtaining fresh supplies, even by the discreditable means to which he had been compelled to apply.

Had even his hopes of finally reducing Tournay been strengthened as the siege advanced, it is probable that he would have struggled still to maintain his power, till the capture of that city should afford some compensation for all the wealth, and labour, and time, and blood, that he had already expended. But Tournay still held out, and seemed as far from its fall as ever. That it possessed some secret means of obtaining supplies was evident; and it was also clear that, exactly in the proportion wherein Edward's wealth decreased, the zeal of his allies decreased also. He now learned the hard lesson, which the interested selfishness of the great mass of mankind sooner or later teaches to all who attempt great things, that gold is the fire by which the enthusiasm of friendship may be made red-hot; but that it requires a continual renewal of the fuel to keep the same affection from cooling.

Every thing, therefore, — the danger of his territories on the Continent, the peril of his Scottish frontier, the perfidy of his agents at home, the growing indifference of his allies abroad, and the hopelessness of the undertaking in which he was engaged, — all disposed him to peace; and after many a vain effort and reluctant delay, he consented that plenipotentiaries on his part should meet those of the French king, in the chapel of Esplechin, in the fields between the two camps, for which purpose a cessation of hostilities was agreed upon for three days.*

The personages deputed to conduct the negotiation for the King of France were, John, the noble, wise, and chivalrous King of Bohemia, to whose councils many, if not the whole of the nobler, acts of Philip's government are attributed, Charles, Count of Alençon, the brother of the King, the Bishop of Liege, the Count of Armagnac, the Duke of Lorraine, and the Count of Savoy. For the King of England appeared the Duke of Gueldres, the Marquis of Juliers, John of Hainault, and the Duke of Brabant; while the presence of Joan of Valois was added, as the undoubted friend of all, to soothe irritations and promote concession. The three days first granted sufficed for the negotiation; and a truce of nine months † was concluded, comprehending all the vassals and allies of the two kings. Each party was to hold what he possessed, and the treaty was to be made known in Aquitaine within twenty, and in Scotland within twenty-five, days from that date, the 25th of September. ‡

It would farther appear, that some other con-

* Froissart, chap. cxliii.

† The first truce was signed on the 25th of September, 1340, and was to be in force till the 25th of June, 1341. The Flemish annalists insinuate that the interests of Flanders would have been neglected but for a spirited remonstrance made by Artevelde.

‡ Rymer, tom. ii. part iv. p. 83.

vention, not now extant, was entered into for providing more fully for the pacification of Flanders *, restoring the Count to his territories, holding the Flemings free of the penalty they had incurred by taking arms in favour of England, and raising the interdict which the Pope had cast upon their country. It was also agreed, that a conference, between plenipotentiaries from Edward and Philip, should be held at Arras, to treat, under the mediation of two papal legates, concerning a more stable and decided peace. Various other acts took place afterwards, in consequence of this truce, which, though generally supposed by the contemporary writers to have been determined upon, like those mentioned above, at the conference held between Tournay and Pont à Bovines, are not to be found stipulated in any public document, and were, very probably, the result of after negotiations.†

No sooner was the treaty signed than the allied army began to decamp from before Tournay, the forces of the Duke of Brabant being those which first hastened from the field.‡ The English, the Flemings, and the Hainaulters, quitted the siege with more regret; and Edward, seeing his plans overthrown and his hopes destroyed, retired to Ghent

* D'Oudegherst, chap. clix.

† Barnes declares that the Earl of Salisbury was liberated at this time, and not, as Froissart says, afterwards in exchange for the Earl of Murray. See Barnes, p. 209. It is not, indeed, impossible that he might visit England on parole to obtain a ransom; but we find by Rymer (tom. ii. part iv. p. 124.), that he was not absolutely freed from prison until the middle of the year 1342.

‡ Froissart, chap. cxliv.

to wait the arrival of those sums which would have enabled him to prosecute the war had they arrived earlier, but were now destined to pay the fruitless expenses already incurred.

Philip of Valois with joy dismissed his troops, and removed from the unhealthy situation in which he had remained so long, having once more seen an immense and well-provided army forced to retreat from his dominions without success. The allies endeavoured to console themselves by boasting, that they had lain two months within the pale of France, without the French king having offered them battle; but the more substantial glory rested with Philip, of having defeated their purposes, and thwarted all their endeavours, protected his subjects, saved his dominions, and driven forth his enemies without concession.

The disgrace which had attended his efforts upon Tournay irritated the mind of the English king to an extreme degree; and the continued neglect of the officers of his exchequer in England, the indecent forgetfulness of his necessities, and contempt for his anger, which they displayed, together with the daily importunities of his creditors on the Continent, must have rendered the two months which he spent at Ghent more painful than any previous part of his existence.* No sums of any consequence arrived even now; and at length Edward, wearied out, departed privately from Ghent, with his queen and a small retinue, and arrived suddenly at London, on the night of the 30th

* Barnes, p. 212.

of November. He landed, a little before daylight, at the Tower, where his son, the Duke of Cornwall, was supposed to hold the court which his rank, both as heir-apparent and custos of the realm, rendered necessary, notwithstanding the tenderness of his age. But the monarch found, with indignation and surprise, that his return having appeared remote and uncertain, relaxation and neglect had taken place, both in his household and in the state. No guards, no signs of reverence and respect, waited his son and the representative of his own person; and on the King's unexpected arrival at the Tower he found only three ordinary servants as the attendants upon his children. His first act was to order the instant arrest and committal of the Lord Nicolas de la Beche, Constable of the Tower, for his shameful negligence; and he then proceeded, with all speed, to enquire into and punish the authors of those defalcations which had embarrassed all his movements, and dashed the cup of victory from his hand when his lip was at the brim.

Thus ended Edward's first great attempt to enforce by arms his claims to the French throne; an attempt in which he had shown both courage and skill, and in which his troops had uniformly distinguished themselves, wherever they found an opportunity. He had been repelled and disappointed, it is true, but the causes of his failure had been more the treacherous instability of one of his chief allies, and the grasping peculation of his servants, than any weakness on his own part, or any great vigour in the efforts of his enemy. This was so evident throughout Europe that, although the French king had met with complete success, and had repulsed the efforts of his competitor, Edward obtained more renown by his endeavour than Philip by his resistance. The King of England also acquired experience; and found that, however small in comparison might be the armies which he could raise in his own country, on them he must in future depend; that to engage mercenary allies was but to hire treachery and buy defeat; and that by relying on his native forces, while he could better calculate his means, he had a greater certainty of accomplishing his object: his expenses would be lessened, at the same time that their result would be rendered more sure; and a temporary delay of pecuniary supplies could never defeat great schemes, or overthrow a nearly accomplished purpose.

CHAP. IX.

PROCEEDINGS OF EDWARD III. AGAINST DEFAULTERS, ETC. — INSOLENT RESISTANCE AND HUMILIATION OF THE ARCHBISHOP OF CANTERBURY. — EXACTIONS OF THE PARLIAMENT. — EDWARD GRANTS THE STATUTE REQUIRED. — ANNULS IT AFTER THE SESSION. — ADVANTAGES GAINED BY PHILIP DURING THE TRUCE. — THE DEATH OF JOHN DUKE OF BRITANNY, AND ITS CONSEQUENCES. — THE TRUCE RENEWED. — RETURN OF DAVID BRUCE TO SCOTLAND. — WAR RENEWED IN THE NORTH OF BRITAIN. — EDWARD INVADES SCOTLAND. — STORY REGARDING THE COUNTESS OF SALISBURY EXAMINED.

The irritation under which the King of England laboured before his return to London, and the additional causes of offence which he met with on his very first arrival, hurried him away into the commission of some acts of violence, which gave the defaulters he intended to punish an opportunity of meeting his accusation with complaint. Edward's indignation fell principally upon the great officers of the crown; and though he arrested and imprisoned a number of inferior persons, the chief of those whom he proceeded against were, the Bishop of Chichester, Lord Chancellor; the Bishop of Coventry, Lord Treasurer; and the Archbishop of Canterbury, amongst the clergy: together with many laymen, of whom were Aubry, Lord Mayor of London; Sir John St. Paul, Keeper of the Great Seal; Sir John Stonore, Lord Chief Justice; the Lords Molins and

Wake *, and a number of the clerks of the Chancery and Exchequer, amongst the laity. All the sheriffs of counties also, and other public officers concerned in levying the late subsidies, were dismissed and disgraced; and the lay functionaries, who are named above, were cast into prison, as well as several of the inferior clergy. The Bishops of Chichester and Coventry only escaped the same fate, by representing to the King that the canons of the church prohibited the imprisonment of bishops; and the Archbishop of Canterbury, it is supposed, would hardly have found even that plea available, had he not contrived to escape from his palace at Lambeth, and take refuge in the midst of his province of Canterbury.

Against that prelate the mind of the King was peculiarly exasperated, inasmuch as, after having been one of the principal movers of the war with France, and one of the most active agents in all the first steps of the English invasion, he had suddenly cooled in his zeal, relaxed his efforts, and permitted, under his administration, the most fatal remissness, and the most culpable peculation.

Foiled in the expectation of arresting him at Lambeth, the King sent messengers down to Canterbury, to summon him either to pay the sums for which, in his former enthusiasm for the French war, he had become bound to the Duke of Brabant and other persons on the Continent, or immediately to pass over into France, and deliver himself up as a surety,

* Walsingham, pp. 147. 150.

which he had also formerly undertaken in case of default.

The Archbishop, now finding that the whole weight of the royal indignation was about to descend upon his head, and perceiving that he might have some difficulty in exculpating himself if he submitted to trial, resolved to meet the storm boldly, and oppose to the power of the sovereign the authority of the church. It would be tedious to follow the monarch and the prelate through all the warfare of words and threatenings which ensued. Edward, however, soon recovered from the irritation which had urged him into some imprudent measures; and, combining calmness with vigour, he firmly pursued his design of humbling the Archbishop. That prelate, on his part, would have willingly been a Thomas à Becket, without the honours of martyrdom; but he found that the days of Becket were past, that the people were very indifferent to his fate, and the parliament resolved to give him no support.

The contest lasted from the time of the king's return till the end of April; at which period, the prelate, after various ineffectual efforts to stir up the populace, and overawe his sovereign, was obliged to humble himself before Edward, in presence of the parliament, and to cast himself upon the mercy of the monarch whom he had insulted and betrayed. Edward, however, was now very willing, on every account, to receive the Archbishop once more into favour. His personal talents, and his influence with the great body of the clergy from whom Edward had derived and still expected very liberal supplies, rendered him an able and useful minister; and the monarch justly hoped that he would become a more obedient servant, after having learned by his unsuccessful attempt that he was not likely to obtain either the honours of a saint or the authority of a demagogue. The prosecution already begun against the Archbishop now dropped; and the parliament granted to the King a new subsidy to defray the expenses which the embezzlement of the money formerly voted had left undischarged. Both lords and commons, however, took advantage of the King's necessity, to wring from him several concessions, which were embodied as a statute, and acted upon for the time. These exactions gave rise, subsequently, to a very dangerous abuse of the royal prerogative. Towards the beginning of October, in the same year, Edward, without any other form than the simple expression of his will, revoked and annulled the statute; honestly but daringly acknowledging that, in giving his consent, he had dissembled, for the purpose of inducing the parliament to proceed quietly in the affairs which then occupied them. This abrogation of a part of the statute law, by the mere proclamation of the monarch, remained in active force for two years, without any confirmation, till at length the statute was formally repealed by the parliament itself, in the year 1343.*

* Joshua Barnes gives a copy of this famous abrogation, as he says, "for the rarity of the case;" and as it afforded, I am afraid, a precedent to many a weak and imprudent attempt at an after period, when the

Although it may not be uncommon for kings to dissemble, it is not very usual for them to ac-

---

country and the world were in a different state, it may not, perhaps, be unnecessary here to transcribe it also. I therefore copy it from Barnes, whose translation is sufficiently correct. It may be premised, however, that the common method of making statutes, at that time, was as follows:—At any period after the opening of Parliament, either one or all of the bodies of which it was composed presented a petition to the King, praying the redress of certain grievances and their prevention for the future, sometimes touching upon general principles, and sometimes confining themselves to individual cases. The King gave his answer, negative or affirmative, to the several items, in general, while the parliament was yet sitting, and those which were granted were subsequently put into the form of statutes by the law officers of the crown, and transmitted for publication and execution to the sheriffs of the counties. The following is the act of revocation:—

"Edward, by the grace of God, King of England and France, and Lord of Ireland, to W. W. Sheriff of Lincoln, greeting: Whereas, at our Parliament summoned at Westminster, in the XV. of Easter last past, certain articles expressly contrary to the laws and customs of our realm of England, and to our prerogatives and rights royal, were pretended to be granted by Us by the manner of a statute, We, considering how that by the bond of our oath We be bound to the observance and defence of such laws, customs, rights, and prerogatives, and providently willing to revoke those things which be so improvidently done to a due state, Counsel, and a treatise thereupon had with the earls, barons, and other wise men of our said realm, and for and because We never consented to the making of the said statute, but as then it behoved Us, We dissembled in the premises, by protestations of revocation of the said statute, if indeed it should proceed, to eschew the dangers which, by denying of the same, We feared to come; forasmuch as the said parliament otherwise had been, without any expedition, in discord dissolved, and so our earnest business had likely been, which God prohibit, in ruine, and the said pretended statute We promised then to be sealed.

"It seemeth to the said earls, barons, and other wise men, that sithence the said statute did not of our free will proceed, the same should be void, and ought not to have the name or strength of a statute.

"And, therefore, by their counsel and assent, We have decreed the

knowledge it in their public acts; nevertheless, if ever the necessities of policy can afford a fair excuse for deceit — which indeed can never be — Edward might palliate the commission of such a fault by the urgency of the circumstances under which he acted. The truce with France was now not far from its termination; a variety of circumstances had tended to strengthen the power of his enemy and decrease his own means of warfare; the eye of a vigilant foe was upon him; and the only chance that existed of concluding an honourable peace, or even prolonging the cessation of arms upon reasonable terms, was by the appearance of union between the monarch and his subjects, and of that capability of speedy and vigorous action which internal peace and harmony can alone display. Such, probably, were among the causes which induced Edward to treat leniently the number of defaulters whose peculations had produced so evil an effect on his late expedition; and such, we may conclude, was one of his strongest motives in yielding so readily to the exactions of the parliament.

---

said statute to be void, and the same, inasmuch as it proceeded of deed, We have brought to be annulled: willing, nevertheless, that the articles contained in the said pretended statute, which by others of our statutes, or of our progenitors, kings of England, have been approved, shall, according to the form of the said statute, in every point, as convenient is, be observed. And the same We do only to the conservation and redintegration of the rights of Our crown, as We be bound; and not that We should in any wise oppress our subjects whom We desire to rule by lenity and gentleness. And, therefore, We do command you, that all these things you do to be openly proclaimed in such places within your bayliwick, where you shall see expedient. Witness myself at Westminster, the first day of October, the XV. year of Our reign." — See Barnes, p. 235.

Still, though England soon re-assumed an aspect of general tranquillity, Philip had already gained many advantages which placed him in a much more commanding position than that which he had occupied at the commencement of the truce; and thus, before that truce expired, he would have been enabled to exact more and concede less, had not internal difficulties sprung up unexpectedly in France, to moderate the demands of the French monarch, and to render him as desirous of repose as his adversary.*

* Although the priority of one event to another does not of course establish the first to the cause, and the second the effect, yet many historians, and those especially it would seem who have written upon the life of Edward III., appear to have forgotten that the cause must precede the effect, and therefore that an exact attention to chronology is absolutely necessary to correct conclusions. As I have taken a different view of the motives which immediately affected both Philip of Valois and the King of England about this time from that given by the generality of other writers, I subjoin a chronological detail of the events to which I refer, wishing to show that their dependence upon one another, as stated in the text, is probable from their dates as well as from their nature.

Nov. 30th, A. D. 1340.	Edward returned to England.
Dec. 1st.	Measures were taken against the Archbishop and others.
April 9th, A. D. 1341.	The parliament met at Westminster.
April 10th.	Edward gave powers to commissioners to treat for a peace or a renewal of the truce, which was to expire on the 24th of June.
April 19th.	The King was reconciled to the Archbishop.
April 21st.	The parliament presented their petition of grievances.
April 30th.	Died John the Good, Duke of Britany, whose death was speedily followed by a contest which involved most of the great barons of France.
May 20th.	A safe-conduct granted by Edward to Charles de Montmorency and Matthew his brother, to come to his court on business.

The first advantage which Philip had gained appeared to be, the separation of the Emperor from the interests of the King of England, by inducements which are not to be traced exactly; but which were, in all probability, the hope of recovering his place in the bosom of the church through the influence of the King of France, and of removing every plea for rebellion from the refractory electors. Whatever were the means, the success of Philip with the Emperor was very great, and the letters of Louis of Bavaria are extant, in which he informs Edward of his alliance with the French monarch, and cloaks his desertion of the English cause under the desire of negotiating a peace between the two crowns of France and England.

Edward perceived his motives through the thin *

June 18th.	Edward announces to the Flemings that the truce is prolonged to the first of August.
June 25th. A.D. 1341.	The Emperor revoked the powers granted to Edward as vicar of the empire.
July 14th.	New powers given to treat with France.
Sept. 27th.	The prolongation of the truce till the 24th of June, 1342, proclaimed in England.

The proofs of these dates are to be found in Rymer's Fœdera, and in the Benedictins' History of Britany. In regard to the meeting of the parliament there was some doubt; but it would appear certain, from the best authority that I can find, that it first met on Easter Monday, which fell that year on the 9th of April. However, even supposing that the date be really the 23d of that month, as there is some reason to believe, it will not at all affect the inferences I have drawn.

* That the negotiations between Philip and the Emperor began almost immediately after the conclusion of the siege of Tournay is proved by a treaty preserved by Leibnitz, dated Jan. 1341, by which Louis of Bavaria binds himself to the French king in the most solemn manner; and it is clear that Edward was aware of the defection of his

disguise with which he attempted to cover them, and rejected his mediation with calm moderation. The benefits, indeed, which he had received from his alliance with the Emperor, when rightly estimated, were too small to cause him any great regret on seeing that alliance terminate; and, although the union of his former ally with his adversary, especially if the vigour of internal tranquillity were by that means restored to Germany, might give a terrible preponderance to the power of Philip, new views were springing up to the eyes of the English king, which, by giving him greater confidence in his native strength, made him less fearful of the leagues against him. A short space of repose was all that he desired, to improve the trade and renew the energies of his own dominions; and for this purpose, though he would by no means make those concessions which might have led to a final peace, he showed every disposition to prolong the truce from time to time, upon the basis on which it was already founded.

The second advantage which Philip gained, and which was much more likely to prove beneficial than the heartless and lukewarm alliance which he had formed with Louis of Bavaria, proceeded from a new

---

imperial ally before any public announcement thereof took place, from a letter which he addressed to the Duke of Austria, dated the 12th of June. Muratori shows in his Annals (Ad. Ann. 1335, 1337,) that long before this Louis had attempted to effect a reconciliation with the Holy See, but had been prevented by the entire domination which Philip held over the popes during their sojourn at Avignon, and the ungenerous use he made of that power.

impulse given to the spirit of independence which he had kept alive in Scotland. Divided amongst themselves, abandoned by their king, and supported by very scanty reinforcements from France, the Scottish nobles had continued to maintain the war of resistance with perseverance and success. They had, indeed, gladly taken part in the truce lately negotiated, and thus given themselves time to prepare against the return of a potent adversary now free to use his whole strength against them; but the promises of support and countenance which they received from Philip determined them, as soon as possible, to recommence the struggle, and it is evident that they did not become parties to the renewal of the truce.

Philip of Valois had, beyond doubt, assured himself of their resolution in this respect beforehand; and, allied with the Duke of Brabant and the Emperor, employing every means to detach John of Hainault from the English cause, and supported by every continental power but the small states of Flanders and Hainault, he saw the certainty of Edward's being soon entangled in the toils of a Scottish war, which he determined to prolong to the utmost by supplies and reinforcements.

Such a position, had it not been accompanied by a weighty evil to counterbalance its many advantages, might have enabled the French monarch to dictate, at no very distant period after the arrangement of the truce, the terms of a peace much more advantageous to himself. But the death of John the Good, Duke of Britany, which followed almost immediately after the separation of the armies before Tournay, and the contest for that prince's succession, which immediately ensued, soon engaged Philip in an internal strife, far more bloody and destructive than that which he had so eagerly fomented on the frontiers of his adversary.

In regard to the struggle in Britanny I shall soon be obliged to speak at length. It is sufficient here to notice it as the cause which induced Philip so willingly to consent to the prolongation of the truce, when from every other circumstance he had reason to suppose that a renewal of hostilities would prove greatly favourable to his cause.

The truces were thus extended from time to time, and it would appear that frequent conferences were held at Arras for the purpose of concluding some final measure of pacification; but as the effect produced was merely temporary, it will not be necessary to notice these transactions more particularly. Benedict XII. during his life continued to exert himself with worthy perseverance to moderate the pretensions of two ambitious kings, and to restore peace to Christendom; and Clement VI., who succeeded to the papal chair on the 7th of May A. D. 1342, embraced the same humane policy as his predecessor. Annibal Ceccano, Cardinal Archbishop of Naples, and the Cardinal of Preneste were sent to conduct the negotiations for a peace; but the drop of Christian charity which they let fall into the cup of human passions and interests proved a weak antidote to all the poisons with which it overflowed.

In the meantime the effects of Philip's negotiations with the Scots began to appear. David Bruce, after a period of seven years spent in exile, returned to his dominions, and landed in Kincardineshire in the month of May 1341. His presence restored confidence and hope to his troops; and his partisans in every part of Scotland exerted themselves to make head against the invaders who had so long oppressed their land.* No sooner had the termination of the

* The task of disentangling this part of Scottish history is most difficult; nor have I, after long examination, been able to satisfy myself very completely. It is more than probable that the doubts which my mind has received from the innumerable discrepancies in the writings of the old historians, and from the perfect incompatibility of the most frequent statements with the facts as proved by the dates of Edward's state papers, may have led me to omit many occurrences which did nevertheless take place. But this I the less regret, as I have confined myself to general terms in speaking of the Scottish wars throughout; and at the same time have not stated any thing which cannot be established by proof. It may be necessary, however, to say a few words as to why I have rejected the account given by Froissart, by Barnes, by Rapin, and many other writers.

They all with one accord declare, that Edward made two expeditions to Scotland, the one in the end of 1341 and the beginning of 1342, to relieve Stirling, which failed on account of the dispersion of the English fleet; the second in 1342, but after David Bruce, whom Froissart represents as returning in that year, had invaded England, and which terminated in a truce of two years. This statement is proved to be totally erroneous in every respect by the State Papers. David Bruce returned in May 1341; and the Fædera show that Edward was at Newcastle and in that neighbourhood on the 4th of November 1341, having been in Westminster on the 28th of October previous. From Newcastle he went to Stamford, and returned to Newcastle by the 4th of December; by the 27th of December he had advanced to Melrose. On the 22d of January 1342, he had returned

first truce, negotiated before Tournay, left the Scots at liberty to act, than Stirling was besieged and taken; and the King of Scotland, with an army of 60,000 men, composed of Scots, French, Danes, and Norwegians, advanced rapidly towards the English frontier.

The first tidings of the siege of Stirling called Edward from repose; and, making what levies he could, he hastened towards Scotland, in order to relieve the besieged town, and to protect the territory which Baliol had ceded to him in former years. By the time he had arrived at Newcastle, however, the news of the fall of Stirling reached him, together with more certain information than he had hitherto received concerning the power and

into England as far as Morpeth; and on the 14th of February he was in Westminster. From that period until he set out on his expedition into Britanny, he was never absent more than forty miles from London for three weeks together. The whole of Edward's military operations, therefore, against Scotland, must have taken place between the 4th of November 1341, and the 10th of February 1342; and as in the letter of summons to William de Bohun Earl of Northampton, recited in Rymer (tom. ii. part iv. p. 115.), and dated 4th of November, Edward implies that he had already considerable forces with him on the frontier, and also shows that he expected a daily invasion of England by the Scottish forces, I am inclined to think that the incursion of David Bruce took place before the assembly of the English reinforcements appointed to meet at Newcastle on the 24th of January; and that Edward, without waiting for the fresh troops he expected, pursued the Scots across the Tyne and the Tweed, and had taken up his quarters at Melrose before the beginning of 1342. The six weeks that intervened before his return to London might well be employed in opening the negotiation of the truce of two years, which certainly took place, although we have lost all exact trace of the particulars.

proceedings of the Scottish monarch. The numbers of the adverse army, which he discovered to be advancing rapidly against his dominions, led him instantly to call upon his barons to bring their retainers to his aid as speedily as possible; and the 24th of January 1342 was appointed by his summons as the day of their assembling at Newcastle. Edward also appears to have entertained the design of bringing a naval force to co-operate with the army in his proceedings against the northern portion of the island; but his fleet was dispersed by a tempest, before it could reach its destination; and David Bruce led his troops into the County Palatine of Durham, took the city of that name, and ravaged a great part of the country round, ere any force could be brought to oppose him. The King of England, however, with the army which was already collected joined to the array of the border counties, marched against the invaders, who retired at his approach, and drew toward the great forest track of Jedwood, or Jeddard, which had for years afforded a safe asylum to the gallant gentlemen defending the independence of Scotland. Taking possession of such fastnesses throughout the country, it seems to have been the design of David Bruce and his advisers to content themselves with the many advantages they had gained, and avoid risking a general battle, by which the whole might be so speedily lost. A short halt, however, which they made before the Castle of Werke, upon the Tweed, had nearly defeated this purpose, and brought about an engagement. That small fortress was then held for the Earl of Salisbury, who had not yet returned from his imprisonment in France by his brother Sir William Montague. The garrison had at various periods given great annoyance to the border Scots, and it would appear had both harassed them in their present retreat from Durham, and re-captured a part of the spoil with which they were laden. A weak desire of avenging this affront is said to have induced the leaders of the royal army of Scotland to besiege so insignificant a place; and for three days the castle was pressed by close investment and continual assaults. William Montague at length took upon himself the task of making his way through the enemies' lines and carrying to the King of England the news of the danger of Werke, and information regarding the position of the Scottish army; which difficult enterprise he accomplished in safety, and returned from Berwick, accompanied by the King and all the forces which Edward had assembled at that time.*

Before their arrival David Bruce and his adherents had raised the siege; and the only farther tidings which could be obtained of the movements of the Scots went to show that they had taken possession of the strong parts of the country to the west, and were prepared to wage against England the same desultory but detructive warfare, which had been so long poured forth upon the border from the bosom of Jeddard forest. As this warfare was likely, from the magni-

* Froissart.

tude of the force now engaged therein, to assume a far more dangerous character than it had hitherto done; as the affairs of Britanny had now taken an aspect which called for the most attentive and anxious watchfulness on the part of Edward; and as the fast waning truce with France promised a speedy renewal of hostilities on the Continent; — it became necessary for the English monarch either to terminate the war with Scotland, by the complete and immediate subjugation of that country, or to obtain an interval of tranquillity on his northern frontier by the conclusion of a peace. The dispersion of his fleet, the unconquerable fortitude of his foes, the difficult nature of the country, and the alluring prospect of the conquest of France, all led Edward to abandon the idea of even attempting the former alternative; and we consequently find that before he set out for London, early in February, he had already opened a negotiation with David Bruce. As it was necessary, however, that the King of Scotland should obtain permission to abandon the war from Philip of Valois, to whom he had strictly bound himself by treaty, Edward, immediately on his return to London, gave a safe conduct to the Earl of Murray, in order to facilitate his passage into France for the purpose of obtaining this sanction.*

How soon this was procured does not appear; but

* Rymer, tom. ii. part iv. p. 119. Dated 22d February, 1342.

on the 20th of March following, a safe conduct* was granted to the ambassadors sent by the King of Scotland to treat for the truce, and in the beginning of April we find that the negotiations were finally concluded.†

Such was the only expedition to Scotland which Edward III. made in the interval between his return from Flanders and his invasion of Britanny. Nevertheless, one anecdote must be noticed here, which has been grafted upon this expedition, and upon a short halt which he made at the castle of Werke.

Two or three chapters of Froissart are devoted to an account of the love of Edward for the Countess of Salisbury, who was at that time in the castle of Werke, and to a display of the virtuous resistance of that lady. But it would appear from the accounts given by our best genealogists, that in all probability some mistake exists in regard to the whole tale. Catherine, the wife of the Earl of Salisbury, then prisoner in France, was, at the time of Edward's visit, many years older than himself; and, whatever beauty she might still possess, it could scarcely be supposed so great as to produce the sudden and also lasting effect which is attributed to it by Froissart. We have reason to suppose, indeed, that the beautiful and celebrated Joan Plantagenet, daughter of the late Earl of Kent, and consequently first cousin

* Rymer, tom. ii. part iv. p. 120. † Idem, p. 122.

to the monarch, was also in the castle of Lord Salisbury at the time it was relieved by the King of England; and by some she is said to have been at that period undoubtedly promised to William, the son and heir of the imprisoned Earl; but the tender years of both parties had hitherto prevented a union, which was ultimately relinquished altogether. The age of the Fair Maid of Kent, as the princess was afterwards called, she not having as yet seen thirteen years, is more conclusive in regard to Edward's passion as affecting her, than the more mature years of the young Earl's mother in regard to the King's sudden attachment. Certain it is, however, that the story must have had its foundation in some rumours strongly current at the time, for we cannot attribute such a tale to the mere imagination of Froissart; and he also dwells too long upon the subject, and connects it too frequently with other occurrences, to permit of our supposing that it was the mere idle report of some chance traveller to the Continent.

It cannot be doubted either that it was of the elder lady that the chronicler of Hainault intended to speak; for he not only frequently refers to the imprisonment of her husband, but pointedly marks the ingratitude of Edward in seeking to destroy the domestic happiness of a man who had so zealously served him. It is but just, however, to remark, that whether these anecdotes, in regard to Edward and the Countess, be true or false, it is positively certain that the monarch evinced no want of gratitude towards the Earl in other respects; and almost immediately after the period at which Froissart represents him as endeavouring to seduce his wife, we find by the public records that the King consented to lose his invaluable services against the King of France for ever, rather than add an hour to his captivity.

CHAPTER X.

THE STATE OF FRANCE. — DEATH OF JOHN III. DUKE OF BRITANNY. — CLAIMANTS OF THE DUCHY. — THEIR CLAIMS CONSIDERED. — NOT AFFECTED BY THE SALIC LAW. — MEASURES OF JOHN III. TO SECURE THE DUCHY UNCONTESTED TO HIS NIECE, JOAN OF PENTHIEVRE. — THE COUNT DE MONTFORD ASSUMES THE TITLE OF DUKE, AND GAINS THE CITIZENS OF NANTES. — TAKES POSSESSION OF THE TREASURES OF LIMOGES. — ATTACKS AND TAKES THE TOWNS OF BREST AND RENNES. — HENNEBON TAKEN BY STRATAGEM. — VANNES, AURAY, AND GUY LA FORET, SURRENDER. — LA ROCHE PERIOU MAKES GOOD ITS RESISTANCE. — CARHAIX ON THE SEA SURRENDERED BY THE BISHOP OF QUIMPER. — DE MONTFORD'S APPREHENSIONS. — VISITS ENGLAND IN SECRET, AND DOES HOMAGE TO EDWARD III. AS KING OF FRANCE. — RETURNS TO FRANCE, AND ATTENDS THE COURT OF PEERS — FINDS HIS CAUSE PREJUDGED, AND HIS VISIT TO ENGLAND KNOWN. — MAKES HIS ESCAPE FROM PARIS BY STRATAGEM, AND RETIRES TO NANTES. — CHARLES OF BLOIS TAKES THE FIELD WITH GREAT FORCE. — NANTES BESIEGED. — THE BURGHERS AND GARRISON BETRAY DE MONTFORD. — NANTES SURRENDERED. — DE MONTFORD MADE PRISONER.

It is now time to examine some points in the state of France, the circumstances of which country now began to affect England more directly than they had done since the conclusion of the siege of Tournay. Almost immediately after the departure of the allies from before that city, Philip of Valois dismissed the various nobles who had come to do him feudal service in the past war. Amongst the rest, John III. Duke of Britanny, who had appeared at the French muster with large forces and great splendour, retired with the purpose of marching towards his dukedom. At Caen, in Normandy, however, he was taken ill, and expired on the 30th of April, 1341; leaving behind him one of the most important feofs of the crown of France to be contested by his brother and his niece. In order to obtain a clear notion of the claims of these competitors, it may be necessary to state that Arthur II., the father of the late duke, had been twice married. By his first wife, Maria de Limoges, he left three sons; John the late Duke, Guy Count of Penthievre, and Peter. His second wife, Jolande de Dreux, who brought the county of Montford into the house of Britanny, gave him one son, John Count of Montford. The eldest son succeeded to his father as John III. Duke of Britanny; the second died, leaving one daughter, Joan; the third died without issue; and thus, at the death of John III., who was also childless, his youngest brother, the Count of Montford, and the daughter of his second brother Guy, were all that survived of the family of Arthur II. These then were the claimants of the vacant dukedom, but their claims were founded upon rules which require some investigation.

In the various provinces and feofs of France, the laws of succession were very different, depending entirely upon the custom of the county, dukedom, or lordship; which custom was affected both by the form of grant which had conveyed the territory to its first feudal possessors, and by the mode in which the province had been acquired by the kings of France themselves. This distinction is the more important in the present instance, as upon these circumstances alone depended the rights of the son and the granddaughter of Arthur II.

Joan claimed the duchy as the daughter of the elder brother; but two objections might be urged against her. The first was founded on the general Salic law of France, by which females were excluded from all male feofs; and the second was supported by the common custom of many provinces in France which did not admit of what is called *representation*, or, in other words, did not allow that the contingent rights of an individual descended to his heir at his death.* In regard to the Salic law, it had become by this time modified and virtually annulled in many parts of France, by various circumstances, into which it is perfectly unnecessary to enquire here, because in Britanny it never existed. That duchy formed a part of the ancient Armorica, the inhabitants of which had not been conquered by the Franks, whose law the Salic law was, but had been blended with the invaders on terms honorable to the Armoricans, and advantageous to the Franks. Whether the fact, that the Salic law did not obtain in Britanny be or be not justly attributable to this early incorporation of the Armoricans with the Franks, I will not pretend to say; but

* Thus A. possessing an estate, and having B. and C. for his children; if A. died before B., B. would inherit the estate, and not C.: but if B. died before his father A., leaving a son, D., the son D. would not succeed to his father's contingent rights on the death of A., but the estate would go to C., the second son, to the prejudice of the grandson. Of this law we have already seen an instance in the case of Robert of Artois.

I believe it is certain, that no instance is known of its having been brought into use in that dukedom. A thousand examples of a contrary practice were to be found in the history of the province. The first objection therefore to the claims of Joan was null; and the second was equally invalid, as various cases were afterwards brought forward to show that representation was the custom of Britanny, though it happened that the proof could not be so easily established at the moment.

John II. had during his life shown a strong partiality to the orphan daughter of his brother; and wisely foreseeing that, after his death, the ambition of the Count of Montford might lead to a struggle, he took care to secure for Joan the strongest support which the realm of France could afford, by marrying her to Charles de Chatillon, commonly called Charles of Blois, a younger son of Guy Count of Blois, by Margaret, sister of the reigning King of France. To remove from her path also every difficulty that her situation might produce, he induced the states, or provincial parliament of Britanny, to acknowledge her husband as his successor in the dukedom; and left no means unemployed to give notoriety and authority to his neice's claims upon the succession.*

Such measures, though they certainly provided a powerful support for the orphan princess, did not obviate the evils which the Duke had foreseen. No sooner did the news of his death reach the Count de

* Argentré, Hist. de Bretagne.

Montford, than assuming at once the title of Duke of Britanny though he had failed to urge his claims during the life of his brother, he flew to Nantes, engaged the citizens to do him homage; and thence proceeded to Limoges, in which city the late duke had accumulated immense treasures, the fruits of a wise and tranquil reign. The Count de Montford entered the city of Limoges with all the pomp of arms, and with that display of splendour and authority which was likely to captivate or overawe; and the magistrates and clergy of the town, whether dazzled or alarmed, yielded him at once the treasure which was so much the object of his desire, notwithstanding the known claims of the Duchess Joan.

Furnished with the surest means of success, De Montford returned to Nantes, in which city he had left his wife, the famous Countess of Montford, sister of the Count of Flanders, a woman who seems to have concentrated in her own person the talents and energies which were denied to the rest of her family. Immediately after his arrival, the nobility of Britanny were summoned to partake of a splendid banquet at Nantes, and to celebrate the accession of De Montford to the dukedom; but the vacancy of his tables gave a lamentable proof of how little he might calculate upon the affection of the nobles. Only one knight of any renown, named Henry de Leon, presented himself at the feast; and the Count and Countess de Montford were obliged to fill the places they had prepared for the barons of the land with the burghers and city dames of Nantes, a mortification which the haughty spirit of feudal times rendered not only painful but ominous.

Having now learned that willing obedience was not to be obtained from the lords of Britanny, John of Montford determined to enforce submission with the the sword; and knowing how great a step is possession, he prepared to act with energetic rapidity. The wealth which the treasures of Limoges had placed at his disposal enabled him to levy large forces; his own resolution and activity were supported by those of his fearless and heroic wife; and he took the field with a large army, offering peace and protection to all who acknowledged his right, but instant attack to every town or fortress that resisted his authority. The first place assailed was Brest, defended by a gallant knight named Walter de Clisson, the representative of a younger branch of the powerful family of that name. The garrison having boldly refused to acknowledge the Count de Montford as Duke of Britanny, his troops were led to the attack with skill and impetuosity. Walter de Clisson, on his part, defended his post in the manner which might be expected from one of his race and reputation; but being shut out by the portcullis, while covering the retreat of his companions after the outer barrier had been lost, he was so severely wounded ere the garrison could rally and rescue him, that on entering the fortress he was obliged to resign the command to another. His death followed within a few hours after his return to the town; and the assault being renewed, the place surrendered on the third day.

The important city of Rennes was next besieged; but De Montford, having taken Henry de Spinefort, the governor of that town, in one of the occasional skirmishes which diversified the siege, threatened to hang him before the chief gate if the resistance were prolonged. The love which the common people bore their commander was opposed by the determination which the chief burghers had formed to hold out to the last. A tumult and contest between the two parties took place in the streets; several persons were slain; and Rennes having surrendered, its inhabitants universally plighted their faith to John de Montford. Some means were found of gaining even Henry de Spinefort himself; and that knight almost immediately afterwards obtained possession of the strong town of Hennebon, for the party of De Montford, by a stratagem which even the license of war could scarcely justify.

Setting out with six hundred men at arms, he appeared before that city, in which his brother commanded, and rode to the gates with his own banners displayed. The governor, not knowing the fate of Rennes, immediately concluded that his relation had come with friendly purposes, ordered the gates to be thrown open for his admission, and rode to meet him in the street. There he was instantly arrested in the name of the Duke of Britanny, and only liberated on embracing the party of De Montford at the earnest request of his brother. Vannes, Auray, and Guy la Forêt, also surrendered; but la Roche-Periou was held out by Oliver de Clisson; and after a siege of ten days, De Montford was obliged to abandon his proceedings against it, and retire unsuccessful. A more important acquisition, however, compensated in some degree for this disappointment; for, at the persuasion of Henry de Leon, the first noble who had joined him, De Montford was acknowledged as duke by Alain le Gal, Bishop of Quimper, who delivered into his hands the town and castle of Carhaix on the sea. The bishop, indeed, made a politic reservation in his submission, declaring beforehand that if any other claimant appeared whose title proved to be better than that of De Montford, he would consider himself free to withdraw his homage, and surrender his territories and fortresses to the hands of their legitimate sovereign.

Although his progress through the dukedom had been very successful, and although he was supported by large forces and large supplies, John of Montford felt that he had much still to apprehend. His fortunes were far from decided; and he well knew that his rival, Charles of Blois, would seek aid and assistance in a quarter where he was sure to find them. To the French Court of Peers was the only legal appeal which could be made by the adverse claimant to the coronet of Britanny; and in that court, where the uncle of his opponent presided, the Count of Montford could expect no favour, and might apprehend some injustice. If the decision of that court were against himself — and he little doubted that by some means it would be rendered so — the whole forces of France, now perfectly unemployed, would of course be brought into the field to support the judgment of the peers, and establish the nephew of the King in the disputed dukedom.

To submit to the award of that court, if it proved unfavourable to himself, never entered into the contemplation of De Montford; and the only question which presented itself was, to what power he might best apply for efficient aid in resisting the execution of a decision the nature of which he already anticipated.

The open enemy of Philip of Valois, the rival claimant of the crown of France, the immediate neighbour of the Dukes of Britanny, and the most talented and ambitious, if not absolutely the most powerful prince of the age, was the ally on whom the eyes of De Montford ultimately rested; and he determined to make a personal application to the King of England for assistance in case of need.

Although the passions of the English monarch, and the facilities afforded to his ambition by an easy entrance into the very heart of France through the province of Britanny, were of course calculated upon by De Montford, when considering the probability of obtaining the aid he sought, yet he felt that some stronger inducement still must be held out to the young King of England, in order to ensure that immediate and powerful assistance of which he stood in need; and he determined at once to tender his homage to Edward, as King of France: a bold step;

but one by no means unwise, if he considered his case hopeless under the decision of the peers.*

By that measure he practically denied the competency of Philip's court, and appealed his cause to a judge who was sure both to decide in his favour, and to support his judgment by force of arms.

Having after some deliberation determined upon this measure, he embarked at a small port † on the coast of Britanny, and arrived shortly after in Cornwall, accompanied by a retinue of only twenty knights.

* It has been asserted that no trace of the homage now rendered is to be found in the state papers of the time; and that Froissart, who states the fact, must allude to an act of homage undoubtedly performed at a later period. This assertion is not quite correct. Though I find no paper absolutely and solely referring to either this visit of De Montford to England, or to the homage he there performed; yet I find allusions to both in other documents. Thus, in the cession of the county of Richmond (in September 1341), Edward says,—"Cum illustris Johannes, Dux Britanniæ et Comes de Monteforti, consanguineus noster carissimus, attendens injuriam per dominum Philippum de Valesio, super detentione regni Franciæ, nobis factam, zelo justitiæ contra dictum Philippum, nobiscum fœdus pepigerit," &c. &c. I have, in consequence, in speaking of these events, adopted the account of Froissart, whose statement, in regard to the principal fact, is undoubtedly correct. It is more than probable that the silence of the state papers on this subject proceeded from the desire of secresy, which it was natural the Count de Montfort should entertain in regard to negotiations which were in the highest degree dangerous, as they must have taken place previous to his visiting Paris in August 1341; for he had but time to escape from that city, return to Britanny, and prepare for defence, ere he was besieged in Nantes, from which place he never went forth again but as a prisoner. It is, therefore, utterly impossible that he could have visited England after the decision of the Court of Peers against him.

† Froissart calls this port Gredo, but it appears that for more than a century the existence of such a place has been unknown.

With these he took horse, and proceeded as fast as possible to Windsor, where his reception at once showed him that his views would meet with every favour from the English monarch. He explained to Edward his situation, engaged him by the most solemn promises to maintain him in the duchy of which he had taken possession, and did homage for it to that monarch as King of France; though, from some cause which it is difficult to explain, he did not receive till some time after the investiture of the county of Richmond* in England, which had been long held by various members of his family, but which had been resumed by the English sovereign on the death of the late Duke of Britanny. The splendour with which he was entertained, however, and the distinction with which he was treated in every other respect, gave him the most convincing proof of how well his pretensions and designs accorded with the passions and the interests of the King of England; and after a short but gratifying visit to the court of that monarch, he returned to France in time to

* In regard to the earldom of Richmond, it would seem to have been granted to the Dukes of Britanny upon a particular tenure, for on the death of John III. Edward took possession of it, and only granted it to De Montford as an act of grace and favour, not of right, though it had long belonged to his family. He shackled the grant also at first with various conditions, which, however, were afterwards removed; and it was thenceforward held by him on the same terms as it had been held by his brother. According to Dugdale, John II. ceded the county of Richmond in England to Arthur II., from whom it descended to John III., and at his death was claimed by De Montford, to whom Edward yielded it in compensation for the loss of the county of Montford, and in whose family it remained till it was confiscated in 1380 or 1381. — *Dugdale*, vol. i. p. 86.

receive at Nantes the messengers sent from Paris to summon him to appear before the Peers.*

His journey to England therefore, and the negotiations which he had carried on with Edward, he considered as still secret; and trusting that they would remain concealed long enough to enable him to visit Paris and return without personal danger, he determined, after some deliberation, to obey the summons and present himself before the Peers of France. He accordingly set out from Nantes with a train of four hundred horse; and on reaching the capital went at once to his own hotel, where he passed the rest of the day and the following night. Early on the subsequent morning, however, he proceeded to the palace, where the King, who had been informed of his arrival, awaited his coming with the principal peers. De Montford passed through the ranks of the other nobles, who, we are told, received him universally with distinction and respect; and, advancing to the King, before whom he inclined himself with every appearance of humility and obedience, he said,

* De Montford's visit to England must have taken place at some period between the 19th of May 1341 and the end of July in the same year; for on the former day we find from Rymer (tom. ii. part iv. p. 100.) that Edward took possession of the county of Richmond, and appointed the revenues thereof to be applied to the maintenance of some of his younger children, showing clearly that at this time the negotiation with De Montford had not commenced; and on the 7th of September sentence was pronounced against the count by the French Court of Peers, fourteen days previous to which De Montford had made his escape from Paris. The journey from Windsor to Paris, visiting Nantes by the way, could not have occupied less than a month, considering the mode of travelling then used; so that De Montford must have concluded his negotiations at the English court before the end of July.

"Sire, at your command and good pleasure I am here."

"Count of Montford," replied Philip, "that you have come pleases me well; but I am not a little surprised that you should have dared to take by your own will alone the duchy of Britanny, where you have no right, inasmuch as there is a nearer heir than yourself, whom you wish to disinherit. And the better * to strengthen yourself also, you have gone to my enemy the King of England, and to him have done homage for the duchy, as I am told."

"Ha, dear Sire! believe it not," replied the Count; "for truly you are ill informed; and it would cost me no small pain to do such a thing. But as to the nearer kin of whom you speak, I believe, Sire, craving your pardon, that you mistake; for I know none nearer of kin to my brother, lately dead, than myself; and if it were judged and decided that any other be nearer than myself, I shall neither be obstinate nor ashamed to resign my claim."

The King replied still dissatisfied; and dismissed the Count with a command not to quit Paris for fifteen days, which De Montford promised to obey. On his return to his hotel, however, a number of reasons presented themselves to his mind, which convinced him that if his journey itself had been imprudent, after the steps he had taken in regard to Edward,

* It is more than probable that Philip of Valois received the news of De Montford's visit to England through the Lords of Montmorency, in whose favour there is a safe conduct from the King of England still extant, dated the 20th of May 1341.

his stay would be the height of folly after he found that those steps were discovered.

It was sufficiently evident from the first words which Philip had addressed to him that his cause was already prejudged, at least by the King; and he might well feel sure that if the decision of the peers was against himself, Philip would immediately confine him, till the whole of Britanny should be reduced to the sway of his rival. Nor was long imprisonment all he had to fear, as his treaty with the King of England, and his homage to that monarch as King of France, placed him within danger of the law of high treason. Neither was Philip a man to hesitate a moment in putting that law in force, especially where it might remove a rival from the paths of his nephew.

On these considerations his resolution was instantly taken to return to Britanny as speedily as possible, if he could accomplish his escape from Paris; and the only difficulty was to plan that escape in such a manner as not to induce immediate pursuit. He accordingly spread a rumour that he was ill; and, choosing but a small party to accompany him, he gave strict charge to his domestics and followers that the same appearance of activity and bustle should be kept up in his hotel that had been displayed during his presence. He then secretly withdrew himself from Paris; and so well was the secret kept, so accurately was the drama he had taught performed by his servants, that for several days no suspicion of his absence was entertained by the King, or by his rival Charles of Blois.

Although their anger and vexation when they discovered his evasion were equal to the want of caution they had displayed in permitting him to remain unwatched, and though the certainty that he was preparing for vigorous resistance aggravated their wrath, they were obliged, in order to observe all the usual forms, to wait for the time previously appointed for the trial. At the end of the fifteen days, the peers met at Conflans, a palace of the kings of France, about a league and a half from Paris, and there the procurator of De Montford was permitted to offer on his behalf whatever proofs could be adduced to show that representation, in regard to noble feofs, was not admitted by the custom of Britanny. On the other hand, Charles of Blois, in right of his wife, brought forward a number of instances to establish the contrary position, and to show that the children of an elder brother succeeded to noble feofs, as the representatives of their father, when his death had taken place prior to lapse of the last life.

This was proved to the satisfaction of the peers; and though it was afterwards asserted that some formalities were wanting to give legality to their decision, there can be no doubt that they unanimously pronounced sentence against De Montford, and in favour of Charles of Blois.

No sooner was their judgment declared, than Philip of Valois called his nephew into his presence, and thus addressed him, "Fair * nephew, you have judg-

* I have given these speeches as I find them in Froissart, not exactly believing them to be the precise words spoken by the persons to whom

ment for you in regard to this wide and beautiful heritage. Hasten, therefore, and strive to reconquer it from him who holds it wrongfully, and pray all your friends that they will aid you in your need. For my part, I will no way fail you, but will lend you gold and silver, and will bid my son the Duke of Normandy make head with you. And more! I pray and command that you will make good speed; for if the English king *, our adversary, of whom the Count de Montford pretends to hold the duchy of Britanny, should come thither, he might cause us great evil, and could not have a better entrance to come farther still than when he has all the towns and fortresses of Britanny at his command."

Charles of Blois wanted no incitement to action, and the principal barons of his uncle's court promised without hesitation to aid him with all their power. It may be as well here to name the chief leaders who

---

they are attributed, but because they may have been so, and at all events display the manners of an age possessing a peculiar interest in the eyes of both French and English.

* It would appear that Edward most anxiously desired to fulfil his promise, and yield immediate support to his ally, though the renewal of hostilities with Scotland retarded the execution of his design. For the purpose of bearing reinforcements to Britanny we find that so early as the 3d of October (before Nantes could be besieged), he had ordered the seizure of all vessels in the ports of Somersetshire, Dorsetshire, Devonshire, and Cornwall, as well as all that could be found between London and Sandwich. These were to be armed and provisioned, and ready to sail from Portsmouth by the 10th of November. Again, on the 10th of November, though then engaged in hostilities with Scotland, we find the King providing for the expences of several leaders about to set out for Britanny, of whom the principal were Robert of Artois and Walter de Mauny.—*Rymer*, tom. ii. part iv. pp. 112. 116.

engaged themselves on the part of that prince, as few of them were ever, from the commencement of this war, without some share in the struggle between France and England.

The first of these nobles was John Duke of Normandy, the son of Philip of Valois, and heir to the French crown; a bold and warlike prince, whose heart was much better calculated to receive and nourish the noble sentiments of chivalrous honour, than his mind to acquire or practise the difficult maxims of military science. The second in point of rank was Charles of Valois, Count of Alençon, the uncle of the prince; a hasty, and somewhat vindictive man, but one who, in the wars of Aquitaine, had shown himself a commander of some skill. Besides these two princes, the Dukes of Burgundy and Bourbon attached themselves strongly to the cause of Charles of Blois, as well as the Count of Blois, his brother, the Counts of Eu and Guisnes, and the Viscount de Rohan. Added to these, was a young nobleman who generally bears the title of Louis of Spain; and it may not be unnecessary to pause at this place upon his history, which has been very frequently mistated. He was the son of Alphonso de la Cerda, the rightful heir to the throne of Castille and Leon; from which, however, he had been excluded by the caprice of his grandfather, Alphonso X. That monarch, preferring his unworthy child Sancho, called the Brave, declared him his heir to the prejudice of the two children of his eldest son, Ferdinand, who had died in 1275. Alphonso de la

Cerda, the first of these disinherited princes, retired to Paris, whither his mother Blanche, the daughter of St. Louis, had preceded him; and, attached by that tie to the royal family of France, he chose for his country the land that had given him an asylum. He soon after married, and by his first wife had Louis of Spain, Prince of the Fortunate Islands, Count of Talmond, and afterwards Admiral of France, —the commander of whom I now speak.* Though it is not possible to discover what troops he brought into the field, or whence they were derived, his aid was of very great benefit to the cause of Charles of Blois, who found in him an able, adventurous, and indefatigable officer; though as a man he proved himself to be cruel, barbarous, and ungenerous. To the troops which the various princes themselves could raise, Philip added a body of three thousand Genoese mercenaries, led by Antonio Doria and Carlo Grimaldi, who had been for some time in the pay of France; while Stephen de la Baume, grand master of the cross-bowmen of France, conducted to the support of Charles of Blois a considerable body of the peculiar troops under his command and a mass of irregular infantry.

The place appointed for the assembling of these troops was the town of Angiers, on the Loire, upon the frontiers of France and Britanny; and when the whole were collected, they mustered five thousand men at arms, besides the infantry, — a force quite

* St. Marthé, Hist. General. de la Mais. de France.

sufficient to terminate the contest if no foreign power had come to the assistance of De Montford.

While these preparations had been in progress, however, De Montford had not failed to employ the moments that were still his own to provide for the defence of the territory, as well as his means permitted. Every town and castle throughout the whole of Britanny, which had acknowledged his sway, he now took means to secure: strong garrisons, resolute officers, and abundant supplies, were thrown into all; and nothing that his own skill or experience could foresee, or that treasure and labour could secure, was left unprovided for or unobtained. He himself, confiding in the inhabitants of Nantes, who affected towards him the greatest possible degree of attachment, remained in that city, while his wife repaired to Rennes; and, thus prepared, he awaited the gathering of the storm without much apprehension.

The Duke of Normandy led his army forward into Britanny as fast as possible; and having passed the Loire, attacked the castle of Chantoceaux, which surrendered after a vigorous resistance. He next directed his march straight for Nantes, and laid siege to that city. A variety of rencontres of no moment followed; but one sally made by the burghers of the town produced results which render it worthy of notice. This sortie was directed to carry off some provisions which a small escort was leading to the camp of the besiegers. The guard was soon put to flight; and the captured carts, which contained the provisions, had nearly reached the city gates, when a detachment issuing from the camp endeavoured to recover them. Reinforcements poured out of the town in aid of the captors; the contest grew fierce; the combatants multiplied on both sides; and, at length, Henry de Leon, the chief adherent of De Montford in Britanny, finding himself engaged with almost the whole French army, judged it expedient to draw off his troops, and effect his retreat into the city.

This was accordingly done; but it could not be accomplished without great loss, which fell most heavily upon the burghers of the town, whose wives and mothers filled the place with lamentations, on finding the number of the first citizens who remained behind upon the field, or in the hands of the enemy. De Montford also, unwisely and apparently unjustly, attributed the fate of the two hundred persons who had been made prisoners to the hasty retreat of Henry de Leon; and in the heat of the moment much was said that, without producing any benefit, left an irritated prince and a lukewarm adherent.

The greatest evil, however, which the cause of De Montford suffered by this unfortunate sally, was the loss of so many of the burghers. The people of the town began to feel all the inconveniences of a siege: glory, which at a distance had shone as a jewel of inestimable value, lost its splendour in their eyes as soon as they were called upon to surmount all the obstacles which impede man's course towards it. Every family in the city had to regret the death or the captivity of some relative; murmurs grew loud, even amongst those who had remained faithful; and a large body of those whose friends were in the hands of the enemy, conspired in secret to deliver the place to Charles of Blois.* Henry of Leon also, it is supposed, negotiated with the besiegers; and De Montford, finding that he could neither rely upon the citizens nor the soldiers, with anguish of heart, took the ultimate resolution of forestalling† the traitors by whom he was surrounded, and treating with the Duke of Normandy himself. ‡

* Froissart. † Dom. Morice, Hist. de Bretagne.

‡ I am by no means unaware that William of St. André, an author of considerable value, has given a circumstantial account of the conditions on which Nantes was delivered by De Montford to the Duke of Normandy, which conditions he declares to have been violated in the grossest manner by the imprisonment of the Count. There are, however, so many reasons for doubting this statement, that I cannot but believe St. André had his account from some very prejudiced adherent of the faction of De Montford. The whole conduct of John then Duke of Normandy, whether before or after his accession to the throne of France, showed that, though often a cruel and always a rash and somewhat haughty prince, he had the highest and noblest sense of chivalrous honour. No proof is brought forward by St. André; no treaty with the terms he speaks of is any where to be found; and he is contradicted in this point by authors fully as worthy of credit as himself. Add to these considerations the known character of the prince, and the little probability which exists that when the town was about to be surrendered by the citizens the Duke of Normandy would grant the most favourable conditions that ever were heard of to the enemy and rival of his cousin, simply for the purpose of breaking them as soon as granted, and it will be clear that the account given by St. André is perfectly incredible.

That some treaty was entered into, however, is evident, if my conjectures hereafter stated, in regard to an error in our copy of the treaty of Malestroit, be correct; and the negotiations which subsequently took place under the mediation of the pope would seem to imply that one article of the treaty of Nantes insured the liberation of De Montford within a certain time, though what were the real conditions I am unable to discover.

It may as well be remarked here, that in regard to all the wars in

Though the precise terms which he obtained cannot be clearly discovered, it would appear that they extended no farther than to his personal safety. The burghers, on their part, received a promise that their friends should be delivered free of ransom; and no farther resistance being offered, a body of French troops entered the place, seized the person of De Montford, and carrying him peaceably out of the city, delivered him into the hands of the Duke of Normandy. By him he was conveyed not long after to Paris, where he was placed in close confinement in the tower of the Louvre. The town of Nantes was treated in no respect as a conquered city. The inhabitants received the enemies of De Montford with the same facility and rejoicings that they had displayed on his own arrival, and gave them the same assurances of attachment and fidelity, with doubtless the same sincerity.

Festivity and amusement succeeded to the horrors of war; and the French leaders remained in the town or the vicinity of Nantes till late in December. They there took measures for securing the part of the territory which they had already obtained, appointed officers and governors for the King in Britanny, and repaired the damage which the siege had occasioned to the fortifications of the capital of the duchy.

The approach of winter put a stop to any farther

France (except those of Flanders), I have rejected the authority of the Chronicle of Flanders, as that of the most confused and worthless record of all the many which have been employed to confuse and embarrass history.

military operations; and as feudal armies, especially when bound together by no tie but voluntary service, as in the present instance, were ever impatient of long campaigns, the Duke of Normandy dismissed his forces, after engaging them to re-assemble in the following spring; and leaving Charles of Blois with sufficient forces to maintain himself at Nantes, he set out for Paris, carrying along with him the unhappy claimant to the contested duchy.

CHAP. XI.

HEROIC CONDUCT OF THE COUNTESS DE MONTFORD.—SHE SENDS TO IMPLORE AID FROM THE KING OF ENGLAND.—EDWARD DESPATCHES SIR WALTER DE MAUNY TO HER ASSISTANCE.—SIEGE OF RENNES. —THE INHABITANTS RISE AGAINST THEIR GOVERNOR, AND DELIVER THE CITY TO CHARLES OF BLOIS.—SIEGE OF HENNEBON. —EXPLOITS OF THE COUNTESS DE MONTFORD.—THE CITY STRAITENED.—TREACHERY OF THE BISHOP OF QUIMPER.—THE GARRISON TREAT FOR A SURRENDER.—THE ENGLISH FLEET ARRIVES.—CONFIDENCE RESTORED.—DESTRUCTION OF THE FRENCH BATTERING ENGINE.—EXPLOITS OF SIR WALTER DE MAUNY.—THE SIEGE RAISED.

Consternation and surprise spread amongst all the garrisons and adherents of De Montford as the tidings flew through Britanny that Nantes had so speedily surrendered, and that the Count himself was taken. Terror, that most infectious of all mental diseases, affected both the soldiers and the allies of the prisoner; and the duchy would have been lost for ever to himself and his family, had not his enemies allowed time for the panic to subside, and had not the courage and firmness of a woman roused the ardour and revived the resolution of his troops. Of all the towns in Britanny, the city of Rennes felt the alarm most strongly, and yielded itself most completely to fear and despair; and the presence of the Countess of Montford, who experienced with deep and painful acuteness all the same apprehensions which the citizens entertained, aggravated by fear for her husband's life, did not at first seem to afford them any support.

No sooner, however, did Joan of Flanders learn the fatal and enervating despondency into which De Montford's adherents had sunk, than shaking off at once, by the exertion of a great and vigorous mind, her griefs, her anxieties, and even the common terrors of her sex, she presented herself to the fearful multitude, carrying in her arms her infant son, and with a face of confidence and resolution exhorted them to cast away their vain and fruitless alarm.

"Be not afraid and confounded, nobles," she cried, "because we have lost our lord. He was but one man; and, behold, here is my child, who, with God's help, shall be his avenger and work you good enough. I have also still wealth in plenty to share with you, and I will soon find you such a leader and such a protector as shall comfort and defend you all." Her words and looks inspired those present with new courage; and, judging of the other cities of the duchy by the example of Rennes, she saw the necessity of immediate and energetic action, and hastened without loss of time from fortress to fortress, carrying resolution and vigour wherever she went. The garrisons were reinforced, the provisions were increased, the defences were strengthened, the troops were accurately paid; and even after she had retired to Hennebon, which she did not do till she had restored confidence to all the adherents of her husband, she maintained the same spirit through the whole duchy by constant messages and supplies. More adherents were gained to the

Count de Montford by the noble and dauntless activity of his wife, during the first winter of his imprisonment, than he had hitherto obtained; and when early in the year the French army re-assembled, not one strong place in Britanny was unprepared to offer a long and vigorous resistance.

Nevertheless that resistance could not be prolonged for ever; and the Countess clearly saw that without such an addition to her forces as would enable her to keep the open field against the French army, her fortresses would soon be captured, however brave might be her garrisons. Britanny of course did not afford sufficient troops to give battle to the whole power of France; and the Countess at once determined to take advantage of her husband's treaty with England, and to claim the promised aid which her situation so strongly demanded. For this purpose Sir Almeric de Clisson, who had newly joined the party of De Montford, and had been appointed guardian of his son, was despatched to the English court at a very early period of the year, charged to propose, as a new inducement to the King of England, a marriage between the infant heir of the house of Montford and one of the daughters of that monarch.

Edward, however, required no fresh motive. Had it but been to weaken his adversary by protracting the intestine strife which now troubled the tranquillity of France, and to retaliate upon Philip of Valois the policy which had led him to support the Scots, Edward would have willingly acceded to the demands of the Countess. But, added to these inducements, was the still more potent motive of securing an easy entrance into France, and an ally whose interests could never be detached from his own, so long as the monarch who had decided against the house of Montford occupied the throne of France. The claims of Edward upon the sceptre of France, and of Montford upon the coronet of Britanny, formed a tie between them which never could be dissolved as long as those claims lasted and were opposed by the same persons; although, strange to say, Edward founded his pretensions to France upon the right of representation in the most unlimited degree, and Montford held Britanny alone by the very opposite principle, and to the exclusion of such a right.

Almeric de Clisson arrived in London in the latter part of February 1342 *, and met with the most distinguished reception. His request was immediately granted; and Edward proceeded to fulfil with all the

* Edward III. does not appear to have returned to London from the Scottish frontier till the middle of February 1342, as I have before noticed; and the troops he granted to Almeric de Clisson were prepared for embarkation by the 15th of March of the same year. The whole time, therefore, between his own return and the departure of the forces sent to the Countess of Montford could be little more than a month, during which time the negociations were carried on and the preparations made.—See *Rymer*, tom. ii. part iv. p. 118. 120.

I also find an order for the seizure of ships for Britanny, dated the 20th of February, which would imply that Aimery or Almeric de Clisson had by that time arrived in London. (Idem, p. 119.) Although Rymer is not always accurate in regard to dates, he is generally so; and had I attempted to verify all the state papers I have cited, by comparison with the manuscripts, the *enormous* sum which the preparation of this work has already cost me would have been more than trebled, owing to the charges at the record offices. I have, however, seldom relied upon these dates for any leading fact, without corroborative evidence.

active zeal which the envoy could desire the promises he had made to De Montford himself.

The difficulty of obtaining money seems to have been at this time the greatest obstacle in the way of the King's designs, but this was removed by a quantity of silver which the Countess de Montford still had at her disposal; and Edward agreed that his troops should be accompanied by minters * in order to strike coin in the duchy. As this might have formed a dangerous precedent, however, in feudal times, De Clisson demanded and obtained a formal declaration that this act was not intended as the assertion of any right, and was not to be construed into any precedent for the future. † Edward also on his part required that, for his own security, some of the strong towns and sea ports of the duchy should be given into his hands, which was immediately conceded; and Sir Walter de Mauny, the officer appointed to command the English force, was empowered to receive and hold the fortresses specified ‡, in the name of the King of England.

These arrangements having taken place, permission was immediately granted to all the gallant gentlemen of England who loved high deeds and sought fair

* The operation of coining was in that age a very simple one. The metal was first made into bars; then cut into square pieces, of exactly equal weight, which were afterwards beaten round; and then received the impress of the die by the stroke of the hammer. — *Leake's Hist. of Eng. Money*, p. 76.

† Rymer, tom. ii. part iv. p. 120.

‡ The letters patent of Edward refer to a treaty between him and De Clisson, in which the towns are mentioned at large; I have not, however, been able to discover that treaty.

renown, to volunteer in behalf of the heroic Countess of Montford *; and six hundred and twenty men at arms, amongst whom we find many of the noblest names in English history, were speedily prepared to take the field. Added to these, by the King himself, was a body of six thousand picked archers, under the command of the renowned Walter de Mauny. The whole force set sail towards the end of March; but it unfortunately happened † that the rapidity with which Edward had despatched this very necessary reinforcement was destined to be counteracted by the opposition of the elements; and, owing to a violent storm, with continual contrary winds, the armament destined to support the Countess of Montford was detained for sixty days upon the high seas.

In the mean time Charles of Blois led a large and well equipped army from Nantes to Rennes; which city, situated on a fine and extensive plain that offered no advantage to besiegers, furnished with abundant stores, defended by a strong garrison, and commanded

* Barnes, p. 256.

† The expedition of Bohun Earl of Northampton, supposed by Barnes to have been the same with that led by Sir Walter de Mauny, was wholly distinct; for I find that the whole transactions closed with Almeric de Clisson on the 15th of March, and that the ships summoned to carry him and De Mauny to Britanny were prepared at Orwell on the Wednesday after Palm Sunday (Rymer, tom. ii. part iv. pp. 119, 120.); while the first order for seizing vessels to carry the Earl of Northampton is dated on the 27th of March, nearly a fortnight after the last mention of De Clisson in England, and does not appoint the preparation of the vessels till several weeks afterwards. In addition to these facts, two letters, cited hereafter, prove that the Earl of Northampton was in England till the 22d of July 1342; and in the patent appointing that nobleman the king's lieutenant in Britanny, Sir Walter de Mauny is alluded to as already there.

by a valiant officer, called William of Caddoudal, promised resistance proportioned to its importance and its size.

The troops of France seem to have been sufficient completely to invest the town, which was accordingly done at a very early period of the year; and the Spaniards and Genoese*, who, like other mercenary troops, were never spared by their employers, were ordered to storm at any point that appeared practicable. A variety of assaults were accordingly made; but the defence was so skilfully and resolutely conducted, that the storming parties were repulsed on every occasion. The siege nevertheless continued; the burghers met with many losses, and were obliged to submit to many privations, and they became anxious to follow the example of the Nantois.

They were withheld for some time, however, from carrying this desire into effect by the reasonings and authority of the governor; but at length, determined to undergo no longer the inconveniences to which they had been subjected, they seized the person of Caddoudal, and, throwing him into prison, negotiated a treaty with Charles of Blois for the surrender of the place. They stipulated, indeed, for several conditions, which somewhat redeemed the dastardly submission they thus made long before the place had become untenable; and one of the articles of capitulation was, that the soldiers and partizans of the Countess of Montford might retire in security to whatever asylum they chose. The terms being agreed

* St. Palaye.

to, they opened their gates to Charles of Blois*; and on his entrance the late governor, being set at liberty, retired immediately to rejoin the Countess of Montford, notwithstanding many an effort to draw so gallant an officer to the party of the conquerors.

Sir William de Caddoudal himself bore to Hennebon, in the beginning of May, the news of the fall of Rennes, and the probable approach of the victorious army. No tidings had yet been received of the succour from England; and the Countess of Montford saw loss following loss, and her hopes decay while her dangers multiplied. She yielded not to adversity, however; but boldly prepared to struggle to the last, and to make good Hennebon, towards which Almeric de Clisson had been directed to lead any reinforcements he might obtain.

Immediately upon the fall of Rennes, which had been besieged after Nantes, as the second city in the duchy, Charles of Blois naturally directed his march upon the town into which Joan de Montford had cast herself. He now entertained great hopes of taking the wife and son of his rival, and of thus terminating the war at a blow, by getting the whole adverse race into his power. In Hennebon, however, the Countess had collected a large body of her most faithful followers; and the number of the military garrison in proportion to the burghers, seemed to leave no danger

* Froissart says that the same lords joined Charles of Blois in this campaign who had formerly supported him at the siege of Nantes; but nevertheless it would appear that neither the Duke of Normandy, the King's son, nor the Count of Alençon, his brother, were present during any part of the earlier events of this year.

of the same internal treason which had proved the ruin of Nantes and Rennes, giving this city also into the power of the enemy.

The aspect assumed by the garrison from the very first, announced to Charles of Blois that the most difficult siege he had hitherto undertaken was before him. No sooner were his forces seen approaching than the *ban cloche,* or great alarum bell, rang out from the watch towers; and by the time he had advanced to within a bow-shot of the city, a crowd of armed men presented themselves at the pallisades to bid him defiance. Some skirmishing took place on the very day of his arrival, which terminated greatly to the disadvantage of the assailants; but the next morning by day-break a more regular attack was begun upon the barriers, and a combat commenced which lasted till noon. At that hour, however, the storming parties of the French had suffered so greatly that their leaders judged it necessary to retire, which they did not effect without very serious loss. Notwithstanding the number of killed and wounded, the retreat of these parties gave great dissatisfaction to the principal commanders, who caused the assault to be instantly renewed by fresh troops; but these were also met by the most invincible resistance, and the contest recommenced with additional fury. The Countess of Montford herself, armed and mounted, rode from place to place, encouraging her troops to spare no effort in defence of the town; and matrons and girls, ladies of high rank and the wives of simple fishermen, were all employed in carrying up stones to the battlements for stronger hands to dash down upon the heads of the assailants. Such a spirit would defend a mole-hill against a lion; and Joan of Montford soon found the means of forcing the besiegers to abandon their first attempt to storm the town.

Climbing from time to time one of the highest towers of the city, to watch the dispositions of the enemy, she at length perceived that the whole of the French army had been drawn out to a distance from their camp, some to aid in the assault, and some to gaze at its progress; so that the tents and baggage of her adversaries remained with a very slight defence. With that rapidity of combination and boldness of resolve which instantly sees an advantage and seizes the means of obtaining it, she perceived the rashness of her opponents, and determined to improve the opportunity that their negligence afforded. Descending in haste from the watch-tower, she mounted her horse; and, collecting a party of about three hundred men, issued forth from one of the gates which was free from attack. By a circuitous route, and a covered path, she gained the rear of the enemy without being discovered; and, entering their camp, set fire to it in every part finding none to oppose her but a few servants and horse-boys. Thus, before the French commanders were aware of their camp being in flames, or could reach it to extinguish the conflagration, every thing was destroyed; and though the whole army at once abandoned the attack of Hennebon, and ran with all speed to ascertain the cause and the extent of the damage, nothing presented itself but fire and confusion. Don Louis of Spain was the first who was informed that the Countess of Montford herself was the person who had executed so bold an enterprise; and, gaining intelligence of her route, he pursued her with a large force, and the prompt activity of vengeance. The Countess in the meanwhile had perceived the first movements which the French army had made in their hurry to reach their camp; and finding herself cut off from the city, had shaped her course in the opposite direction. Well aware too that safety could alone be found in speed, she hurried on without pause; and though several of her followers, whose horses were less swift than the rest, fell into the hands of the Spaniard and his companions, she herself reached Auray * in security, and was received with joy, which was heightened by the news of the exploits she had just performed.

The siege of Hennebon continued, notwithstanding the great inconveniences which the assailants suffered from the loss they had sustained in their tents and baggage; and, hutting themselves in cantonments nearer the town, they seemed disposed to press the city more vigorously than they had hitherto done. Their measures must nevertheless have been very ill-judged; for at the end of five days the indefatigable Countess of Montford found means again to pass the French army, and throw herself into Hennebon, with a reinforcement of five hundred men. The success of these enterprises on the part of Joan of Montford of course greatly discouraged her ad-

* Froissart says Brest; but the distance renders that statement incredible; while the historians of Britanny, collected by Dom Morice, with greater probability, name Auray as the place of refuge chosen by the Countess. Hist. de Brétagne; D. Morice, tom. i. p. 256.

versaries; and, finding that in all their attempts to take the town by assault, they lost large bodies of men, without gaining a single advantage, it was at length determined to send to Rennes for twelve of the immense engines used in battering walls, which had been left behind upon a false report of the weakness of Hennebon.

During the space of time required to carry this resolution into effect, Charles of Blois with one division of the army proceeded to attack Auray; while Don Louis of Spain continued to carry on the siege of Hennebon, with forces which were supposed fully sufficient to compel its surrender after the necessary engines for battering the walls had arrived.

These were speedily conveyed from Rennes; and from the moment that they reached the camp of the assailants, they were worked against the walls without intermission, and with terrific effect. The most gallant defenders of the town began to lose hope; and the Bishop of Quimper *, who was within the walls, as a partizan of the house of Montford, now seemed to think it would be expedient for him to take advantage of the stipulations he had made on surrendering Carhaix, and go over to the more

* Froissart calls him Guy de Leon, but the historians of Britanny prove, beyond a doubt, that his name was Alain le Gal, Bishop of Quimper; and Dom Morice, a careful and diligent antiquary, seems to doubt that he was at all related to Henry de Leon, as Froissart declares. I have, however, retained the statement of the latter in this respect, because the influence that the prelate and the knight seem, on various occasions, to have exercised over each other warrants the supposition of some near connection.

powerful party. His nephew, Henry de Leon, who was now with the force besieging Hennebon, we have before seen attach himself to Charles of Blois, after the fall of Nantes and the capture of De Montford; and with him the Bishop opened a parley to insure himself recompence, whatever his defection might be worth. To render it more valuable, he was also induced to negotiate with the rest of the nobles and commanders in the city; and so powerful did his exhortations prove, that one after another forgot the zeal which had inspired them and the fortitude which had ennobled their zeal, and began only to think of the present danger, and the best means of obtaining immunity and reward. So much can the voice of one cold traitor sometimes do, to dull the finest enthusiasm and sink the most daring courage.

The unhappy Countess of Montford, who saw the designs that were working to her ruin, wept and petitioned in vain. Voice after voice was joined to the faction of the Bishop. Henry de Leon had notice that all would soon be arranged, and drew near with his forces to receive the surrender of the town. A faint refusal only was opposed by those who still held their honour and the house of Montford dear; and in a few minutes the gates of Hennebon would have been opened, and the wife and child of the imprisoned Count would have been given into the hands of his rival and his foe.

Joan of Montford herself had at length yielded to despair; and while the proceedings were taking place which seemed doomed to seal the destruction of her house and name for ever, she sat at a high window of the castle looking over the wide melancholy sea, which her eyes had so often explored for the long-promised and withheld aid from the English shore. As she looked, she beheld the mast of a vessel rising above the distant waves; another and another came rapidly upon her sight, as a strong and favourable wind wafted them towards the coast of France; ship after ship appeared, straining their canvas for the shore, and a mighty fleet covered the bosom of the waters.

"I see the succour so long desired," she, cried — "I see the succour so long desired!"

Her voice first called the attention of others; the tidings spread like lightning through the town; windows, and battlements, and loopholes, were instantly crowded with anxious spectators, while sailing gallantly on the English navy approached the port of the distressed city. *

* Though it is impossible to state, with any degree of accuracy, at what precise time Sir Walter de Mauny landed the army he brought to the aid of the Countess of Montford in Britanny, we have every reason, from various causes, to feel certain that it took place towards the middle of May 1342. It is proved that every thing was prepared for the departure of the troops in the middle of March. Froissart declares that the fleet was delayed sixty days by contrary winds, which would place their arrival about the 15th of May. We find also that by the 20th of July news had been received in England from Sir Walter de Mauny, who, Edward expressly says (in his letters patent appointing the Earl of Northampton his lieutenant in Britanny; Rymer, tom. ii. part iv. p. 131.), had already concluded a general treaty with the Countess de Montford. These letters, as well as some other papers connected with the early transactions in regard to Britanny, will be found at the end of this volume. I have been induced to give them at large, because I have found nothing but confusion and error reigning in the writings of

No one now dreamed of surrender but the Bishop, who soon discovered that his power was gone; and, disappointed and angry, he retired from the city, bearing the news of the change which had taken place in the situation and designs of the garrison, to the besiegers without.

The efforts of the assailants were instantly renewed with redoubled energy, in order, if possible, to force their way into the town before the reinforcements which approached could reach the port; but the

---

those historians who have entered at all into the detail of these events. Our greater historians, who, from the long series of years they have embraced, have been obliged to confine themselves to a general narrative, have preserved a more correct outline of the facts, though in some instances they have suffered themselves to be misled by very inferior authors. Rapin, never mentioning the expedition of Sir Walter de Manny, represents Joan of Montford as coming to England for assistance, and returning with Robert of Artois: declares that the Earl of Northampton took the command on the death of Robert of Artois, and that the siege of Stirling took place on account of the breach of the truce occasioned by the English invasion of Britanny.

That Joan of Montford did not come to England at all in 1342, is evident by the letters of Edward to the Earl of Northampton, in which he speaks of the negotiations held with that princess in Britanny, but never mentions any other. That she must have come before the date of those letters (22d of July) is clear, if, as Rapin states, she returned with Robert of Artois; for that prince was ready to embark on the 3d of the month of July, and had reached Britanny, performed a multitude of actions which must have required a long space of time, had been severely wounded, written to England after his wound, and was in great danger of death by the beginning of October. (Rymer, tom. ii. part iv. p. 136.) It may be, therefore, decidedly asserted that she never did quit Britanny during 1342, and that Froissart antedated an after visit. The Earl of Northampton was despatched to Britanny long before the death of Robert of Artois, even if he did not accompany him, as I feel sure he did; and it has been before shown that the renewal of war with Scotland, so far from being caused by Edward's aid to De Montford, prevented that aid from being despatched so early as the King intended.

hopes which were now re-awakened within the walls set all their attempts at defiance; and while the knights repelled the assault, and the Countess joyfully prepared a splendid reception for her deliverers, the English fleet sailed on with a fair and powerful breeze, and soon anchored under the walls of Hennebon.

Notwithstanding the massive stones which during the whole night were cast with fury against the outer defences of the city, joy and festivity reigned within; and early in the following day, Walter de Mauny, having viewed the capabilities of the place, and the dispositions of the enemy, proposed to the leaders of the garrison to sally forth and destroy the largest of the battering engines, which had now been brought close to the walls of the town. None held back, and in a few moments the principal knights were armed and ready for the field. The commander of the English forces, however, conducted his sortie with more skill and caution than we have hitherto seen; and, while fearless to a fault of his own person, he exposed himself wherever danger was to be found, he took care to provide for the support of his party in case of necessity, and to secure the means of retreat when his object should be accomplished. A large body of archers were in the first place drawn out along the fosse in the neighbourhood of the gate from whence the knights proposed to issue, and a band of three hundred more were ordered to precede the men at arms. These dispositions being made, De Mauny issued forth, and marched slowly forward towards the engine, against which his archers directed a murderous discharge, that soon drove the greater part of those who were working it from their station. Those who remained were put to the sword by the men at arms, and in a moment the immense machine itself was hewn to pieces. This being done before the rest of the French army were even aware that a sally had taken place, De Mauny and his companions dashed forward to the outer tents of the camp, killed the first opponents that they met, and, setting fire to the pavilions, retired slowly towards the city.

They were not destined, however, to re-enter the town unpursued. The French army by this time were alarmed, and getting under arms; and a number of knights might be seen issuing from the camp, and spurring like madmen after the small body which had performed so daring a feat.

The gate was near, and the way open; but the spirit of chivalry prevented De Mauny from taking advantage of the means of retreat, without fighting. "May I never be saluted by my lady love," cried he, "if I take refuge in castle or in fortress, till I overthrow one of these comers, or am myself overthrown!" and turning his bridle with lance in rest, he galloped forward upon the enemy. The other knights and esquires followed his example, and in a moment a number of cavaliers on both parts were cast to the earth.

The French party, however, increased every moment; and after maintaining a severe combat for some time, De Mauny found it necessary to draw off his troops and retire towards the town. This he accomplished slowly and in good order, till, reaching the fosse, he wheeled his forces and presented a firm face to the enemy, the knights interposing to cover the entrance of their followers, and receiving the whole weight of their adversaries' charge. It was now, however, that the archers who lined the edge of the fosse effected the purpose for which they had been thus stationed. Their arrows flew like lightning amongst the advancing array of the French. Men at arms, who thought themselves secure in their armour, were struck through the bars of their visors, or the defects of their mail. The horses, though loaded with iron, fell headlong under their riders, or, mad with stinging wounds, carried confusion through the ranks; and the French commanders, finding their loss every moment increasing, drew off their troops, while De Mauny, still without the gate, remained in possession of the field.

He did not retire himself till the enemy had re-entered their camp; and then, with this day's exploits adding immensely to the renown he had formerly acquired, he rode back to the castle, amidst the acclamations of the people. The Countess de Montford met her deliverers at the gate, and, with the curious simplicity of chivalrous times, kissed them each, one after the other, as the best means of expressing her gratitude and admiration.

With such succour she could no longer doubt of ultimate success. In one day, the engine which had caused the greatest damage and danger to the town had been destroyed, the French had been repulsed with great loss, her friends had recovered more than their former courage, her enemies had been deprived of the support of success; and she doubted not, either to maintain the town till the fresh reinforcements promised from England arrived, or to force the assailants to raise the siege by the efforts of her present force. She knew not, however, how soon that object was to be accomplished, without any farther exertions on her part.

The landing of such reinforcements as the garrison had received, of course put the besiegers and the defenders of Hennebon in a new relative position; and the proofs of skill and vigour given by the leader of the English, as well as the terror occasioned by the fearful effect of the British arrows, shook the resolution of Don Louis of Spain, who commanded the assailants, as well as dismayed his troops. Separated as he now was from Charles of Blois, and deprived of one half of the forces with which the siege had first commenced, he judged it most prudent to abandon an attempt which promised little ultimate success, and in the prosecution of which his troops were each day suffering immense losses.

He accordingly called to council the Viscount de Rohan, together with the Bishop of Quimper, Henry of Leon, and the chief of the Genoese mercenaries; and finding that all voices were in favour of decamping from before Hennebon as speedily as possible, he made his preparations to that effect. The following morning, being the third which had shone since the arrival of Walter de Mauny, the siege was raised, and the French commander marched to effect his junction with Charles of Blois, before the castle of Auray. Cries of mockery and derision saluted his forces as they decamped; and some parties issued from the town to harass them in their retreat. The pursuers, however, were promptly met, and were driven back to the walls with defeat and loss; while Louis of Spain continued his march uninterrupted, leaving Hennebon to restore its defences, and to renew its supplies in tranquillity.

CHAP. XII.

DON LOUIS OF SPAIN RAVAGES BRITANNY. — IS PURSUED AND DEFEATED NEAR QUIMPERLÉ BY SIR WALTER DE MAUNY.—UNSUCCESSFUL ATTEMPTS OF THE BRITISH FORCES AGAINST LA ROCHE-PERIOU AND FAOUET.—AURAY AND VANNES TAKEN BY CHARLES OF BLOIS.— AFFAIRS OF SPAIN.— SECOND SIEGE OF HENNEBON. — CRUELTY OF DON LOUIS OF SPAIN TOWARDS TWO PRISONERS.— EXPLOITS OF ALMERIC DE CLISSON AND WALTER DE MAUNY. — THE PRISONERS RESCUED. — THE EARL OF NORTHAMPTON AND ROBERT OF ARTOIS SAIL IN AID OF JOAN DE MONTFORD. — NAVAL ENGAGEMENT OFF GUERNSEY. — VANNES RETAKEN BY THE ENGLISH. — LEFT WITHOUT SUFFICIENT DEFENCE. — RETAKEN BY THE FRENCH. — DEATH OF ROBERT OF ARTOIS.

THE forces which the Countess of Montford could bring into the field, even after the arrival of Sir Walter de Mauny, were so greatly inferior in number to either of the divisions of the French army, that her only hope of winning any advantage over her enemies, previous to the coming of fresh reinforcements from England, lay in the skill and activity of her officers and partizans.

That activity, however, could not prevent the fall of many small towns and castles, which were besieged and taken one after another by the two armies with which Charles of Blois now occupied the open country. While he himself continued the siege of Auray, that prince directed Don Louis with his division to attack the small town of Dinan; and in his march thither the Spaniard made himself master of an old fortress called Conquet*, the walls of which were speedily pierced, and the garrison put to the sword. On this occasion, notwithstanding the inferiority of his forces, Sir Walter de Mauny had resolved to risk even a battle in order to save the brave men who held out Conquet for the house of Montford; and no sooner had he heard that it was attacked, than he had made all speed to afford it relief. Before he could reach the spot, however, the place had fallen; and having placed a garrison of sixty Spaniards to defend it, Don Louis had continued his march to Dinan. It was now again captured by De Mauny, as easily as it had been taken by the enemy; and, convinced that it was indefensible, that officer left it void.

* There seems to be great difficulties in regard to the account given by Froissart respecting the course of Don Louis, which was as erratic, according to his account, as can be well conceived. Proceeding from the southern to the northern side of Britanny, he is represented as taking Conquet, a place of which name is now found near Brest, in the very extreme west. He then returns to Guérande in the south; and then, by sea, again proceeds to the west. Nevertheless, as it would appear that the plan of Don Louis was to scour the country, and gain what advantages he could by sudden movements, it is not at all improbable that in these respects the account of Froissart may be right. In regard, however, to the distance of places from each other, he is undoubtedly wrong in many instances, unless we suppose that the names of the towns have changed throughout the whole country. Respecting Conquet, indeed, it is not unlikely that it was a different place from that at present known by the same name, as the account of it given by Froissart varies from the circumstances of Conquet near Brest more in other points than even in position, and more especially as the fortress mentioned by Froissart is stated to have then been in such a decayed condition as to be untenable. I am not aware whether the sea be advancing or receding upon the coast of Britanny in the present days; but from the accounts of all the old chronicles, it would appear that within the last 500 years a vast tract of land, bordering the coast, has been left dry, so that we find many places mentioned in the fourteenth century as situated upon the shore which are now several miles removed from sea.

While De Mauny returned to Hennebon, which had remained during his absence with too weak a garrison to defend it for any great length of time if attacked, Don Louis proceeded to Dinan; and having made himself master of that town, he returned to Guérande. Here he met with a vigorous resistance; but having obtained possession of the neighbouring port, he assailed the place on all sides; and taking it by storm, gave it up to the fury of the soldiery. Five churches were burned in the course of the pillage. But for this species of outrage Don Louis had a greater horror than for excesses equally brutal; and, in punishment of the sacrilege, he caused twenty of those who had committed it to be hung in the market-place.

He now determined to take the sea with the vessels which he had captured in the port of Guérande; and having sent back to Charles of Blois the greater part of the French lords who had accompanied him thus far, he embarked, with the Genoese and Spanish troops, to the number of near eight thousand men, and sailed direct for Quimperlé, a rich and populous town in Lower Britanny. Anchoring in the river Laita, he disembarked his troops; and leaving a guard to protect the vessels, he marched into the interior, plundering and desolating the country, and from time to time despatching the booty he obtained to swell the immense mass which he had brought in his ships from the pillage of Guérande.

The distance from Quimperlé to Hennebon is so insignificant, that news of the arrival and proceedings of the Spaniards and Genoese soon reached the ears of Walter de Mauny and Almeric de Clisson; and taking with them a number of other knights, and a body of English archers, amounting in all to three thousand men, they embarked in the ships which were in the port; and entering the Laita, soon made themselves masters of the enemies' fleet and all the treasure of which they had swept the country. Not contented, however, with this acquisition, De Mauny and Clisson disembarked their troops; and dividing them into three bodies, proceeded in search of their adversary. Such a disposition would undoubtedly have been highly faulty, considering the superior number of their enemies, had not the means of speedy communication and mutual aid been concerted between the various divisions before their march began. That such cooperation had been arranged is evident; and in this order they proceeded to search for Don Louis and his army.

The news that the English were marching to attack him, was not long in reaching the ears of the Spanish commander; and he immediately attempted to effect a retreat to his ships. By this time, however, the people of the country had risen on every side, to take vengeance on his troops for the devastation and violence they had committed; and large bodies of peasantry were hovering around his army, armed with clubs and pikes, and watching their opportunity to cut off any stragglers, or attack any small detachment. He was thus obliged to conduct his march with great care and circumspection; but before he reached the sea shore, he perceived one division of the English forces, and instantly prepared for battle. The commander of the French now only paused to create several new knights, amongst whom a nephew of his own, called Alphonso, was one; and then at the head of his troops charged the handful of English, who attempted to dispute his passage. There can be no doubt that, with the fearful odds of seven to one on their side, the Spaniards and Genoese might have annihilated their foes in a very short time, had not the other two bodies appeared upon the flanks. These fresh troops, however, were quickly brought into action ; the aspect of the battle was speedily changed ; and a severe and long-protracted struggle took place, which ended in the complete destruction of Don Louis's army.

His forces were broken and dispersed ; the armed peasantry put every fugitive they could overtake to death ; and, of seven thousand men with which the Spanish general had begun the battle, only three hundred accompanied him in flight. His nephew had fallen on the field ; and he himself, severely wounded in several places, turned his horse's head towards his ships, not knowing that they had fallen into the hands of the enemy. Finding such to be the case, he embarked on board the first small vessel he could meet with, and made his escape to Redon*, chased

* A small town on the Vilaine, which serves as a port to Rennes, from which it is distant about sixteen leagues. Some copies of Froissart, it is to be remarked, read Vannes instead of Rennes, a distance of about twelve leagues. I have adopted the supposition, however, of the generality of the historians of Britanny, that the town to which Don Louis fled was Rennes, notwithstanding the additional distance; because it does not appear either that Vannes had yet been captured by Charles of Blois, or, if it had been so, that the news had yet reached Louis of Spain.

by De Mauny, and the British forces which had followed him from the field of battle to the port.

No time was allowed the fugitive to pause at Redon, for the indefatigable foe came fast upon him; and procuring what horses the place afforded for himself and his followers, he spurred on to Rennes, to the very gates of which city he was pursued by English and Breton men at arms.

Retiring from before a place which he had not sufficient forces to reduce, Walter de Mauny endeavoured to return to Hennebon by sea; but finding the wind contrary, he landed, and made several unsuccessful attempts upon different fortresses in the vicinity of the coast.

From one of the fortresses attacked, called La Roche-Periou, he was drawn off by the bold stratagem of an officer called Regnier de Maulin, brother of the governor of La Roche, and himself commander of a fort in the vicinity named Faouet. This officer, hearing that his relation was besieged, advanced to within a very short distance of the English army; and finding two wounded knights, called John Boteler and Hubert de Fresnoy, who had been carried to the rear, he made himself master of their persons, and bore them away as prisoners to Faouet, with the greater part of those who had been left to attend them. The news was almost instantly communicated to De Mauny; and ceasing the assault of La Roche-Periou, he pursued the party of Regnier de Maulin, in order to deliver his wounded companions. That officer, however, had already reached his castle; and the fatigue which the English soldiers had already suffered prevented the assault of Faouet from being severely pressed before night.

In the meanwhile, Gerard de Maulin who commanded in the neighbouring fortress, attributing the departure of the English from his own walls to the right cause, issued forth, and rode with all speed to Dinan, in order to return the service his brother had rendered him by leading a sufficient force to his relief. Six thousand men were speedily assembled, and marched early the next morning for Faouet; but before their arrival Walter de Mauny had received intimation of the danger which threatened him, and, though with great regret, had been forced to raise the siege. He now turned his steps towards Hennebon once more; but passing near the castle of Goy la Forêt on his way, he took the sudden resolution of attacking it, notwithstanding the weariness of his troops. The garrison defended the place with the utmost bravery, although their commander was absent at the time; but De Mauny leading the assault in person with an ardour which nothing could withstand, the ditches were filled up, in spite of all the efforts of the defenders; and a considerable part of the wall being thrown down, the Bretons and the English rushed in, and terminated the contest within the fort by the death of all who resisted. From that place De Mauny led his troops straight to Hennebon, where he was received with no small joy, as many events had occurred which rendered it highly probable that the Countess de Montford would have to undergo another siege, in the city which she had before so gallantly defended.

By this time Charles of Blois had made himself master of Auray, the garrison of which, after living for many days upon the flesh of their horses, had endeavoured to force their passage through the besieging army. Most of them perished in the attempt; but Henry and Oliver De Spinefort made their way with a few followers to Hennebon, and brought the tidings that the French army was increasing every day.

Vannes, a much more important conquest, followed quickly upon that of Auray, the burghers having treated with Charles of Blois shortly after the siege commenced, notwithstanding all the efforts of the famous Geoffrey de Malestroit, who with difficulty effected his own escape to Hennebon. Carhaix was next besieged, and was soon forced to surrender; and still it appeared that every day added something to the numbers of the French force, a fact which may require some explanation.

During the wars between France and England, a struggle even more sanguinary had been carried on in Spain, between Alphonso XI., King of Castille and Leon, and the Moorish Princes, who still held under their sway some of the finest portions of the Peninsula. The gallant monarch of Spain had on many occasions applied to France and England for support; and the spirit of the crusades was not yet so far extinct that the chivalry of either land could behold, indifferent, the strife between a Christian king and infidel adversaries. No sooner then was the truce of Tournay concluded, than a great number of French and English nobles set out to aid in the war of the Peninsula; and many *, we are told, arrived in time to be present at the battle of Tariffa, in which Alphonso, with an army of 35,000 foot and 14,000 horse, defeated a Moorish force, which, whatever was was its real number, poets and historians have magnified to 600,000 men. The whole details of this victory as related by contemporaries, though great and extraordinary it certainly was, are somewhat more miraculous than credible; the account of the Moorish loss varying from 200,000 to 450,000 men, while the best historians only allow that 20 were killed upon the part of the Christians.

Such a splendid triumph drew the eyes of all Christendom to Spain; and from France, especially, a crowd of knights and gentlemen hastened to share in the glories of the war with the Moors. From this period till the siege of Algesiras, which followed, and was protracted for some time by the determined resistance of the garrison, a long series of hostilities took place between the Christians and the Moors of Spain; and thus a war which engaged a multitude of the boldest and most enterprising of the French nobility, and from which they did not feel themselves at liberty to withdraw, was prolonged for several months after the struggle had begun in Britanny be-

* Such a fact is possible; the truce having been proclaimed on the 25th of September 1340, and the battle taking place on the 30th of October of the same year, leaving thirty-five days for the journey.

tween the houses of Montford and Blois. Occasional truces, however, supervened between the Spaniards and the Moors, which were gladly seized by many of the volunteers as opportunities of returning to their own land; and the French army, in the neighbourhood of Carhaix and Vannes, received daily reinforcements of veteran troops from Spain.

The news of the increasing strength of the adverse force, and the demonstrations which Charles of Blois made upon Hennebon, showed to De Mauny and the Countess of Montford the absolute necessity of an immediate application to Edward III. for some fresh support. That monarch had already promised the aid of a much larger body of men than he had sent at first, and had intimated that thereunto he would ultimately add his own presence in defence of the house of Montford; but many pecuniary difficulties had impeded the prompt execution of his engagements, and messengers were now despatched by the Countess to hasten the arrival of whatever troops were prepared.*

A very considerable force had by this time been raised; and being placed under the command of the Earl of Northampton and Robert of Artois, it sailed for Britanny either in the end of July, or the beginning of August.† Twenty-seven bannerets and

* Rymer tom ii. part ii. page 131. Froissart, chap. clxxxv.

† It will be seen from the papers concerning Britanny, at the end of this volume, that if Robert of Artois and the Earl of Northampton did not set forth together for Britanny, a space of nineteen days was all that intervened between the periods of their departure. To me, however, it appears clear that Robert of Artois commanded no separate expedition, notwithstanding the assertion of Froissart; for from the 3d of July

2,000 men we find distinctly specified on this occasion; and in the list are some of the most famous names in history, whose very renown must have proved of infinite advantage to Joan of Montford in the perilous crisis through which she was now about to pass.

Before the English armament could reach the shores of Britanny, however, Hennebon was once more besieged; but by an army greatly superior in force

---

1342, on which day Edward signed an order for certain sums towards defraying his expences, we find day after day various matters of the same kind transacted in regard to other noblemen, showing that some expedition was in preparation of which they were all to form a part, till at length on the 22nd and 23d of the same month came the full powers of Vicegerent in France and Britanny, directed to the Earl of Northampton as commander in chief. From the 1st of August all reference to the expedition ceases in the public papers of the period, till Edward, on the 15th of August in that year, speaks of it as "Exercitus in partes transmarinas jam transmissus," while ordering another army to be raised to accompany himself. All the troops thus levied received regular pay, the amount of which we find stated in the King's letters addressed to the collectors of wool in the various counties of England, but more particularly in the order in favour of Ralph of Stafford (Rymer, vol. ii. part ii. p. 1202, edit. of 1821), in which the pay of each banneret is calculated at four *solidi*, that of each knight two *solidi*, of each squire 12 deniers, and each horse archer six deniers. Twenty solidi went to the pound, and twelve deniers to the solidus; but it is very difficult to tell the exact value of the solidus or sol at a time when the currency was undergoing very great changes, and prices were continually varying. Le Blanc, who wrote in the reign of Louis XIV., calculated that in the time of Philip of Valois it was nearly ten times more valuable than in his day; and I find by the tables at the end of his work that in April 1342, the price of the marc of silver was 13 livres 10 sous. (Le Blanc, Traité des Monnoyes, pages 24. and 317.) I am led indeed to believe that the relative value of our money, compared with that of the times to which I allude, is about one twelfth; and therefore that the solidus, or twentieth part of a pound, may be looked upon as rather more than twelve shillings; but I speak from a very limited knowledge of the subject.

to that which had before sat down beneath its walls. Nevertheless, that city also possessed advantages on the present occasion which it had been without before. Time had been given to construct engines, and lay up provisions and military stores. A much larger garrison was within the walls than that which had maintained it during the former siege; and this garrison was commanded by an officer of whose fidelity, fortitude, and skill, there could be no doubt, whose high renown was plighted to the most energetic defence of the place, and whose constant success gave confidence and vigour to his companions and to the soldiers. At the same time the city itself had undergone an active siege, and repelled a powerful enemy — the strongest inducement and the surest pledge to do the same again.

The troops of Charles of Blois invested the fortress on every side; but it must be remembered that, on this occasion, it was merely by drawing his camp round it that he attempted the blockade, and that no strong lines, as in a modern siege, at once protected the assailants and restrained the garrison. The defenders of Hennebon perceived the approach of the enemy unalarmed; and Charles of Blois soon found that although his engines continued night and day to batter the walls, such means of precaution had been taken, while the town had remained in tranquillity, that little effect was produced upon the defences, and none upon the place itself. A few days after the commencement of the siege, Don Louis of Spain, now recovered from his wounds, arrived in the camp of the besiegers, thirsting for vengeance upon the victors of Quimperlé, and breathing nothing but wrath and destruction against those who had given him so signal a defeat. The garrison of Hennebon, however, only aggravated the motives for anger which they had before afforded; and brutally insulted their enemies when they approached the walls, by shouting to them to seek their friends in the fields of Quimperlé.

This ungenerous mockery raised the passions of Don Louis to a pitch of desperate cruelty, almost unexampled in the history of chivalrous warfare. Hearing that Sir John Boteler and Sir Hubert De Fresnoy* had been captured before la Roche-Periou, and were still kept as prisoners at Faouet, he one morning entered the tent of Charles of Blois, which was nearly filled with the nobles of France; and, according to a very frequent custom of those times, demanded a boon in requital of all his services.

Charles of Blois at once acceded, when, to his horror and surprise, Don Louis replied, "Many thanks, my lord. I pray and require you then to cause those two knights, Sir John le Boteler and Sir Hubert de Fresnoy, who are now in your prison at Faouet, to be brought hither and delivered to me, that I may work my will upon them. This is the boon I demand. They have pursued, discomfited, and wounded me, and killed the nephew whom I loved so well; and as I have no other mode of vengeance, I will cut off their heads before their companions who lie there within."

* There seems to be some doubt in regard to the Christian names of these two knights.

Charles of Blois, and all his followers, were struck dumb with amazement and grief at a demand so contrary to all the chivalrous customs of the times; and as soon as they recovered from their surprise, attempted by every means in their power to turn their savage ally from his purpose: but their endeavours were used in vain; and after reasoning and beseeching for a long time, but with no effect, they were obliged to choose between the breach of a promise so inadvertently made and so cruelly employed, and an act of base and ungenerous brutality. Unfortunately their ideas of honour induced them to prefer the greater crime to the less; and the unhappy knights were sent for, and told by the mouth of Don Louis himself that their last day had arrived. At first they would scarcely believe that so notorious an infraction of all the laws of war and honour could be seriously proposed; and when they could no longer doubt that it was the intention of their ungenerous enemy to put them to death, they represented to him in the strongest terms what a stain such an act would leave upon his name as a knight, and how fearful might be the consequences were such a new system of warfare once begun.

The Spaniard, however, was not to be turned from his purpose, either by their remonstrances or by the reiterated petitions of his own companions; and allowing them only a few hours to prepare for death, by performing the ceremonial duties of their religion, he appointed their execution, or rather murder, to take place immediately after the dinner of the army.

All that had occurred was soon made known in Hennebon by some of the many spies, who in those days enjoyed an extraordinary degree of toleration in all camps and armies; and horror and anger took possession of the English and Breton leaders, on the news of the ignominious death about to be inflicted upon their gallant but unfortunate comrades. A council was immediately called, and various methods were proposed for compelling the enemy to refrain from their savage design; but at length Walter de Mauny declared his purpose, which, though the boldest of all, was both the most feasible and the most effectual.

His exordium alone showed the gallant spirit in which the plan was conceived, and which, calculating the very worst consequences that could follow, set a generous object against the fear of captivity or death, and hesitated not for a moment.

"Lords companions," he said, "it would be great honour to us if we could save these two knights; and if we put ourselves in risk and peril, and succumb, still will our Lord, King Edward, hold us high, as well as every gallant gentleman who hears our deeds in time to come; because we have done to the utmost of our power."

He then went on to detail his plan, which was instantly adopted; and without loss of time Almeric de Clisson, on whom the execution of one part of the design rested, issued forth from the great gate of Hennebon, accompanied by 300 men at arms, and 1000 archers. The latter were instantly ranged along the ditches; and the men at arms rode direct towards the enemies' camp, which was undefended, the whole army being within their tents at dinner. Plunging into the midst, the Englishmen and the Bretons began to overturn the pavilions, and run down with their lances every one they met, till the whole army were alarmed. Not knowing the extent of the danger, or the smallness of the attacking force, the French knights sprang up from table; and, mounting their horses, hurried to encounter the assailants. They on their part for some time maintained their ground, till finding that the whole camp was on foot, Almeric de Clisson began to retreat towards the town, fighting step by step; and, notwithstanding the inferiority of his numbers, occupying a great part of the French army by the tremendous exertions he made to defend each hillock on his return. As they approached the town the archers began to draw their bows; and it seemed so evidently the design of De Clisson to risk a general battle under the walls, that the whole French force crowded to the spot.

In the meanwhile Sir Walter de Mauny, with 100 men at arms and 500 horse archers, issued from a distant sally port, and with all speed directed his course to the rear of the French camp. There he found none to oppose him but valets and camp followers; and making his way straight to the tent of Charles of Blois, where the two knights were confined, he soon freed them from their bonds. The joy of men so suddenly delivered from the near apprehension of an ignominous death needs no description. Without wasting the precious moments of which so few remained for escape, Sir Walter de Mauny mounted his two comrades upon fleet horses, which had been brought for the purpose; and turning again towards Hennebon he was out of danger, and had nearly reached the postern before the fugitives from the camp announced to the French commanders his bold enterprise, and its complete success.

The army of Charles of Blois immediately retired from a skirmish the object of which was now explained. Two of the principal Breton leaders, however, the Lord of Landremans and the Castellan of Guingant, had fallen into the hands of the French in the course of that morning's strife. Towards these knights no cruelty was exercised; and Charles of Blois found means to win them from the service of De Montford to his own, with a degree of facility which did not enhance their reputation with either party.

Both the events of that morning, and the information given him by his new friends, showed so clearly to Charles of Blois the undiminished spirit of the garrison, that considering the abundance of provisions which Hennebon received by water, and that the country around afforded him by this time scarcely any supplies, he determined once more upon raising the siege, and attacking some other place where he was not likely to be opposed by such formidable obstacles.*

* I have before noticed the inaccuracy of Froissart in regard to this part of the wars in Britanny. He here states that the siege of Hennebon was raised late in the year 1342, and yet makes the Countess of Montford go to England afterwards, and arrive in London towards the middle of August; the expedition of Robert of Artois he places in 1343, though we find by the state papers that he was dead before the 20th of November 1342. In marking the mistakes committed by Froissart, I mark those of Barnes, who has followed him blindly through all his

This resolution was put in force the next day; and drawing off his troops to Carhaix, he allowed them some time to repose. The strong town of Jugon was soon after betrayed to him by one of the burghers, who had been taken prisoner by Robert of Beaumanoir; and the castle, which attempted to hold out, was forced to surrender from want of the necessary provisions.

In the mean time *, the report that a large armament under the Earl of Northampton had set out from England, for the purpose of reinforcing the Countess of Montford, reached the French army; and Don Louis, together with the Genoese and other Italian mercenaries, embarked on board a fleet of large vessels, which had been collected on the coast, and put to sea for the purpose of intercepting the English transports. The two fleets met off the island of Guernsey; and a severe engagement took

errors in regard to this war, amongst which are the supposed voyage of the Countess de Montford, a truce which is said to have taken place between her and Charles of Blois at this time, and which could not have taken place, and her presence at the combat off Guernsey, as well as the placing the latter event and even Edward's own expedition in the spring of 1343, when it is evident that they were both concluded in the autumn of 1342, as may be seen by the state papers published in Rymer.

* I have received the account of Froissart in regard to a naval engagement between Don Louis and the fleet under the Earl of Northampton, because it is confirmed by the historians of Britanny, and because other contemporary accounts mention such a battle without giving the same details; but not believing, as I have before stated, that the Countess of Montford visited England at all, I have rejected Froissart's statement, so far as it refers to her. I do not find it absolutely asserted that Louis of Spain set out with the purpose of encountering the English fleet; but I conclude from the haste with which he must have embarked, and the course which he steered, that he must have received intelligence of the Earl of Northampton's departure from England.

place, which lasted till night. During the darkness that ensued, a tremendous storm divided the hostile armaments; and Louis of Spain, having captured the next day four small vessels charged with ammunition and horses, which had been separated from the English fleet, was driven by the tempest to the coast of Spain.

Robert of Artois and the Earl of Northampton in the mean time pursued their way to Britanny *, and

* Froissart states the numbers of the English on this occasion to have amounted to 1000 men at arms and 3000 archers (chap. 199.), and the History of Bretagne raises them to 4000 men at arms and 6000 archers. The numbers mentioned in the various state papers that I have met with do not amount to quite 800 men at arms and less than 1000 archers; but as Edward himself speaks of the force as *magnus exercitus armatorum*, it is certain that many of the orders have been lost, or are withheld from the public. I subjoin, as affording a curious insight into the economy of the English armies, an account of the various forces brought into the field on this occasion by the nobles specified in Rymer.

Names of Leaders.	Total of Men-at-arms.	Of whom there were				Total of Archers, Horse or Foot.
		Earls.	Bannerets.	Knights.	Squires.	
Ralph Lord Stafford	50		3	16	31	50 horse.
Robert of Artois	120		5	29	86	120 foot.
William of Kildesley	50		1	10	39	100 foot.
Earl of Suffolk	51	1	1	14	35	50 horse.
Reginald Lord Cobham	40		1	9	30	40 horse.
Philip of Weston	20		1	3	16	20 horse.
Thomas of Hatfield	20		1	3	16	20 horse.
Earl of Warwick	80	1	1	18	60	100 horse.
Earl of Oxford	40	1	1	9	29	30 horse.
Michael of Ponynges	15		1	4	10	12 horse.
Thomas of Bradstone	20		1	4	15	20 horse.
Maurice of Berkley	20		1	4	15	20 horse.
Courtney Earl of Devonshire	50	1	1	12	36	60 horse.
Audley Earl of Gloucester	100					
Hastings Earl of Pembroke	60	1	2	12	45	100 horse.
Robert Ferrers	40		1	14	25	40 horse.
Totals,	776					782

landed not far from the city of Vannes, to which they immediately laid siege. The news of their arrival brought Sir Walter de Mauny to their aid from Hennebon; and, after various efforts to storm the town, a general assault was given on three different points, which lasted the whole day, and completely exhausted the garrison with fatigue. Towards nightfall, Robert of Artois and the Earl of Northampton withdrew to their camp; and Oliver Lord of Clisson, who commanded in the town for Charles of Blois, though many of his family were attached to the adverse party, suffered his weary troops to quit the walls, and retire to seek refreshment and repose. Nothing, however, was farther from the intention of the besiegers than to abandon the assault; and, as soon as they had given the garrison time to disarm, two strong parties, at the suggestion of Robert of Artois, were directed to attack the principal entrances of the town, while Walter de Mauny and the Earl of Oxford, after lying concealed till the whole disposable forces of the place were drawn to the defence of the gates, proceeded to attempt an escalade on the opposite side. This plan was completely successful; and while, at the first alarm, the weary garrison armed in all haste, and flew to the points where the enemy appeared, Oxford and De Mauny made their way into the town unopposed, and attacked the defenders in the rear. Terror and confusion immediately followed. All resistance was abandoned; and those thought themselves most happy who could effect their escape into the country through the various sally ports. Amongst these were the two chief knights to whom the defence of Vannes had been entrusted, Oliver de Clisson and Hervé de Léon *, both of whom, at no very distant period, contributed to avenge the defeat they had this night sustained.

Robert of Artois now established himself in Vannes, and the troops which had come to his aid from Hennebon returned thither with all speed; while the Earl of Salisbury †, accompanied by about 4000 men, proceeded to lay siege to Rennes, from which city Charles of Blois had retired to Nantes a few days before.

The forces thus left with Robert of Artois were but scanty for the defence of a town, the inhabitants of which were not very strenuous in their affection to the house of Montford. At the same time much wrath and indignation was felt throughout the party of Charles of Blois, that so strong a city, well supplied with provisions, ammunition, and men, should have been so easily captured by the English. None felt more bitterness of spirit on the occasion than Hervé de Leon and the Lord of Clisson; and, determined to make every effort to wipe out the effects

* I find this officer here called Hervé, while, on former occasions, we have seen a Henry de Leon acting as a most serviceable friend, first to Montford and then to Blois. Whether the same person was meant, but the name mispelt, I cannot tell.

† The Earl of Salisbury had received permission from Edward to pledge himself not to bear arms against Philip of Valois within the territory of *France, in case his liberation could not be procured on other terms* (Rymer, tom. ii. part iv.). The language in which the oath required of him is stated admits of no doubt that such a war as that in Britanny was included in the stipulation, as Philip not only states that he was not to appear in arms against himself, but against any of his adherents. It would appear, then, as the Earl of Salisbury was certainly employed in these wars, that notwithstanding the first demands of the King of France, and the permission given by Edward, he found means to obtain his liberty without yielding to such a galling condition.

of their surprise, they proceeded through the country, raising volunteers from amongst the soldiery in all the neighbouring towns and castles, till at length towards the end of September, they sat down before Vannes with an army of 12,000 men. Thither also came the famous Beaumanoir, Marshal of Bretagne for Charles of Blois; and an immediate assault was determined on, lest the troops besieging Rennes, and those which had retired to Hennebon, should return before the garrison were forced to surrender if slower means were adopted. Shame and anger made a number of the commanders and soldiers amongst the assailants perform feats of valour and daring which nothing but the desire to wipe away disgrace could prompt. Such an example had of course its effect upon the rest. The barriers were soon won, notwithstanding every effort of the garrison; the gates were forced after a tremendous slaughter on both sides; and the partisans of the house of Blois pouring into the town, the small garrison which the place contained met with the usual fate of those who have failed in repelling an assault. One of the Le Despencers received quarter, but it was only to die of his wounds at the end of three days. The Lord Stafford contrived to cut a passage out for himself and Robert of Artois, whom he conveyed by a postern into the open country and thence removed severely wounded to Hennebon.

Grief for his defeat, embarrassment in regard to various debts he had contracted since his arrival in Britanny*, and the memory of a life of lost advan-

* Rymer, tom ii. part iv. p. 136.

tages and perished hopes, weighed down the wounded frame of Robert of Artois, and contributed to hasten his fate. He wrote, it would appear, to Edward, stating his circumstances; and that monarch, with the kind feeling which he had always shown towards the unhappy exile, did all in his power to sweep away such of his difficulties as any earthly hand could remove.* This kindness, however, was exerted in vain: not long after Robert of Artois arrived at Hennebon, the dysentery was added to the other evils under which the wounded knight laboured, and he died before Edward himself reached the shores of Britanny.†

Thus ended the life of Robert of Artois, a prince over whose character hangs a veil which may probably never be removed. That he was brave, courteous, and liberal, is proved beyond a doubt; but some of the most severe and dishonouring accusations which can be levelled at man, were brought

* It is not very clear on what day Robert of Artois died, though it must have taken place within the first ten days of November, 1342. He was not expected to live on the 6th of October (Rymer, ubi supra), and he was said to be dead on the 20th November (Rymer, tom. ii. part iv. page 138.). It is scarcely necessary to say that the whole of the story given by Barnes and others of his having been brought to London, and of Edward undertaking the expedition to Britanny in order to avenge his death, is perfectly erroneous. Edward had reached Britanny before the 12th of November; and the death of Robert of Artois was still doubted in London on the 20th of that month, though it proved that the reports received of his death were accurate. Edward had positively embarked, also, by the 4th of October, although in all probability he did not sail for some days afterwards (Rymer, tom. ii. part iv. p. 135.); and the first letters patent of his son as guardian of the realm in that year refer to Robert of Artois as living; so that Edward of course did not sail to avenge the death of a person who was still alive.

† Knighton, col. 2582.

against him during his life; and though they rest, as we have them before us now, upon the very doubtful testimony of interested persons, they cannot be disproved by any thing but general inferences. Some facts, however, seem certain—that he was wronged in regard to the county of Artois, that he was unfortunate, and that he was a traitor.

CHAP. XIII.

EDWARD III. SAILS FOR BRITANNY IN PERSON.—TAKES PLOERMEL, MALESTROIT, REDON, ETC., AND BESIEGES VANNES.— THE LORDS OF CLISSON, LOHEAC, MACHECOUL, AND RETZ, COME OVER TO THE PARTY OF DE MONTFORD. — THE POPE SENDS LEGATES TO TREAT CONCERNING PEACE. — THE EARLS OF NORFOLK AND WARWICK ATTACK NANTES. — RAISE THE SIEGE AND RETIRE ON THE APPROACH OF THE DUKE OF NORMANDY. — THE ENGLISH STRAITENED IN THEIR CAMP.— THE LEGATES OBTAIN A TRUCE. — THE TREATY OF MALESTROIT. — VIOLATED BY PHILIP, WHO PUTS TO DEATH FIFTEEN BRETON NOBLES. — INDIGNATION OF THE KING OF ENGLAND AND OF THE FRENCH NOBILITY.—SEVERAL OF THE NOBLES OF NORMANDY PUT TO DEATH BY PHILIP.— GODFREY OF HARCOURT MAKES HIS ESCAPE, AND ULTIMATELY TAKES REFUGE IN ENGLAND.

THE bodies of troops which Edward had hitherto sent into Britanny were intended alone as a temporary aid granted to the Countess of Montford in order to support her in her struggle to maintain possession of the duchy, till the English king could himself lead his forces into France in the more immediate pursuit of the grand object of his ambition. The armament under Robert of Artois and the Earl of Northampton had scarcely quitted the port, when Edward himself began active preparations to follow them with far more considerable forces. Where he obtained the necessary resources does not appear *;

* Immediately after Edward's departure, very large sums were borrowed from the clergy by Prince Edward and the council, in order to supply his father's expences beyond sea. A long list of the bishops

for we find no new parliamentary grants, and in the beginning of the year in which all these vast efforts were undertaken, the King is seen pressed by his creditors from Cologne, and placed, by the difficulty of fulfilling his engagements, in a situation which may well be looked upon as both hurtful and degrading even when affecting a private individual.* It seems probable indeed that, trusting to future successes to discharge debts already contracted, Edward applied the greater part of the means which had been especially granted for the liquidation of old encumbrances to the execution of the new enterprises to which he had bound himself.

Large forces were collected, ships were prepared, an army of observation was stationed upon the Scottish frontier; and the Prince Edward being once more appointed custos of the kingdom, the monarch himself proceeded to Sandwich in order to embark. Thither also were brought from the Tower all the large and tremendous engines for battering besieged towns, which had been used with signal effect in the wars of Scotland ; but the number of vessels collected not being sufficient to transport both the royal army and those implements of destruction, Edward was obliged to leave behind the means of prosecuting any siege with vigour and rapidity.†

---

and abbots who were obliged to make these involuntary loans, together with the sums extorted from each, may be found in Rymer, vol. ii. part iv. page 137.

* Rymer, tom. ii. part iv. p. 118.

† Ibid., p. 134.

Although we have reason to believe that the forces which accompanied the monarch must have been very considerable, from the number of vessels employed in their transit, and from the various great enterprises that they immediately undertook, Edward, whose designs extended much farther than the mere establishment of the house of Montford in the duchy of Britanny, had taken every precaution to ensure the arrival of large and continual reinforcements; nor did he, during the whole time of his stay on the Continent, cease for any length of time to encourage and command the levying of men throughout England, and their speedy embarkation for Britanny.* Such precautions afforded abundant materials for the war in which he was now about personally to engage, and of course enabled him to undertake many enterprises of much greater importance than had hitherto been attempted in favour of the Countess de Montford.

On what precise day Edward sailed from the port of Sandwich† is doubtful, but he had arrived in Britanny early in November; and marching forward through the country, soon reduced‡ Ploermel, Males-

* Rymer, tom ii. part iv. pp. 137. 139, 140.

† Edward must have sailed either the 5th or 6th of October. A memorandum of the delivery of the great seal into his hands on board the George, on the 4th October, then on his passage to Britanny, is preserved in Rymer, tom ii. part iv. page 135.; but we find in the same page the letters patent appointing Edward the Black Prince custos of the realm, bearing date the 5th, and on the 6th we find (from the following page) the custos began to exercise his power, showing that the King had set sail.

‡ It will be seen that in all points where the letter of Edward him-

trait, Redon, and the rest of the province, in the vicinity of Vannes.* That city, as the strongest seaport in the hands of the enemy, and as the third town in point of importance in Britanny, Edward next besieged with his whole army; and while Charles of Blois, and Philip of Valois made every exertion to raise sufficient forces for its deliverance, the Count of Valentinois, who commanded in the place, and the garrison with which it was furnished, showed their resolution to defend it to the last with the most persevering fortitude. As the troops which accompanied him were far more than sufficient to carry on the siege, Edward despatched a considerable body, under the Earls of Norfolk and Warwick, in the direction of Nantes, with orders to reconnoitre the country, and take advantage of any opportunity which might offer. Nor was it alone Edward's intention to gain strong places and

---

self, preserved in Robert of Avesbury, differs from the account of Froissart, I have of course followed the former; and although Monsieur Dacier has endeavoured to reconcile the two narratives, they appear to me in almost all particulars totally irreconcilable. Especially the important point of the adherence of the Lord of Clisson and his companions is represented quite differently by the two, Froissart declaring that they were taken in the latter part of the siege of Vannes, while Edward states that they had made voluntary submission immediately after his arrival. On this very point the war was afterwards renewed. Let no one whose mind is imbued with the details given by Froissart, and copied by other historians, conceive that I am incorrect in the statements here given, without consulting the letter of Edward to his son, a document of the authenticity of which there can be no doubt; remembering at the same time that on the 5th of December, when it was written, Edward could not have the slightest object in misrepresenting the facts to which I allude.

* Robert de Avesbury, p. 98.

cities by force of arms; but every means of persuasion were tried to bring over adherents to the Countess of Montford, and to weaken the party of Charles of Blois. In this object the King was more successful than even in his warlike operations; and in his letters to his son he announces, almost immediately after his arrival, that the Lords of Clisson, of Loheac, of Machecoul, of Retz, and several others, had given in their adherence to the party which he protected.

In the meanwhile other events were bringing about a temporary suspension of hostilities. The news of the warlike preparations of the King of England had reached the Continent long before he himself appeared; and Clement VI., who had succeeded in the beginning of the year to the papal chair *; vacant by the death of Benedict XII., proceeded in the same charitable course wherein his predecessor had led the way, and seemed determined, by every means within the scope of his new authority, to put an end to the hostilities between France and England. Scarcely had Edward been three days before Vannes, when missives from the Holy See presented themselves in his camp, desiring letters of safe conduct for two cardinals legates, who had already advanced some way on the road to Britanny; Edward immediately granted the demand, permitting their approach as far as Malestroit. In the mean time, however, he paused not in his military operations; but even while carrying on the

* L'Abbé Chron. Technic. 1342.

siege of Vannes with vigour and activity, he made himself master of a number of other towns in the duchy, sometimes proceeding against them in person, sometimes detaching towards them a part of his forces under the command of an experienced leader.*

* The account of these events, as given by Froissart, cannot be correct, and therefore it may be as well to mark the few dates by which his statement may be rectified. He declares that Edward first attacked Vannes, and, while the siege was going on, proceeded to join the force which was assailing Rennes; thence marched to Nantes, and besieged it for some time; left it attacked by several of his officers, and marched to Dinan, which he captured; and then returned to Vannes, where the Duke of Normandy soon after appeared to raise the siege. After this the cardinals legates arrived, and concluded the truce. The following dates are derived from public documents and the letter of the King himself, and therefore are not subject to the same dubiety.

By the 12th November 1342, Edward had arrived in Britanny.

By the 5th December, he had taken Ploermel, Malestroit, and Redon; had besieged Vannes for some days; and had despatched the Earls of Norfolk and Warwick towards Nantes, but had not heard any tidings from them.

By the 21st of December the cardinals had reached the army of the King before Vannes, and never ceased to go from one host to the other, exhorting the monarchs to peace, till they had obtained a suspension of hostilities, which ended in the treaty of Malestroit, dated 19th of January 1343.

The only period then in which Edward could have moved from Vannes to Rennes, from Rennes to Nantes, from Nantes to Dinan, and from Dinan back to Vannes, lies between the 5th and 21st December; and as the distance by the nearest calculation was 300 miles, it will at once appear impossible that Edward could march a large army that space, besiege three cities, and stay before each of them several days, in the space of a fortnight. In regard to the general facts, it is probable that Froissart was correct; and that Dinan was taken, as well as that Rennes was besieged and Nantes attempted, by the English: which latter fact we know from other sources was really the case. It is improbable, however, that Edward was present at any one of those sieges, and impossible that he could have undertaken them in succession, as described by Froissart.

The Earls of Norfolk and Warwick, during the course of these proceedings, approached Nantes, and laid siege to it with the forces which had accompanied them. As their numbers, however, were not sufficient to invest the town, they were obliged to confine their operations to various attempts to take it by storm; and these also, they were soon induced to relinquish by the news that John Duke of Normandy was marching in force from Angiers, for the purpose of raising the sieges of Nantes and Vannes. This intelligence, which also reported the force of the Prince at forty thousand men, with the prospect of its hourly increase, immediately decided the Earl of Norfolk to fall back upon the royal army, which he executed without difficulty.

Shortly after this retreat, the Duke of Normandy appeared at Nantes; and, being joined by Charles of Blois, marched forward upon Vannes, and encamped at a little distance from the English army. The numerical force of the French, which appears to have been about four times that of the English, now required the recal of all Edward's parties; and the siege of Rennes was in consequence raised, having been distinguished by very few matters worthy of record, except some of the first exploits of the noble Bertrand du Guesclin, afterwards so famous as the deliverer of France.

After the junction of all these detachments, the English force still continued greatly inferior to that commanded by the Duke of Normandy; and the arrival of Philip of Valois, who soon after followed his son as far as Ploermel with considerable reinforcements, rendered the situation of the King of England still more precarious.* The Duke of Normandy entrenched his camp strongly, and seemed resolved by rendering the capture of Vannes utterly hopeless, either to force Edward to attack the French army under great disadvantages, or to drive him forth by weariness and want of provisions, a growing scarcity of which was already felt in the English host. To render this latter difficulty the more urgent, Don Louis, with a large fleet, was ordered to scour the seas, and almost all the supplies from England were cut off before they reached the shores of Britanny. A number of historians assert that Philip, after his arrival at Ploermel, despatched a herald to Edward, calling him to a general battle. The fact, however, is more than doubtful, as no authentic document has been brought forward to establish it, and as such a proceeding did not at all harmonise with the course of policy which Philip and his son were then pursuing. Neither was it to be expected that Edward would accept such a defiance, with the great disparity which existed between his own troops and those of his adversary, especially when Philip had once evaded and once declined a general battle, at a time when no such disparity had obtained.

The army of the Duke of Normandy † could have

* Hist. de Bretagne, tom. ii. p. 267.

† On the 5th December no intelligence of the proximity or even preparations of the Duke of Normandy had reached the King of England; and the cardinals arrived within fourteen days afterwards; so that, allowing the necessary time for the march of the French army, but a

been but a very few days in presence of that of Edward of England, when the Cardinal Bishop of Preneste, and the Cardinal Bishop of Tusculum*, appeared before Vannes in the exercise of the best and noblest function of their sacred office—the promotion of peace. For a length of time, however, their mediation proved fruitless; but not to be repelled in their holy zeal, they went from camp to camp, exhorting, praying, and reproaching; representing alternately, to each ambitious king, the scandal and desolation which their rivalry caused in Christendom, the insolence and advantages of the infidel, the waste of noble powers, the devastation of once happy provinces, and the effusion of innocent blood. Still the skirmishes between the two armies continued; the supplies were almost totally cut off from the English army; the foraging parties were annihilated, unless they issued forth in immense bodies, and the besiegers of Vannes might be said to be besieged in their own camp. The French forces also were destined to have their share of suffering. Their tents had been pitched in the meadows while Edward occupied the hill. An uncommonly wet season set in; the cold was intense, the rain was incessant; a pestilence destroyed the greater part of

---

short space could have passed after its appearance at Vannes before the cardinals also approached that city.

* Froissart says that the second legate was the Cardinal Bishop of Clermont; but we find by Baluzius, and also by the correspondence between the Pope and Edward, that this was not the case; and that the envoy was the same Annibal Ceccano, Bishop of Tusculum, who had before been employed in mediating between France and England.

their horses; and their encampment being flooded, they were obliged to spread themselves over the neighbouring fields, each one seeking where he might find some dry ground for the erection of his pavilion.*

These distresses had their effect on both commanders; and as the sufferings of either host increased, the cardinals found their exhortations more willingly received, and their entreaties more faintly rejected. A suspension of hostilities was at length agreed upon; commissioners were appointed to treat of a peace or of a truce; and the Dukes of Burgundy and Bourbon, on the part of the King of France, having met the Earls of Lancaster, Northampton, and Salisbury, on behalf of the King of England, a convention was entered into, the principal stipulation of which was a general truce, to continue from the date of the treaty to Michaelmas next ensuing, and to be prolonged from that day for the full term of three years more. †

The particulars of this convention, however, must be more fully detailed in this place, in order that the cause of its failure may be more clearly understood hereafter. The first clause then imported, that ambassadors from both monarchs should be sent to Avignon before St. John's day following, to treat for a general peace, under the mediation of the Pope ‡; though Edward at the same time positively refused to submit his claims to the judgment of the

* Froissart, chap. ccxi.

† 19th January 1343.

‡ Walsingham, p. 117. Robert de Avesbury, p. 102.

pontiff*, and merely admitted his interference as a moderator.†

The next clause provides a truce, for the period above mentioned, between the belligerent parties, including the Kings of England, France, and Scotland, the Count of Hainault, the Dukes of Brabant and Gueldres, the Marquis of Juliers, John of Hainault, the Count of Flanders, and *all the adherents of each and every of the contracting parties*, in all their lands and territories thenceforward, from the date of the treaty till the conclusion of the term.

The clause that follows declares that each of the allies of the two monarchs shall have right and liberty to send ambassadors to the congress held before the Pope, though the treaty shall in no degree be staid or retarded in case of their neglecting so to do.

It is next clearly stated, that the truce is to hold good in Britanny between the kings and all their adherents, without prejudice to the titles of either of the parties claiming the dukedom; and that the city of Vannes shall be given in pledge into the hands of the cardinals, to dispose of in the end at their pleasure.‡

* Barnes, p. 283.

† Barnes is confirmed in this statement by all the powers granted by Edward to treat before the Pope; in the very titles of which, the King takes care to guard against any assumption of judicial authority on the part of the Holy See, by inserting the words, "De tractando coram Papa (ut persona privata) super pace, &c." — Rymer, tom. ii. part iv. page 144. "De tractando super pace coram Papa (ut privata persona), non in forma judicii, sed extrajudicialiter."—Idem, page 150.

‡ The French copy of this treaty, as given by William of Avesbury, page 102., possesses the following singular and indefinite clause in regard to John of Montford: —

The fifth clause relates to Flanders alone.

The sixth provides that in case any of the lords, adherents to either party within the duchies of Gascony and Britanny, *do levy war against any others, neither of the monarchs shall either directly or indirectly meddle therewith*, nor shall the truce be at all broken thereby. No leagues, contracts, or endeavours for obtaining advantages, by any means whatever, for carrying on the war after the expiration of the truce, shall be permitted to either party: the truce shall extend to sea as well as land, and shall be proclaimed at various places stated, within a certain time.

The seventh clause declares that all prisoners taken on either part, after a certain period, shall be set free.

"Item que a Counte de Mountfort solent regardes lez choses que luy fusrent promys devaunt la citee de *Vannes* ou de deinz, par le Duc de Normandie, de queux homme purra estre apris resonablement."

Although the orthography of the French language was by no means fixed at that period, yet there are here evidently two or three errors of transcription, of which the most important is the substitution of Vannes for Nantes. I should have been led to believe that some conditions had been promised to the Count of Montford in a prior negociation under the walls of Vannes, had not the words *ou de deinz*, which follows the name of the place, rendered it almost certain that Nantes was meant. Whether the error lies with Hearne in transcribing from a manuscript in all probability difficult to decipher, or with Avesbury in copying the original treaty, I do not know. At all events, the clause in its best form shows but a small regard for the interests and feelings of the unhappy De Montford; and the consequences of its very vague and ambiguous language was his detention in prison for more than two years afterwards, as Philip of Valois easily found excuses sufficient to parry the repeated applications of the English King for the liberation of De Montford, and to satisfy his spiritual servant, the Pope. Frequent allusion to the subject is made in the correspondence between Edward and Clement VI. — See Rymer (tom. ii. part iv.), where Philip's cavils are stated at large.

The eighth, that no damage or evil shall be attempted by one party against another during the truce.

The ninth proceeds to state that the kings and their allies are to remain in possession of all that they hold, or may have acquired by any means up to that date.

The tenth especially sets forth, that all the subjects and *adherents* of the contracting parties shall have full liberty to go and come in safety from one country to another, by land or water: excepting only those fugitives from Flanders who have taken part with the King of France in his wars, and those exiles who are under sentence of banishment for other causes than the contention between these parties.

The eleventh clause includes in the truce Spain, Catalonia, Provence, Genoa, and Cambresis, together with the Lords of Albret, Fronsac, Tricoleon, Vernon, and Roy.

Such was the treaty signed at Malestroit on the 19th of January 1343; and almost immediately afterwards Edward embarked for England, with the greater part of his troops. The Countess of Montford and her son either followed or accompanied him; and the possessions of her husband in Britanny were left to the guardianship of her partisans in the duchy, and of a small but chosen body of Edward's forces.* The towns which Edward now possessed we find to have been Brest, Quimper Corentin, Quemperle,

* Rymer, tom. ii. part iv. pages 156, 157.

Hennebon, Redon, and Guérande *; and notwithstanding that part of the treaty which placed Vannes in the hands of the cardinals, the King of England appears to have exercised from the first some jurisdiction within its walls.

His expedition to Britanny, therefore, had been any thing but fruitless; and for a short time the truce was observed inviolate by both parties. Britanny began to recover from the devastation which such a war must ever occasion; and the nobles attached to the rival houses, though occasionally taking advantage of those clauses in the truce which permitted private hostilities † to carry on a desultory warfare with each other, in general courted repose, and employed the space of tranquillity allowed them in recruiting their forces and economising their finances.

Edward, on his part, undoubtedly proposed to keep the truce with honour and good faith. A number of his most renowned leaders received permission to visit the Holy Land; and many more were despatched

* The names of these towns are taken from documents in Rymer, implying that they were possessed by the English. Amongst other letters, we find one addressed by Edward to the Lord of Loheac, whom he mentions in his former letter from Britanny as having joined the party of De Montford with Oliver de Clisson. As far as there are any means of judging, the cases of these two nobles are perfectly parallel. Froissart mentions them both (chap. cvii.) as the partisans of Charles of Blois; and Edward announces almost immediately after his arrival, that, like many others on both sides, they had changed their party and come over to the Countess of Montford. All such, however, as well as those who had abandoned her cause, were included in the truce, and therefore had every right to expect perfect immunity and safety.

† It must be remembered, that the right which the French nobles claimed of waging private war with each other was recognised by every code of feudal law.

on distant embassies.* The military preparations which he had been engaged in making were instantly dropped; the renewal of trade and prosperity seemed to engage his chief attention; and, from all the state papers of the time, it is evident that the English monarch calculated upon a long interval of peace.

Not so Philip of Valois. Enraged at beholding his greatest efforts produce so little effect against the superior fortune of his rival; seeing the troops of that adversary holding calm possession of a part of his kingdom, and preserving a constant inlet into his dominions, whenever war should be renewed; foiled by the inclemency of the season in his purpose of driving forth his enemy with disgrace; and beholding daily many partisans in Britanny falling off from the party he espoused, and turning to that upheld by a more brilliant and chivalrous monarch, — he seems to have lost all sense of the dignity of a king and the honour of a gentleman, and to have suffered wrath to deviate into frenzy.

Notwithstanding the clear provisions of the truce, which insured immunity to all the allies and adherents of either party for actions committed during the course of the war, Philip's animosity towards those nobles who had latterly abandoned the cause of his nephew could not be held down by the solemn engagements under which he was bound. The Lord of Clisson especially, described by Edward himself as one of the most potent barons of Poitou, after having redeemed his military renown by recapturing Vannes,

* Vide Rymer, tom. ii. part iv.

had joined the party of De Montford shortly after the arrival of the English monarch in Britanny, and was consequently an object of the most deadly hatred to the French King. Almost all accounts state that he was taken prisoner by Edward; and that, as the Lord of Landremans and the Castellan of Guingant *, with a multitude of others, had done in regard to Charles of Blois, he had abandoned his former party, and had been persuaded to go over to that of his captors.

Perhaps the severe and unmerited reproaches which the fall of Vannes had called upon him from the adherents of Charles of Blois, had cooled his zeal in favour of that prince; but it is evident from the letter of Edward III. to his son that, long previous even to the conferences for a truce, the Lord of Clisson had openly joined the supporters of the house of Montford †; and that instead of his adhesion to that family being concealed, it was a matter of open rejoicing and gratulation. De Clisson, therefore, had every right to suppose himself secured by the articles of truce against all penal proceedings in consequence of his abandonment of the party of Charles of Blois.

Towards the end of the year 1343, however, Oliver de Clisson, with fourteen other nobles of Britanny and Normandy ‡, were arrested by order of the French

* Froissart, chap. clxxxii.: but it must be remarked that Edward makes no mention of his capture in his own letters; but, on the contrary, implies that he had voluntarily come over to the English party.

† Robert of Avesbury, in loc. cit.

‡ These were the Lords of Malestroit, Avaugour, and Laval; Thibalt Lord of Montmorillon, John of Montauban, Allain of Quedillac; William, John, and Oliver of Brieux; Denis of Plessis, John of Malart, John of Senedavy, and Denis of Calac, together with the son of the Lord of Malestroit.

King; and without any form of trial, as far as has hitherto been discovered, were decapitated in Paris with every adjunct of ignominy and disgrace.*

The place and manner of their arrest are differently stated by different authors. The French chronicles declare that De Clisson and his companions were lured to Paris by the announcement of a tournament; and admit that De Clisson acknowledged boldly that he had allied himself to the English King. Edward, however, in an indignant letter to the Pope, in which he complains of the arrest and death of his adherents, to the manifest violation of the truce, states that they were taken in Britanny; and Clement, although he endeavours by all the subtle evasions which the church of Rome could command to cover the crime of Philip, admits in his answer, that this base act of aggression took place within the territory more particularly specified in the treaty.†

* Froissart, chap. ccxii.; Chron. de France, chap. xxxii.; Fabian, p.272.

† I have reasoned particularly upon the case of De Clisson, because it presents peculiar features; but there is every reason to believe that all the other persons executed were equally injured. On the 5th of December 1342, Edward wrote to his son, stating that the Lord of Clisson, with many other nobles and knights, "*sount rendux a nostre pees,*"—the general expression which he uses for offering fealty. On the 19th January 1343, was signed a treaty insuring safety and peace to all the adherents of either party up to that date, with liberty to come and go in security through the realms of France and England, for the space of three years and nine months; and yet, on the 29th November of the same year, Philip puts to death the Lord of Clisson, the adherent of the English King, without form of trial, as well as the Lord of Malestroit, who from a very early period had been one of the most strenuous adherents of the house of Montford. (See Froissart, chap. clxxx.) Were this case not sufficiently clear, the correspondence between Edward and the Pope, in which the King assumes as a matter beyond all doubt that the sufferers were his known adherents, together with the

Nevertheless, though the circumstances which attended this bloody deed may serve as an aggravation,

---

reply which Clement states that Philip had made to Edward's accusation, would set the matter at rest for ever. As the papal epistle is too long for insertion as a whole, even amongst the proofs, I subjoin the part containing Philip's reply, in which it will be seen that he first declares the execution of the nobles was on account of various acts of hostility committed in Britanny since the truce; which, be it remembered, was no excuse for his conduct, as it is especially stipulated in the treaty that the various nobles of Britanny and Gascony might pursue the warfare if they pleased, but that neither of the kings were to take any part, directly or indirectly, in their proceedings. He then proceeds to quibble about De Montford in a manner the most disgraceful. The following is extracted from Rymer, tom. ii. part iv. p. 182.

"Rursus, super eo quòd, propter captionem et punitionem illorum nobilium, in eisdem litteris asseruntur prædictæ Treugæ violatæ, alias tuæ magnificentiæ scripsisse, et tuis nunciis dixisse, meminimus, quod præfatus Rex ad invectivas Litteras nostras, missas sibi super hoc, sic respondit, quòd illi Nobiles, violando ipsas Treugas manifestè, in partibus Britanniæ, ac homicidia, depopulationes incendia, et alia horrenda maleficia committendo ibidem, flagrantibus hujusmodi et aliis criminibus capti, propter præmissa et alia sua facinerosa scelera, et deinde puniti, exigente Justitiâ, extiterunt; quòdque dicti Nobiles asserebant se non tecum, sed cum Delecto Filio Nobili Viro, Johanne de Britannia Comite Montisfortis, confæderationes habere.

"Qui quidem Comes, tunc existens Parisius, se etiam tecum colligatum nullis confæderationibus asserebat."

Such was the base and degrading manner in which Philip of Valois attempted to cover over an act that admitted no justification; and I feel sure that any one who reads attentively the original documents, will at once perceive that De Clisson and his companions were the adherents of Edward before the truce; that they were lawfully secured by that truce; that their capture in Britanny and their death in Paris was a notorious violation of the truce; and that the excuses of Philip for his conduct were as invalid as the proceeding was illegal and the action base.

It is unnecessary to refer to the opinion of Rapin, who fancies that De Clisson must have joined the party of Edward after the truce; or to the account of Froissart, which both Edward's letters to his son and that to the Pope prove to be incorrect, as far as regards De Clisson in every particular. The Flemish chronicles are proved by the state papers to be wrong in every particular touching this affair.

they in no degree alter the general facts, — that De Clisson, as well as each of his companions, had become an adherent of De Montford, and consequently of Edward, before the signature of the truce; that the articles of the treaty secured immunity to all persons so situated, not only in Britanny, but in all the realms and territories of the contracting parties; and that, in notorious violation of that treaty, Philip of Valois arrested and put him to death, in a manner which, besides being illegal and unjust in itself, was base from the motives by which he was actuated, and dishonourable from the breach of faith by which it was accompanied.

The natural indignation which a gallant nation like the French must always feel at such shameful act, of injustice, at once raised hosts of enemies against their perpetrator; and numbers fell off from the cause of Charles of Blois, while Edward prepared to avenge the adherents of the house of Montford, and murmurs and discontent spread through the whole of France.

Deeds of blood and violence must ever be maintained by the same means; and either as a part or a consequence of this first butchery, a number * of other nobles followed De Clisson to the scaffold in the beginning of the succeeding year. † These were principally ‡ chosen from Normandy; but the last who

* These were Richard of Percy, the Lord of Rochetesson, William Bacon, and Henry of Malestroit.

† Chron. de France, cap. xxxii. 1344.

‡ Barnes, in describing the death of these nobles, has fallen into an egregious error in regard to their fate, which for the honour of human

suffered was a Breton, the brother of the Lord of Malestroit, one of those who fell with De Clisson. His death was accompanied by circumstances of greater cruelty than attended that of his companions in misfortune, and the state which gave him hopes of immunity only served to aggravate his fate. Originally destined for the church, he had taken the first orders; and, in his clerical capacity, was claimed by the Bishop of Paris, and thus saved from the axe. Philip of Valois, however, with that persevering and fiend-like spirit of vengeance which had so bitterly manifested itself in the case of Robert of Artois, pursued his purpose with implacable determination, obtained that the unhappy Henry de Malestroit should be degraded from his ecclesiastical office; and, as if to compensate for the delay which the gratification of his passions had sustained, he raised him on a scaffold in the midst of Paris, and caused him to undergo the horrid death of lapidation.*

One only, it would seem, of all those nobles on whom the indignation of the violent monarch fell, escaped the fate he had prepared for them. This

---

nature must be rectified. Froissart, in mentioning the circumstances, says, "Encore assez tot après furent mis à mort, par fame, je ne sais si elle fut vraie ou non, quatre chevaliers." The word *fame* has been translated hunger; and Barnes declares that Philip of Valois starved his prisoners to death. I need not point out to any one who understands old French that the word Fame does not at all mean hunger, but is always employed in the sense of rumor or report. The correct translation of Froissart may be something to the following effect: — "Still farther, shortly after, there were put to death, according to report, I know not whether true or not, four knights."

* Chron. de France, cap. xxxiii. 1344.

was Godfrey of Harcourt, Lord of St. Sauveur en Cotentin, who, warned by the fate of his companions, refused to obey the summons of the King, and fled at once to the Duke of Brabant, towards whom he stood in some distant degree of relationship. An edict of banishment was instantly pronounced against him, and Philip seized his whole possessions in France; but having inherited some property in Brabant, he continued for several months in that country, while the Duke made vain efforts to procure his pardon from the King. That monarch, however, was inexorable; and Godfrey of Harcourt, following the steps of Robert of Artois, fled to the English court, and did homage to the enemy of his persecutor.

Although human beings, with their dim and feeble intellect, which can neither ascend to remote causes, nor descend to ultimate effects, see not in a multitude of events that occur that special providence which rules the world; yet sufficient instances of retribution and compensation, even in this world, are frequently afforded for an assurance of eternal justice, here or hereafter, and as a step to lead reason up to faith.

It is seldom that a bad man is seen to go on prosperously even to the end; but, if this be evident in ordinary life, it is much more strikingly displayed in the consequences which invariably follow the evil actions of monarchs, as they lie before us recorded in history. Nor, as I have before observed, do many stronger examples of the crimes of great men producing the natural fruit of their own destruction, occur in the annals of the world, than in the life of

Philip of Valois. Had he left Robert of Artois to mourn over his exile, in the first asylum to which he fled, that great but unhappy noble, dependent on the bounty of a petty prince, would, in all probability, have sunk down the oblivious stream of time, forgotten and unsupported. Philip, however, pursued him with fire and sword; drove him from land to land; cast him in despair into the arms of a great and dangerous rival; and reaped the harvest of his own violent passions in a war of many years.

In the contest for Britanny we find the same intemperance, and the same consequences. We have seen him avenge the dereliction of the Breton nobles from the party of his nephew, in defiance of law, of justice, and of good faith; and we shall soon have to mark his ravaged territories, his captured towns, his defeated forces, the loss of Aquitaine, and the route of Cressy.

CHAP. XIV.

EDWARD III. RESISTS THE PRETENSIONS OF THE HOLY SEE.—FRUITLESS NEGOTIATIONS BEFORE THE POPE CONCERNING A FINAL PEACE.—EDWARD COURTS THE FLEMINGS.—NEGOTIATIONS WITH THE DUKE OF BRABANT CONCERNING THE MARRIAGE OF THE BLACK PRINCE.—NEGOTIATIONS WITH THE KING OF CASTILLE.—WITH THE KINGS OF PORTUGAL AND ARRAGON.—A BRIEF ACCOUNT OF THE STATE OF SOCIETY IN THE FOURTEENTH CENTURY.

On the return of Edward III. from Britanny*, every thing promised, if not a secure and stable peace, at least a long interval of tranquillity; and the efforts of the monarch naturally applied themselves to two great objects—namely, to encrease the general prosperity of his dominions; and to maintain the military skill, spirit, and reputation of his people, during the suspension of hostilities. Of the latter of those two objects I shall have to speak at length hereafter; but as, in pursuit of the former, Edward was led into many negotiations with foreign states, and to many internal regulations affecting the condition of society in England, it may be better to pause for a moment here, and touch upon these subjects briefly, ere we follow Edward the Black Prince to the more busy scenes in which his active existence as a historical character really began.

* A. D. 1343.

A parliament, which had been summoned before the King's return from Britanny, met at Westminster in the month of April; and the treaty with France having been laid before the members, both nobles and commons petitioned the King, with the most urgent entreaties, to use every means to obtain a final peace.* They advised him strongly to send the promised ambassadors to treat before the Pope; but, at the same time, they marked in the noblest manner their willingness to support their monarch in the prosecution of the war, in case peace should not be attainable by the mild means of negotiation. Nor did they express any desire that Edward should submit his claims to the arbitration of the supreme Pontiff, the corruption of whose court was too notorious to afford any security that justice would be observed in his decision; but on the contrary, they upheld the King in the resistance which he showed himself at this time determined to make against the grasping ambition of the Romish See.

Two great causes of evil and injustice had arisen in England, partly from the concessions of weak monarchs, partly from the gradual encroachments of the church of Rome; and these causes Edward now determined to remove. The first of these was the right of occasional presentation to churches, abbeys, and priories in England, which had been long claimed by the Pontiffs; and the second was that of judging, in ultimate resort, all cases of patronage in the English territory. It would be tedious to investigate what

* Rymer, tom. ii. part iv. p. 184.

were the concessions which had really been made to the Roman Bishops up to this time; but it is sufficient to say, that they had overstepped the most extreme bounds which the occasional weakness of the English monarchs had yielded to them. Scarcely a benefice in the kingdom was left to the disposal of its legitimate patron; and sometimes more than one reversionary appointment was made by the Pope to a living in England which was not yet vacant, and to the gift of which, when it did become vacant, he could have no just claim. The kingdom was thus overrun by a swarm of foreign ecclesiastics, avaricious in their views, licentious in their manners*; despising the people on whom they were sent to prey, hateful to those whom they were bound to teach; ignorant, superstitious, luxurious, and depraved. Against this

* The moral state of the city of Avignon, at this time, is described by Petrarch in his letters. "In this town," he says, "there is neither piety, nor reverence, nor fear of God, nor faith, nor charity, — nothing that is just, equitable, or humane. Why should I speak of truth, where not only the houses, palaces, courts, churches, and the thrones of Popes and Cardinals, but the very earth and air seem to teem with lies! A future state, heaven, hell, and judgment, are openly turned into ridicule as childish fables. Good men have of late been treated with so much contempt and scorn, that there is not one left amongst them to be an object of their laughter." Perhaps from the beginning of the preceding century till the days of Luther may be considered as the darkest period of the Roman Church. It should never be forgotten, however, that to it Europe is indebted for many most invaluable boons, especially for the preservation of light when all the rest of the world was in darkness. Nor should we fail to remember, that though many of the Pontiffs and Prelates have shown the full portion of human vices in a more glaring light from elevation of station and assumption of infallibility; yet many have given examples of virtue and magnanimity, which lent lustre to their high office rather than derived splendour from it, and added the character to the name of saint.

"army of provisors*," as Edward justly termed them, the monarch determined to make a vigorous stand; and he published, in the middle of 1343, a proclamation, forbidding his subjects to encourage or yield to their exactions, and threatening the provisors and their agents with severe punishment if they set their foot upon English ground.†

A long correspondence ensued between the King and the Pope; and Clement at first showed a strong inclination to assert his title to confer such provisions, by all those means then usually resorted to by the church of Rome in order to compel the refractory to submit to its extortions.‡ But a law was enacted in England, by which any person was subject to fine and imprisonment, who should sue for or receive such reservations or provisions from the court of Rome; and it was further decreed, that, being so imprisoned, he should, before his liberation, find good and sufficient security not to prosecute any man in the Papal court on account of the execution of that statute. This

* Rymer, tom. ii. part iv. p. 151. † Idem, ibid. sed p. 149.

‡ Shortly after the first signs of open resistance shown by Edward, 12th May 1343, various procurators from the church of Rome visited England, and proceeded, without regard to the King's remonstrance, to levy the dues claimed by the various dependants on the Holy See as before. This open contempt of his authority, however, called forth an indignant warrant from the King, ordering the instant apprehension of all such persons; in which, after alluding to their arrival and proceedings, he says, "Nos (tatia tolerare non valentes) assignavimus dilectos et fideles nostros Thomam de Rokeby, Rogerum de Blakeston, et Hamonem de Sesseye de Eborum, conjunctim et divisim, ad omnes hujusmodi Procuratores ubicumque inventi fuerint, in comitatu prædicto, sive alibi, infra dictum regnum nostrum Angliæ, sive fuerint infra libertates, sive extra, insequendum arestandum et capiendum, et ad ipsos coram nobis et concilio nostro, ubicumque fuerit, ducendum indilatè, justitiam super hoc, ibidem recepturos. — Rymer, tom. ii. part iv. p. 146.

act was followed some time afterwards by the famous statute of *præmunire*, by which imprisonment and confiscation were awarded to any subject of the King of England, who should carry a cause within the cognizance of the King into any foreign court whatever; and the whole of this proceeding in opposition to the Pope, when compared with the events which took place both in England and France less than 150 years before, shows one of the most remarkable steps in the progress of society which the whole range of history can display.

The vigour of Edward's measures, and the determination evinced by his people to support him strenuously in their execution, taught Clement that the staff of the church would break like a reed upon the shield opposed to it, if he attempted to strike, as he might have done, at a weaker or more timorous adversary. He determined, therefore, to pursue that more calm and insiduous policy, of gradually winning back again what had at first been gradually obtained. He suffered the dispute to drop, exercised the privilege he claimed with prudent caution, and allowed time to wear away the spirit of resistance.

It may well be supposed that such bold and successful opposition was not at all calculated to render Clement favourable to the cause of the English monarch; and we consequently find in all instances where Philip of Valois and Edward III. appealed to the Holy See, in any of their manifold accusations against each other, that Philip found a ready and eloquent advocate in the supreme pontiff, and Edward but a lukewarm friend. In regard, however, to the negotiations pending at the court of Avignon between the two kings, the earnest desire for peace seems to have rendered the Pope willing to appear at least impartial. He addressed to both monarchs pacific exhortations innumerable, and exposed to both the evil consequences which arose in Christendom from their continual dissensions; but these public declarations, which were undoubtedly as much addressed to the eye of the world as to the hearts of the contending princes, had little effect upon the course of the negotiations, while his obvious leaning to the party of Philip led him to support that monarch in all his unjust demands, and to palliate all his most criminal actions. Had the Roman bishop, indeed, nobly and boldly heard the causes of the two monarchs, and, without arrogating a title to temporal jurisdiction, judged as a Christian and a man, each several claim of those ambitious princes; had he represented to Edward the evident illegality of his assumed right to France, and reprobated the fruitless and criminal expense of human blood which its pursuit had already produced; had he exposed to Philip of Valois, in their true colours, the base encroachments which he and his predecessors had made upon the territories of the English monarchs in Aquitaine; had he traced thence, and laid open to his view, the long series of sorrows, and crimes, and desolations, which had been poured forth on France from that spring of bitterness, instead of attempting to defend actions that were indefensible, and glossing over aggressions and injuries too mighty to be hid,—his voice might have brought conviction to the hearts of men impressed with his impartiality; and the omnipotent power of truth would, at all events, have given a dignity and authority to his mediation which no earthly station could bestow.

This, however, he did not do; and even before the envoys from the two kings reached Avignon, many a complaint was made on either part of the violation of the truce by the adversary.* William of Norwich, Dean of Lincoln, Sir William Trussel, and Andrew of Ufford, professor of civil law, were despatched to Avignon, with the remonstrances of the English King; but very little effect was produced; and De Montford, whose liberation from prison seems now to have become one great object of the negotiations, was still detained on various shallow pretences by Philip of Valois.

To the envoys named above, Hugh le Despencer, Lord of Glamorgan, and Ralph Lord Stafford, were added as ambassadors to treat of peace; and to these were afterwards joined, amongst many others, the Lords Neville, Burghersh, Grey de Ruthvyn, Cobham, and Bradiston, as well as the Earls of Warwick, Arundel, and Henry of Lancaster, Earl of Derby, though other letters of the same date show that the last was at the very time absent at the court of the King of Castille.

The names of the ambassadors, however, were frequently changed, and it is perhaps unnecessary to investigate who were really the persons that conducted a negotiation which produced no results. The con-

* Rymer, tom. ii. part iv. p. 144.

ferences, which were delayed till late in the year 1343, broke up in November without determining any thing; and a renewal of the attempts to treat in August of the following year was equally without effect.*

While these proceedings were taking place at Avignon, Edward did not forget his northern allies; and he found many motives to cultivate the friendship of the Flemings, both in the advantages which were thence derived to his relative position with other continental states, and in the manifold benefits which his commerce received from a connexion with Flanders. England, at the accession of Edward, was an agricultural and pastoral country. Manufacture for the purpose of export was hardly known; wool was the chief commodity of the land; and even the revenues of the crown were often dangerously affected by the state of that article of produce.

This wool, exported in large quantities, furnished the looms of Flanders with matter for the great Flemish manufacture of cloth; but, very soon after his accession, Edward perceived the immense advantages which might accrue to England, if the art of producing the wrought fabric could be combined in one land with the abundant growth of the raw material; and he pursued with the most diligent, active, and persevering wisdom, the introduction of a better system of weaving into his own kingdom. It had been said at a former period by Matthew of Westminster, that the looms of Flanders and the wool of England supplied the world with clothing; but now

* Rymer, vol. ii. part iv. p. 164, 165.

foreign workmen were encouraged to settle in the land, which hitherto produced little but the unwrought material. The populace, with the blindness of passion and prejudice, on many occasions endeavoured to defeat the will of the sovereign, and to drive forth the strangers, whom they believed to be brought over not to instruct but to rival them; but Edward, well knowing that the manufacture he sought to introduce, once fully established, would fall into the hands of his own subjects, and that the whole benefit would ultimately be their own, followed up his purpose by a variety of wholesome laws, which secured to the foreigners he encouraged the tranquil prosecution of their art, and the peaceful possession of their wealth.

As from Flanders, however, these workmen were procured, and to Flanders was the principal export of the immense quantities of wool, which as yet could not be wrought in English manufactories, with that country Edward courted the nearest alliance, and even, it would seem, sought to render it a permanent appendage to the crown of England. During the truce of Tournay and the first campaign in Britanny, continual negotiations and reciprocal assurances of regard and support took place between the King and the Council of the Flemish towns; and every measure which could be devised to encrease and promote the commerce between the two countries, was attended to with a minute and scrupulous accuracy, which proves how important that commerce was considered by both parties.* The Flemings still

* Rymer, tom. ii. part iii. iv. passim.

continued to acknowledge Edward as King of France and their liege lord; and notwithstanding many efforts on the part of Philip of Valois to detach them from the interest of his rival, they remained firm in their attachment to the King of England till after the truce of Malestroit, as we find from many of their letters at this period.*

With the Duke of Brabant also, notwithstanding the tergiversation which he had shown in the former wars, Edward now renewed those amicable relations which had been interrupted, but not totally destroyed. The marriage of the young Prince Edward with one of the daughters of the Duke was again spoken of; and either in the hope of winning completely a powerful ally from the King of France, or of removing any obstacles from his own designs upon Flanders, Edward seems really to have desired the alliance, and to have made use of every effort to obtain a dispensation from the Pope†, the Prince and his proposed bride being within the third degree of consanguinity.

It is very apparent from the papal letters in reply to those which Edward wrote upon the subject, that the motives which induced the supreme pontiff to evade granting the dispensation required, originated more in the interest which he took in Philip of Valois, than in his respect for the canons of the Roman church. The negotiations, however, continued, and were prolonged till the war again broke out with encreased animosity.

* Rymer, tom. ii. part iv. pp. 138. 147.

† Idem, part iv. p. 174.

In the more southern parts of Europe, on the other hand, no means of establishing friendly relations were neglected. No sooner had the truce been signed with France, than we find that the King of England despatched the Earls of Derby and Salisbury to treat with Alfonso, the gallant monarch of Castille, still under the walls of Algeziras.* The negotiations first began in reference to vessels mutually captured by the English and Castilian cruisers, but they proceeded with success to a renewal of former conventions which had bound the two countries strictly to each other, and also to a treaty of marriage between the eldest son of the Spanish monarch with Joan the daughter of Edward and Philippa.†

It is sometimes, indeed, painful to look into the means employed to produce beneficial results; but nevertheless it is not the less necessary on some occasions to lay them open to the world. In the long and intricate correspondence between Edward III. and Alphonso of Castille, we find the heir of the Castilian throne absolutely set up to auction between the Kings of France and England‡; while Edward on his part has recourse to a flattering negotiation with Eleanor of Gusman, the mistress of the Spanish King, through whose means the treaty was finally arranged. His letters to the King of Castille, to that monarch's Queen, to his minister, and to his

* Knighton, col. 2583. Barnes, p. 285. Rymer, tom. ii. part iv. p. 146.

† Something similar had been proposed before.

‡ Rymer, tom. ii. part iv. passim.

concubine, by which plain name he boldly addresses her, stand side by side, as a curious instance of the tortuous and unholy policy which reigned even in those days in such affairs; while the chivalrous actions of the English ambassadors, Lords Derby and Salisbury *, under the walls of Algesiras, form a strange contrast with the pitiful bargaining of the negotiations, and the whole transaction affords a curious picture of the times and of the men.

With the King of Portugal and the King of Aragon also, Edward entered into treaties and correspondence at the same time; and much of his attention was given to courting the maritime states of Italy.† The whole series of papers on these subjects afford a picture of commercial relations much further extended and much more important than has generally been supposed to have existed at that epoch; and in this respect, even in regard to France ‡, the trade with which country was interrupted by continual wars, we find that an ex-

* Edward himself, in one of his letters to Alphonso, speaks of the presence of the Earls of Derby and Salisbury at the siege of Algesiras.

† Rymer, tom. ii. part iv. pp. 146. 148. 158. 97. 189.

‡ The learned and judicious, but somewhat arid Dr. Henry, is not quite correct in stating that no mention is made of commerce in the treaties between England and France at this time. The mention is indeed slight; but in the treaty of Malestroit, reported by both Walsingham and Avesbury, as well as in that of Tournay, will be found the stipulations to which I have alluded in the text. An error even so unimportant as this is not often to be found in Henry's History; and in regard to commerce, of which I am about to speak, I beg to acknowledge, that the information on which the greater part of the next five or six pages have been written was derived from his work, with a few additions which I have noticed in the margin.

press stipulation was made in the treaty of Malestroit, for the security of merchants trafficking between the two kingdoms, on their paying the customary dues.

It may be necessary to notice how this traffic, of which I have been writing, was generally carried on in Europe at the time to which I refer. Large towns, especially sea-ports, were always, of course, emporiums, at which traders sooner or later met with a market for their goods; and long prior to this time, the German* merchants had already ob-

* In regard to the establishment of the German merchants in London, and the great privileges they enjoyed, I cannot do better than make some extracts from Stowe, in his account of the Steelyard. "Next to this lane (Cosin-lane) on the east, is the Steelyard (as they term it), a place for merchants of Almaine, that used to bring butter, as well wheat, rie, and other graine, as cables, ropes, masts, pitch, tarre, flaxe, hempe, linnen cloth, wainscots, waxe, steele, and other profitable merchandizes. Unto these merchants, in the yiere 1259, Henry the Third, at the request of his brother Richard, Earle of Cornwall, King of Almaine, granted that all and singular the merchants, having a house in the city of London, commonly called Guilda aula Theutonicorum, should be maintained and upholden through the whole realme, by all such freedoms, and free usages or liberties, as by the King and his noble progenitor's time they had enjoyed, &c. Edward the First renewed and confirmed that charter of liberties by his father." He goes on to record a dispute between the Mayor and the Hanstown merchants, concerning the repairing and defence in time of need of the Bishop's gate, to one third part of which, in men and money, they were bound on account of certain privileges, which he thus specifies:—

"And for this agreement, the said maior and citizens granted to the said merchants their liberties, which till of late they have enjoyed, as namely, amongst other, that they might lay up their graine, which they had brought into this realme, in *Inns*, and sell it in their garners by the space of forty days after they had laid it up, except by the Maior and citizens they were expressly forbidden, because of dearth or other reasonable occasions. Also, they might have their aldermen, as they had been accustomed, foreseen alwaies that they were of the city, and presented to the maior and aldermen of the city so oft as they should

tained a permanent establishment in London, which aided not a little, both in nourishing the rising commerce of England, and in consolidating and strengthening the growing power of the Hans Towns themselves. The greater part, however of the trade of Europe was still conducted at public markets, called fairs, a degraded remnant of which custom has descended to the present day; the fairs, however, of the reign of Edward are not to be confounded with those of our own times. The nearest approximation to what they then were is to be found at some places in Germany; but even these large marts are but faint shadows of the great and splendid commercial assemblies which took place in the thirteenth, fourteenth, and fifteenth centuries.* The great fair of St. Giles's Hill near Winchester, may be given as an example of the immense extent to which the commercial transactions were carried on

---

be chosen, and should take an oath before them to maintain justice in their courts, and to behave themselves in their office according to law: and as it stood with the customes of the city.

"Thus much for their privileges: Whereby it appeareth that they were great merchants of corne, brought out of the East parts hither, insomuch that the occupiers of husbandry in this land were enforced to complain of them, for bringing in such an aboundance when the corn of this realme was at an easie price. Whereupon it was ordained by Parliament, That no person should bring into any part of this realme, by way of merchandise, wheat, rye, or barley, growing out of this said realme, when the quarter of wheat exceeded not the price of 6*s.* 8*d.*, Rye 4*s.* the quarter, and barley 3*s.* the quarter, upon forfeiture, the one half to the King, the other half to the seisor thereof." — *Stow, Survey*, p. 249.

This is the first protective corn law that I remember to have met with.

* Ducange, Glos. in voc. Mercata.

these occasions.* During the sixteen days to which it was limited, all trade was prohibited in the neighbouring towns; the fair itself took the appearance of a large city, containing a multitude of streets and lanes, thronged with merchants from every land in Europe, and presenting in different places every species of merchandise from a jewel to a slave. Nor was this institution at all confined to England. Fairs were the general resorts of commerce throughout all Europe; and the advancement of internal traffic was not more the object of these assemblies than the congregation of foreign merchants and the promotion of external commerce. In France the edicts and regulations promulgated from time to time for the government of the fairs which took place throughout the country, formed one of the greatest branches of the law of the middle ages; and the great fair of the Landit, held at St. Denis, was attended not only by merchants from every part of Europe, but even from Armenia.†

Whatever might be the origin of fairs, many causes combined to encourage this method of conducting the affairs of commerce when they were once established. For more than two centuries Europe had been gradually emerging from the barbarous state of a mere military society, where few arts were cultivated but those which were absolutely necessary to the support of life and the prosecution of warfare. The first attention bestowed upon any

* Henry, vol. viii. p. 320.

† Ordonnances du Louvres.

branch of the arts, as the mind of man took its spring towards a renewal of civilisation and luxury, was of course turned to those most nearly connected with the state from which society was emerging. Agriculture and chivalry succeeded to the rude exertions for the support of life and for its defence, which marked the character of the tenth and eleventh centuries; and the necessity of commerce also began to be felt in the twelfth and thirteenth, without a just appreciation of the means necessary for facilitating its progress. These, however, gradually developed themselves under various monarchs; and the first and most natural method, the protection and encouragement of foreign merchants, was resorted to by almost all the sovereigns of Europe.

The spirit of external enterprise is the characteristic of republics. The geographical position of Italy, and the advantages which it thereby possessed of communicating with the only parts of the world where trade had never entirely ceased, and where arts lingered unextinguished from the time of their birth to the period of their revival in the West, — I mean with India, Palestine, and Greece, — had enabled a number of cities on the Italian shores to outstrip the rest of Europe in the commercial arts. The merchants of Italy, therefore, were the first who received any great favour from the monarchs of more western countries; and, exempt from a great number of petty dues which were exacted in every lordship and territory from other traders, they monopolised a great part of the traffic of the world. The benefits thus produced led to greater encouragement still, and it soon became a part of the policy of every king to draw foreign merchants to his country by all the means in his power. But cities were still few in number, and limited in extent, and the regular supplies which they might require were generally provided for at this period by companies of merchants possessing particular privileges. The great body of a nation lived remote from towns; and some other mart was therefore wanting to adventurous traders, where they might procure a certain and speedy market for their commodities. This was to be obtained alone at fairs*; and as a certain fixed period was appointed for the holding and duration of the mart, all who desired to purchase flocked to the nearest fair, while every one proceeded thither also who had goods to sell, the profits on which might remunerate the trouble and expence of carriage.

Edward III., however, not contented with the system which he found established, resolved, as far as possible, to render the great towns of his kingdom places of general traffic; and though he did not in any degree discourage the temporary markets which were afforded by the fairs, he determined to create

* I am inclined to think that fairs were the first efforts which the spirit of commerce made in Europe amongst all the savage nations which swept away the civilisation of the South in the fourth and fifth centuries. They can be traced up to a very early period in France: and even amongst the fierce and untameable hordes which frequented the shores of the Baltic, far beyond any point to which Roman civilisation ever extended, we have every reason to believe that a general and regular assembly took place for the purposes of commerce, which can only be looked upon as a fair.

emporiums, in a number of particular cities, with which foreign merchants might be encouraged to trade by the certainty of finding at all times the objects and the means of commerce. For this purpose he appointed certain towns as the sole places for receiving the customs granted to him by Parliament upon the principal productions of the country, and for exporting that portion of such commodities which was not required for internal consumption. These staple towns, as they were called, were fifteen in number; and Newcastle, York, Lincoln, Norwich, Westminster, Canterbury, Chichester, Winchester, Exeter, Bristol, Caermarthen, Dublin, Waterford, Cork, and Drogheda, received the privilege of trading in wool, wool-fells, leather, lead, and tin, which right was guarded and extended by a number of laws and provisions.*

It may be doubted whether Edward saw the whole consequences of this measure, but it was accompanied by one far more extraordinary; he absolutely and entirely prohibited the exportation of staple commodities by English merchants †, and the whole views of his commercial policy seem to have been directed to the attraction of foreign traders to our shores.

* Statutes, 27 Edward III.

† Statuta nova Edward III. ann. 27. cap. 3. Even after having read the statute attentively as it exists in the original French, I could not satisfy myself that such was the precise meaning, and fancied that by the third clause Edward might have meant to guard against the export of staple commodities by English merchants, only when they had not passed the staple towns: but the statute of the 43d of the same monarch, cap. 1., explains the former one, and shows that the prohibition was strict and unqualified.

Whether, in a deliberate conviction of the great communication which this law would bring about with foreign nations, he lost all fear of hampering a commercial spirit which he saw must inevitably arise amongst his own subjects and burst all restraint, or whether he merely provided for the moment, and enacted the statute to encourage the merchants of other countries without considering the temporary inconveniences which might flow from it to his own subjects, must ever be in some degree problematic. An unity of purpose, however, seems to exist between this law and the measures which he took to introduce foreign arts into England by the importation of skilful workmen from other lands, which goes far to justify us in believing that both measures were the fruit of thought and foresight. In pursuit of his commercial views he evinced little anxiety to promote an adventurous spirit amongst his own people; and in regard to manufactures, he took no heed of the complaints and resistance of native artisans. But his policy has been justified by very extraordinary results; and, in ignorance of many of his motives, it would be hard to say that those parts of these laws which seem most objectionable, and which caused the most frequent murmurs, were not necessary at the time they were enacted.

Long prior to his accession, numerous companies of foreign merchants had been established in London; and during the two preceding reigns, we find that Rome, Genoa, Florence, Lucca, and other Italian states, possessed regular trading establishments in the English capital.* The ancient hatred of the populace towards these strangers, however, had not abated; and, on the new provocation afforded by Edward in the introduction of such immense numbers of foreign artisans†, it required all the power and vigilance of that great monarch to prevent the commission of the most brutal outrages.

In other respects, though the arts were not very generally diffused at this period, they were by no means unknown; and the sciences, though confined to the bosoms of a few, had advanced much farther than modern vanity has been willing to allow. It may be sufficient to mention some of the discoveries which had been made at the beginning of the fourteenth century, to show what great steps knowledge had taken, and how nearly the unaided investigations of a few powerful minds had arrived at the same magnificent conclusions which have since been reached by the accumulated experience of many. The first grand principles of optics, catoptrics, and dioptrics were known in England as early as the middle of the thirteenth century; and Friar Bacon, in his Opus Majus, not only describes correctly the method of preparing lenses and specula, but shows, from the train of his reasoning, that the general causes of the phenomena he describes were familiar to him, as well as the results he details. The treatise on perspective left us by that great man is a curious evidence of the progress which his mind had made, in paths where

* Henry, vol. viii. pp. 336, 337.

† Rymer, vol. ii. part iv.

there were few to guide or assist its efforts; and the correct account which he furnishes of the construction and effect of telescopes*, proves that what has been considered a far more modern invention owes its origin to a period much anterior. We find that glasses for aiding feeble or impaired vision were amongst the first results of the discovery of a magnifying power; and the quadrant, as well as the astrolabe, were known in Europe before the commencement of the epoch under our consideration.† Both these instruments, however, appear to have been derived originally from the East; and mention is made of the latter in Arabian authors of a much earlier period.

It must be remarked, that the optic or spying glasses, as they were called, of the thirteenth and fourteenth centuries, were undoubtedly applied to celestial as well as terrestrial objects, though unhappily the results which might have been obtained were lost, in consequence of the observers being turned from the pursuit of real knowledge, at the very point where they might have most easily acquired it, by the idle but poetical dreams of astrology.‡

* Opus Majus, 357. † Tiraboschi, vol. iv. pp. 169. 199.

‡ Friar Bacon mentions a number of mechanical inventions, which, if we are to take his account without reserve, far exceeded any thing that modern times have produced: instruments by which the largest ships could be moved with the greatest rapidity, guided by only one man; chariots so constructed as to proceed with immense velocity, without the aid of any animal; instruments for flying in the manner of birds; instruments of a very small size, by which the greatest weights might be raised; instruments by means of which men were enabled to walk under water without danger. All these, except the instrument for flying, he declares he had seen. Some of them we have

The science of mechanics was by no means unknown; and that the power of moving great bodies with extreme rapidity was in the possession of the engineers of that age, is evinced by the immense masses cast with vast force, and to great distances, by the military engines employed in sieges.* The art of clock-making† also was by this time practised in Europe, especially in Holland; and there is every reason to believe that it was exercised in England. At all events, it is very evident from all the writings of the time, which are full of allusions to the striking of the hour, the regularity of clock-work, &c., that clocks were common throughout the country in the early part of the fourteenth century; to which period may also be attributed the invention of the mariner's compass, by a citizen of Amalphi.‡

As the scientific part of the mechanical arts, and still more the discovery of optical theories, and the

---

seen ourselves; and as there is every reason to believe that Bacon was an ardent lover of truth, the only causes we have to doubt that such things existed in his day, is the fact of their not having been mentioned by other authors, and that of their not having been transmitted direct to after times, both of which, however, might depend upon circumstances not yet discovered.

* Walt. Hemingford, p. 205.

† Henry mentions the art of watchmaking, and cites the account of the watch of Robert Bruce in the Archæologia; but as there still linger doubts in my mind, I have not placed that art amongst those which were certainly cultivated in the fourteenth century.

‡ There has been much dispute upon this point. I state the conclusion of my own mind. I am not unaware that Albertus Magnus interpolated an account of the use of the magnet in the works of Aristotle, nor that James of Vitry alludes in a distant manner to its utility to seamen; but still it seems certain that the compass, properly so called, was not invented before the year 1302.

construction of optical instruments, implies absolutely a knowledge of mathematics, we cannot doubt that many persons had made themselves acquainted with the general principles of that science. Nevertheless, there is reason to suppose that it was much neglected; for I cannot believe that a profound knowledge of mathematics could be co-existent, in our great seminaries of learning, with that gross system of sophistry which was then mistaken for logic. Metaphysics and moral philosophy * were all poisoned from the same perversion of reasoning; and the subtleties of Aristotle †, with the absurdities of his commentators, were received throughout Europe with blind rever-

* Dr. Henry brings forward a curious instance, which may at once tend to show the system of sophistry that was then substituted for logic, and its effect upon moral philosophy. He writes as follows: "Nicolas de Ultricuria, a famous professor in the University of Paris, A.D. 1300, laboured in his public lectures to convince his scholars that in some cases theft was lawful and pleasing to God. 'Suppose,' said he, 'that a young gentleman of a good family, meets with a learned professor (meaning himself) who is able, in a short time, to teach him all the speculative sciences, but will not do it for less than one hundred pounds, which the young gentleman cannot procure but by theft, in that case theft is lawful. Which is thus proved: whatever is pleasing to God is lawful—it is pleasing to God that a young gentleman learn all the sciences—he cannot do so without theft; therefore theft is lawful and pleasing to God.'"

† The absurd worship of Aristotle in the schools in the thirteenth and fourteenth centuries, is strikingly displayed by the oath exacted from the students of the University of Paris at that period, to defend the opinions of Aristotle and his commentators on all occasions. "The philosopher" was the name given to him in all disputes, to show that there was none other worthy of the name but himself; and even this was sometimes curtailed to "He," as if no other person could be cited upon a matter of science. His writings formed the text book of every school, and the words "ipse dixit" were conclusive in all sorts of disputes.

ence; while the demonstrations of Euclid, and the effects of experiment, were unemployed and neglected.

In regard to other sciences, geography had made some progress; but astronomy remained much in the same state in which it had been for many years. The speculative part had made no great advance, and the practical branch of the science was still confounded with astrology. Chemistry had made greater strides towards perfection than might have been supposed; but in this science alchymy, which at first sight seems to stand in the same relation towards it that astrology does to astronomy, had in reality produced very different results. Astrology, by persuading men that the means they already possessed might, by just application, produce certain results, led the mind away from the improvement of means to the pursuit of an unattainable object; but alchymy, on the contrary, teaching that the means were yet to be found, led to continual experiments, in the course of which an immense number of valuable discoveries were made. Thus, in the pursuit of the grand elixir for extending life to an indefinite period, one of the great speculations of the alchymists, a multitude of medicines were produced, which tended to relieve it from the effect of many diseases.*

Medicine, of course must always receive great benefit from the improvement of chemistry; but it does not appear, notwithstanding the long and severe

* The same may be said of the researches designed to discover the philosopher's stone and the powder of projection.

study which was then peremptorily exacted from all persons intending to practise as physicians, that any very striking progress had been made in that science. For the knowledge which the Europeans did possess, they were probably indebted to the Arabians, who, again, are supposed to have derived it from the Greeks. The Medical Rose of John Gaddesden, the most famous work of the kind which has come down to the present times, certainly shows some improvement during the reign of Edward II., and gives a complete view of that science in the fourteenth century. That view, however, is any thing but favourable to the physicians of those times, taking it for granted that all were equally superstitious and ignorant with the author, of which very little doubt can be entertained.

In regard to architecture, it may be merely necessary to say that the style which we call Gothic was advancing rapidly towards its highest degree of perfection. More on this point would be superfluous, and I shall therefore briefly proceed to notice some of the pleasing and ornamental arts which were at this time practised. The method of working all the metals then known was skilfully exercised in England; and we have reason to believe, that the number of goldsmiths and jewellers which London alone contained was immense.* The works produced

* Rymer, tom. ii. part iv. The quantity of gold and silver plate which we find in use shortly after this period is hardly credible; for when the palace of the Duke of Lancaster was burnt, in 1381, it was declared upon oath that the silver and gold plate would have loaded

from their furnaces were often richly wrought, embossed, and enchased, but displaying far more skill and industry than taste. The practice of gilding other metals also was common; and we find statues of copper gilt still existing, which are clearly attributable to this age, and display no small genius on the part of the artist. The art of the sculptor, indeed, had been greatly improved in England during the thirteenth century, and was much encouraged under the reigns of the three Edwards; so that no models were wanting to the founder, and a great advance was evidently taking place towards a better taste than had hitherto prevailed. * What degree of progress painting had made at this time can scarcely be told. The art of illuminating manuscripts with miniatures, representing various actions of the persons spoken of, is of a very ancient date, and towards the present time arrived perhaps at the highest pitch of perfection which it ever obtained. Much more laborious works, however, were undertaken by the pencil, especially in the reign of Edward III.; and we find long descriptions of pictures, representing battles, processions, and ceremonies, which must have contained an immense number of figures. These were

---

five carts; and yet Edward, the father of the Duke, in the early part of his reign, was obliged to pawn his crown to procure money for prosecuting the war, which shows an extraordinary change in the situation of the country, effected during his life. In different places in the fourth part of the second volume of the Fœdera, we find allusions which prove that the trade of goldsmith was at this time one of the most prosperous in England.

* Montfaucon, Mon. de la Monar. Franc.

generally painted upon the walls; and it would seem that the halls and chambers of all men of competent fortune were thus adorned, as well as the interiors of the churches and of the royal palaces. Scarcely a vestige of these performances now remain, whereby to form an opinion in regard to the taste and skill of the artists; but it appears from Chaucer's description of one of his Canterbury pilgrims, that painting was amongst the most esteemed accomplishments of the age.*

Music also had by this time obtained a high place in public estimation, and there is every reason to believe that it was cultivated with great care. What effect a piece of music of those days, performed by musicians of the fourteenth century, might have upon the ears of a modern audience, is very difficult to say. It is nevertheless clear, that it was sufficiently tuneful to charm and delight those who heard it; and its effect upon the passions was so well known, that we seldom find that an army was unaccompanied by a military band. The musical scale had been previously invented by Guido Aretini; and before the epoch to which I allude, some person —it would seem an Englishman †—had invented the method of de-

* In speaking of the Squire, the Knight's son, he says, that he could

"Well endite,
Just, and eke daunce, and well portraie and write."

The original portrait of King John of France existing in the royal library at Paris, and engraved in "D. Dibdin's Bibliographical Tour," is a favourable specimen of the arts of that time.

† Much doubt exists as to the person who first made this great improvement on the discovery of Aretini, some attributing it to Franco

noting the division of time by fixed characters, as Aretini had marked the division of sound. Music had now, therefore, become a written language, if I may use the expression; and as such it was taught in all ecclesiastical establishments, a great part of the ceremonies of the Romish church deriving additional attractions for the multitude from the sweet sounds which accompanied them. In colleges and large cities also music received the greatest encouragement; and none of the poets of the day describe any character in which they wish to interest the reader, without endowing him with some knowledge of that art. The principal instruments of music at that time in use were the psaltery, the guitar, the lyre, the cymbal, the flute, the pipe and tabor, the nakyre, the fiddle, the bagpipe, the hautbois, the systrum, the solemn organ, the war-stirring drum and trumpet, and the immemorial harp. Several others are mentioned in the writers of those days, with regard to the nature of which we have no information.

The manners of a particular period can best be learned from the actions of the time; and therefore I shall only further pause to notice the dress and language of the English at the time of which I am now writing, together with some of the customs which I do not casually mention elsewhere.*

---

one of the musicians of the cathedral of Liege, who has left a treatise upon the introduction of harmonics into music, 1066; and some giving the credit of it to John de Maris, not earlier than the fourteenth century.

* Those who feel an interest in the customs and manners of nations

There never perhaps, in the annals of the world, was a period when extravagance in dress was carried to a greater pitch than in the reign of Edward III. The common habits of the higher classes consisted of cloth of gold and silver, rich furs, silks, and velvets; but as the fashions were then, as now, continually changing, only a few parts of the costume can be at all particularised. In the dress of men, it was the custom in general to tighten the clothing round the waist in a manner which called forth the ridicule and reprobation of all the moralists of the time; while the short breeches, reaching but half way down the thigh, exposed the whole of the leg in its tight hose, of which one was generally of one colour, and another of a different hue. The feet were covered with a sort of shoe, called amongst the French *soulier à la poulaine*, which, though differing greatly in size at different times, were uniformly extravagantly long in the points, almost always embroidered, and very frequently so absurdly lengthened that for the mere possibility of walking the tips were looped up to the knees by gold or silver chains. The coats were often particoloured, like the hose; and on the head was worn a hood of silk, buttoned under the chin, jewelled and embroidered with a variety of ridiculous figures. This was put back upon the shoulders, or drawn forward, as convenience

---

at remote periods, will find an extraordinary fund of entertainment and instruction in the "Histoire des Français de divers Etats," by M. A. Monteil.

required; and was always pushed from the face in sign of salutation, or in speaking to a superior. The hair, at the period of which I speak, was frequently worn very long behind, and, even amongst the men, tressed in the manner of the female peasantry in some of the Swiss cantons. It was generally, however, close-cut upon the forehead, especially by those whose pursuit was war. The beard also was suffered to grow, though I do not find it represented in any of the illuminations of the time as of an immoderate length. In some respects the male apparel at this time, and during a long series of subsequent years, was barbarously indecent.

The dress of the ladies of the fourteenth century was as fantastic as that of the men; and the old miniatures are full of fair dames whose garments are exactly divided into two sides of different colours. Sometimes we find the family coat of arms embroidered on the petticoat, giving it much the appearance of a herald's tabard; and a thousand varied extravagances might be cited, which display the profuse luxury of expanding civilization struggling with the barbarous taste of a preceding epoch. Europe at that time, as far as regarded costume, appears like a savage set down with unlimited means in the midst of an immense bazaar, and left to adorn himself according to his own taste. One of the most grotesque parts of the female apparel was the high cap, which was common during a considerable portion of the reign of Edward III., and which was sometimes raised in the form of a cone to the height of three feet above the head, with streamers of silk flowing from the top to the ground. This part of the costume of the times has still maintained its ground in some parts of Normandy; and a very good idea may be obtained of the head-dress of an English lady, in the beginning of the fourteenth century, from that of some of the rich farmers' wives of the *pays de Caux*. A gold or silver girdle, with an embroidered pouch, and a small dagger, completed the apparel. But in regard to the female dress, as well as that of the men, a continual change was taking place; so that by the year 1350*, the tall caps had dwindled away to nothing, and many a lamentation was poured forth by the praisers of past times upon the indecent scantiness of the ladies' coifs.†

Since the Norman conquest, three languages had hitherto been commonly used in England by different classes. These languages were French, Saxon, and Latin, each more or less corrupt. Latin was employed in the courts of law, and also amongst learned men as a general means of communicating their ideas to their brethren of all nations. French was the tongue of the court and the gentry; and a species of adulterated Saxon was the

* Knighton, col. 2597.

† It would seem that the high caps returned into fashion more than once; for, notwithstanding the accounts of the pettiness of the ladies' head-dresses, I find many persons represented in towering structures of a conical form at a much later period. I am also inclined to believe, from my own reading of Knighton at the passage referred to, that he did not mean to say that the ladies of England had in general abandoned the high cap, but only those particular masculine dames of whom he was then speaking, though the passage has been generally understood differently.

language of the people. But a change was now taking place, which Edward III. was wise enough to favour; the tongue of the many was gradually becoming the tongue of all; and the Saxon, daily enriching itself by the incorporation of many Norman and Latin words, was gaining great advantages over the other two languages. The justice of letting the people comprehend what was urged on either side in the pleadings of causes *, introduced the vulgar tongue into the courts of law. Latin was confined to the writings of learned men, upon abstruse and uninviting subjects; and, as English became popular in the writings of Gower, Chaucer, and Wickliff, French was forgotten even by the court, or learned alone as an accomplishment.

In regard to diet, the English of this period, as well as their neighbours of France, seem to have been very profuse in expenses of the table; but, without entering into discussions, which might prove tedious, concerning the particulars of their banquets, it will be sufficient to say that in general they seem never to have made more than two meals in the day, the first, called dinner, a few hours after sun-rise; the second, named supper, not long before bed-time. To persons of high rank, however, and to their guests, spiced wines were served, together with cakes and comfits, as they were about to lie down to rest.

Bull-baiting, cock-fighting, wrestling for a ram, pitching the bar, the use of the foot and hand ball,

* Stat. at Large, anno. 1362, c. 15.

and archery, were the diversions of the lower classes; while their superiors in station practised the games of chivalry, or sought entertainment in dancing, mummeries, or disguisings, pageants, and mysteries, as well as in the tricks of jugglers, and the songs of minstrels.

Such a sketch of the state of society at the period when Edward the Black Prince first issued forth into the great scenes in which he was now about to act, seemed necessary in order to give the reader some idea, however faint, of the customs and manners to which he may find reference hereafter.

CHAP. XV.

ENTRANCE OF EDWARD THE BLACK PRINCE INTO ACTIVE LIFE.—HE IS CREATED PRINCE OF WALES.—A FEAST OF THE ROUND TABLE PROCLAIMED.—DEATH OF THE EARL OF NORFOLK.—JEALOUSY OF PHILIP OF VALOIS.—VIOLATION OF THE TRUCE OF MALESTROIT.—THE BRITISH PARLIAMENT SUPPORT THE KING.—EDWARD'S REMONSTRANCES AND THREATS.—THE EARL OF NORTHAMPTON COMMANDED TO DECLARE WAR AGAINST PHILIP.—EDWARD'S MANIFESTO.—DE MONTFORD ESCAPES FROM IMPRISONMENT.—DOES HOMAGE PUBLICLY TO EDWARD FOR THE DUKEDOM OF BRITANNY.—GODFREY DE HARCOURT ARRIVES AT THE COURT OF ENGLAND.—DOES HOMAGE FOR HIS LANDS IN FRANCE.—THE EARL OF NORTHAMPTON SAILS FOR BRITANNY, TOGETHER WITH DE MONTFORD.—THE EARL OF DERBY SAILS FOR AQUITAINE.—SECRET EXPEDITION OF THE KING AND THE BLACK PRINCE.

THERE was now before Edward III. the task of initiating his eldest son into active life, and of guiding him through the first of those great scenes in which he was afterwards destined to mingle; a task combining in itself manifold joys and apprehensions. Each individual, in setting out in existence, has in his favour both that ignorance of the ills with which his voyage is beset, which is in itself a blessing, and those glorious and buoyant expectations which bear him lightly over so many of the waves of adversity. Not so a parent, who sees his child emerging from the calm days of infancy into the tempestuous season of manhood. In his case, the sympathies of the human heart are roused to the highest pitch, without any of that consoling ignorance which renders the experiment of a new state of being so brilliant in the eyes of youth. Memory of his own feelings may enable him to place himself easily in the situation of the being he is about to lead forth into the world; but the same act of memory must call up all the bitter and manifold disappointments of the past.

Nevertheless, there are grand joys attached to the task where, as in the case of the King of England and his son, the spirit of the child repays the efforts of the father: there is the daily watching of the expanding mind, the sight of great qualities finding subjects for action, of the intellect taking its first flights and growing stronger on the wing; and, where bright capabilities of mind and body are combined, there too is the surpassing delight of giving to each its truest purpose, and its most vast expansion, of opening the way for high endeavour, and of bringing forth mighty deeds from mighty aspirations.

From the time of the King's return from Britanny to the end of his own life, and almost to the termination of his father's reign, Edward the Black Prince continued to mingle in all the events, and to perform the greatest deeds of the day in which he lived. He was now in the thirteenth year of his age, a time of life at which the young men of noble families generally began that chivalrous education which, by inuring the body to fatigue, and the limbs to the continual use of arms, gave them that skill and those powers of endurance*, which were necessary in the laborious and hazardous life for which they were almost always destined. We have every reason to believe that his previous education under Doctor Burleigh had been by no means neglected; and though we find no proof of his having acquired stores of knowledge more extensive than those usually possessed by the princes of his age, we cannot doubt, from a variety of after occurrences, that his acquaintance with the learning of the day was such as befitted his station.† Active and robust in person, he gave promise already of all those corporeal powers which fitted him so well for the career before him; and he brought to his military studies all that generous ardour, those high-toned feelings, and noble sentiments, which were required by the original institutions of chivalry, and which rendered it one of the most beautiful means of softening and ameliorating a barbarous state of society that the mind of man, or a concurrence of extraordinary events, ever produced.

* St. Palaye, 1ère Partie.

† In regard to many of the minor particulars concerning the private life of Edward the Black Prince, I have relied upon Barnes, who cites as his authority a manuscript of Corpus College, Cambridge, entitled "Acta Edwardi, Filii Edwardi Tertii." A gentleman of very high acquirements, and to whom I beg to offer my best thanks, was good enough to search for the manuscript, which was found in a state of great decay. It must have been more legible in the days of Barnes, though even then it had suffered much from time; but, as there is every reason to believe that he was perfectly incapable of misquoting any work, I have taken his citations as sufficient authority in this instance, though in all others I have considered it a duty to consult the original sources.

His initiation into active life may be dated from the time at which he was created by his father Prince of Wales, which took place on the 12th of May, 1343.* The ceremony was performed in the presence of the Parliament, and the Prince was invested with his new dignity by the symbols of a coronet of gold, a ring, and a silver wand. Nor was the title, thus for the first time bestowed upon the son of an English King, unaccompanied by the means of maintaining his station with that splendour and liberality which his high rank required. All the royal domains held in north and south Wales; all goods and chattels belonging to the King within the principality; all debts, arrears, rights, claims, and dues of the crown, in that district, were granted in full unto the young Prince, and a noble revenue was thus provided for the increased expenses which he was now likely to incur.

The maintenance of military skill, and a military spirit amongst his people, and the extension and support of the national renown in a chivalrous age, went hand in hand with Edward's purposes in regard to his son. Pomp and display, examples of gallant daring and enthusiastic zeal, the spirit-stirring voice of multitudes, the applause of the beautiful and the brave, were all called up to nourish and keep it alive, to breathe deep into the bosom of his son, and to guard in all its brightness amongst his subjects that chivalrous spirit, which was yet to bid the

* Cart. 17 Ed. III. m. 24. n. 27.

hosts of other lands fall before the scanty bands of England.

No means were left unemployed, nor did Edward entertain any fear of raising the ardour of his nobles to too high a pitch. The renewal of the institutions of chivalry, with greater splendour than ever they had yet possessed, was now the great object of all his endeavours; and his natural disposition, combining with his own peculiar powers, his political views, and the character of his barons, prompted him to efforts and designs which had a striking and extraordinary effect upon the age in which he lived, and which have transmitted memorials through five centuries of change.

The first institution which Edward founded with this object, and which evidently gave rise to a greater one that we shall have to notice hereafter, was the appointment of an annual tournament to be held at Windsor. Such military ceremonies, however, were so common in those days, that in order to give splendour and distinction to that which he now proclaimed, the English monarch joined a thousand adjuncts of magnificence and display to the attractions which a royal tournament always held out to the youth of Europe. He announced it to the world as a feast of the round table *, to perpetuate the memory of King

* Barnes, page 292. This feast of the round table was by no means the first that had been given in Europe; but none had been proclaimed for many years. Many had been celebrated in the thirteenth century; but the last which I can discover prior to that mentioned above was one given by the Duke of Brabant in 1295, in which he himself was killed. Ducange, Dissert. VII. The last which had been previously celebrated in England was instituted by Roger Mortimer, in 1279–80, at Kennilworth, where

Arthur and his knights; and the heralds which he sent to proclaim it in all parts of Europe, gave out that the feats of arms there to be performed, would have for witnesses and judges, the Queen of England and 300 of the noblest and most beautiful ladies of the land.*

The rumour of such a meeting, and the announcement that honour and safe conduct would be accorded to every knight or squire, during the festival, and for fifteen days after †, from whatever country he might come, spread far and wide amongst the chivalry of Christendom. At this period the romances of Arthur and his knights, and the lays which were sung of great deeds and splendid passages of arms, formed all the lighter literature of Europe; and, while a few of the sceptics of that day might be bold enough to doubt the authenticity of the British King's history, and disbelieve the wonderful adventures of his companions, the great bulk of the people looked upon such suspicions as a heresy in chivalry, and believed as firmly

---

he entertained for three days, at a round table, 100 knights and 100 ladies in a sumptuous manner. Walsingham and Matthew of Westminster both notice the festival; and the History of the Priory of Wigmore, which was dependent on the family of Mortimer, affords a long and tedious description of the whole proceedings. It would be equally tedious to attempt to trace the origin of this custom, and it may be sufficient to say, that the sports implied by the proclamation of the *mensa* or *tabula rotunda*, consisted, according to Ducange, in a number of knights answering separately, for a certain number of days, the challenge of all comers; without admitting the mêlée, in which a great number fought at once.

* Froissart, chap. ccxiii.

† Rymer, tom. ii. part iv. p. 157.

in the tales of the round table, and the pursuit of the Sangrael, as in the power of absolution and the infallibility of the Pope.*

The renewal, then, of that famous institution in the very castle wherein Arthur was supposed to have held his court, woke up all those bright enthusiasms which lie beneath the wings of fancy; and for many weeks Europe became a thoroughfare towards England. Every land sent forth her knights; and for the reception of so many guests an amphitheatre of 200 feet in diameter was erected, by the King's command, in the immediate proximity of Windsor castle†, the birth-place and favourite residence of Edward III. The festival surpassed in splendour all that had been anticipated; and, though many of the most promising of the English youth lost their lives in the course of the military games,—though many a heart was taught to ache, and many an eye to weep, for the loss of the husband, or the lover, or the son,—the ideas of honour which were entertained in those days enjoined the

* Even in the days of Camden an immense round table was shown, in Winchester Cathedral, as the round table of King Arthur. Camden's Britannia.

† Walsingham, Ypodigma, p. 117. It would seem, from the account of Walsingham, that this amphitheatre itself received the name of the Round Table. He says, "Rex Eduardus fecit convocari artifices ad Castrum Windesore, et cœpit edificare domum quæ Rotunda Tabula vocaretur. Habuit autem ejus area à centro ad circumferentiam, per semidiametrum centum pedes, et sic diametrum 200 pedum erat." It appears, however, that the first building was merely a temporary structure; as the order for pressing workmen to build the more solid amphitheatre, which was afterwards raised at Windsor, bears a later date than the first festival. — Pat. 18. Ed. III. p. 1. m. 39.

concealment of such grief; and individual accidents were not suffered to trouble the joy of the assembly.*

One death, however, is said to have occurred at this first feast of the Round Table which, if it really took place, must have seriously affected the King, by depriving him of one of his most gallant and skilful leaders,—William Montague Earl of Salisbury, who, after signalising himself in the exercises of the first and second day, is reported to have died eight days afterwards of the injuries he received.† This event is very doubtful; but not so the death of Thomas Earl of Norfolk, a gallant and successful soldier, who had accompanied the monarch in almost all his wars, and escaped the dangers of many a hostile encounter to die in the midst of rejoicings, and in a time of peace.

* Froissart, chap. cxcii.

† Barnes, p. 295. I am strongly inclined to believe that this statement of the death of Lord Salisbury is entirely incorrect. Walsingham, from whom I imagine the whole account to have been borrowed, calls him Marshal of England, and evidently confounds him with Thomas Earl of Norfolk, who did indeed die during the tournament at Windsor. The office of Earl Marshal was immediately granted by the King to the Earl of Warwick, and was never enjoyed by the Earl of Salisbury. See Rymer, tom. ii. part iv. p. 159, 160. William Earl of Salisbury is named amongst the founders of the order of the Garter in 1349, and I cannot conceive that the person receiving this high honor was the son of William Earl of Salisbury, of whom Walsingham now speaks; as at the institution of the garter he could not have been more than nineteen. Edward appears uniformly to have chosen the knights of that celebrated order for their military services, without any regard to rank, except in cases affecting the blood royal; and at the time of the institution, the young Lord Salisbury could boast of no great exploits, though his father could boast of many. I am inclined, therefore, from every circumstance, to believe that the general account of the death of the Earl of Salisbury at this time is perfectly erroneous, and that it did not take place for several years afterwards.

Such occurrences, as I have before said, cast no damp upon the gaieties of the meeting; nor did they at all serve to diminish the youthful ardour of the aspirants to chivalry, to instruct and encourage whom was one great object of these games. On the contrary, the dangers, the wounds, the slaughter, which always attended a tournament, familiarised them early, in the midst of sports and pastimes, with all that can render war horrible, and robbed the monster of the additional hideousness of novelty.* Each one who bore a share in such encounters might say, in the splendid words of a poet of the present day, —

"—— Death and I have met in full, close, contact;
"And parted, knowing we should meet again;
"Therefore, come when he may, we 've looked upon
"Each other, far too narrowly, for me
"To fear the hour when we shall so be join'd,
"That all eternity shall never sever us."

Miss Kemble.

The fall, therefore, of some of the sharers in these exercises, though we may well suppose it was not desired by the English King, was far from counteracting his purpose of maintaining during peace the bold and chivalrous spirit of his people; nor, indeed, were any of his designs left unfulfilled by the tournaments at

* It is to be remarked that Froissart gives two accounts of two separate tournaments held by Edward; the one, in the middle of August 1342, the other in 1344. Neither of these accounts can be received as exact, as in the first he names a number of knights and gentlemen who were at that time in Britanny, and in the second he confounds the feast of the Round Table with the institution of the Garter. It is evident that Froissart had received some vague rumours of great military spectacles in England, without having any very precise information on the subject.

Windsor. The general renown of the English nation was, perhaps, more raised throughout Europe by the military exercises of the Round Table, than by her splendid actions and great endeavours in the field; while at the same time the passion for similar games and spectacles spread with such fury through the land, that Edward was obliged to watch and restrain, rather than encourage its progress, lest every petty town throughout his dominions should forget all else in jousts and tournaments.

In the meantime, Philip of Valois perceived with bitterness of spirit the increase of Edward's renown. A sort of fatality seemed to hang upon him, and retard him in that race of eager competition, which he urged with all the strenuous efforts of rivalry against the happier King of England. Peace saw him sink below his competitor; war left him less in fame. His most successful efforts gained him less renown than the fruitless but glorious attempts of Edward; and accident, which is seldom always adverse, never seemed to favour him. Three great causes, indeed, combined to render the advantages he gained infructuous, at least in reputation. In the first place, he wanted that creative energy which devises great undertakings, — the most magnificent quality in the mind of his rival. In the next place, his successes were almost always dependent more upon what he did not, than upon what he did do. In the third place, he was throughout the passive party in the war; and therefore wanted the glory of activity; all that he did attempt beyond the mere defensive was either petty, like the ravages committed by the French fleet upon the English coasts, or unsuccessful, like the attempt made by the same fleet to repel Edward from the Flemish shores.

He now marked with fear and envy the measures of the English King; and he determined, as far as possible, to rob them of effect. For this purpose he strictly forbade all his subjects from attending the festival given at Windsor *; an act which might be prudent, and which was certainly mean. In the next place, he resolved, by instituting an assembly of the same kind at Paris †, to imitate his rival; a purpose which in itself, like every other kind of imitation, implied inferiority of conception. At the same time, however, one wise measure issued from his council; he granted a licence to all ship-builders ‡ to fell timber in the royal forests; and much evil thence accrued in after years to his rival, with the collateral advantage that the depression of an enemy of course produced to himself.

It appears plain, from every circumstance recorded in the more credible historians of the time, that Philip of Valois never entertained the purpose of terminating the truce by a treaty of peace; and, before the end of the first year after the signature of the convention of Malestroit, that conviction must have forced itself upon the mind of Edward also. Both parties complained that the other violated the articles

* Froissart notices the fact of no French knight being present, chap. ccxv.

† Barnes, p. 299.

‡ Walsingham, p. 164.

which had been stipulated; and Philip of Valois even made the Pope the medium of his accusation against the English King. Edward, however, recriminated with indignation, asserting boldly that the convention was notoriously infringed by Philip's agents, even in the presence of the cardinals sent to enforce its execution.* The charges might be false on both sides; but Edward descended to particulars, Philip kept to vague generalities; and while, at the end of the truce, we find no clear act of infraction proved against Edward, while he possessed no cities or castles, which we do not clearly find he did possess within the first six months after the signature of the treaty, we meet with a number of instances in which Philip had grossly violated the promises he had given.†

* Rymer, vol. ii. part iv. p. 155.

† It would seem more impartial, but would be less just, to acknowledge, with some writers, that Edward and Philip mutually broke the truce as they found it inconvenient; but I do not find that such was the case. The war, as the treaty permitted, was carried on in many parts of Britanny between various adherents of the two parties of Montford and Blois: but it is clear, from every historical record of authenticity, that Edward did not afford any aid to either, nor did he even, as far as I can discover, make any efforts to lay up provisions in the towns, or strengthen the fortresses which he held, till Philip had violated the truce by the execution of the Lords of Bretagne. Even in regard to Guienne, before he despatched the Earl of Derby thither, Philip had collected a large and menacing force upon the frontier; and still Edward, in his private commands to his Generalissimo (as I shall show hereafter), gave the strictest orders that the truce should be infringed by the English on no pretence whatever, and that whosoever attempted any thing against it should be punished. (Rymer, tom. ii. part iv. page 162.). The same had previously been done in regard to Scotland. The city of Vannes, as I have before stated, was under Edward's authority in 1343, as we find by his very first letters to Britanny.

No sooner did Edward clearly perceive that the war was absolutely to be renewed, at the end of the temporary suspension of hostilities which had been granted, and that his rival did not intend to suffer the period of repose to pass over without seeking to strengthen his own position and weaken that of his enemies in the very country in which all such attempts had been foresworn, than he determined to prepare against the event also, by making alliances wherever he could find friends or adherents.* News reached him about the same time, that on the confines of Aquitaine a large French force was assembled, and that those nobles who maintained the cause of his adversary in that province were wasting the country †, and subduing all the smaller castles, with which that part of France was thickly strewed. While this information evinced the hostile purposes of the French King, the tidings of the unhappy fate of Oliver de Clisson and his companions showed that Philip would hesitate at no action, however base, to gratify his vengeance, or to weaken his adversary. The feelings which Edward experienced on receiving the latter part of this intelligence, combined general horror and indignation with personal disappointment and regret; and he was almost tempted to commit an act equally ungenerous, in order to revenge the unmanly cruelty which had been displayed towards his adherents. According to the account of Froissart,

* Rymer, tom. ii. part iv. p. 4.

† Froissart, chap. ccxv.

Henry de Leon *, who had been taken by Sir Walter de Mauny, and remained still an unransomed prisoner at the English court, had nearly been sacrificed in retaliation for the death of the Breton nobles; but the chivalrous and gallant Earl of Derby interposed to save his life; and, representing to the enraged monarch that no provocation whatever could justify the slaughter of an honourable adversary, taken in fair fight, he persuaded Edward to refrain from his unworthy purpose. Edward's first emotions were almost always fierce; but better feelings lay below, and, whether it proceeded from the heart or the head, — whether it was the effect of noble sentiments, or wise calculations, — a more generous conduct generally succeeded to the first outburst of passion. It was like the coming down of floods from the hills—first a red and turbid torrent, gradually followed by a clear but rapid stream.

By the advice of Lord Derby, Edward called before him his prisoner; and, after pouring forth his indignation against Philip in words, he told the Breton knight that, although his first intention had been to put him to death, he would now, on the contrary, give him his liberty, and acquit him of a large part of his ransom, upon condition that he proceeded forthwith

* In Monsier Buchon's edition of Froissart, this prisoner is here called Hervé de Leon, while the famous Breton captain is called Henry. I believe, however, that the name Hervé has been written by mistake. I find no celebrated person of that name in other authors. I do not find that such a person was ever taken by the English; and Knighton expressly states (col. 2581.), that Henrius de Leon was captured by De Mauny in a small fortress near Brest.

to the court of France, and carried a message of bitter accusation to his adversary. The task itself was not without danger, when the character of the French King was considered; but to Hervé de Leon it appeared a relief after the apprehensions which the news of Philip's violence had already occasioned, and he willingly undertook to be, in this instance, the messenger of the King of England.*

Edward at the same time addressed many an angry remostrance to the Pope; and to guard the English possessions in Aquitaine, he commissioned his cousin Henry of Lancaster, Earl of Derby, to lead a considerable army into that province, with orders to protect in every honourable and rightful manner the territory truly appertaining to the English crown; but by no means to break the truce, or overstep the strict defence of his sovereign's rights.†

The departure of Lord Derby, however, was delayed for some months, in consequence of a new series of negotiations opened at the papal court, which proved as unfruitful as the former, and only served to postpone the open declaration of hostilities.‡ Philip, on his part, neither paused nor receded in his various acts of aggression; efforts innumerable were made to win either by bribery or force the castles and towns which Edward held in Britanny; and the English monarch, soon after the opening of the new conferences at Avignon, received intelligence that the

* Froissart, chap. ccxiv.
† March, 24 A. D. 1344. Rymer, tom. ii. part iv. p. 161, 162.
‡ Ibid, tom. ii. part iv., p. 164.

last act of the tragedy of the Breton nobles had been completed, by the barbarous execution of Henry of Malestroit.*

Before this time Edward had joined threats to remonstrances; nor had those threats been made without preparation for their execution in case of the failure of the negotiations and of the continuance of aggression on the part of his adversary. Orders had been given for collecting armies and providing ships †; the strictest injunctions had been issued for the most watchful guard of Britanny; and the English monarch loudly proclaimed his intention of immediately passing the seas, in order to succour his subjects and allies with a strong hand. He even, it is said, despatched fresh troops into Britanny ‡: but I find no public record of such an act §; and as his so doing would in all pro-

* Barnes, in speaking of Henry of Malestroit, declares that he came over to England, after the decapitation of his brother, and urged Edward to avenge the fall of the Breton nobles. Edward, he farther states, gave him a post in the city of Vannes, which was then held by England; but after the rupture of the truce, the city being given up by the cardinals to the King of France, Henry of Malestroit was found in it, and carried to Paris, where, being degraded from his clerical rank, he was put in the pillory and pelted to death. It is only necessary to observe upon this story, that according to the Chronique de France (chap. xxxiii.), the best authority for what took place in Paris at that time, Henry of Malestroit was lapidated, in the end of August or beginning of September 1344; whereas the truce was not broken till April 1345.

† Rymer, tom. ii. part iv. p. 166.

‡ Froissart, chap. ccxv.

§ Froissart declares that Thomas of Agworth was sent to aid the Countess of Montford in Britanny with 100 men at arms and some archers. Against this it is stated by Robert of Avesbury (p. 109.) that Thomas Agworth was already commandant in Britanny, and had been so since 1343. This, however, was not the case, as in 1344 I find

bability have brought on an immediate renewal of the war, it is not likely that such was the case.

The most effectual measure, and the principal step taken towards hostility, was the calling a Parliament to consider the state of the English relations with France. The tone of all the deliberations which followed was decidedly warlike, and was probably in every respect accordant with the wishes and expectations of the King.* A stronger determination than ever was evinced by the clergy, the nobles, and the commons, to oppose the papal encroachments; and though the three estates counselled the monarch if possible to terminate the war by a solid peace, yet they prayed him, if hostilities became inevitable, to prosecute the war to some decided conclusion, without being tempted to grant any more such hollow truces as then existed, even at the solicitation of the Holy See. This advice was followed by grants which showed how little they expected a pacific result, and how determined they were to support their monarch to the utmost in every just and reasonable enterprise.

A number of desultory negotiations now ensued; and though the Pope evinced a very marked partiality

---

that Edward names John of Hardeshul as his locum tenens in that duchy. Whether Agworth was really sent or not I do not know; but it is certain that the Countess de Montford was in England during a great part of 1344, and I am inclined to believe that she had left Britanny with Edward in the preceding year, according to the statement of most of the old English historians.

* June 7. 1343. Barnes, page 303. Rot. Parl. 18 Ed. III. Walsingham, p. 164.

towards France*, he left no apparent means untried to bring about a peace. His exhortations to Edward were manifold, and couched in a variety of forms; he held up to his eyes the prospect of victories over the infidels; he displayed the danger of war and the happiness of peace; he showed the criminality of shedding Christian blood; and he even sent legates to negotiate with the English King in his own dominions. But he neither persuaded Philip of Valois to restore Ponthieu, nor to yield the grasp he held of Aquitaine, nor to offer amends for the death of the Breton nobles: and to the cardinals commissioned to open a separate negotiation with Edward, the English monarch constantly replied, that he would enter into no treaty without the knowledge and participation of all his adherents on the Continent. †

At length, on the 24th of April 1345, Edward having determined to suffer his rival no longer to enjoy the advantages which this ill-kept truce afforded him, issued his commission to the Earl of Northampton to defy Philip of Valois in his name, for the notorious violation of the treaty between the two countries. He constituted that nobleman also his locum tenens in France and Britanny; and in a letter to the Pope, he set forth at large his motives for proceeding to hos-

* He this year created Don Louis of Spain, who was then one of the ambassadors on the part of Philip of Valois, Prince of the Fortunate or Canary Islands. The Pontiff might certainly have motives for conferring this empty honour totally unconnected with France, but it would have been more decent to have deferred such a distinction till another time.

† Rymer, tom. ii. part iv. p. 172.

tilities, and once more stated his title to the crown of France. These acts were followed by a proclamation addressed to the French people, asserting his right to the throne occupied by Philip, and promising to revive the laws and institution of St. Louis, in case of his being enabled to obtain the actual sovereignty of the country; while at the same time a manifesto, containing a general defiance of Philip of Valois, was published both in England and Britanny.*

The escape of the Count de Montford † from the tower of the Louvre, and his arrival in England, together with the appearance of the banished Godfrey de Harcourt ‡ at the court of Edward, served to hasten the actual recommencement of hostilities. De Montford immediately acknowledged Edward once more as legitimate King of France; and his solemn act of homage for the duchy of Britanny was taken down in form.§

* Robert of Avesbury, p. 114.

† From the Pope's letter to Edward (Rymer, tom. ii. part iv. page 144.), and from Du Tillet (Recueil des Traités, p. 235.), it would appear that De Montford had been kept in prison by Philip, contrary to express agreement, and even against the decree of the Parliament of Paris; from the same documents it is evident that the method Philip employed to give this proceeding a semblance of justice was, by constantly refusing on some pretence every sort of security De Montford could offer for his return to prison at the expiry of the truce, in case it was not followed by a general peace including himself. Many of the old English chroniclers declare, that De Montford was liberated by Philip previous to his flight to England; and that he pledged himself not to set foot in Britanny, which promise he afterwards broke. Of this fact, however, I can find no proof; and it seems clear to me that he made his escape from prison without having been liberated in any manner.

‡ Barnes states that the cause of De Harcourt's banishment was a quarrel with one of the officers of the King — a cause hardly equal to the effect.

§ Rymer, tom. ii. part iv. p. 177.

Godfrey of Harcourt too, — who, fearful of being pursued even to the court of the Duke of Brabant, had, as we have seen, quitted the first asylum which he had sought in the preceding year *, — now did homage also to the English King †; and, breathing nothing but revenge, prepared to give him that counsel and assistance which his knowledge of the state of France, and his influence in Normandy, enabled him to furnish, and which produced much greater results than even the aid and intelligence formerly afforded by Robert of Artois.

Almost immediately after the arrival of these nobles ‡, the Earl of Northampton set sail with a small army for Britanny, and was, in all probability, accompanied by De Montford himself; but the greater operations of the war were not destined at present to be carried on in that quarter. The principal event of importance which occurred in Britanny for some months, was the death of the unhappy claimant of the duchy, who, with more than even the usual misery of ambition, had not only never known one year of tranquillity since first he set his foot in that thorny path, but had never seen one year even of success. His escape from prison, his safe flight to England, the favour and distinction that awaited him there, and his armed return to the country he claimed, were the brightest events which had be-

* Chronique de France, chap. xxxii. Froissart, chap. ccxlvi.

† Rymer, tom. ii. part iv. p. 179.

‡ The Earl of Northampton had not set out on the 4th of June (Rymer, tom. ii. part iv. p. 178), but we find in the following page that he had taken his departure before the 11th of the same month.

fallen him for many a year; but they were all comprised in less than five months, and he died at Hennebon on the 26th of September, leaving to his son a contested coronet and an inheritance of strife.*

The ships which bore the Earl of Northampton had no sooner spread their sails for Britanny, than the Earl of Derby took his departure, with a much larger force, for the defence of Guienne†: but at the same time the more extensive preparations made for an expedition, to be conducted by the King and the Prince of Wales in person, of course occupied a considerable part of the forces of the realm. What was the original object of this expedition, where it was intended to land, and whether that original purpose was or was not fulfilled by the course which it did take, will probably remain for ever in doubt. Edward certainly kept its destination secret in the first instance, and he afterwards declared that the direction in which he led it was determined by sudden intelligence‡; but it is very clear from the results, though the papers connected with the transaction seem to have been lost, that he had kept up a close though secret correspondence with Artevelde in the country to which he now conducted his forces. As this expedition however is not only remarkable in itself, but produced events totally apart from the general history of the war, the circumstances connected with it are worthy of separate notice.

* He appointed Edward III. by will guardian to his son. Rymer, tom. ii. part iv. page 189.

† Rymer, tom. ii. part iv. p. 179.

‡ Idem, p. 185.

CHAP. XVI.

MOTIVES AND PROCEEDINGS OF JACOB VAN ARTEVELDE. — EDWARD III. ARRIVES AT SLUYS.—CONFERENCE WITH THE FLEMISH COUNCILS ON BOARD THE KING'S SHIP.— ARTEVELDE PROPOSES TO RAISE FLANDERS TO A DUKEDOM, AND GIVE THE CORONET TO EDWARD THE BLACK PRINCE. — DIFFICULTIES OF THE BURGHERS.—CONDUCT OF ARTEVELDE.— HE GAINS BRUGES AND IPRES.—NEGLECTS GHENT.—MACHINATIONS AGAINST HIM IN THAT CITY. — HE RETURNS TO GHENT. — IS BESIEGED IN HIS HOUSE. —HIS DEATH AND CHARACTER.—EDWARD SAILS FOR ENGLAND.

THE efforts of Philip of Valois to detach the Flemings from the interests of the English King had been unwearied before the concession of the truce of Malestroit; and, notwithstanding their previous unfruitfulness, had not been relaxed after the suspension of hostilities. There is every reason to believe that the Pope also had added his influence; and at all events it is clear that before the renewal of the war had become inevitable, the people of Flanders, though not absolutely inimical to their former ally and acknowledged sovereign, had become far less zealous in his cause than they had previously shown themselves.

Nevertheless with Artevelde the influence of Edward was as great as ever; and the power of the demagogue over his fellow-countrymen was not apparently diminished in any respect*, except in that of maintaining their attachment to the King of England. This point, however, was a most important one to the popular leader. The reunion of the states of Flanders to France implied as a matter of course the return of the Count to his territories; and that return the abasement of Artevelde from his commanding station, the destruction of his power, and probably the punishment of his offences. Whether we look upon Artevelde as the defender of his country's liberty against the efforts of a prince who was tyrannical because he was weak, or whether we regard him as one of the many men of genius who have made use of the real wrongs of their native land merely as steps to individual aggrandisement, we shall still see that it was imperative upon him, in the position he had assumed, to maintain the predominance of the English interest in Flanders, at any hazard.

If he were merely an ambitious demagogue, he had no choice; and if he were really a patriot, the advantages which were offered by the commerce of

* It is not impossible that a very powerful party had been formed against Artevelde, in the city of Ghent, upon motives totally unconnected with the attachment of that extraordinary man to England. On a Monday, in the month of May, 1345 (see d'Oudegherst, tom. ii. p. 462.), the weavers and the fullers, who had been long at enmity, met in the great market of Ghent to the number of many thousands, and a severe conflict took place, in which 1500 of the fullers were slain. The weavers, who remained masters of the field, were ever one of the most powerful of the trades, and it is not improbable that their dean, Gerard Denis, who afterwards slew Artevelde with his own hand, had long been jealous of that power to which the victory of his trade and its great predominance gave him such strong pretensions. This, however, is all conjecture.

England, her system of government, far milder and more popular even then than the purer feudalism of France, and the excellent fact of her having nothing to forgive or to avenge in regard to Flanders, all impelled him strongly to maintain, even by the sacrifice of national independence, the union between the Flemings and the English. The progress, however, which the French monarch was every day making in Flanders admitted of no delay; and Artevelde perceived that he must either hurry forward his yet undecided countrymen to some irretrievable step in favour of England, or see them ultimately fall back into the arms of France, and yield themselves to the same rule, and probably to the same exactions, as before. The step he meditated could not be taken without some sacrifice of his personal power; but such a sacrifice was of course calculated to make his conduct appear the more disinterested; and, confiding still in his habitual influence with the Flemings, and his tried powers of persuasion, he determined to urge them to throw off in words, as they had thrown off long before, in fact the authority of their native prince, and yield themselves entirely to the sway of England.*

* Froissart fixes the whole agency of this sheme upon Artevelde, and declares that the first incitement for Edward to visit Flanders at this time was given by him. Of this fact no doubt can exist; but the letter of Edward after his return, preserved in Rymer (tom. ii. part iv. p. 185.), proves that the whole was conducted with the most profound secrecy on all parts, although d'Oudegherst, vol. ii. p. 463., declares that Artevelde had previously opened his views to the council of Ghent, and had been strongly opposed by Gerard Denis. D'Oudegherst, however, I have never relied on without collateral proof, as he is contradicted by state papers on very many occasions.

Such a measure, he knew, must be taken at once, if at all; and he felt sure that if it were submitted to long discussion, the host of cold doubts, and fears, and hesitations, which might be arrayed against it by the partisans of France, would overawe that timid and fluctuating mass which always forms the bulk of popular assemblies. On these grounds he cautiously concealed his plan from his own countrymen; and giving Edward III. a clear picture of the danger which menaced him of losing Flanders for ever, he at the same time assured him that if he would immediately visit that country with a sufficient force to give his party even a temporary strength, he would snatch the coronet from the brow of Louis of Nevers, and place it upon that of Edward Prince of Wales.*

Such were the tidings which made Edward instantly determine to visit Belgium; and, accompanied by the Prince and a large force, he sailed from Sandwich on Sunday the 3d of July, and arrived in safety at Sluys after an easy passage.† He did not disembark, however; and it would appear that his coming took the Flemings completely by surprise. Numbers, however, of the burgomasters visited him on board his ship, where they were splendidly entertained; and as soon as his arrival was generally known, the municipal councils of all the great towns, with Artevelde at their head, proceeded to offer him their congratulations. Several days were spent in festivities; and time was

* Froissart, chap. ccxlvii. Rymer, tom. ii. part iv. p. 185.
† Rymer, tom. ii. part iv. p. 184.

given for the young Prince of Wales, in all the beauty and grace of youth, and gifted in the highest degree with that chivalrous courtesy so engaging in a prince, to win the affections of the Flemish citizens.

At length one day, when all were assembled, Artevelde, with his usual specious eloquence, addressed his countrymen; and setting forth the virtues of the Prince, the obligations which Flanders was under to Edward, the advantages which must arise from a nearer connection with England; and contrasting therewith the weakness of the Count, the many ills which his adherence to France had produced to the country, and the dangers that menaced them if his power should ever be renewed, he proceeded boldly to propose that they should solemnly cast off their allegiance to that weak sovereign, and bestow the vacant coronet upon the heir of the British throne. Flanders, according to his plan, was to be raised to a dukedom; and Edward Prince of Wales was to have the defence and government thereof, with the aid of a Flemish council.

Artevelde, however, had calculated upon greater influence than he now possessed; time had really diminished his power, and the point on which he endeavoured to exert it was exactly that in which it was most weak. There were besides various difficulties in the way of the measure which he proposed, that were likely to prevent many independent citizens from giving him assistance, as well as those who had been actually gained by France. The burgher councils had tasted for a long time, each in their particular town, the sweets of uncontrolled power; and what Artevelde demanded was plainly an immediate and direct resignation of a part of that power; while, on the other hand, the dangers with which he sought to alarm them in regard to France were, however certain, distant and obscure, and therefore much preferable in their minds to the instant deprivation with which they saw themselves menaced. In addition to this obstacle, it is certain that, notwithstanding the long feuds between themselves and their lords, notwithstanding their turbulent and ungovernable disposition, feelings of reverence for the feudal system were not totally extinct in the hearts of the Flemings*; and those feelings were all opposed to casting off the nominal jurisdiction of a prince whom they had long ceased to obey. There is not a better established nor a more extraordinary fact in the his-

* Although I believe I might, without any other authority than the general character of man, have stated this reverence as one of the motives which induced the Flemings to hesitate upon the proposal of Artevelde, yet I have not done so unsupported by proof; and I rather seek to give it as one of the most extraordinary historical instances of that peculiar propensity in man's mind to adhere to even the shadow of his old institutions, to which I immediately after refer, than intend the subsequent observations as corroborative of my statement. Froissart, and all the other chroniclers of the time, speak of the feelings of the Flemings in this respect as if they had never shown one act of disobedience to their princes. His expressions are — "Dont ceux du pays n'etoient mie bien d'accord au roi ni à Artevelde, qui preschoit sa querelle de desheriter le Comte Louis leur naturel seigneur, et son jeune fils Louis, et heriter le fils du roi d'Angleterre. Cette chose n'eussent ils fait jamais." And again — "Dont commencèrent toutes gens à murmurer sur lui; et ne leur vint mie bien à plaisir cette requête; et dirent que s'il plaisait à Dieu, ils ne seroient ja sçus ni trouvés en tel deloyauté que de vouloir déshériter leur naturel seigneur, pour hériter un etranger." Chapters ccxlvii. and ccxlviii.

tory of that contradictory thing, human nature, than that men will adhere tenaciously to the shadow after they have long cast away the substance, especially in regard to old institutions. Hope, and expectation, and enterprise, and the spirit of improvement, and ignorance of the future, and the sense of inconveniences present, still hurry mankind on to change; but memory hangs fondly round the past, and often calls back the fugitive in all the impetuosity of his onward career.

The Flemings had hated, and despised, and trampled upon their lords; but when it was proposed to them calmly and formally to break the strongest feudal ties, and verbally deny the force of institutions they had often substantially violated, they shrunk from the undertaking, and only sought how they might best evade giving a decided answer in presence of a monarch they feared to offend. After a short and murmuring consultation amongst themselves, they fell upon an often-used excuse. They professed their great attachment to the King, and their love and admiration for the gallant and generous prince proposed for their acceptance*; but they set forth at the same time, that not having been themselves aware of the great changes about to be submitted to them, they had come unprepared with any knowledge of the sentiments of the general people, of whom they were the representatives. On a matter of such moment to Flanders, they dared not, they said, return any positive

* Froissart, chap. ccxlvii., d'Oudegherst, tom. ii. p. 463.

answer without consulting their fellow-countrymen and learning their opinion; but they promised that, on a certain day, they would return the King a more decided answer; and with many professions of affection and zeal, they took their leave.

Whatever were the sentiments of Edward on the reply of the Flemings, Artevelde no longer deceived himself; but saw that in the undecided state of the minds of his countrymen, the day would soon be lost to him and to the English cause for ever, unless he could by some real and substantial power, support the authority he had raised upon the unstable basis of popular opinion.

After the councils of the Flemish towns had retired, he remained some time in consultation with the English monarch; and though it is not now possible to ascertain the exact plan determined upon, with a view to overcome the scruples of the Flemings, it is evident that it comprehended both the means of persuasion and intimidation. In pursuit of the first, Artevelde, fancying himself more secure of Ghent, as the place of his own particular residence, proceeded to Bruges and Ipres, and found his oratory still so powerful, that the citizens of those two cities yielded themselves implicitly to his guidance.* He had, however, committed a great error in postponing the impetration of Ghent to any other consideration. That city was decidedly the largest and most influential of the Flemish towns; and, having once

* Froissart, chap. ccxlviii.

engaged it to commit itself to the prosecution of his designs, he could not have failed of success with the rest of the country. His enemies also were more numerous and more powerful in Ghent than in the other cities; and it was there that the battle between his influence and that of France was sooner or later to be fought. To delay his journey thither, therefore, one day after the arrival of the municipal council, now furnished with a knowledge of his designs, was to afford his adversaries time to choose and fortify their position; and this they did not fail to do, with the utmost celerity and effect. A burgher of the name of Gerard Denis, dean of the great trade of weavers, a man perhaps less ambitious and certainly less talented than Artevelde, but equally daring and equally factious, put himself at the head of the opposite party, and easily found means to stir up the multitude against him who had once been their idol. All the ordinary means of decrying a public man, which have been used for long centuries in the past, and will undoubtedly be employed for long centuries in the future, were turned against Artevelde; and whether true or false — for the verity of an accusation is of little consequence to an excited populace — he was charged with engrossing the whole power of Flanders, with embezzling the public money, and conveying the proceeds of the taxes to a foreign country, in order to prepare for himself a safe refuge and enormous fortune in England. Day after day the same tale was repeated with aggravated circumstances; and the people, receiving it all as truth, wrought themselves into a phrensy of hatred towards Artevelde.

Intelligence of all these proceedings reached the falling demagogue before his return to Ghent, and he communicated them to Edward, petitioning at the same time for some armed assistance to support him in authority, till he could recover the false step he had made.* The interests of the English King and his son were too deeply affected to allow of hesitation; and it can be hardly doubted that had Artevelde judged it necessary, Edward would have disembarked his troops and entered Ghent at the head of his army. Nor can it be doubted that Bruges, Ipres, and the rest of the country being secured, this policy, though bold, would have been the most effectual in the state of mind to which the people of Ghent had been by this time excited. But Artevelde still fancied his power greater than it really was, and that of his enemies less. He doubted not that a small force to secure the persons of his principal opponents would be sufficient, and that his eloquence would soon have its wonted effect upon the people. Under this conviction, all he asked and all he received was a guard of 500 English soldiers, and with these he proceeded towards Ghent. Fearful, however, of finding the gates shut if he presented himself accompanied by a military force, he left the soldiers in concealment at a little distance from the town; and entered it attended only by his usual suite.†

* Chron. de Flandre, p. 177.

† Such is the opinion to which I have come after a minute examin-

In passing through the streets, he clearly saw that the animosity of the populace was much more strongly excited against him than he had anticipated.* Those who had been accustomed to push back their hoods and bow low as he passed, now turned their backs without any sign of reverence, and re-entered their houses. He was suffered to proceed uninterrupted, however, to his own dwelling, where he was immediately induced, by evident signs of a change in popular opinion, to call together all those friends and retainers who had too deeply participated in all his schemes and actions to hope for immunity in the event of his fall. A hundred and forty persons were thus assembled in his house; and as signs of tumult began to manifest themselves in the town, the doors and windows were barricaded, and every means were taken to fortify it as effectually as the time would permit.

The apprehensions of Artevelde were not unfounded. Gerard Denis, it would appear, had gained information of his measures in regard to the guard he had obtained; the gates of the city were closed, the people were called to arms; and in a short time the dwelling of the popular leader was surrounded on every side by a furious multitude, crying loudly for his blood.† Every

ation and comparison of Froissart, D'Oudegherst, Meyerus, and various public records. But it may be necessary to state that some chronicles assert the English soldiers accompanied him into the town, and were massacred with him.

* Froissart, chap. ccxlviii.

† Chronique de Flandres.

means were now employed to force a way in; and Artevelde and his companions showed on their part the determined resistance of despair. But the number of assailants rendered defence hopeless; and after repelling the first efforts, the demagogue presented himself at one of the higher windows, and once more used those powers of eloquence which had so often ruled the multitude that now clamored for his death. His influence, however, was gone; and his oratory proved ineffectual, though tears and entreaties were added to arguments and protestations.*

Finding that no mercy was to be expected, and that resistance could not repel from a weak dwelling many thousands of armed and infuriated men, Artevelde determined to fly to the only refuge which his circumstances permitted him to seek; namely, the sanctuary of a church which was situated nearly behind his own house.† With this design, he closed the window, and endeavoured to reach a back door, from which his escape to the church would have been comparatively easy; but before he could gain it, the barricades were driven in, and in a moment several hundreds of people poured into the house, dealing death to every one they met. Artevelde was instantly surrounded; and while a number struggled

* Froissart, chap. ccxlviii.

† His house, which was situated in the *Padden hoek*, or Toads' Corner, was not, as has been generally supposed, demolished by the faction which slew him, as we find it mentioned particularly some years after; but all the records of his government were so completely destroyed, that I have only been able to hear of one document at present in existence which bears his signature. See *Mémoires sur la Ville de Gand*, by Diericx, tom. iv. p. 47.

to obtain possession of his person, Gerard Denis put a period to his existence by the blow of an axe.*

Thus died a man whose imputed faults have outweighed, in the opinions of all historians, many great qualities which his mind undoubtedly possessed. But fresh facts have been discovered which render former accusations doubtful. That he was highly gifted by nature, is evident from the effects which his talents produced in an age when the general state of intellect amongst the lower orders, and the prejudices and policy of the higher classes, were as unfavourable as it is possible to conceive for the exertions by which he rose. That his virtues were greater than have been admitted, and that his vices were less than they have been depicted, we may also reasonably assume, when we remember that his actions have in most instances been chronicled by his enemies, and his character transmitted to posterity by people whose prejudices he assailed. Had his education been equal to his genius, and his means been equal to his designs, it is probable that he would have proved himself one of the greatest men of modern Europe; and even comprehending those designs but imperfectly, and deducing his history from unfavourable sources, it is scarcely too much to class him amongst the greatest men of the age in which he lived.

What were the ulterior objects of the design in

* Chron. de Flandres, p. 177. Froissart, chap. ccxlviii. The honour or disgrace of having killed Artevelde is divided amongst many, as we find from the registers of Ghent that several persons were subjected to the fine hereafter mentioned.

which he fell cannot now be told, but its first appearance was certainly well calculated to arouse the fears of a nation jealous of its liberties; and in the means which he employed, he showed a lamentable want of that prudent caution and knowledge of human nature which had characterised all his preceding political enterprises. As far as we can judge of the interests of Flanders at that time, it would appear that, if it were absolutely necessary — which Artevelde undoubtedly believed it to be * — to choose between the recall of the French domination or submission to an English prince, the Flemish leader was imperatively required, both for his own sake and for that of his country, to fix upon the latter alter-

* That Artevelde was justified in believing that the only alternatives were those stated above, and that he did believe such to be the case, may be inferred from the suddenness of his call for Edward's presence, from the known influence which the French had obtained, and from the sacrifice of his own power which he proposed to make. Nor does the fact that the Flemings did not for a long time follow the course he apprehended at all show that he had not very good reasons to fear they would recall the domination of the French. At the time of his death the position of Philip of Valois was very different from that which it soon became. That monarch, when Edward was called to Flanders by the apprehensions of Artevelde, had removed a number of his enemies in Britanny, had gained many great points in Aquitaine, and was in every respect in a situation to hold out both menaces and promises to the Flemings with a great prospect of their fulfilment. Before the end of the same year, however, his troops had been defeated in Aquitaine, his efforts had failed in Britanny, and his rival was preparing to lead another army into the heart of his kingdom. The Flemings, therefore, had soon reason to feel that—as in their communications with him they had by no means gone too far to retract, and as they had nothing for the time to fear from his enmity, while there was much to lose by that of Edward — a change of policy had become necessary; and they made several concessions to the English King, in order to expiate their negotiations with the monarch of the French.

native. He did so; and had he followed the dictates of that same shrewd policy which had formerly guided him, he would easily have found an excuse to introduce the English monarch and the English army into Ghent, without suffering the French faction even to know the purpose of the royal visit. Small persuasions in the market-place of Ghent, supported by 10,000 armed men, would have effected what no persuasions could obtain on board the King's ship at Sluys; and Artevelde, sacrificing a part of his power to retain the rest, would have transferred the coronet of Flanders from the brow of Louis of Cressy, to that of Edward Prince of Wales, would have conferred a boon upon a mighty king, and probably a benefit upon his native country.

Whether any results could morally justify such an act of deceit, can hardly be a question; but, beyond all doubt, such was the train of policy which the former conduct of Artevelde might have led an observer to imagine he would pursue in the present conjuncture. We almost always find, however, that a long course of success gives a sort of confidence very different from that which arises in a reliance on accurate and extensive views and prudent calculations. Many a man sets out in life with a daring and powerful genius, which, trusting implicitly to the precautions which it has previously taken, and the resources which it feels within itself for the future, grapples with enterprises, and risks consequences, and succeeds in efforts, that would daunt the timid, and be lost by the slow and calculating; but, after a long course of success, the basis of confidence becomes changed to the same man: he trusts to his fortune, not to his genius, grows rash instead of bold, and falls by events for which he is neither prepared nor adequate.

Such I believe to have been the case with Artevelde. His first enterprises, however daring, were conducted with skill, vigilance, and activity; and he met with the meed which such conduct usually obtains, success, — success in enterprises the greatness of which had not dazzled him, and the details of which had been considered by a mind equal to their conception as a whole. The long habit of prosperity, however, taught him to believe that it was inherent in his attempts; and in this persuasion he forgot that wisdom by which it had really been bestowed.

The death of Jacob Von Artevelde at once overthrew the projects of the English monarch, and removed the prospect of the sovereignty of Flanders from the eyes of the young Prince of Wales. No sooner did the tidings reach the fleet, than weighing anchor it bore away for England, Edward vowing in the first heat of the grief and indignation which he really felt for the death of a man who had so faithfully served him, to wreak bitter vengeance on the Flemings ere long for the deed they had just committed.* Time, however, acts on the wrath of monarchs, as on the passions of other men, with a power of mitigation which the most inflexible nature can

* Froissart, chap. ccxlix.

hardly resist; and before he arrived in England, the anger of the English King was sufficiently abated to leave his ear open to the voice of interest. His return was delayed by a tremendous storm, an event which generally attended his passage from the Continent to England *; but when at length he did reach the British shores, policy had so far resumed her sway over his mind as to prevent any allusion in his public papers to the causes of indignation which the Flemings had given. Even in his very first proclamation, he declared that his voyage to Flanders had removed all the perils with which his interests in that country had been threatened, and that the faithful obedience of the Flemings to himself as legitimate King of France was established on a firmer basis than ever. †

In the meanwhile the people of Belgium on their parts perceived the danger and disadvantage which must accrue to their trade from any permanent disagreement with England: the circumstances also which had induced many of them to look upon a reunion with France as an event which might be more advantageous than their alliance with the English monarch, were changed before the end of the year

* The occurrence of a tempest as Edward returned from the Continent was so invariable, that the flatterers of the period declared loudly that it was evident France belonged to the English King, as even the winds and seas opposed his abandonment of each effort he made to recover that territory. Edward in all probability did not discourage such an idea; for although he does not appear to have been greatly influenced by superstition himself, yet many traits of his life evince that he well knew the powerful effect it had upon others.

† Rymer, tom. ii. part iv. p. 185.

by the occurrences which took place in France. Philip every day lost the power of protecting or benefiting his allies, while Edward acquired the means of punishing severely each breach of faith towards him; and the Flemings who, with all their turbulence, generally calculated their interests with great nicety, soon found it necessary to court the favour of the English monarch, and to atone for the violence they had committed by manifold protestations of submission and grief. The death of Artevelde was represented as the act of a frantic mob; severe pecuniary fines were imposed upon the leaders of the party who slew him*; and though the three principal towns declined in respectful language to break the bands which tied them to the Count of Flanders, they offered to make those very ties the means of uniting them more closely to the English monarch. The method by which they proposed to effect this object was by marrying Louis, the son of the reigning Count, to one of the daughters of Edward. As neither of the parties, however, was yet of a marriageable age, the final arrangement of the whole was deferred till an after period; and Edward, who evidently gained some additional power in the Low Countries † by the con-

* See the very learned Mémoires sur la Ville de Gand, by M. Diericx, tom. iv. p. 47, 48.

† This is made manifest by a variety of papers preserved in Rymer, which prove, that the Flemings not only remained sincerely attached to Edward for some time, but that they acted in such a manner as to effect a powerful diversion in Edward's favour, while he carried on the war in Britanny and Gascony, and led his troops in person into Normandy. Thus we find Hugo of Hastings appointed by the King his locum tenens and captain general in Flanders, on the 20th June

cessions which were made as a compensation for the loss he had sustained in Artevelde, contented himself for the time with frustrating the views of Philip in the north, and prepared to carry the war once more into his adversary's territory.*

1346; and by a paper of the same date, it appears that the Flemings had agreed to furnish a certain force to act directly against France, under the command of an English officer. The assertion of the great body of historians is positive that the Flemings, fell off from England after the death of Artevelde (see Rapin, page 423. folio ed.), and made their peace with their own Prince. So far from the truth, however, is this assertion, that we not only find the apppointment of Hastings recorded, but we find also the services in which he was employed, and which were none other than in aiding the Flemings, with a strong body of English troops under his command, to expel from Termonde and other places the garrisons left behind him by the Count of Flanders, after a vain attempt to recover his authority on the death of Artevelde. See the notes of M. Lesbroussart upon D'Oudegherst, tom. ii. p. 466.

* The character of Jacob Van Artevelde has lately been ably defended by the amiable and learned Cornelissen, in his rare but admirable *Mémoire sur les Chambres de Rhétorique:* by the Chevalier Dierickx, in his *Mémoire sur le Droit public et politique de la Ville de Gand*, tom. i. p. 61. 181.; and by Monsieur A. Voisin, in his *Guide des Voyageurs dans la Ville de Gand*, a work which, notwithstanding its unpretending title, bears witness, in every page, of learning, research, and talent. These writers prove beyond all contradiction that Artevelde conferred innumerable benefits on Flanders; that he displayed great military talents on various occasions; that he completely remodelled and wonderfully improved the internal polity of his native country; that he raised commerce, manufactures, and agriculture to a pitch they had never before reached; and that, on various occasions, even where his own passions were most strongly engaged, he showed that reverent obedience to the laws scarcely possible to reconcile with his picture as painted by Froissart. Why Froissart should have so traduced him cannot be now ascertained; but it is clear that, at the very time that the chronicler was accusing him of a thousand crimes, the Flemings were still submitting to the laws he had made, preserving his regulations with scrupulous reverence, and burning a perpetual lamp to his memory.

CHAP. XVII.

EDWARD THE BLACK PRINCE PREPARES TO ACCOMPANY HIS FATHER TO FRANCE. — HIS WANT OF ECONOMY. — DELAYS OF THE EXPEDITION. — IT SAILS FOR NORMANDY. — PROCEEDINGS AT LA HOGUE. — THE BLACK PRINCE KNIGHTED. — VALOGNES, CARENTON, AND ST. LO TAKEN. — STORMING OF CAEN. — LOUVIERS AND THE PONT DE L'ARCHE SACKED. — MARCH TOWARDS PARIS. — PHILIP'S PREPARATIONS. — INEFFECTUAL EFFORTS TO PASS THE SEINE. — THE PASSAGE EFFECTED. — PHILIP IN FORCE FOLLOWS THE BRITISH ARMY. — EDWARD ATTEMPTS TO PASS THE SOMME. — CRITICAL SITUATION OF THE KING OF ENGLAND. — PASSAGE OF THE SOMME, AND BATTLE OF BLANCHE TACHE.

Edward the Black Prince was now entering his sixteenth year. His body, naturally strong and vigorous, had been hardened by the fatigues and exercises of a military education; and his mind, whose original capacity was great, had been stimulated to exertion by many a lesson of honour, by the example of his mother's generous virtues, and his father's ever-growing renown. The bright world of youth was all before him; and his mental and corporeal powers, his period of life, his station in society, the habits he had acquired, and the objects which had been presented to his hopes, all taught him ardently to seek that active employment of his faculties which is necessary to the health, to the happiness, to the existence of man. Opportunity was now about to be presented to him; and while his father hastened the necessary preparations for the invasion of France, which he once more determined to undertake, the Prince, with far more eager zeal, prepared for the first time to mingle with conflicting hosts and tread the field of battle.

The ardour of youth, and youth's unthinking inexperience, led him already to contract debts which, we are particularly told, were incurred in consequence of the immense expense attendant upon the first military expedition in which he was engaged.* Nor, indeed, can we wonder that with credit easily obtained, he followed the example set him by his father, who at the very same time was engaged in compelling very involuntary loans from all who could furnish him with money.† Nevertheless, the habit thus early begun, I mean the habit of undertaking more than his resources were calculated to sustain, is unhappily to be traced throughout the life of Prince Edward; and we do not wonder to find the same person who at fifteen was thus pressed by creditors, and burthened with debt, terminating his career in the midst of difficulties and sorrows, hurried on by the same disproportion between his endeavours and his means. It may be said in his defence that in almost all instances his financial embarrassments proceeded rather from unfortunate circumstances compelling him to incur expense, than from profusion in the conduct of his enterprises; but, liberal and not careful, his error lay in not providing

* Rymer, tom. ii. part iv. p. 201. † Rymer, tom. ii. part iv. p. 191.

for times of exigency by frugality in moments of plenty; and few persons who trace the consequence of events in history will doubt, though parsimony be a vice more contemptible in a monarch than in an individual, that the want of proper economy is a failing in a prince most dangerous both to his people and to himself.

On the present occasion it will be seen that a number of delays, which were imposed upon the Prince of Wales by the circumstances of the country, forced him to maintain a great military establishment for nearly a year in perfect idleness; and thus to free him from the pressure of his debts, his father was obliged, when the time of activity at length arrived, to grant him the privilege of conveying his property by will to executors, who by the same act were invested with power to hold all the lands and revenues which had been granted to him for one year after his death.

The causes of the delays to which I have alluded were various, and must be noticed briefly. The forces which accompanied Edward to Flanders, though perfectly equal to overcome any resistance which the monarch might have anticipated in that quarter, were by no means adequate to encounter the army of a powerful adversary. The monarch's first step, therefore, after his return to Sandwich, was to hasten by proclamation the levying of additional troops throughout England. This of course required time, and the interval was fully filled up by negotiations with the Emperor in regard to the renewal of former alliances; with the Pope concerning the breach of the truce with Philip; with the Kings of Castile and Portugal, in pursuance of treaties already in progress; and with a variety of inferior states and minor sovereigns, for the purpose of thwarting the measures of his adversary, and attaching adherents to himself. In addition to these important transactions, Edward's attention was engaged by two great objects, the provision of money for the immediate expenses of the expedition, and preparation for the defence of his kingdom during his absence. The principal means employed to accomplish the first consisted in somewhat tyrannous exactions from abbots, bishops, and private persons, both lay and clerical*; and in seizing the revenues of what were called the alien priories into the hands of the King.† To guard against threatened invasions from Normandy, which province seems to have resumed the former wild project of conquering England, the King commanded beacons to be established along the coast, and the counties to be placed in a state of general preparation for vigorous and immediate resistance.‡ Nor were these alone the occupations which pressed heavily upon the mind of the English monarch. The death of his brother-in-law, William, Count of Hainault, who was killed in

* Rymer, tom. ii. part iv. p. 191.

† It would seem that the revenues of the alien priories had been partly restored to their former possessors after the truce of Malestroit; but I can find no trace of their having been generally resigned by the King for many years after this period.

‡ Rymer, tom. ii. part iv. p. 193.

Friesland, in 1345, left in dispute the land which had been granted in dowery to Philippa of England, as well as his own territories, and a long train of negotiations ensued of a painful and difficult nature. In the Count himself Edward lost a brave and attached, though rash and obstinate, friend; but his death was followed by an event of still greater importance, namely, a breach of the alliance which had hitherto existed between the King of England and the famous John of Hainault, one of the boldest and most talented of the military leaders of Europe.* How Philip† engaged him in his cause, and detached him from that of the English monarch, whom he had

* Froissart, chap. ccl.

† There is no absolute proof that the dowery of the Queen of England was the original cause of quarrel between Edward and his wife's uncle; but the first claims of Edward upon the territories of the dead Count of Hainault are addressed to John of Hainault, and they seem immediately to have been turned into a different channel by some circumstances of which we are not aware. (See Rymer, vol. ii. part iv. p. 187. 190. 198.) The account given by Froissart of the defection of John of Hainault is that Philip employed the Count de Blois, who had married his daughter, to seduce him by offers of personal advantage; which failing, from that leader's affection for his niece and her husband, the Lord of Fagnoelles, his favourite companion and friend, was next gained to the French interest. Through his means and by his suggestion, John of Hainault was made to believe that the King of England had withheld the pension which he had enjoyed for many years, and that it was his intention to deprive him of it for ever. While his anger on this subject was excited to the highest pitch, Philip's emissaries continued to court him with the most assiduous attention; and he was in the end tempted to abandon the King in whose service he had spent the brightest years of his life, and join himself to that monarch's bitterest enemy. (Froissart, chap. ccl.)

Barnes states, after Villani, that the Marquis of Juliers was slain in Friesland, with the Count of Hainault; but this was by no means the case, as we find him with Edward III. long afterwards.

so long and so faithfully served, is variously stated; but it is not at all improbable, that some slight cause of quarrel, in regard to the dowery of his niece the Queen of England, might be magnified by the artful partisans of Philip into a matter of sufficient importance to justify the rash and angry act which separated him for ever from his former ally.

Thus it appears that the attention of the King was sufficiently occupied; but still the length of time required for levying and arming such a body of troops as the extent of his design demanded, was the principal cause of the monarch's delay; for every document which has descended from those days to the present evinces that Edward's reliance was solely fixed upon his native forces, and that he had now resolved to lead a larger army of Englishmen into France than he had ever yet brought into the field. Every man between sixteen and sixty on the hither side of Trent was called to arms, and commanded to prepare to follow the King in his expedition. The most arbitrary stretch of the royal prerogative* was ventured to swell the ranks of the English army to an unusual extent; and Portsmouth having been named as the place of assembly, the mid Sunday of Lent was appointed as the latest day for the general muster.†

* The King's mandate on this occasion is one of the most curious documents in history; and shows precisely by its various provisions both the extent to which the royal prerogative was sometimes illegally carried, and the rights which the people knew they possessed, and which the monarch in some degree was obliged to acknowledge even while he violated them.

† Rymer, tom. ii. part iv. p. 191.

A tremendous tempest, however, having scattered the whole and destroyed a great part of the fleet collected for the transport of the royal troops, the day of meeting was postponed till Easter.* What was the amount of the forces then assembled it is hardly possible to say; but we know that Edward the Black Prince was called upon to lead from his principality three thousand five hundred and fifty men as his individual quota; while we find orders directed to other nobles holding lands in Wales, which imply the levying of at least three thousand five hundred more. The army raised in the English counties, although it is clear that the mandate of the King was obeyed but very imperfectly, must have been considerable; and before this period, a great part of the British forces had been recalled from Britanny, together with the Earl of Northampton.†

Every thing seems to have been fully prepared for the proposed expedition before the end of April: and we find no reasonable cause for farther delay, except some new efforts made by the Church of Rome to bring about the often-rejected peace.‡ Edward, as well as the very parties who proposed this renewal of negotiation, must have been aware that it would prove fruitless; and he evidently yielded with reluctance to the reiterated solicitation of the cardinals, so that we cannot suppose his movements to have been greatly retarded by those trans-

* Rymer, tom. ii. part iv. p. 192. † Barnes.

‡ Rymer, tom. ii. part iv. p. 199.

actions. In the very outset of such a complicated enterprise, however, as that in which Edward was now engaged, the obstacles to be overcome, and the difficulties to be conquered, were of course great; and we find that his departure for France was delayed for several months after the period to which it had been at first postponed.

At length, in the middle of July 1346 *, Edward sailed from the Isle of Wight, leaving his second son, Lionel, guardian of the kingdom during his absence.† The number of ships which accompanied the monarch on his voyage, is more variously mentioned than can be reconciled with any degree of truth or information on the part of the historians. By some it is stated to have consisted of more than 1000 large and 500 small vessels ‡; and by others the number of ships is reduced to 200. § Of men at arms ||

* Most writers, both French and English, state the departure of Edward to have taken place on the 2d of July, solely because on that day the last transaction in regard to the delivery of the great seal took place in the Isle of Wight. But this could not have been the day on which Edward left that island, as a letter patent, empowering the Council to open letters, addressed to the King during his absence, is dated, "*apud portum Sanctæ Elenæ in Insula Vectæ undecimo die Julii.*"

† Rymer, tom. ii. part iv. p. 202. ‡ Knighton, col. 1585.

§ Barnes, p. 340. I am inclined to believe that the real number was about 500; as in the Harleian MSS., No. 246., we find attached to a list of the principal men at arms, who served at the siege of Calais, a note of the ships which were employed in those wars, together with the number of mariners which they contained. The amount is as follows:— South fleet ships, 433; mariners, 9030: North fleet ships, 37; mariners, 805. The handwriting of the MS., however, does not appear very ancient.

|| In regard to the men at arms and archers this account is taken from Froissart. He has been supposed to diminish the number of the English troops; but judging from every collateral fact, I am inclined to

4000, with 10,000 archers, 12,000 Welsh, and 6000 Irish, constituted, according to the best accounts, the whole force which accompanied the King; but these were led by twenty-four of the most famous commanders of Christendom*, famous not alone for their valour but their skill.

---

believe that his statement is very nearly correct. The amount of the men at arms returned from one hundred and thirty places in England, on this very occasion, among which places such considerable towns as London, Hertford, Gloucester, Maidstone, Guilford, Reading, Bedford, Leicester, and Cirencester are comprised, only reaches 1177, which leaves it very probable that the whole force of men at arms did not exceed four or five thousand. Should it seem difficult to make this statement agree with the account given of the great efforts made by Edward to raise troops, we must remember that a considerable force was necessarily left behind for the defence of the Scottish frontier, that a large army was already in Gascony, and that Britanny also was held against the French by English soldiers.

* Barnes gives the names of these leaders from the Cambridge manuscript to which I have before referred. They were, besides Edward himself and Godfrey de Harcourt, Humphry Bohun Earl of Hereford and Essex, William Bohun Earl of Northampton, Thomas Beauchamp Earl of Warwick, Richard Fitz-Allan Earl of Arundel, John de Vere Earl of Oxford, William de Clynton Earl of Huntingdon, Robert Ufford Earl of Suffolk; together with the Lords Roger Mortimer, Gerard Lisle, Reginald Cobham, John and Roger Beauchamp, John Mowbray, William de Roos, Thomas Lucy, William Felton, Thomas Bradston, Ralph Basset, John Willoughby de Eresby, Peter Mauler, Thomas Ughtred, John Fitzwalter, William Kerdestan, Roger Say, Almeric de St. Amand, Robert Bourchier, John le Strange, Edward Montague, Richard Talbot, John Mohun, William Boteler, Robert Ferrers, John Seymour, John Grey, William Botreaux, Hugh Spencer, John Striveling, Michael Poynings, Robert Morley, Thomas Morley, Thomas Ashby, John Sutton, Nicolas Cantelupe, John Chandos, Peter and James Audley, Bartholemew Burwash, Thomas Holland, Fulk Fitzwarren, and Richard Pembroke. The Harleian MS. just cited, gives us but little precise information in regard to numbers. The words are, *the principal* men at arms; and the account refers to the siege of Calais, on which occasion fresh troops joined the

In the monarch's own ship, sailed also Godfrey of Harcourt, and Edward Prince of Wales; the latter in his sixteenth year, animated by all the eager hopes of youth, and the aspirations of mighty genius struggling forward towards the fitting field for its active exertion; the former burning with the near prospect of that revenge, which, as it is one of the most purely criminal, is one of the most powerful of the human passions. The instigations of De Harcourt had undoubtedly hastened the steps of the English King; and his persuasions now guided him to that part of the country with which he himself was best acquainted, and where his influence and knowledge might be most serviceable to the cause he had espoused.*

It has been asserted that Edward, up to the time of his departure, and even after he had set sail, proposed to direct his course to Guyenne, in order to expel the French completely from his territories in Aquitaine; and that a contrary wind was the first inducement which led him to listen to the counsels of his Norman ally, and conduct his armament to La Hogue. Such vacillation, however, was totally contrary to the general character of all Edward's other enterprises; and as many of the statements generally connected with the account of his present proceedings

---

King from England. The number, including knights, but no inferior persons, amounts to 1265; of whom were only two German counts and 91 German knights. The MS. is very curious, however, in many respects, and well deserves to be printed, if it have not been printed already.

* Froissart, chap. cclxiv.

are decidedly false, I cannot doubt that this assertion is so likewise, and that long before the monarch set sail, his plan for invading Normandy was fully formed upon the suggestions of Godfrey de Harcourt. It was very natural to ensure his design from being defeated in the outset by the preparation of his adversary's means of resistance, that the monarch and his counsellors should maintain the most profound silence in regard to the real object of the expedition. Nor is it at all improbable, that even a false report of the intended landing in Guyenne was industriously circulated for the purpose of deceiving the enemy, and in the hope of finding the Neustrian coast completely unprepared for resistance; but at the same time I cannot suppose that Edward for one moment entertained a serious intention of conducting his troops to Aquitaine.*

* The motive assigned for this intention by Froissart, and by Barnes who follows his account blindly, is, that the position of the Earl of Derby, or rather the Earl of Lancaster, for his father was now dead, demanded the King's immediate presence in Guyenne. It appears, however, that such was by no means the case, as in the month of May, long after the assembly of the troops, Edward announces to the English clergy that the Earl had been eminently successful against the French, and calls upon them to pray for a continuation of Divine favour. (Rymer, tom. ii. part iv. page 199.). The letters also of the Earl himself show that he was any thing but in a depressed condition. (Robert of Avesbury, p. 141.) The whole account of Froissart, however, is positively erroneous in regard to Edward's voyage. He says that Edward, having sailed from Southampton, was cast upon the coast of Cornwall the third day by contrary winds. He there remained at anchor six days, and then sailed direct for Normandy. Now, as I have shown in a former note, Edward was still at the little port of St. Helens in the Isle of Wight on the morning of the 11th of July (Rymer, tom. ii. part iv. page 202.); and it is proved by other authorities (Robert of Avesbury, the Chroniques de France, and Edward's own letter preserved in the chronicle of Lanercost,) that he arrived at La Hogue on Wednesday

Certain it is that with a favourable wind he stretched his sails for Normandy; and after a short and easy passage, reached La Hogue on the small peninsula of Cotentin. He found the country, as he had been led to expect, totally undefended, and disembarked his troops without opposition *; but as he himself set foot upon the shore, he is said to have fallen with such violence that the blood gushed from his nose. The knights and barons who accompanied him, and who were all more or less tinged with the superstition of the day, besought him to return to his ship, declaring that the accident was an evil omen. Edward, however, with prompt policy recalled the words of Cesar, and replied that it was but a sign that the land desired him.†

For six days Edward remained at La Hogue‡ disembarking his horses and stores. Some repose was also judged necessary by that monarch, and a considerable time was employed in baking bread for the long march which lay before his troops; a precaution the more necessary in those days, as both parties

---

the 12th of July. He was therefore clearly not two whole days and nights on his passage. The Earl of Lancaster, in his letter cited above, makes no mention of having expected the King in Gascony, although he states that he was aware of Edward's having landed in Normandy, prior to the middle of August.

* Walsingham (p. 118.) mentions some opposition; and declares that the Earl of Warwick, with seven inferior soldiers, slew sixty Normans; but I see no cause why we should pause on such a tale for a moment, as Edward, in his own letter, never alludes to any event of the kind.

† Froissart, chap. cclxvi. ‡ Robert of Avesbury, page 123.

ravaged the country through which they passed, and the avant-guard of a royal army often spread desolation and famine for several leagues in advance of the main body, with very little consideration of the evils they inflicted upon their own companions as well as upon the enemy.* Before the English force quitted the peninsula of Cotentin also, a large detachment took and pillaged the town of Barfleur, which had been left without defence and was afterwards burned as well as Cherbourg and a number of small towns and castles. At the same time the fleet swept the sea coast of all those vessels which might have spread the intelligence of the invasion through different parts of the country, destroying more than 100 large ships.

Here, too, at La Hogue, Edward the Black Prince went through that ceremony † which was one of the

* I have followed throughout this account the letter of King Edward himself addressed to the Archbishop of Canterbury (Cotton MSS., Claudius, D. VII.), and that of Michael de Northbury, a personal attendant on Edward, as preserved by Robert of Avesbury. Beyond all question these documents are worthy of greater confidence than the account of Froissart, or that of the anonymous manuscript cited by Barnes, called Acta Edwardi filii Edwardi Tertii; but as their narrative is of course very brief, I have supplied some details from other sources where they are not contradicted by the more certain authority of the letters. All accounts state, however, that Edward landed at La Hogue St. Vast, by which I do not conceive the town of St. Vast to have been meant, as that would imply that the troops turned back from their road into the interior of France to attack Barfleur. I suspect that the cape of La Hogue itself was meant; but I advance the idea with doubt, as Edward says himself that they landed at "*La Hogue pres Barfluz.*" This letter has been published I believe in the Retrospective Review.

† Rymer, vol. ii. part iv. p. 205.

most important events in the life of a young warrior of those days, being dubbed a knight by his father's own hand; and at length, on Tuesday the 18th of July 1346, the King, after having created several others knights*, and conferred various military honours to encourage his young nobility to great efforts in the enterprise before them, struck his tents and began his march into the interior. His force now formed three divisions, commanded by Godfrey of Harcourt, the Earl of Warwick, and himself; while the Earl of Arundel acted as Lord High Constable, and the Earl of Huntingdon, in command of the fleet, followed the army along the sea coast.† Before quitting the peninsula of Contentin, De Harcourt, whose territory of St. Sauveur le Viscomte was situated within its limits, once more did homage for his lands to Edward III., as lawful King of France. But this act of his revenge was by no one mistaken for the effect of conviction, and none of the French nobles were thereby induced to follow his example in an act of rebellion, for which they did not possess the same motives.‡

Upon the march, Edward Prince of Wales accompanied his father; and in the various skirmishes which took place, as the King advanced into the heart of France, he first saw those things practised as a matter of severe necessity, of which the exercises of

* Barnes.

† Froissart, chap. cclxvi.

‡ Barnes, p. 341.

the tournament and the round table were but a sportive mockery. At their first day's halting-place, Valognes, no resistance seems to have been offered, and the town and castle surrendered*; but as they proceeded to Carentan, the breaking down of the bridges gave some signs of a growing spirit of resistance.† An attempt to defend the castle of Carentan appears to have been made; but Normandy, as Godfrey of Harcourt had previously informed the English monarch, had been long without seeing the face of an enemy, and it required time for the inhabitants to recover from the consternation and surprise which the sudden appearance of an unexpected adversary occasioned.‡ The place surrendered almost instantly; but notwithstanding all the efforts of the King of England, the town was pillaged and partially burned. §

Crossing the Vire, the royal army of England now attacked and took St. Lo; and under the guidance of Godfrey of Harcourt,—whose intimate knowledge of the country, as well as his skill in warfare, rendered him invaluable as a leader, while his peculiar circumstances placed his fidelity beyond doubt,—the English host advanced by rapid marches upon Caen, plundering as usual the country for six or seven leagues on either side of the line of march. Much more booty was obtained than any one then present had ever acquired by the same means before, as the

* Cotton MSS., Claudius, D. VII.

† Northbury, Robert de Avesbury.

‡ Froissart, chap. cclxvii.

§ Avesbury, p. 124.

towns of Normandy had become garners of the abundance of the land during a long continuance of prosperity and peace. Gold and silver were cheap in the English camp, and valets and grooms learned to despise fine cloth and gowns of fur.

In the meantime, the news of Edward's landing in Normandy flew to Paris; and the direction of his march seems to have been instantly divined by Philip of Valois, who, having been long aware of the great preparations which the English King was making for a renewal of the war, was in some degree ready to meet the storm wherever it might fall; though, from the great force he had detached to Gascony, it is probable that he had judged that province would be first exposed to its fury. No sooner, then, did he learn that the English had actually landed in Cotentin, than he despatched the Count d'Eu, then Constable of France, with the Count of Tankerville, and as numerous a force as he could collect at the moment, with orders to oppose the farther advance of Edward at Caen.

The Bishop of Bayeux had already thrown himself into that city; the castle was garrisoned by 300 Genoese, commanded by Sir Robert de Warignies; and the commons showed a zealous determination to defend their town to the last, which resolution was strengthened and confirmed by the arrival of the two Counts with 600 men at arms. Immediate preparations were made to raise new defences; but it would appear that the place, which was altogether unfortified except by a citadel, was incapable of resisting a powerful army; and that the only chance of delaying Edward before it was by opposing the passage of the river Orne, which flowed between the principal quarters of the town and parts which were then merely suburbs. The bridge, therefore, was barricaded; strong wooden towers were erected to gall the enemy in his approach; and such was the confidence of the inhabitants and their leaders, that all the offers of Edward were rejected with scorn; although he sent written promises of protection in person and property to the citizens, by the hands of Geoffrey de Maldon, a friar of the order of St. Austin.*

At length, on the 26th of July the English monarch, without having halted one day since he quitted La Hogue, arrived within two leagues of Caen; while the fleet, under the command of Clynton Earl of Huntingdon, came round to the mouth of the Orne, and anchored at the little port of Estreham. After sleeping in the fields, and gaining by his scouts what information he could, concerning the attitude of the enemy, Edward drew up his army for the attack, and marched forward towards the bridge. The suburbs were found deserted; and it became evident that upon the passage of the river depended the success of the day.† The attack was immediately begun, and

* Barnes, p. 344.

† This account, it will be perceived, is totally different from that of Froissart, who declares that the citizens of Caen went out against the will of the Constable and the Count of Tankerville to meet Edward in the open field; but fled upon the first appearance of the

the bridge was defended for some moments with great gallantry: but, at length, the barriers being forced, the commons fled in every direction; and the English poured in with overpowering numbers. Plunder and slaughter to a fearful extent were, of course, the consequences; and a multitude of knights, as well as citizens, were pursued and slain in the streets and gardens; though, from the horrid custom of instantly stripping the bodies, it became impossible to tell to what class the dead had in general belonged.* Nevertheless the spirit of chivalry in some degree ameliorated even the outrages inflicted on a town taken by assault; outrages which, in a time when men's minds were but half emancipated from the ferocity of the dark ages, would have been dreadful indeed, without some softening principle. Quarter was very generally given, after the first momentary fury of attack had subsided; and besides the Constable †, and the

---

English forces without striking a stroke. I found, however, that the French account (Chroniques de France, chap. xxxvii.) agreed in every material particular with that of Edward himself, and that of Michael Northbury, an Englishman, who was present; and, therefore, of course I preferred their united evidence to that of Froissart, who received his statement from another person (Jean le Bel) who was not present on the occasion himself. So far from the people of Caen having made a feeble defence, Edward (Cot. MSS., Claudius, D. VII.) gives them the highest praise for gallantry and good conduct.

* Villani states the number of the slain at five thousand.

† Edward, it would appear, bought the Constable of his captors for the sum of 80,000 florins. If Sir Thomas Leigh did take the Constable, as some have asserted, it was under the command of Thomas Lord Holland. See Rymer, tom. iii. part i.

Count of Tankerville, 140 knights *, and from 120 to 140 squires were made prisoners.† The loss of the English was very inconsiderable, the death of only one person of any note being recorded. ‡

The plunder collected was immense, and was more than sufficient to compensate for the expenses of the present expedition. § This being placed on board the vessels at Estreham, with the wealth which had been previously acquired, was despatched to England; and Edward prepared with all speed to march forward in search of new conquests. ||

He directed his steps, in the first place, towards Lisieux, from whence, it would appear, he proposed to march upon Rouen ¶; but at the former place he was met by two cardinals** commissioned to make such

* Edward's letter (Cot. MSS., Claudius, D. VII.).

† Robert of Avesbury.

‡ I have rejected the statement of Froissart, who says that an immense number of the English were killed and wounded, and that Edward commanded in revenge that the city should be given up to fire and sword, because his account does not agree with the King's own statement, with that of Northbury, who was present, nor with the Chronicle of France. The gentlemanly courtesy of Mr. Woodthorpe having lately placed the archives of the city under my inspection, I find in Vol. F. fol. 120. a contemporary account of the taking of Caen, in which it is especially marked that the city was captured *saunz perd de noz gentz.*

§ Henry.

|| Michael Northbury declares that the citizens of Bayeux sent to Edward to offer submission; but that the King refused to receive them to his fealty: but the letter which follows from Edward's confessor seems to imply the contrary, by the words, "Civitas Bajocensis se sponte reddidit, timens ne consimilia paterentur."

¶ Froissart, chap. cclxxii. Robert of Avesbury, p. 127.

** These were Annibal Ceccano, Cardinal Bishop of Tusculum, and Stephen Albert, Cardinal of Saint John and St. Paul. Rymer, tom. ii. part iv. p. 204.

offers as the Roman pontiff judged might produce a peace.* Their proposal, however, merely implied a restitution of the duchy of Aquitaine, in the same position as Edward's father had held it; with the prospect of greater concessions, if he would conclude a treaty of alliance by marriage between a member of his own family and one of the race of Valois.

Edward's original claims upon Aquitaine, however, were much greater than the offers of the cardinals were calculated to satisfy. It had been his invariable demand, as it was his unquestionable right, that the duchy should be restored in the same state, and to the same extent, as it had been originally held by Eleanor, whose marriage with Henry II. had conveyed it to the Kings of England; and now accompanied by a great and conquering army, amidst a career of glory and success, he was not likely to listen to any more limited concession. Of truces he knew the fallacy, and of delay he knew the danger; so that rejecting the mediation of the cardinals at once, he marched on to take advantage of the unprepared state of his adversary's territories.

Finding, during his halt at Lisieux, that Rouen had been put in such a state of defence as to promise a long and vigorous resistance, and unwilling to undertake any enterprise which might either delay his advance or tarnish the brightness of his previous success, he abandoned the design of attacking that city, and directed his march upon Evreux. Here also he

* 3d August 1346.

found preparations had been made for defence; and turning once more towards the Seine, he descended the beautiful valley of the Eure, in which Louviers and the Pont de l'Arche were completely sacked by his soldiers.*

The monarch's proceedings since the taking of Caen had been, perhaps, more bold than prudent; for it must be remembered that there is a great difference between the warfare of modern and that of feudal times, which difference was decidedly unfavourable to Edward. At present, a very considerable length of time is required for the formation of any thing like a regular army; but at that period, every man being by profession a soldier, and bound to take arms at a moment's notice, the materials for cutting off an invader's retreat were always ready in every part of the country, and could be organised with great rapidity. Such was the case in the present instance. While Edward was marching onward from Caen, the garrison of Rouen formed a nucleus for the collection of a larger force.† The Count of Harcourt, brother of the exile, and the Count de Dreux, called the whole of Normandy to arms; every feudal lord summoned his vassals to his banner, every vassal put his foot in the stirrup; and before Edward reached the banks of the Seine, a formidable army was gathering in his rear.‡ As his ships had by this time left the coast,

* Froissart, chap. cclxxiv.

† Robert of Avesbury, p. 128.

‡ Dr. Henry says that Philip was at Rouen in person; of this, however, there is not only no proof, but the positive assertion of Froissart, as

Edward had now only the choice of retreating through Normandy upon Britanny, or of attempting to force the passage of the Seine and fight his way to Flanders. He instantly chose the bolder alternative, and marched along the left bank of the river towards Paris *, seeking some passage for his troops, but in vain. The enemy followed him step by step on the opposite bank of the river; all the bridges were broken down; the fords destroyed; and the most watchful precautions were used in every way to guard against the possibility of his succeeding in this design.

Still he marched on, with a resolute countenance, ravaging the country through which he passed, and burning the towns of Vernon and Mantes†, as well as all the villages on the left bank of the Seine between the Pont de l'Arche and Poissy. At the latter place the bridge was found broken ‡; but

well as every sort of collateral evidence, against it. Henry is usually so extremely accurate, that so slight an error even as this is very uncommon. I am inclined to think, therefore, that he must have been misled by some bad edition of Froissart, as at the same place I find another mistake; namely, the assertion that Edward appeared in arms before Rouen. It is proved beyond doubt that he never approached nearer to that city than the Pont de l'Arche, whence he turned upon Paris.

* Froissart, chap. 273.

† Froissart declares that Edward also destroyed in marching to Poissy the towns of Meulan and Vernueil. I have omitted the first, because, being situated on the right bank of the Seine, it would have required the passage of the English army to have burned it; and this was the very object for which Edward was striving in vain. Vernueil also, being about fifty miles out of his line of march, seems to me to have been inserted by mistake, perhaps meaning Vernon.

‡ Robert of Avesbury, pp. 129. 136. Froissart, chap. cclxxiii.

the piles on which it rested were still in the river, and the facilities for its reconstruction which this circumstance afforded determined Edward to make the attempt. He accordingly halted at Poissy for five days; and to cover the real purpose of his pause, he detached considerable bodies of troops in various directions, burning and ravaging the country to the very gates of Paris. St. Germain, St. Cloud, Bourg la Reine, and a multitude of the small towns and hamlets that always gather around a capital, were given to the flames; and terror and anxiety spread amongst the Parisians at the bold approach of so successful an enemy. Poissy, which had given birth to St. Louis, had long been a favourite residence of the Kings of France; and several of the last monarchs of the Capetian race had taken pleasure in ornamenting it with a number of splendid buildings. One of the most beautiful specimens of the Gothic architecture of the period was to be found in the Dominican priory adjoining the King's palace, the prioress of which was always of noble and frequently of royal race. At the present time one of the sisters of the reigning monarch presided over the ladies of Poissy *; but the good nuns had fled to Paris on the approach of the invaders, and Edward found both the palace and the convent void. It was here, however, that he fixed his residence, during his stay in that town, whilst Edward Prince of Wales held a

* MS. Vet. in Bib. C. C. C. Cantab., tit. Acta Edwardi Filii Edwardi Tertii.

second court at another royal palace in the vicinity. Provisions of every kind were plenty in the town; and the English monarch and his son here celebrated the festival of the Assumption *, one of the solemn days of the Roman church, with as much pomp as if they had sat in the palace of the English capital.†

In the meanwhile Philip of Valois had issued a general summons for all his nobles to meet him with their armed vassals at St. Denis ‡, for the purpose of giving battle to the invader; and zealous troops were flocking in every day from all parts of the realm of France. It was not indeed that Philip was by any means a popular monarch, that he was loved, or that he was respected; for his late acts of insane violence had deprived him of what little esteem he had ever enjoyed amongst the nobles of France, and we shall soon have cause to see how little his commands were attended to, on occasions even of the most vital importance. There was never yet, however, an instance when the prospect of an immediate engagement did not find a French army ready to seek the field; and within a very few days after Edward had

* Froissart, chap. 273.

† Froissart breaks off his account of the military proceedings rather drolly to describe Edward holding his court in the Abbey of Poissy, *en draps fourrés d'ermines, de vermeille écarlate sans manches*. In regard to the manuscript Life of the Black Prince which I have cited above, I wish it clearly to be understood that I have not seen it, and that I trust to the exactness of Barnes's quotations, as he had access to it when it was in a far more perfect state.

‡ Froissart, chap. cclxix.

taken advantage of the old piles at Poissy to throw his bridge over the Seine, a force fully sufficient to givehim battle was collected at St. Denis.

Whether the generals who had hitherto watched his motions had been called to join the troops commanded by Philip himself, on account of the strong demonstrations made by Edward upon Paris and the prospect of a general engagement, or whether by a feigned movement the English king deceived them, as has been stated by some historians, and led them farther up the river, while the passage of his army was effected at Poissy, I do not know.*

As soon as it was possible, and apparently before the bridge was fully constructed†, Godfrey of Har-

* Henry declares that Edward deceived the French by marching a part of his forces up the river. All that Froissart says upon the subject is, "et tant allèrent qu'ils vinrent jusqu' à Poissy et trouvèrent le pont rompu et défait; mais encore étoient les estaches et les gites en la rivière. Si s'arrêta le roi et y sejourna par cinq jours. Entrementes fut le pont refait, bon et fort pour passer son ost, aisément et sans peril." At the same time, he marks that the previous appearance of the English detachments so near Paris as St. Cloud, &c. had not deceived Philip, who assured the citizens of the capital that Edward would approach no nearer. Michael Northbury makes no mention of any other movements to deceive the enemy; and yet it is impossible to suppose that Philip, after having taken so much pains to oppose Edward's passage, would have suffered him to construct a bridge and pass his men over without he had either deceived himself or had been deceived by Edward. Michael Northbury and Froissart both mention the engagement between a part of the English army and the burghers of Amiens; but the first declares that it took place while the bridge was yet in the act of being built, which, as the Amienois were certainly on the right bank of the Seine, implies, as I have stated in the text, that a part of the English force had passed the river before the bridge was absolutely finished.

† Froissart, chap. cclxxiv.

court, with the English advance guard, crossed the river, and shortly after fell in with a strong body of the burghers of Amiens, who were hastening with all diligence to join the King's muster at St. Denis. The English, fewer in number, were probably better disciplined; but the Picards wanted neither courage nor resolution, and they not only boldly* encountered the adverse force, but maintained the combat long, leaving full five hundred dead upon the field.† Notwithstanding all their valour, they were at length discomfited and dispersed; and the van of Edward's army, after pursuing the fugitives for some time, brought back to the monarch towards night the gratifying intelligence of this new success against the forces of his foe. Before the whole army had crossed also, Robert Lord Ferrers is said to have found means to convey his own retainers to the opposite bank, and, descending the river, to have taken by assault the strong fortress of La Roche Guyon.

On the 16th of August, Edward himself passed the river with his whole force‡, and immediately marched

* Froissart, chap. cclxxiv. Robert de Avesbury, p. 136.

† Michael Northbury says that this skirmish was fought by the Earl of Northampton; but that worthy clerk never mentions the foreign officer at all, although we know that he had a very great share in some of the chief actions of the campaign; and at the same time Froissart's account is so perfectly consistent with the situation he had before assigned to Godfrey de Harcourt, that I have adopted it in preference. Froissart, however, states that twelve hundred of the Amienois fell on this occasion.

‡ Rapin declares that Edward decamped from Poissy to frustrate Philip's design of enclosing him between the Seine and the Oise; which

upon Beauvais, with the apparent view of reaching Flanders*, where reinforcements might be expected. Beauvais itself was too strongly fortified and garrisoned to become an easy prey; and after some skirmishing at one of the gates, the two divisions which had made demonstrations of attacking it more seriously, contented themselves with setting fire to the suburbs, and followed the division of the King and the Prince of Wales.

In the meanwhile, Philip of Valois quitted St. Denis, on the first news of the English army having passed the Seine; and by parallel marches to the north, he endeavoured to interpose between Edward and the frontiers of Flanders. As his force

---

statement any one who looks into a map of France will perceive must be erroneous, as Poissy is on the left bank, and the Oise falls into the Seine from the north considerably higher up.

* We find it stated in Mezeray's history, a work indeed on which small reliance can be placed, that Edward sent a herald to the King of France from Poissy, bearing his defiance, and offering to meet him where he would, in fair field of battle. The Chronicles of France (chap. xxxviii.), on the other hand, represent Philip as striving at the same time to force Edward to an engagement. Between these conflicting accounts, I have omitted the offer of battle on Edward's part, because I find no good authority for the statement; while, at the same time, it must be perfectly evident to every one who considers Edward's movements for one moment, that he entertained no wish to avoid a battle, though, of course, he desired to choose his own field. It seems clear also that Philip had been joined by no sufficient force to justify him in seeking an engagement before Edward had crossed the Seine. We find, indeed, that even by the time Philip reached Coppigny, near Amiens, a great part of the reinforcements which he expected had not yet arrived; although the forces which were already collected, and those on whose speedy coming he could count with certainty, justified him in offering Edward battle within two days after he had crossed the Seine.

was every hour increasing, he at length despatched messengers to Edward, then in the neighbourhood of Beauvais, offering him battle within a few days, on condition that he would cease to ravage the country.* This proposal Edward declined, alleging that Philip himself, by breaking down the bridges, had avoided a battle so long that he could not fairly demand such conditions; but the English monarch added, that whenever his enemy really sought a battle, he on his part would not evade it, and with this reply led his forces forward towards Poix.

The two armies, though not yet sufficiently near to render an engagement inevitable, were nevertheless, during the whole march, within a few leagues' distance of each other, and continual skirmishes took place between bodies detached from both hosts. At Grandvilliers, a large force, levied by the old King of Bohemia, was engaged by a small number of the English men at arms, who were almost immediately discomfited, and would in all probability have perished to a man, had they not been speedily succoured by the Earl of Northampton, who on his part overthrew the victors, and pursued them nearly to Amiens. The commons of the country, also, rose in masses as the English advanced, and more than once attempted to make a stand against them. They were defeated, however, on all occasions, with great loss; and Edward, now followed by Philip at the distance of about a day's march, still directed his steps

* Acta Edwardi filii Ed. III.

towards Poix, and approached the banks of the Sômme.

The principal towns in the English line of march were found deserted *; and even Poix, which offered great capabilities of defence, had been left nearly ungarrisoned. A part of the English army made themselves masters of the town, meeting with little resistance; and some of the soldiery forced a way into the two castles by which it was defended. In one of these were the beautiful daughters of the Lord of Poix, who was in person with the royal army; and their unprotected situation would have subjected them to the brutal passions of the soldiery, had not the arrival of Sir John Chandos and Sir Ralph Basset freed them from a fate compared with which immediate death would have been a blessing. Those two knights, with the excellent spirit of their order, rescued the unhappy girls from the hands of the men who had seized them, and conveyed them in safety to the presence of the King. Edward, with the same chivalrous courtesy, soon taught them to forget their cares by his gentle and generous demeanour; and asking them in what part of the country they could find a more secure asylum, sent them at their own desire to Corbie, under a safe and honourable escort.

In the meanwhile, the burghers of Poix had agreed to save their town from the fate which had been inflicted on other places in the same circum-

* Michael Northbury, apud Avesbury.

stances, by paying a sum of money, which was to be delivered as soon as the English forces were withdrawn. A few soldiers were in consequence left behind to receive the ransom; but the citizens seeing themselves free from the presence of that power which had terrified them into profusion, now determined to break their word, and attempted to put the party to death which had remained in expectation of the promised payment. This piece of treachery met with its due reward.* The alarm was conveyed to the rear guard of the English army, which was yet within recall; and Lord Reginald Cobham, with Thomas Lord Holland, immediately spurred back to the city with their followers, nor quitted it till blood and ashes were all that remained of Poix and her inhabitants.†

The next halting place of the English monarch was at the small town of Airaines, where he paused for several days, while the marshals of his army, with 1000 men at arms and 2000 archers, explored the banks of the Sômme, in hopes of finding some passage unguarded. Philip of Valois, however, had by this time arrived at Amiens, with a force of 100,000

* Froissart, chap. cclxxv.

† It does not appear to me that this account, as given by Froissart, is at all irreconcilable with that of Michael Northbury, who, as Monsieur Buchon justly observes, could not in the short space of a letter enter into all the details of the events he narrates. His knowledge of what took place at Poix also would greatly depend upon the division of the army which he accompanied; as he says that it was the rear guard of the English force which attacked and took the city, after the van and main body had passed.

men. His design seems now to have been to coop up the English king between the Sômme and the Seine, and either to starve his army, by keeping him amongst the marshes which fill the valley of the Sômme, or to oblige him to fight at a great disadvantage. The passages of the Sômme, therefore, were guarded with greater care than even those of the Seine had been, and the marshals found all the bridges which had been left standing so strongly defended that no possibility existed of forcing a way across. They made the attempt, indeed, at Pont à Remy, but after a severe skirmish were forced to retreat; and then having examined the bridges at Long, and even as far up as Pequigny*, and destroyed several villages and towns on the banks of the river, they returned to Edward, bringing the intelligence that no practicable passage existed towards Amiens. The situation of the English monarch was now very critical; advancing through a difficult country, where he was liable continually to be taken at a disadvantage, where the people were daily arming against him, with a river defended at every passage before him, and on his rear and flank an adverse army more than treble his own in number. To force the passage of the river at some point, before Philip could overtake and attack him in the attempt, appeared now absolutely necessary; and quitting Airaines in great haste early in the morning after the return of the marshals, he led his forces towards the sea,

* Froissart, chap. cclxxvi.

and halted for the night at Oisemont. A multitude of the armed peasantry had flocked thither from the neighbouring cantons; and confiding in their numbers and some slight defences which had been added to the place, they attempted to hold out against the English army. The town, however, was carried in a moment, and a number of prisoners were made, chiefly from amongst the actual inhabitants of the country. The Earl of Warwick and Godfrey of Harcourt had during this time pushed forward as far as the gates of Abbeville and St. Valery, but had found the passages at those places as strongly guarded as elsewhere. It would appear, however, that they had gained some intelligence of a ford not far below Abbeville; for immediately after their return Edward called the prisoners belonging to that part of the country before him, and demanded, "Is there any man among you who knows of a passage, said to be below Abbeville, where we and our army can pass without danger? If any one will undertake to show it, we will free him from prison, and twenty of his companions for his sake."*

Amongst the captives was a peasant called Gobin Agace, a name which will be remembered while France and England exist; and stepping forward from the crowd he replied, "Yes, sir, in the name of God I promise you, at the peril of my head, to bring you to a place where you and your host may pass the river Sômme without danger. There are

* Froissart, ch. cclxxviii.

certain parts where, twice between day and night, twelve men can go abreast with the water up to the knee. For when the tide, which comes twice a-day, is rising, it drives up the river so that no one can pass; but when it has ebbed away again, the river remains there so narrow and so small, that one may pass easily on horseback or on foot; which is what cannot be done any where else but at the bridge of Abbeville, a strong large town well furnished with men at arms. And at the passage which I speak of, my lord, the bottom is of strong white marl, so that one can pass over it easily, and for that they call it the White Spot, — La Blanche Tache."

This news, as may well be conceived, was very gratifying to Edward, who on that side of the Sômme was every day getting himself more and more embarrassed amongst strong fortified towns and marshes; and in order to take advantage of the ebb, he decamped from Oisemont at midnight, and reached La Blanche Tache by daylight the next morning. By some miscalculation, however, it proved that the river was quite full, and he was obliged to wait impatiently, seeing it slowly ebb away. Another obstacle was still destined to oppose his passage. The ford was as well known to Philip of Valois, as it was to the peasant who guided the King of England; and as soon as he learned that Edward had shown a disposition to descend the river, he detached Godemar du Fay, the officer who had so gallantly defended Tournay, to guard the right bank of the Sômme, at the only spot where the English army could hope to cross. A thousand men at arms and 5000 foot were put under his command by Philip, and from Abbeville and Tournay he had received considerable reinforcements, which placed 12,000 men at his disposal.* When first Edward approached the river, no adverse force was visible; but before the ebb had rendered the water fordable, the opposite bank was occupied by an army. There was now, however, no retreating. Philip was by this time at Airaines, and the salvation of the English troops depended upon their forcing the passage. But twelve men could traverse the stream abreast; and any one who has seen the ford must know that at the lowest ebb the river is of considerable breadth. Godemar du Fay had thus very great advantages over the enemy, who now plunged into the water to attack him; but he did not display that skill and resolution in opposing the passage of the English at Blanche Tache which he had evinced in defence of Tournay.† The archers of England proved on this occasion as serviceable as in every other military effort. Their

* Froissart, chap. cclxxix.

† The Continuation of William of Nangis and the Chronicle of Flanders imply, as Monseiur Buchon has stated, that the troops under Godemar du Fay fled after very little resistance. That they did resist strenuously, however, is proved by the fact of their having left 2000 men dead upon the field, as well as by the whole account of Michael Northbury, and by that of Froissart, both of which agree in stating that the French fought most gallantly. Their want of success is universally attributed to the bad dispositions of their commander, who had certainly defended Tournay resolutely; but the defence of a walled city is a very different post from that which Godemar du Fay occupied at Blanche Tache.

arrows, discharged in one uninterrupted shower, confounded and embarrassed the French men at arms, and favoured the passage of the English. The Genoese cross-bows did far less execution; and Edward, calling to his knights, "Let those who love me follow me," spurred forward through the water, while the marshals and the most famous men at arms eagerly rode on upon the French gentlemen, many of whom had come down into the river to meet them.* The battle thus began in the bed of the Sômme; but the English pouring on, gradually bore back their opponents upon the dry land, who now feeling that they were defeated, lost all order, and fled over the country in every different direction. Two thousand of the enemy's men at arms were killed in the battle and the flight, and a much greater number of the foot were slain in the fields around.† The battle was just won in time; for it was scarcely over when the light troops under John of Hainault and the old King of Bohemia, who had both by this time joined the French monarch, appeared upon the opposite bank, and several stragglers from the English army were killed. The main body of the French, however, did not appear, and those who had reached the bank carried back to the King the tidings of the English success.

Thus was won the passage of the Sômme, on the 24th of August 1346; and Edward, having freed

* Barnes, p. 352.

† Robert of Avesbury, p. 138. Froissart, chap. cclxxx.

himself from the difficulties which had encompassed him on the other side of the river, prepared to make a stand in the first favourable position he could find, and risk that battle which all parties now most ardently desired.

CHAP. XVIII.

THE BATTLE OF CRESSY.

THE rumour of the first movements made towards the bold enterprise which saved Edward's army, had afforded to Philip of Valois a delusive prospect of the most brilliant success. No sooner had that monarch heard that his rival had decamped from Airaines, than at once divining that he would be led to attempt the passage of Blanche Tache, and trusting that he would be repelled with ease by Godemar du Fay, Philip instantly commenced his march from Amiens, with the certain assurance of completely enclosing his adversary in such a manner, as to render unequal battle or immediate surrender the only alternatives left for the choice of the English king. Had Philip's calculations been correct, his army would have arrived in the rear of Edward's power at the very moment in which that power, repelled by the force of Godemar du Fay in front, had found the passage of the Sômme impracticable. The strong garrison of Abbeville at the same time, on the east of the English army, and that of St. Valery on the west, afforded the greatest facilities for Philip's design; and it appeared clear that by taking up his own position at Airaines, the fate of his adversary, as far as human calculations could be relied on, would be in his hands. At Airaines*, tables still covered for the morning meal, provisions half cooked, bread yet in the oven, and many other signs of his enemy's hasty departure, showed to the French monarch that Edward was fully sensible of the difficulties of his own situation, and perhaps inspired Philip with that triumphant confidence which induced him to make a fatal delay. Instead of pursuing the English with all speed, he halted for the night at Airaines, convinced that no means of escape had been left to his enemy. The next morning his march was resumed; and with the troops of his earliest friend, the King of Bohemia, and of his new ally, John of Hainault, thrown forward to reconnoitre, he advanced towards the ford of Blanche Tache, not doubting to find the English upon the banks of the river.

His mortification and surprise were very great on perceiving that 12,000 soldiers had not been sufficient to guard a narrow passage by which scarce twelve men could advance abreast; and as the tide had risen before the news of the defeat of Du Fay, and of the English success reached him, he was obliged to direct his march upon Abbeville, in order to pass the Sômme by the bridge at that city.†

In the meanwhile Edward marched on, and at first

* Froissart, chap. cclxxviii.

† Froissart, chap. cclxxx. Robert of Avesbury, p. 138.

directed his course upon the town of Noyelle; but learning that it belonged to the Countess of Aumale*, daughter of his dead ally Robert of Artois, with a generous forbearance unusual in matters of war or policy, he turned his steps another way, prohibiting under the severest penalties that any one should injure that lady's territories, though her husband was serving at the time in the army of his adversary. Nor did he forget to recompense the guide who had been the means of delivering him from the difficult situation in which he had been placed on the other side of the Sômme; and his first act, after returning thanks to God for his success, was to free the peasant and all his companions, presenting Gobin Agace with a good horse and 100 golden nobles, as a recompence for his service. †

While Edward, now proceeding towards Hesdin, advanced into the forest of Cressy, and halted for the night in the open fields, Hugh Le de Spencer, with a considerable force, was detached to Crotoy, which town he took by assault after a severe conflict, in which 4000 of the French men at arms were slain.‡ The capture of that city removed all danger of want from the English army; for large stores both of wine and meal were found therein, and were immediately transported to the main body of the forces then lying

* Froissart and most other writers call the Countess of Aumale sister to Robert of Artois. It is proved, however, by the Histoire Genealogique de la Maison de France (tom. i. page 388.), that she was the daughter of that unhappy prince.

† Froissart, chap. cclxxxi.

‡ Michael Northbury, in Robert of Avesbury, p. 138.

in the forest, a little to the west of the small town of Cressy.

The possession of Crotoy and of the mouth of the Sômme would now have rendered it easy for the English monarch, had he been so inclined, to transport his troops to England, and to leave a country through which he had made one of the most daring and most successful marches that are recorded in the annals of warfare. But he could now choose his own ground; his confidence in his troops and himself was great; his men were animated with the memory of many triumphs; and he resolved to make a stand in Ponthieu *, notwithstanding the immense numerical superiority of the enemy. In pursuance of this intention he despatched the Earl of Warwick on the morning of Friday the 25th of August, 1346, together with Godfrey of Harcourt and Lord Cobham †, to examine the country and make their report concerning the capabilities of the ground; and the result of the information they brought back was the

* It must be remembered that Edward laid claim to Ponthieu, and that his title thereunto was as undisputable as that of any gentleman in France to his estates: though his warfare as an independent monarch had of course been made an excuse for confiscating this property, to which he was entitled as a private individual. It is clear, however, that at Cressy he considered himself as fighting on his own ground. That the conduct of the King of France, in regard to Edward's French possessions, was contrary to the feudal notions of justice and right, is shown by Villani, who says "Lasciamo stare il torto fatto al re d'Inghilterra e altri suoi baroni d'occupare loro retaggi, e signorie," &c.; and again, in regard to the present war, he speaks of Philip as "faccendo guerra contro i signori cristiani inguistamente." (Giov. Villani, lib. 12. cap. lxvii.)

† Froissart, chap. cclxxxii.

choice of the famous field of Cressy. The plan of the battle was drawn out by the King and his counsellors; and Edward, who seems to have appreciated fully the character and talents of his son, resolved, as the greatest and most chivalrous favour he could confer, to yield to the prince the place of danger and of honour, and, in his own words, "*to let the day be his.*"

He was not, however, without a parent's anxiety; and in the division which the Black Prince was appointed to command, we find most of the famous knights of the English army; while the Earl of Warwick and the renowned John Chandos * were commanded to direct and aid, and never to quit the gallant heir to the English throne, who had then just completed his sixteenth year.

On the night of the 25th, all the principal leaders of the British host were entertained by Edward in his tent; and no sign of doubt appeared upon the monarch's countenance. Nevertheless, when the feast was over, and the guests were gone, the King retired to his oratory and prayed fervently and long. † He then lay down to rest, and rose early in the morning to hear mass with his son. They next confessed, and the Prince received the sacrament with his father and many other knights and nobles; after which the trumpets sounded, and the army marched to take up the position which had been previously selected.

* Barnes, page 354. † Froissart, chap. cclxxxiv.

The ground which had been chosen was an irregular slope, between the forest of Cressy and the river Maie, not far from the small village of Canchy. The declivity looked towards the south and the east, from which quarter the enemy was expected to arrive; and some slight defences had been added to the natural advantages of the ground. According to the instructions given before, the Prince of Wales, with his division, consisting of 800 men at arms, 4000 archers, and 6000 Welsh foot *, occupied a post nearly

* The numbers of the English throughout, as given by Froissart, are so greatly inferior to those which he says accompanied Edward on his landing, that I cannot help correcting his account by others. Froissart makes the division of the Prince of Wales to have consisted alone of three thousand eight hundred men, that of Lord Northampton he estimates at seventeen hundred, and that of the King at two thousand seven hundred, amounting to eight thousand two hundred in all. Had there been any cause for such an extraordinary diminution of the English force since its disembarkation in Cotentin, this account might be credited; but in the skirmish with the burghers of Amiens the defeated party only lost five hundred men, in the storming of Caen we are told that very few perished, and the passage of the Sômme is stated to have been effected without great loss. Now the troops that landed in Normandy amounted, according to the same Froissart, to thirty-two thousand men; so that if there were no more than eight thousand two hundred at Cressy, nearly twenty-four thousand must have perished in the march, which is incredible. The account of Villani, which makes the numbers of the English army at Cressy about thirty-four thousand, tallies much better with the first statement of Froissart; and I cannot but think that an error or a corruption has been made by the early copiers in the manuscripts of the Chronicler of Hainault, who, in almost every other particular regarding the battle of Cressy, is confirmed by the best authorities. I am the more strongly persuaded that it is so, because he himself, in another place, gives the proportion of French to the English on this occasion as eight to one; and we learn from the best accounts that when Philip arrived at Amiens he was accompanied by more than 100,000 men, after which he was joined by several reinforcements.

at the bottom of the hill.* The archers, as usual, were placed in front, supported by the light troops of Wales, and by the men at arms in the midst of whose ranks appeared the Prince himself. With him were the Earls of Warwick and Oxford, Godfrey of Harcourt, and the Lords Stafford, Delawarre, Holland, Cobham, Burwash, Mohun, Bourcheir, Chandos, and Clifford. This division occupied the right; while on the other hand, commanded by the Earls of Arundel and Northampton, appeared the second division, with its extreme left extended towards the village and the river, and its flank farther protected by a deep ditch.† About 7000 men are stated to have composed this corps, though the accounts of the numbers vary so greatly that it is hardly possible to arrive at any thing like precision. The King himself had taken up his position on a rising ground, surmounted by a windmill; and the place is so well remembered, that to the present day one may stand upon the field of Cressy, and with great certainty trace where five centuries ago were placed the King of England and his gallant son. Twelve thousand men, under the command of Edward himself, were here held aloof as a reserve; and, somewhat in the rear of the force intrusted to the Prince, an enclosure of stakes had been formed, in which were ranged all the waggons and baggage of the army‡, guarded by a small body of

* Barnes, p. 354. Villani, 612. cap. lxix.

† It would seem that this division was posted somewhat higher on the rise.

‡ Froissart, chap. cclxxxiv.

archers. Here, also, were placed all the horses of the army, Edward having determined that the battle on his part should be fought on foot, a resolution which not a little contributed to the success of the day.

When all the arrangements were complete, and all his forces had taken up the position in which they were destined to meet the enemy, the King, mounted on a small palfrey, and holding a white leading staff in his hand, rode from rank to rank, exhorting his soldiers to do their duty gallantly, and defend his honour and his right. His countenance, we are told, was cheerful and smiling; and there was so much glad confidence in his words and manner, that the most timid heart in his army received hope and strength from his address.*

It was nearly noon before the King had passed through all the lines; and permission was then given for the soldiers to refresh themselves while waiting the approach of the enemy. This was accordingly done, the men eating and drinking at their ease, and afterwards lying down in their ranks upon the soft grass, with their bows and their basinets beside them.

While such dispositions were in progress in the English army, Philip of Valois had not been inactive. He had been forced to make a retrograde movement upon Abbeville, which town he reached late on the Thursday which had seen the passage of the English across the Sômme; and here he remained during

* Froissart, chap. cclxxxiv.

the Friday following, collecting into one mass the various bodies of his troops, whose very numbers were embarrassing under the bad system of military organisation which then prevailed. Considerable re-enforcements were hourly arriving; and amongst others, a body of men at arms under the command of the Count of Savoy, from which great efforts were expected, did not make their appearance till late on the Friday. It is probable, however, that Philip, who had marched from Amiens with more than 100,000 men, would not have waited for the arrival of any fresh forces to crush the small army of England, had he not learned from the officers whom he sent forth to reconnoitre his enemy's position that Edward showed the most unequivocal determination of halting to give him battle.* According to a common custom, on the eve of an engagement Philip invited the whole of the nobles in his army to a splendid banquet on the night of Friday, which, being the festival of St. Louis, was held as an auspicious day, and concluded with joy and revelry. The French monarch took this occasion to beseech his nobles, whose feuds and enmities had so often proved ruinous to France, to lay aside all private animosities, and as friends and brothers to strike together for their native country.

On the following morning, August 26th †, the King, accompanied by his brother the Count of Alençon, the old King of Bohemia, and his son the

* Chron. de France, chap. xxx. Froissart, chap. cclxxxiii.

† Muratori, I know not on what authority, fixes the battle on the 24th; but he is undoubtedly in error. The date is fixed by the tomb of Louis, Count of Flanders, who fell at Cressy.

Marquis of Moravia *, the Duke of Loraine, the Count of Blois, the Count of Flanders, and a multitude of other feudal princes, heard mass at the Abbey of St. Peter, and then issued forth to begin his march upon Cressy. A great part of his troops had been encamped without the town; and very little order appears to have prevailed in the French army during the first part of the march. The Monarch himself, with the King of Bohemia and John of Hainault, advanced with great deliberation, giving time for the other bodies which were spread over the neighbouring country to come up; and each party, under its own chief, followed as best it might.

At length one of the leaders † suggested to Philip that it would be better to gain some information concerning the enemy's dispositions, and to put his own forces into array, before he proceeded farther: in consequence of which advice, four knights, headed by an officer of the King of Bohemia, called Le Moyne de Basele, were sent forward to reconnoitre the English position. They approached within a short distance of the adverse army, and gained a very exact knowledge of Edward's plan of battle; the English both seeing their movements, and comprehending their

* He had already been elected King of the Romans in the end of July, by a part of the electors assembled under the authority of the Pope, Clement VI., who followed up the proceedings of the former pontiffs against Louis of Bavaria with more fury than charity. His election, however, was not recognised by many of the electors, who termed him the Priests' Emperor. — *Muratori, Ann.* 1346.

† It does not appear by whom this suggestion was made.

object, but taking no measures to interrupt their reconnoisance.

Le Moyne de Basele, who bore the character of one of the most prudent and judicious officers of the day, rode back as soon as he had fulfilled his task, and reported what he had seen to Philip, whom he met still slowly advancing. He also advised the King immediately to halt his troops, alleging that, as it was evident the English were determined to give battle, as they were fresh and vigorous, and as the French were wearied and hungry, it would be far better to encamp and delay the engagement till the next morning, when the forces of France would be refreshed, and when there would be plenty of time to make every arrangement, and take advantage of every accidental circumstance.

Philip immediately saw the wisdom of following this counsel; and ordered his two marshals, the Lord of St. Venant and Charles of Montmorency, to command a halt. The one instantly spurred forward to the front; and the other galloped towards the rear, commanding the leaders to halt their banners in the name of God, the King, and St. Denis. Those in advance obeyed at once; but those who followed still rode on, declaring that they would not pause till they were amongst the foremost. The parties in front, seeing those of the rear pressing up behind them, moved on again. Disarray and confusion succeeded; the King commanded, and the marshals stormed, threatened, and entreated in vain. Very little respect was left even in the bosoms of his own nobility for the monarch they pretended to serve, and there were many princes in the field over whom he had no general authority. Each one chose to be first, no one was willing to be commanded; and thus rushing forward in disgraceful disorder, they hurried on, dreaming of nothing but their own jealous competition, till suddenly opening a small wood, detached from the forest of Cressy, they found themselves in the presence of the English army. The surprise was so great, that the first line recoiled in confusion; the second fancied that the first had been engaged with the enemy and were already defeated, and still more fearful disarray was the immediate consequence. The common people, who crowded the road from Abbeville to Cressy in incredible numbers, served only to increase the tumult, drawing their swords and shouting "A la mort! a la mort!" though they as yet beheld no one.

Thus arrived the French army on the field of Cressy, the leaders in as great confusion as their soldiers; and had Edward's troops been sufficiently numerous to have justified a charge at that moment, it is probable that the battle would have been sooner terminated than it was eventually. Notwithstanding the lamentable state in which his adversaries' forces appeared, however, Edward still kept his position on the rising ground; and the only movement which was seen was the rising of the English soldiers from the grass, occupying, in fair and martial order, the hill-side, with the standard of the Black Prince in front of the line.

In a few minutes after, Philip himself reached the field; and when he beheld the English "his blood was moved," to use the words of Froissart, "for he hated them; and nothing could have prevented him then from giving them battle."

Some few arrangements were now made for conducting the attack with a degree of order. The army was divided into four * bodies, of which the Count of Alençon commanded one, the King of Bohemia a second, Philip himself a third, and Amè Count of Savoy † the last. Separate from the mass of the French forces was a band of 15,000 mercenary cross-bow-men of Genoa, who were now commanded to advance from behind the cavalry, and by their missiles to break the firm front of the first body of English archers, who were drawn up in the form of a harrow before the Prince of Wales's men at

* I find but one authority for stating, as I have done, that the French army attacked in four separate divisions, while historians in general assert that it was divided into three. Michael of Northbury was present; but I have chosen his account in preference, not only because he was an eye-witness, but because it is the only one which can be reconciled with the particulars of the battle as gathered from other sources. Had the King of Bohemia been found in command with the Count of Alençon, he would have clearly understood the movement made by that prince to attack the Prince of Wales, which by every account he did not for some time comprehend. Had he been with Philip, he would have heard the order given to charge through the Genoese. It is perfectly evident from the whole account of Froissart, who had his statement both from the English and from the followers of John of Hainault, that Michael Northbury was correct; and that the French, although in the highest degree disordered and irregular in their array, did attack the English in four great divisions.

† Barnes, p. 357. The French word *herse* has been drolly enough translated *a coffin* by some of our learned antiquaries.

arms. These unhappy Italians, however, had made a weary march, in the heat of a summer's day, from Abbeville to Cressy, a distance of about four leagues, loaded with their armour and their heavy crossbows; and they remonstrated with their constables on the orders they had received *, representing that they were in no fit condition to do good service without some repose.

The Count of Alençon, furious at their hesitation, ordered them up with many bitter words, and after a short delay they were brought forward; but in the meantime the sky became clouded, and while the Genoese advanced with their cross-bows in their hands, a severe thunder storm came on, accompanied by torrents of rain, which slackened the strings of the arblasts, and rendered many of them unserviceable. The darkness and the lightnings were terrible; and several ravens were remarked hovering over either host, a fact in which the superstition of the day was prone to find matter for apprehension. At length the cross-bow-men were ranged in front, supported by a gallant and glittering body of cavalry; and the order was given for the battle to begin.

The Genoese now advanced with shrill cries, intended to terrify their enemies; but the English

* The commanders of the Genoese were, according to Villani, Charles Grimaldi and Otho Doria, who both died on the field of battle. The number of the cross-bow-men the same author states to have been only six thousand. (Giov. Villani, lib. xii. cap. lxvii.) The copy of Villani consulted by Barnes must differ essentially from mine, but I have had no opportunity of judging which is the most correct.

archers paid no heed to noise, and waited calmly for the attack, while the clouds cleared quickly away, and the sun approaching the west shone out bright and clear, pouring his rays obliquely from behind the English position, in the faces of the French. Having arrived within a certain distance, the Genoese drew their cross-bows, and began to discharge the quarrels with which they were loaded at their impassable enemies; but at that moment the English bows were brought forth from the cases which had protected them from the rain *: each archer stepped forward a single pace, and a flight of arrows fell at once amongst the Genoese which, piercing their heads, and arms, and faces, threw them instantly into confusion; and, some cutting their bow-strings, some casting down their cross-bows, they recoiled in disarray, amongst the horsemen behind them.

Philip, with the passionate and savage haste which so constantly inflicted its punishment on himself †, beholding the confusion of the Genoese, instead of endeavouring to rally them by gentle means, at once ordered the men at arms in their rear to fall upon them.‡ The Italians rushed back amongst the cavalry;

* Even had they not been thus protected, the English bows would not have suffered from the moisture so much as the cross-bows; for the string of the latter was so much more thick and unpliable than that of the long bow, that it was generally fastened firmly to the steel band which formed the bow, and therefore could not be tightened with ease and facility. The machine for tightening or slackening the cross-bow at pleasure was an after invention.

† Froissart, chap. cclxxxvii. Ægidius li Muisis says, that the Genoese had left their defensive armour in the waggons behind.

‡ Froissart expressly states that the order to charge the Genoese

the men at arms plunged in amongst the masses of the cross-bow-men; and a scene of horror, confusion, and disarray ensued, impossible to be described; whilst still amidst the wild and reeling crowd of their mad enemies, the English archers poured the incessant flight of their unerring arrows, and not a bow-string was drawn in vain.

In the meanwhile *, the Count of Alençon separated his division into two bodies; and, avoiding the scene of confusion in the front, swept round on one side himself, while the Count of Flanders did the same on the other, and prepared to attack the troops under the Prince of Wales in somewhat more regular array.

---

was given by Philip himself, and not by the Count of Alençon, as a number of modern writers have since declared; nor do I find in any account, worthy even of comparison with that of Froissart on the present occasion, authority which could lead to a doubt of the fact.

* This is evident from the words of Froissart, who represents Philip as demanding from John of Hainault what he had best do, seeing the inextricable confusion into which his front had been thrown by the strife between the men at arms and the cross-bow-men. He then proceeds "Le roi qui tout fremissoit d'ire et de mautalent ne repondit point adonc, mais chevaucha encore un petit plus avant; et lui sembla qu'il se vouloit addresser devers son frère le Comte d'Alençon dont il véoit les bannières sur une petite montagne; lequel Comte d'Alençon descendit moult ordonnément sur les Anglois et les vint combattre, et le Comte de Flandres d'autre part. Si vous dis que ces deux seigneurs et leurs routes en costiant les archers, s'en vinrent jusques à la bataille du prince et la se combattirent moult longuement et moult vaillament." (Froissart, chap. cclxxxix.) The fact of the men at arms and the cross-bow-men being still in confusion together, shows that this took place in the early part of the battle; and the whole account proves that the troops commanded by the Count of Alençon were not those engaged with the Genoese, as Rapin and others have stated. The expression, "*et le Comte de Flandres d'autre part,*" I do not think could imply any thing but that the division had separated into two parts.

From the narrowness of the field, and the circuitous path he had been obliged to take, the Count of Alençon appeared upon a rising ground towards the flank of the archers of the Black Prince, and avoiding the arrows of the English, charged at once the men at arms immediately around the heir of the British throne. The chivalry of England, however, headed by the gallant boy on whose young efforts the whole weight of the day's strife was cast, met the impetuous charge of the French knight with equal valour, and with greater success. Each man fought where he stood; and still the ranks were formed anew as every headlong effort of the French deranged them for a moment. No one quitted his place to make a prisoner or pursue a foe; but every man at arms who hurled himself against the English line was met by a strong arm and a resolute heart, and growing piles of dead told the effects of discipline united to courage and to vigour. The Count of Alençon and the Duke of Loraine fell early in the battle. The young Count of Blois, dismounting with his household knights, fought his way forward on foot to the very standard of the Prince of Wales *, and it would appear fell by the hand of the young commander himself. The Count of Flanders was also slain; and confusion and terror began to spread amongst

* For this anecdote of the Count de Blois I am indebted to a contemporary poem on the battle of Cressy, published by M. Buchon, to whose efforts in elucidation of Froissart we owe so much. It is stated in the old MS. from which it is taken to have been composed by one of the attendants of John of Hainault, and is to be found in the manuscripts of the Bibliotheque du Roy, No. 6271.

the troops, whose leaders were now lost, and whose companions were every moment falling under the blows of the enemy. Philip had by this time reached a position from which he could behold the efforts of his followers, and he would gladly have led on his own division to support the large body which was already engaged with the English; but the Genoese cross-bow-men, still struggling with the men at arms, lay obstructing the way, and the very multitude of his troops embarrassed the monarch's movements in the narrow and difficult field on which his foes had taken up their position.

It is probable that about this time took place the charge of a large body of German cavalry, under the command of Charles of Luxemburgh, the son of the old King of Bohemia, and afterwards Emperor of Germany. Bearing down upon the archers of the Prince of Wales with gallant firmness, the German nobles, and the French with whom they were joined, endured the terrible flight of arrows which had already proved fatal to so many, and, assailing the bowmen in front, cut their way through, and poured in upon the men at arms.* With a steady countenance, however, the young Prince and his companions received the shock; and the fight was renewed hand to hand, with more energy than ever. Nearly 40,000 men must at this period have pressed round the little phalanx of the Black Prince; and seeing the impossibility of his sustaining alone such a tremendous attack, the Earls of Northampton

* Froissart, chap. ccxc.

and Arundel moved up with the second division of the English army to support the van.

At the same time the Earl of Warwick *, seeing fresh bodies of the enemy pouring down upon them every moment, despatched a knight, called Thomas of Norwich, to the King, who still remained with his very powerful reserve, viewing the progress of the battle from the windmill above.

On reaching the presence of the monarch, the knight delivered the message with which he was charged, displaying in strong terms the overpowering force by which the Prince was assailed, and praying the immediate aid of the King's division.

"Sir Thomas," demanded Edward, "is my son killed, or overthrown, or wounded beyond help?"

"Not so, Sire," replied the knight. "But he is in a rude shock of arms, and much does he need your aid."

"Go back, Sir Thomas, to those who sent you," rejoined Edward, "and tell them from me, that whatever happens, to require no aid from me, so long as my son is in life. Tell them also that I command them to let the boy win his spurs †; for, God willing, the day shall be his, and the honour shall rest with him, and those into whose charge I have given him."

* Barnes, p. 358.

† I should have been inclined from this expression to adopt the opinion of M. de St. Palaye, and several other authors who have written on the history of chivalry, namely, that Edward the Black Prince did not receive the order of Knighthood till after the battle of Cressy, did I not find in Rymer (vol. ii. part iv. page 205.) a declaration that he had been knighted at La Hogue, signed by the Bishop of Durham, the Earls of Northampton, Arundel, Oxford, Suffolk, and a great many other noblemen present with Edward at the siege of Calais.

This message inspired the Prince and those around him with new ardour. Shame for having sent at all became a fresh incitement to fortitude, and a stronger motive than ever for exertion; and efforts surpassing all that had preceded them were made by the English soldiers to repel the forces that were incessantly poured upon them from behind the confused front of the French army. Still, as the French men at arms dashed down upon the English ranks, they met the same fate as those who had preceded them; and wounded, slain, or hurled from their dying horses, they lay upon the field of battle encumbered with their armour; while troops of the half-armed Welshmen * rushed hither and thither through the midst of the fight, putting to death every one who was once smitten to the ground. The Count of Harcourt, with his nephew the Count d'Aumale, and his two gallant sons, fell together on the same bloody plain, notwithstanding all the efforts made to save them by their unhappy relation, who fought on the part of the victors; and Charles of Luxemburgh, seeing his banner down, his troops routed, his friends slain, himself severely wounded in three places, and the day irretrievably lost, turned his rein and fled, casting off the rich surcoat of his arms to avoid being recognised. †

* Villani represents the Welsh as armed with short lances, wherewith they slaughtered a great number of the horses of the French men at arms; and it seems certain that by their activity and daring they contributed not a little to the success of the day.

† Villani, p. 878.

In the mean time that prince's father, the veteran King of Bohemia, who in his day had fought in almost every quarter of Europe, now blind and old, but full of fire and valour, sat on horseback at a little distance from the fight, inquiring anxiously into the events that were taking place before those eyes which could no longer mark the wavering progress of a well-contested field. The knights who stood around him told him all the truth, to follow the picturesque simplicity of Froissart, saying, "Thus is it, my Lord, and thus — The Genoese are defeated and the king has given orders to kill them all; and still between our people and them there is sad disorder, for they fall and stumble one upon the other, and retard us but too grievously."

The veteran monarch soon comprehended that the day was lost to him and his; and at length demanded tidings of his son; to which his attendants were forced to reply that they could give him none — that the King of the Romans was not in sight, but that doubtless he was somewhere engaged in the melée.

"Lords," said the old man, drawing his own conclusions from what he heard, and resolving not to quit so sad a field alive, "Lords, you are my vassals, my friends, and my companions; and on this day I command and beseech you, to lead me forward so far, that I may deal one blow of my sword in the battle."*

* Barnes asserts that after the first and second attack upon the force of the Prince of Wales, the English men at arms, with the archers upon the wings, advanced against the French, and thus became the assailants instead of the assailed; but this is so totally contrary to the apparent plan of Edward, whose purpose was evidently to maintain the advan-

His faithful friends, to whom his honour, and the renown he had won, during so many years of glory, were dearer than his life, at once obeyed his commands; and with his old companion, Le Moyne, beside him, they placed him in the midst. A number of others ranged themselves around; and lest they should lose their Lord in the battle, they tied their horses together by the bridles and galloped down into the field. Advancing directly against the Prince of Wales, the blind monarch was carried into the midst of the thickest strife. He was there seen fighting gallantly for some time, till at length the standard of Bohemia went down. John of Luxemburgh was found next day dead upon the field of Cressy, and all his friends around him, with their horses still linked to one another by the bridles.*

---

tageous position he had gained, that I have without hesitation adhered to the more probable assertion of Froissart, whose words are, "Et sachez que si les Anglois eussent chassé, ainsi qu'ils firent à Poitiers, encore en fut trop plus (de François) demeuré, et le Roy de France même: mais nennin; car le samedi oncques ne se partirent de leurs courois, pour chasser après homme, et se tenoient sur leur pas, gardants leur place et se défendoient à ceux qui les assailloient."

* I have long hesitated whether to adopt the account usually given in regard to the three feathers, now called the Prince of Wales's feathers, and said to have been won by Edward the Black Prince from the old King of Bohemia, on whose banner they were borne. The statement rests solely I believe upon the authority of Camden, who does not mention whence he derived it; but he is in general so accurate, that I can scarcely doubt that he himself received it from some source worthy of confidence. It is true that this emblem formed no part of the arms of Bohemia, but John of Luxemburgh laid claim to so many small sovereignties in Italy and other countries, that it might well form a badge of authority of which he might be the more anxious to retain the symbol, as he had in almost all instances lost the reality. In a number of miniatures in my possession, from the earliest MSS. of Froissart, which I have been able

During the sanguinary strife which had been taking place since three o'clock, Philip had made more than one effort to give efficient succour to those who were actually engaged; but before he could effect a passage in person to the real scene of strife, it was growing dark. Terror and confusion had already spread amongst his people; those who could extricate themselves from the battle were seeking safety in flight; and still the unremitting showers of English arrows continued pouring like hail on all who approached from the side of Abbeville. As the monarch at length made his way forward, he found his followers falling thick about him: many fled and left him to his fate; and at length his own horse was slain by an arrow.

John of Hainault, who had remained by his side during the whole day, and who had already more than once urged him to quit a field so irretrievable, now furnished the unhappy monarch with one of his own horses, and again pressed him to fly, while there was yet sufficient light to guide them from the enemy. Philip, however, still persisted, and made his way * into the melée, where he fought in person for some time, with that dauntless courage which was, perhaps, his greatest quality; till, at length, seeing the King†

---

to discover, a person is to be seen in all the battles — whom, from the arms, we distinguish as the Black Prince — bearing uniformly a plume of white feathers on the helmet; but it is to be remarked that on the seals of a number of other princes of his house the same emblem is likewise to be found. The motto "*Ich diene*, I serve," might well be used by John of Bohemia after his reverses.

* Villani, p. 877.

† Walsingham, 119.

wounded in two places, the troops immediately round his person almost annihilated *, and death or captivity the certain consequence of longer delay, John of Hainault seized the bridle of his horse, exclaiming, "Come away, sire; come away, for it is full time you should. Do not lose yourself thus foolishly. If you have lost this day, you will win another;" and forced him unwilling from the field.

His flight was accomplished in safety; and having spurred on for some time after night had absolutely fallen, Philip reached the castle of Broye, where he found the gates closed and the drawbridge up. Sad tidings from the field of Cressy had already reached the captain of the garrison, and he refused admittance to all, till the voice of the king himself exclaiming, "Open, open the gates, Castellan; it is the unfortunate King of France †," convinced him of the monarch's presence. The drawbridge was instantly lowered, and Philip, with the Lords of Montmorency, Beaujeu, Aubigny, and Monsault, together with John of Hainault and sixty men at arms who had accompanied him from the field of

* Adam Murimouth declares that the royal standard-bearer of France was slain before the King's face; and that the standard itself was only saved by a knight cutting it from the lance to which it was attached, with his sword, wrapping it round his body, and thus carrying it from the field.

† All the printed copies of Froissart read, "It is the fortune of France," which, unless it be meant for poetry, is very nearly nonsense. Monsieur Dacier, however, in a note upòn the passage, declares that he has found no such expression in any of the manuscripts which he has examined, and gives as the true reading in all, the more rational phrase which I have inserted above.

battle, found a place of temporary security. Towards midnight, however, the King again set forth; and, provided with sure guides to conduct him in safety across the country, he rode on till dawn, nor ever drew a rein till he entered the city of Amiens.

In the mean while, Edward Prince of Wales held firmly his station in the midst of the battle; and from three o'clock, till night, maintained the fight without yielding a single step to all the efforts of the French. Gradually, however, the assailants became less numerous, the banners disappeared, the shouts of the leaders and the clang of arms died away; and the silence which crept over the field, announced that victory was complete in the flight of the enemy. An immense number of torches were now lighted through the English lines, to dispel the darkness which had by this time come on; and the monarch of the victors, quitting for the first time his station on the hill, came down to clasp his conquering boy to the proud bosom of paternal affection. "God give you perseverance in your course, my child!" exclaimed the king as he held him in his arms. "You are indeed my son! Nobly have you acquitted yourself, and worthy are you of the place you hold!"

The young hero had hitherto felt alone the urgent necessity of immense exertion. He had fought for his father, for his country, and for his own honour; and in the energy and excitement of the fearful strife in which he had been engaged, had probably forgotten every thing but the immediate efforts of the moment. But now, clasped in the mailed arms of his father and his king, he must have felt, for the first time fully, that he had passed nobly through an arduous enterprise, had fought a great battle, and won a mighty victory; and overcome by his own sensations and his father's praise, he sank upon his knees before the monarch, and prayed his blessing after such a day of glory and of peril.

In the same spirit of humility, Edward and his host rejoiced over their victory. No songs of triumph, no feasting and merriment, were permitted: but the King and his soldiers, by the solemn service of the church, offered up their thanks to God, for the success that he had granted; and thus ended the battle of Cressy.*

* In describing this battle, I have followed, throughout, the account of Froissart, except where it is contradicted by the letter of an eye-witness, Michael Northburgh. Villani has occasionally furnished particulars not mentioned in Froissart; and Knighton and Walsingham have also afforded some information; but I have still given a preference to the statements of the Chronicler of Hainault, because, as he especially mentions, his account was derived both from the English who were present on the one hand, and from the followers of John of Hainault on the other. It may be necessary to remark, however, that in quoting Froissart I refer to several passages which will not be found in the very imperfect printed copies of his works, which are generally met with. The edition which I have used, as I remarked in the preceding pages, is that published by Monsieur Buchon, and prepared by Monsieur Dacier, from the most extensive collation of the original manuscripts ever made; and which edition contains nearly double the matter usually found in Froissart. Thus the 288th and 289th chapters, referring to the battle of Cressy, are curtailed in the old editions more than one half; the 290th is considerably mutilated, and the 293d is omitted altogether.

In the account I have given it will be seen, that I have made no mention whatever of the use of cannon at the battle of Cressy. I find not the slightest reason, except the assertion of Villani, who very evidently had but a faint idea of the engine he mentions, to suppose that they were employed upon that occasion, and every reason to suppose that they were not. The march of Edward through Normandy, and his retreat upon Cressy were so rapid, that it is impossible his army could have been encumbered with any of the great military engines at that time in use. The care with which he avoided attacking any fortified place would seem to prove that he had none even of the usual implements for siege along with him; and the passage of the Sômme at Blanche Tache presented an obstacle to the conveyance of artillery which, in those days, must have been insurmountable. The mistaken idea that he had carried a train of cannon from England I believe to have originated in the use he made of them in the subsequent siege of Calais; but at that time, it must be remembered, he had every opportunity of receiving them from England; whence he was daily supplied with men and ammunition. Had cannon been used at Cressy, Froissart could not have avoided mentioning the fact, especially as he states the various arms employed, and examines particularly which sort of troops effected most against the French: nor is there any recorded instance of cannon having been used, except in the attack or defence of fortified places, for many years after this period.

CHAP. XIX.

DISPERSED PARTIES OF FRENCH DEFEATED.—NUMBER OF SLAIN. —EDWARD UNDERTAKES THE SIEGE OF CALAIS.—PREPARATIONS FOR THE SIEGE.—PHILIP OF VALOIS MAKES NEW EFFORTS.—DETERMINES TO RECALL HIS TROOPS FROM ACQUITAINE AND BRITANNY.—NEGOTIATES WITH THE FLEMINGS—AND WITH DAVID KING OF SCOTLAND.

THE English army lay all night under arms *; and a number of scattered parties of the French, wandering about in the darkness, got entangled in the adverse lines, and were either slain or taken prisoners. The dawn of the following morning was obscured by a thick fog; and intelligence having been received by Edward that a large body of the enemy were advancing upon the English position, the Earls of Northampton, Warwick, and Norfolk, were detached to reconnoitre with 500 men † at arms and 2,000 archers. This party soon found that the tidings which had reached the King were correct; for shortly after, in the misty twilight of the early morning, an immense force, consisting of the citizens of Beauvais, Rouen, and some other places, was descried wandering on through the fields, and totally ignorant that it was approaching the spot where a great battle had been fought and won.

* Michael Northburgh. Robert of Avesbury, p. 140.

† Froissart, chap. ccxciv.

These troops were led, it would appear, by the Grand Prior of France, and the Archbishop of Rouen; but by what extraordinary accident, while the whole country was covered with fugitives from Cressy, those leaders were ignorant of the defeat of their monarch and his host, it is impossible to discover. That they were so, however, is evident; and they advanced boldly, expecting to join the King of France, and take part in a battle which they imagined was yet to be fought. The impetuous charge of the Earl of Northampton was the first intimation they received of the presence of a foe; and the advance guard, consisting alone of the commons, was overthrown and scattered in a moment. The second division, which was chiefly composed of men at arms, offered a more determined resistance; but still, taken by surprise, and attacked by forces flushed with victory, it also was completely defeated.* The Grand Prior was killed; and the English pursuing the fugitives in every direction, a vast number were captured †, and still more were

* Froissart, chap. ccxciv. Mich. North. ubi supra.

† Froissart declares that the English granted no quarter either on this or the preceding day; and Barnes, admitting this statement, attempts to justify the conduct of the English, by asserting that the King of France having erected the Oriflamme, which was an intimation that no quarter would be given, Edward erected for his banner what he calls the Burning Dragon, on which symbol the worthy historian affixes the same sanguinary interpretation. In regard to the Oriflamme, which, according to Ducange (Dissertation xviii.), *was* carried to the field of Cressy, that banner was by no means such a token of rigour. That it was not so is evident from the fact of more prisoners having been taken at the battle of Bouvines, where it was also displayed, than on any other occasion that I remember. It is very probable, at the same time, that Edward, whose forces did not amount, we are told, to more than an eighth of the troops of the French King, might command no prisoners

slain.* During the whole of the morning detached parties from Edward's army scoured the country, dispersing and slaughtering the bands of fugitives who still remained in the fields around, so that four times the number of those who perished in the battle are said to have been slain on the succeeding day; and the Earl of Northampton returned towards night with the certain intelligence, that no enemy remained in the vicinity who could offer even a show of resistance to the English force.

On the field of Cressy, in the mean time, the Lords Cobham and Stafford were engaged in the melancholy task of numbering and examining the bodies of the dead; in which they were aided by three heralds †, whose station implied a knowledge of the coat of arms which each man of rank bore above his armour. By this means the quality of the dead was easily distinguished; and the list which the heralds brought back at night showed how busy death had been amongst great names.

Besides the King of Bohemia, nine sovereign princes ‡, and eighty lords displaying their own

---

to be taken; and in the letter of Michael Northburgh we find no mention made of any on the first day, though on the second he states that multitudes were captured. The account given by Villani shows that Edward, instead of drawing on himself a charge of cruelty, obtained at the time a high reputation for humanity by his conduct on this occasion.

* It is implied by Froissart that the Archbishop of Rouen was killed at the same time; but it is elsewhere proved that the ecclesiastic then holding that dignity died at Avignon in 1347.

† Froissart, chap. ccxcv. Robert of Avesbury, p. 139.

‡ The principal persons slain, according to the statement of Michael

banners, remained upon the plain, with 1,200 knights, 1,500 men at arms, and 30,000 foot. Such was the loss on the side of France, while that sustained by the English was small, but we no where find in history any accurate statement of the number. Knighton indeed mentions that three English knights were killed at Cressy *, and implies that Edward had to regret no greater diminution of his forces.

Nevertheless the English monarch and his son felt sincere grief for the fall of so many gallant men as lay dead upon the field of Cressy, even though they had once been foes; and for the King of Bohemia, and the little band of devoted servants who fell around him, the victorious princes sorrowed deeply. In those days the spirit of chivalry often extinguished all feeling of animosity in generous adversaries; and raised admiration of great qualities, even in an enemy, to the height of personal regard. The deceased monarch, we are told, was carried in solemn pomp to the Abbey of Maintenay † accompanied by Edward himself, and the Prince his son, as mourners; and thither

---

Northburgh, were the King of Bohemia, the Duke of Loraine, the Count of Alençon, the Count of Flanders, the Count of Blois, the Count of Harcourt, the Count d'Aumale, the Count of Nevers, the Archbishop of Nismes and the Archbishop of Sens, the Grand Prior, who, by Froissart's account, was killed on the following day, and the Count of Savoy. It has been very generally asserted that James II., the unhappy King of Majorca, who some time before had been dispossessed of his dominions by Peter King of Aragon, was killed at the battle of Cressy; but it would appear that he did not die till the year 1349, when he was slain in attempting to recover his territories.

* Knighton, col. 2588.

† Barnes. Villani, b. xii. cap. p. 7. says Riscamp.

also the bodies of all the other leaders were ordered to be borne, while a truce of three days was granted to the French, for the burial of their dead. On the Monday following *, Edward quitted the position which he had so successfully maintained; and directing his march through the Boulonnois, appeared before Calais on the third † of September following.

The importance which that city derived from its relative position with England, did not escape the eyes of the English monarch; and the proximity of his own country and his own resources determined him to undertake the immediate reduction of a place which would afford him the command of the narrow seas, and a key to the dominions of his adversary.

Passing the night of his arrival in the fields,

* Dr. Henry is wrong in stating that Edward remained three days at Cressy after the battle; as Michael Northburgh positively states that the King marched for Calais on the morning of Monday the 28th of August. His whole subsequent dates are also false till after the commencement of the siege of Calais, which he declares commenced on the 8th of September. Were the letter of Michael Northburgh not sufficient evidence, in regard to these dates, the proclamation published at Windsor on the 6th of September, which states that the siege was already begun, would put the matter beyond all doubt.

† I am very much inclined to believe that Edward's march, at least from the time that his fleet left him, and he began his advance upon Paris, till he arrived at Calais, had been previously laid out upon some general plan, with the details of course contingent upon circumstances, but so far fixed, that a fleet and reinforcements were ready to meet him at Calais, for we find (Rymer, tom. ii. part iv. p. 204.) an order from the custos of England for the regulation of an armament about to join the King beyond seas, dated the 21st of August, five days before the battle of Cressy. The name of Calais, indeed, is not mentioned; but the order shows that a fleet and army were about to set out, and some orders must have been given previously, in regard to the spot where they were to seek the King.

Edward the next morning summoned the garrison to surrender to him as King of France *; and a bold refusal having been returned by John of Vienne, the commander of the garrison, the English monarch prepared to carry on the siege with all the vigour and energy of his character. The position of Calais had ever rendered it an object of extreme solicitude to the kings of France; and its fortifications were in such a state of repair, its garrison so strong, and its means of defence so ample, that Edward soon perceived he must use measures of strict blockade, in order to reduce it without risking both loss and dishonour.

Relying solely upon his own troops, with no indifferent or false allies to thwart his designs by inactivity, or frustrate his efforts by treachery, he employed all those means to secure the capture of Calais, which his own mind suggested, and his own resources could supply. His firm determination to remain under its walls till it surrendered soon displayed itself by the care which he took to guard his soldiers against the severity of the approaching winter, and the attacks of their lately defeated enemy. His lines were immediately drawn round the city; and though it may be unnecessary here to repeat the names of all those points which he occupied,—names, many of which are no longer known upon the spot, it is clear that the blockade of the place by land was soon rendered complete; and that no possible means of egress was left to the gar-

* Barnes, page 366.

rison of Calais, except by the port. Within his own entrenchments *, Edward took every care for the comfort of his troops; and from the woods which were then abundant in the neighbourhood, he caused to be constructed spacious and convenient dwellings of timber, which being thatched with broom and straw, were divided into regular streets, and assumed the appearance, not of a camp, but of a city, to which he gave the name of "Newtown the bold." †

For the supply of provisions, also, Edward had taken every precaution from the very first moment of his arrival before Calais; and we find that though he only came in sight of that place on the 3rd of September, a general proclamation was published in England, on the 6th of the same month, inviting all merchants and traders to carry to the besieging army ‡ every kind of necessary, whether in the shape of food or military stores. This had the desired effect; and constant supplies of all sorts arrived daily, not only from the English, but also from the Flemish coast; while detachments from the besieging force scoured the country, and carried off immense booty, pushing their excursions to the gates of Boulogne and St. Omer. Within the English camp, a market was held, every Wednesday and Saturday, at which objects of luxury, as well as of necessity, were constantly exposed for sale; and such were the preparations and precautions of

* Froissart, chap. ccxcvii.

† Chron. de France.

‡ Rymer, vol. ii. part iv. p. 205.

the English King, that the French historian declares, it seemed to all men that he intended to remain there for ten or twelve years.*

In the mean time, Edward did not neglect the port; and shortly after the commencement of the siege, a considerable fleet, under the command of the Earl of Huntingdon, appeared before Calais, and completed the blockade. Such measures, of course, announced to the garrison the privations which they were likely to undergo, unless the King of France should by some means force his adversary speedily to abandon his design; and John of Vienne, though well provided with necessaries at the time, took the prudent but cruel precaution of driving forth from the city gates 1700 of the poorer classes, who had not the means of purchasing food at the high rate to which the blockade was likely to raise every kind of provisions.

By all the rules of war, and the common, though inhuman practice of the day, Edward would have been justified in driving back this miserable crowd to the gates from which they had been expelled; but his late successes seemed to have opened his heart to nobler feelings than the cold dictates of policy generally inspired; and through the whole siege of Calais, — except, indeed, in the circumstances immediately connected with its surrender, —he displayed, in the highest degree, those finer chivalrous qualities which so highly distinguished his son. On the present occasion, the English King received the starving multitude

* Froissart, chap. ccxcvii.

of men and women who had been driven forth by their countrymen, and after giving them an ample repast, he ordered two small pieces of silver money, called stirlings, to be delivered to each, in order to help them on their way *, and then suffered them to pass in peace beyond his lines.†

While Edward had been pursuing his victorious march from Cressy, and had completed his entrenchments round Calais, the unhappy monarch of France paused at Amiens, to prepare new efforts, and to ascertain what loss he had sustained in the last fatal field, on which he had staked so much. The confusion in which the French army had commenced the attack, and the darkness which in

* Froissart, chap. ccxcvii.

† Such is the account of Froissart, and his account has with reason prevailed in history. Another version of the story, however, has been given by Knighton; and Monsieur de Brequigny, in the papers of the Academy of Belles Lettres, has attempted, even while he showed the absurdity of the statement on which he reasoned, to invalidate thereby the testimony of Froissart, and deprive Edward of part, if not the whole, of the honour which was his due. Knighton (col. 2593.) says that 500 persons alone were driven out of Calais, that the time of their expulsion was the festival of St. John the Baptist, and that they died of hunger and cold because Edward would not suffer them to pass. Now the festival of St. John being at Midsummer, it would require a derangement of the seasons somewhat extraordinary, to kill 500 people of cold at that period of the year. The very expression shows the inaccuracy of the whole passage, which can be proved to be false in other respects; and why Monsieur de Brequigny should take an incorrect statement, even in part, and imagine with manifest inconsistency that Edward should relieve and give money to some, and condemn the rest to a death of horror, when, opposed to such an inaccurate account, there is a clear, direct, and positive assertion, which contains no such palpable errors as the other, and was written for the very persons most likely to contradict it if false — why, I say, he should choose the absurd statement and reject the consistent one, I cannot divine.

the end had fallen over the battle, had prevented the King, or those about him, from learning, before their flight, the full extent of their misfortune; but during the Sunday which he passed at the Abbey of Le Gard, near Amiens, news upon news reached him of the darkest import to himself and France. His troops slaughtered by thousands, his nearest relations fallen before the enemy, his dearest friends and wisest counsellors all dead upon that terrible plain, and the noble army which might have conquered empires, scattered like chaff before the wind, — such were the baleful tidings that poured moment after moment upon his ear.

The first effect of Philip's disappointments generally evaporated in rage, and on this occasion broke forth in the most violent invectives against Godemar du Fay.* Though he does not appear to have thought of punishing him for his defeat till its consequences showed its importance, he now proposed to put him to an ignominious death for his late failure, forgetful of all the advantages which had been reaped from his former success. John of Hainault, however, interposed; and, by reasonings and persuasions, moderated the King's anger, making use, perhaps, of the same simple but cogent argument which is employed by Froissart, and demanding, "How could Godemar du Fay resist the whole power of the English, when the flower of all France had been able to effect nothing against it?"

* Froissart, chap. ccxcvi.

The monarch at length abandoned his cruel and unjust design; and retiring to Paris, after the obsequies of his dead rélations had been duly celebrated, employed himself in wise efforts for remedying the disaster of Cressy, which did him far more honour than any of his previous undertakings.

Yielding not in the slightest degree to despair, notwithstanding the difficult position in which his late defeat had placed him, he immediately strengthened the garrisons of all the towns in the neighbourhood of Calais; and environed the English army by a line of strong places, well supplied with warlike stores, and filled with men eager to signalise their courage and wipe away the memory of their late discomfiture.* For a short time, detachments from Edward's camp ravaged the country at their will, and one body even forced its way into Terouanne; but as the knights and soldiers who had been scattered at Cressy reassembled, and Philip's judicious measures began to take effect, the English commanders could send out no party to forage without the certainty of a severe struggle taking place with some of the neighbouring garrisons; and the English monarch was obliged to depend for supplies principally on his communication with his own country.

While such means of harassing his adversary in his operations against Calais were promptly taken by the King of France, he did not forget the necessity of relieving that city by more direct and

* Froissart, chap. cccix.

effectual efforts; and he prepared to call all the disposable forces in his kingdom to his aid, in making one more great attempt to drive the English from his shores. Many circumstances combined, however, to embarrass him, and to leave him nothing but a choice of evils. In three distinct points of his dominions, the forces of his rival were waging an active warfare against him; and hitherto that warfare had, on their part, been carried on with success, notwithstanding the opposition of large armies and skilful commanders on the part of France. He foresaw then that to recall even a part of his troops either from Britanny or Aquitaine, would be merely to remove the scene of his enemy's success, even if the immediate object of delivering Calais were thereby accomplished; and though no choice was left him but to abandon that important city to its fate, or to march the great bulk of his forces from the south, he felt in choosing the latter alternative that he resigned his hold on Gascony for ever, unless he could effect some diversion which might neutralise the advantage he was thus forced to cast into the hands of his foe. For this purpose he despatched emissaries in every direction, which offered the slightest prospect of calling the forces of his adversary from the siege of Calais; and we find him at the same time treating earnestly with the Flemings through the mediation of the Duke of Brabant, and negotiating with his ancient friend and ally the King of Scotland.

It is more than probable that on the first landing

of Edward in Normandy, Philip had anxiously pressed David of Scotland to break the truce then existing between that country and England, and, taking advantage of the British monarch's absence, to recommence a war, which might both re-establish himself firmly in his own dominions, and recall part of his enemy's troops from the invaded territories of his ally. After the battle of Cressy, however, the necessity of this diversion became more urgent, and Philip's entreaties probably hastened the movements of the Scottish king *, who assembled a very considerable army, and prepared for active hostilities against England. The results must be spoken of more fully hereafter. It is only necessary here to state that, instead of pursuing the wiser course, and seeking to recover complete possession of his paternal dominions, to consolidate his power at home, while his adversary's strength was all employed in efforts from which it could be withdrawn with difficulty, and to provide means of future defence, David Bruce engaged in a rash and fruitless expedition, which ended in his own ruin, without producing any benefit to the King of France.

With the people of Flanders † also Philip opened a treaty, not only for the purpose of detaching them from the interests of the English King, but in the hope of inducing them to espouse his own cause with energy and effect. The course of these negotiations with the Flemings, however, was as un-

* Robert of Avesbury, p. 145.

† Froissart, chap. cccx. Robert of Avesbury, p. 153.

favourable to him as the events of the war; and though they continued in various forms during the greater part of the siege of Calais, the first results must be detailed briefly in this place. The death of the Count of Flanders at the battle of Cressy had left the nominal sovereignty of that country to a boy of the age of fifteen, who remained under the guardianship of the King of France. Frequent negotiations had taken place between Edward and the Flemings, concerning the marriage of this prince with Isabella daughter of the King of England; but the Duke of Brabant, anxious for an alliance between one of his own children and the young sovereign of Flanders, pursued the surer plan of treating with the King of France. Philip at once consented, upon condition that the Duke should bring over the citizens of the good towns to the interests of France *; and this great object having been apparently accomplished in a considerable degree, the young Count, who had imbibed a natural hatred towards the English, was trusted for the first time in the hands of his own turbulent subjects. He arrived in Flanders in the beginning of November 1346 †; and was received by the people with joy and acclamations, which gave him hopes of a more peaceful and easy dominion than any of his predecessors had enjoyed. Almost immediately after his return to his own land, however, the Earls of Northampton and Arundel, together with the Lord

* Froissart, chap. cccx. † Meyer Ann. de Flandres, 150.

Cobham, appeared as the ambassadors of Edward III., having been sent in order to counteract the intrigues of the Duke of Brabant, and recall the Flemings to their alliance with England.

So many motives combined to render the friendship of the English monarch as necessary to the people of Flanders as their aid was to him, that few difficulties opposed the negotiations of the envoys. The counsels of the Duke of Brabant were rejected: it was determined by the authorities of the Flemish towns to persuade or force their young sovereign to the marriage which had been proposed with Isabella of England; and he was in consequence urged in full assembly to give an immediate consent.*

The Prince replied boldly and at once that he would never wed the daughter of a man who had slain his father, were he to give her half of England for her dowry. But the Flemings attributing this determination to his predilection for the French, and to the prejudices he had acquired at the court of Philip, immediately put him under gentle restraint, from which they informed him he should never be free till he cast from him that love for France which had proved the ruin of his father, and till he followed counsels more conducive to the interest of his country and himself.

Thus ended in disappointment Philip's first negotiation with the Flemings, and the failure of his hopes in Scotland was made known to him about the same time; but these circumstances could not

* Froissart, chap. cccx.

now affect his proceedings in regard to his southern and western provinces, for, long prior to this period, he had recalled the chief part of his troops from Aquitaine, and had left only a sufficient force in Britanny to maintain the principal strong places which his nephew had acquired.* . It is not improbable, indeed, that John Duke of Normandy, who commanded the French armies in the south, had received directions to send reinforcements to his father almost immediately after Edward's first landing at La Hogue; but the tidings which he soon heard of that monarch's proceedings caused him to hurry his retreat in person, and the effects of the battle of Cressy induced Philip to leave Aquitaine destitute of any force fitted for active operations. The events, however, which had taken place in that duchy as well as in Britanny since the expeditions of the Earls of Derby and Northampton in 1345, require a more full detail, which must be given here, in order that the history of those future operations at which Edward and his son were present may be fully understood.

* Rymer, tom. ii. part iv. p. 205.

CHAP. XX.

AFFAIRS OF GUYENNE. — THE EARL OF LANCASTER ARRIVES IN GASCONY. — TAKES THE FIELD AGAINST THE COUNT DE LILLE. — TAKES BERGERAC BY STORM. — MARCHES ON PERIGORD. — BOLD EXPLOIT OF THE FRENCH GARRISON OF PERIGUEUX. — CONVENTION WITH THE COUNT OF PERIGORD. — AUBEROCHE TAKEN. — THE DUKE OF NORMANDY ARRIVES TO DEFEND AQUITAINE. — THE FRENCH BESIEGE AUBEROCHE. — THE EARL OF LANCASTER MARCHES TO ITS RELIEF. — TOTAL DEFEAT OF THE FRENCH. — ST. BASEILLE, ROCHEMELLON, MONTSEGUR, AND AIGUILLON TAKEN. — SIEGE AND CAPTURE OF LA REOLE. — FARTHER SUCCESSES. — THE DUKE OF NORMANDY TAKES THE FIELD. — ANGOULEME REDUCED. — THE SENESCHAL OF BEAUCAIRE TAKES ST. JEAN D'ANGELY. — SIEGE OF AIGUILLON. — THE FRENCH REPULSED AT ALL POINTS. — THE SIEGE RAISED. — THE DUKE OF NORMANDY RETREATS FROM GUYENNE. — FARTHER SUCCESSES OF THE EARL OF LANCASTER. — HE SAILS FOR ENGLAND.

While Edward had been employed in collecting in England the army with which he invaded France, won the battle of Cressy, and besieged Calais, his parliament had been encouraged to support him, and his subjects to flock to his standard, by continual tidings of success won by the Earl of Lancaster in Aquitaine. That gallant and victorious prince sailed from Southampton, as I have before mentioned, towards the middle of the year 1345 *, with considerable

* In common with almost all the dates and events of this reign, the expedition of Henry Earl of Derby and Lancaster, has been erroneously

forces and one or two subordinate leaders, whose presence was in itself a host. His arrival at Bayonne, and afterwards at Bordeaux, was celebrated by the inhabitants with a thousand demonstrations of joy; for the threatening position which the French had assumed, and the assembling of considerable forces on the frontier, had given the adherents of England great

---

placed. Dr. Henry divides his campaign into two, and says that after overcoming the Count de L'Isle in 1344, he returned to England in the winter for reinforcements; and it is true that he was despatched for a short time to Gascony as the King's locum tenens early in 1344; but it is equally clear that this in no degree implies that he carried on any hostilities against France during that visit to Aquitaine, for the very letters which empower him to act for the King enjoin him strictly to observe the truce with France, and forbid him to commit any act which might tend to a breach thereof. It is also clear, notwithstanding the erroneous chronology of Froissart (which is generally only arrived at by inference), that no hostilities took place in Aquitaine, except occasional skirmishes of partisans, till 1345; and that during the whole of the preceding year, negotiations were continued for a firm and stable peace, and no mention whatever is made in any of the state papers of warfare having commenced. On the contrary, in 1345, Edward for the first time declared the truce broken, and published the manifesto (Rymer, tom. ii. part iv. p. 179.) which Dr. Henry mistakenly attributes to the former year. After the public defiance of Philip entrusted to the Earl of Northampton, and not before, the Earl of Derby sailed with hostile purposes for France, though on what precise day is uncertain. The letters in Rymer show that he was still in England on the 11th of June, and Robert of Avesbury declares that he set out towards Michaelmas (Robert of Avesbury, p. 121.). The last assertion, however, is certainly incorrect; for Don Vaissette proves that the Earl had taken Bergerac on the Dordogne by the 24th of August (Histoire de Languedoc, vol. iv. p. 254., and note xxi. p. 569.), and the order for paying one half year's salary to the Earl and others for their services in Gascony (Rymer, tom. ii. part iv. p. 190.) implies that he and his companions had set out from London at least, though not from Southampton, by the 10th of June 1345; and I think, from the multitude of events which followed in Gascony before the end of the year, that they must have quitted England very soon after their arrival at the port of embarkation.

and just subject of alarm. The defiance of the French King and the actual recommencement of hostilities had long been anticipated in Guyenne; and no sooner was the arrival of the Earl of Lancaster, with an army sufficiently large to take the field against the power of France, known to the Count de Lille Jourdain, who at that time held the supreme sway as delegate for Philip in Perigord, Saintonge, and Limousin, than preparations were made to resist the further advance of the English, on the very banks of the Dordogne.

It may be as well to notice here the precise situation of the French and English in Aquitaine, that the encroachments which had been made by Philip and the successes afterwards obtained by the Earl of Lancaster may be properly understood. To the north and east of Bordeaux, the French had pushed their posts as far as the Dordogne, on which river they held the two strong towns of Libourne and Bergerac; and on the south-east they were in possession of La Reole on the Garonne, within forty miles of the capital of Guyenne. The English territories, therefore, which had once extended to the frontiers of Britanny and Anjou, to the Pyrenees and Languedoc, were now confined to a narrow tract of sandy country on the shores of the Bay of Biscay, from the mountains to the mouth of the Gironde.

The plan of the Earl of Lancaster was immediately formed for driving back the French upon the north-east, satisfied that if he could extend the frontier of the English territory in that direction, he would easily find means to reduce the adherents of France in the south of Gascony, which would no longer possess the facilities of communicating with the adversaries of England, which had hitherto been afforded by the presence of the Count de Lille Jourdain upon the Dordogne.

His first operations were therefore directed against Bergerac; and his determination in this respect being anticipated, a large force, under the command of the Count de Lille in person, prepared to oppose him at that point. In the beginning of August the Earl, having appointed the famous Walter de Mauny and another distinguished knight called Frank Von Halle the marshals of his army, began his march for the city he proposed to attack.* The English army halted for a day and a night at a village called Moncuq, while the scouts reconnoitred the dispositions of the enemy, which were found to be very simple. At dinner on the second day the reconnoitring parties having made their report, Sir Walter de Mauny, who with other officers was at table with the Earl, exclaimed, laughing, "If we were good men at arms, and sufficiently alert, my lord, we should drink the wine of these French lords at Bergerac for supper."

"You shall not wait for me," replied the Earl; and these few words having been overheard by the other officers, all was in a moment changed to the bustle of preparation. The Earl of Lancaster took

* Froissart, chap. ccxvii.

advantage instantly of the enthusiasm of his troops, and led them to the attack; but at the same time the French, not less confident of their own power, issued forth to meet him, and a severe skirmish took place without the walls. An ill-armed rabble of partisans on foot, however, who preceded the French cavalry, being thrown into confusion by the arrows of the English archers, and utterly routed by the Earl's men at arms, carried flight and disarray into the ranks which followed them. The Count de Lille was beaten back into the suburbs, which, after a severe contest, he was obliged to abandon also; and, passing the bridge, he took refuge in the town. The Viscounts of Chateauneuf, of Bosquentin, and of Castelbon, with the Lord of Lescun, were taken by the English: the Lord of Mirepoix or his son was killed; and the gallant Sir Walter de Mauny, on the other part, engaged himself with the enemy so far before his followers, that he had nearly been carried prisoner into the city.*

After attempting in vain to storm Bergerac on

* Dom Vaissette, in the History of Languedoc, proves that the siege of Bergerac took place in the end of August 1345, though Froissart places it late in the year 1344. I have before shown that this was not the case, as in the autumn of 1344 the Earl of Lancaster was in England; and by this originial error Froissart confounds his whole account. It will only be necessary to remark, in order to correct the principal errors, that all the events in this war of Aquitaine previous to the siege of Blaye are referable to the autumn of 1345, and that those which follow took place in the course of the year 1346: the French army under the Duke of Normandy having assembled at Toulouse on the 3d of February 1346. These facts may be established by an examination of the state papers in Rymer, and of the 4th volume of the General History of Languedoc at the 255th and following pages.

the land side, the Earl of Lancaster commanded the ships which were at anchor at Bordeaux to be brought round into the Dordogne; and by their means a more successful assault was made the next day, which left the town in such a state that the burghers, taking fright, demanded a suspension of arms till the following morning. This was granted by the Earl, upon condition that no attempt to repair the fortifications should be made; and during the interval the Count de Lille, finding that he could not depend upon the inhabitants, and that the defences on one side were nearly ruined, abandoned the city during the night, and left the burghers to make their own terms with the assailants.

The Count himself took his way across the country to La Reole; and, having determined to change his plan of operations, divided his troops into separate parties, which he detached to reinforce the garrisons of the principal towns that held for France. His object, however, was by no means accomplished; for the additional forces thus cast into the strong places of Guyenne appear to have retarded but little the march of the English army.*

The Earl of Lancaster took possession of Bergerac on the 24th of August, and the burghers, swearing fealty to the King of England, escaped without molestation. He then advanced upon Perigord, taking either by assault or composition ten † fortresses of

* Hist. de Languedoc, vol. iv. p. 255.

† The first of these fortresses is said to have been Langon; but as Froissart distinctly mentions that it was situated between Bergerac and

various importance in his way.* After reconnoitring Perigueux with the intention of attacking it, and judging it too strongly fortified to offer him a prospect of success, the Earl directed his march upon a small fort in the neighbourhood, called Pellagrue, and encamped before it. The garrison of Perigueux, however, encouraged by his retreat from their walls, issued forth in the night, and, beating up his quarters, caused a great deal of confusion, and carried off the Earl of Oxford a prisoner to their own city.

This capture proved more advantageous to the Count of Perigord than he had any right to expect; for the liberation of the Earl of Oxford and his companions was esteemed so important by the Earl of Lancaster, that three of the French nobles taken at Bergerac were given in exchange, and a convention was entered into, by which the county of Perigord was freed from the horrors of war for three years.

This being arranged, the English commander drew off his troops from before Pellagrue, which was within the limits of the territory he had agreed

---

Perigord, it could not have been Langon on the Garonne. I know of no spot called Langon so placed; and Langoyne, between Le Puy and Mende, is farther from the line of march laid down than even Langon on the Garonne. I am rather inclined to suppose that Froissart, who is not very accurate in regard to dates, has placed the capture of Langon on the Garonne considerably anterior to the real period of its reduction, and thus thrust in at this place a fact that took place long afterwards. The same may be the case in regard to Lisle en Jourdain, said to have been taken at the same time, but which lies within twenty miles of Toulouse, and, therefore, was still farther from the English line of operations on the side of Perigord.

* Froissart, chap. cccxliv.

to respect; but to wipe away the memory of the check he had received, he immediately led his army against Auberoche, the garrison of which, learning his determination not to quit their walls without victory, yielded after very little resistance.* As an important point upon the frontier of the newly acquired territory, the Earl placed in Auberoche a strong garrison, commanded by Sir Frank Von Halle, Sir John of Lindehalle, and Sir Alan of Finefroide; and then, contented with the splendid success he had obtained, returned towards Bordeaux, making himself master of Libourne upon the march; and thus reducing to submission the whole country within the Isle and the Dordogne, except the small county of Perigord.

Scarcely had he returned to Bordeaux, however, before tidings reached him of immense preparations having been made in all the surrounding provinces in order to wrest from him what he had already obtained, and to crush him under the whole

* It is not improbable that the name Auberoche has been substituted by transcribers for Aubeterre, which, in some points, agrees better with the description given by Froissart. His account is not very satisfactory; for he declares that Auberoche belonged to the Archbishop of Toulouse, and not to Perigord; and yet Dom Vaissette (vol. iv. p. 570. note) shows that this town is in the diocese of Perigueux. This, however, does not absolutely prove that Froissart was wrong. So many changes have taken place, that it is impossible to judge from these circumstances to whom the *lay* dominion of Auberoche belonged; and it might have formed a part of the property of the Archbishop of Toulouse without being in his diocese, as it might be no part of the territory of the Count of Perigord, though it be within the ecclesiastical domination of the Bishop of Perigueux. Perhaps, after all, Froissart spoke of some place which no longer exists; as, from his account of the subsequent siege, it may probably have been merely a castle, and not a town.

power of France, before any reinforcements could arrive from England to his aid.* Already the Duke of Normandy had arrived at Carcassonne, and on the 8th of August the Duke of Bourbon had been despatched with considerable forces to Languedoc.

The Count de Lille at the same time had made fresh levies at La Réole, and marched direct upon Auberoche, trusting undoubtedly to receive strong support from the Dukes of Normandy and Bourbon. But many circumstances prevented those princes from rendering him any effectual assistance; and amongst other impediments was the unprepared state of the neighbouring country. The war had hitherto been principally waged either in Britanny or in the north of France, and a few thousand men had been sufficient to support the partisans of Philip of Valois in the south, and to enable them to make great progress against the feeble garrisons of Guyenne. No fear had been entertained of the English effecting any great enterprise from the side of Gascony; and the fortresses of Languedoc, Touraine, Poitou, and the Limousin, had been left scantily furnished with means of defence. A different scene, however, was now opened to the eyes of Prince John and the other French leaders. The Earl of Lancaster's immense and extraordinary success during the two first months after his arrival spread terror and surprise through the neighbouring provinces; and it became immediately necessary to supply the chief towns

* Hist. de Languedoc, par D. Vaissette.

which might be attacked, with garrisons and ammunition. For the purpose of examining with his own eyes, and putting the surrounding country in security, the Duke of Normandy proceeded rapidly through the districts bordering upon English Guyenne, but the deficiencies he found completely drained his resources; and the troops left in Languedoc with the Duke of Bourbon were only sufficient to insure some defence to that rich province, in case the enemy should turn their steps thither.

In the meanwhile, the Count de Lille appeared before Auberoche with a larger force than he had heretofore been able to bring into the field; and having procured four immense mangonels from Toulouse, he lost no time in pressing the besieged to a surrender.* The desire of effacing his former failures incited him to immense efforts; and the near approach of the King, who visited Angoulême † in the course of October, sharpened his zeal and encreased his activity. The troops before Auberoche were sufficient to render the blockade complete; and declaring that he would accept of nothing but unconditional surrender, the French commander caused his military engines to cast night and day against the castle immense masses of stone, which, destroying the roofs, left the garrison no shelter except such as they could find in the subterranean chambers generally attached to a building of that nature. Sir Frank Von Halle and his companions nevertheless defended their post

* Froissart, chap. ccxxvii. † Histoire de Languedoc, vol. iv.

with gallant determination; but the miscarriage of a scheme for giving intimation of their distressed state to the Earl of Lancaster, put the assailants in possession of a true knowledge of their situation. When reduced to the utmost necessity, one of the knights' servants, or varlets as they were called, offered to carry a letter to the commander-in-chief; and having been let down from the walls during the night, he succeeded in passing through a great part of the French camp. He was at length seized, however; the letters were found upon his person; and the Count de Lille had the cruelty to tie them round his neck, and placing him in the sling of a mangonel, to cast him back into the fortress. He fell dashed to pieces within sight of his masters, while several of the French lords rode round the walls insulting the unhappy Englishmen. They on their part offered to yield one of their knights, to be afterwards ransomed according to the laws of war, if the besiegers would give notice to the Earl of Lancaster, and wait his battle; but this was refused with vain boasts, and the garrison resolved to die rather than surrender at discretion to a commander, who had already shown too plainly the spirit by which he was actuated.

The Earl of Lancaster had in the meantime gained intelligence that Auberoche was besieged; and as soon as he heard of the active measures pursued against that fortress, he summoned the Earl of Pembroke, who was at Bergerac, to join him with all his forces by the way, and marched forward without delay to succour his brave companions. He paused for one night at Libourne, waiting the Earl of Pembroke, who did not appear; and the following morning the Earl of Lancaster, with the troops which accompanied him from Bordeaux, Sir Walter de Mauny, the Earl of Oxford, Lord Ferrers, and several others, 300 men at arms, and 600 horse archers, marched forward for Auberoche, which was assailed by between 10 and 11,000 men.

Knowing the condition of the garrison, they continued their advance night and day, and arrived a little before dawn, on the second morning after quitting Libourne, at a small wood not far from the camp of the besiegers.* Here a consciousness of the great inferiority of their numbers induced them again to pause, in hopes of Lord Pembroke's arrival. He did not appear, however, and after waiting several hours, while their horses fed upon the forest grass, a council was called, at which all agreeing that it was better to risk every thing than suffer the brave knights in Auberoche to perish, it was determined, on the suggestion of Sir Walter de Mauny, to skirt round under cover of the wood, till they were close upon the enemy, and then to display their banners and dash amongst them at once.

This was accordingly done; and it so happened, that at the moment when the English knights emerged from their concealment, the French were merrily employed, taking their evening meal. The banners of England were instantly given to the wind, and shouting "Derby, Derby, to the Earl of Lancaster!

* 23d October, 1345.

a Mauny, a Mauny for the Lord," the assailants galloped on, with levelled lances, into the midst of the French lines. Tents and pavilions were overthrown: the French knights, unarmed and unprepared, made but a faint resistance. The Count de Lille was severely wounded and taken in his tent, as well as the Count of Perigord *: the Count of Valentinois was killed, and his brother made prisoner; and whenever the French soldiers drew out from their lines and attempted to rally in the open field, the arrows of the English archers dispersed them in a moment. In the meanwhile tidings of the attack had spread to that part of the French camp which lay on the other side of Auberoche; and the Count of Cominges, who commanded there, had time to arm and array his men, and lead them up to the field, while the English were completing the dispersion and rout of his comrades. The body now brought regularly to oppose the Earl of Lancaster was fully three times as numerous as his own force; but without giving the impulse of victory time to subside, that gallant commander instantly led his men at arms to the charge, and the fight recommenced with more fury than before. The French knights strove gallantly to recover the day; but the English were full of confidence and vigour: and in the midst of the second engagement, Sir Frank von Halle and Sir John of Lindehalle, hearing the cries of the battle, and seeing English banners mingled in combat

* Histoire de Languedoc, tom. iv. p. 255. note 21.

with the French, mounted their horses, threw open the gates, and leading forth their little garrison, poured a charge upon the flank of the enemy which completed their defeat. *

Flight and confusion succeeded, and we are assured by Froissart, that, had the night not fallen soon after, few if any of the French would have escaped from the field of battle. Of the ten thousand men who had besieged Auberoche, more than one-half were killed or made prisoners by the thousand archers and men at arms which the Earl of Lancaster led against them: and three counts, three barons, seven viscounts, and fourteen bannerets were found amongst the captives †, with such a number of knights and squires, that each man at arms of the victorious party had two or three under his charge.

The prisoners met with greater courtesy from the Earl of Lancaster than their conduct to the garrison of Auberoche deserved. The greater part were suffered to depart upon parole, and the rest he entertained with princely magnificence within the ruined walls of the fortress which they had so nearly captured. The Earl of Pembroke arrived the morning after the battle, and expressed great discontent that it had taken place without his presence; though we do not find that he offered any valid excuse for the delay which had occurred. The reinforcements thus received and the total dispersion of the enemy

* Froissart, chap. ccxxxi.

† Robert of Avesbury, p. 122. The Histoire de Languedoc, tom. iv. p. 255., says nine counts or viscounts.

before Auberoche, enabled the English commander to act with vigour; but the presence of John Duke of Normandy, with large forces in the Limousin, was probably the cause of his leading his victorious troops to another quarter, and leaving the side of Perigueux *, where he had so immensely extended the English frontier. He now turned his arms towards the south with equal success. The Castle of St. Baseille on the Garonne surrendered at once; and though La Rochemillon attempted boldly to resist his progress, yet, by filling up the ditch, and causing three hundred archers to keep up a constant hail of arrows upon one part of the battlements, while two hundred pioneers under cover of pavisses advanced to undermine the wall, he forced an entrance; and the place was taken by assault.

Montsegur delayed him longer; but after a siege of fourteen days, the garrison, through the intercession of Sir Walter de Manny, obtained a convention, by which they agreed to surrender at the end of a month, unless relieved by the King or the Duke of Normandy. The Earl thence proceeded to attack the strong castle of Aiguillon at the confluence of the Lot and the Garonne: but the necessity of assailing it was removed by the cowardly baseness of the governor, who yielded it at once, though in those days it might

* The Duke of Normandy, apprised of the landing of the Earl of Derby in Gascony, had hastened, as we have seen, to put the surrounding provinces in a state of preparation. He arrived at Carcassonne on the 2d of August, 1345; and thence went by Touraine and Poitou to the Limousin; where he remained till the end of October, and then proceeded to meet his father in Angoulême. See Dom Vaissette, tom. iv. p. 257.

well have passed for impregnable. The English troops took immediate possession of the place, while the governor, retiring to Toulouse, met the fate he deserved, and was hanged for his treachery or his cowardice.

The capture of La Réole, towards which city the Earl now directed his march, proved the most difficult enterprise in which he had been hitherto engaged.* The town itself was strongly fortified, according to the science of defence in that day, and the citadel afforded still greater means of resistance against an enemy. The garrison was numerous, and commanded by a brave and skilful officer, called Agout de Baux; and military stores, as well as other provisions, had been plentifully accumulated in the place, while it had been held by the Count de Lille. † For several weeks a number of unfruitful efforts were made to take the place by assault; but at length two wooden towers were constructed, and brought close to the walls, which eventually compelled the town to surrender. These machines, called Beffrois or Belfries, were larger than those usually employed, consisting of three stages, each of which contained a hundred archers; and being covered with boiled

* I was for some time doubtful in regard to the date of the capture of La Réole, and, indeed, as to whether it preceded or followed the surrender of Angoulême and other places to the north of Guienne, which I speak of hereafter, the first mention of its fall by any of the contemporary letters, being made in April, 1346, by the Duke of Bourbon, who refers to it as a very recent event; but I have since been convinced that the victory at Auberoche was followed immediately by the Earl of Lancaster's conquests in the south, by reasoning which I have stated at the end of this chapter.

† Froissart, chap. ccxxxvi. Hist. de Languedoc, tom. iv. p. 255.

leather, they were protected from the fire which the enemy cast down from above.*

While the archers, from the stages of these machines, rendered it almost certain death for any of the garrison to show themselves on the battlements, two hundred soldiers undermined the wall, and soon effected such a breach, that the burghers of La Réole demanded to capitulate. The commander of the garrison, however, refused to be a party to the convention ; and, retiring into the citadel, while the terms were under negotiation between the townsmen and Lord Lancaster, he laid in such stores as would have enabled him to hold out for many days longer had not the means of mining been again employed. Though the rock on which the donjon or keep was built set all efforts at defiance, a small tower was soon overthrown, which served more to dispirit the garrison than to aid the assailants. At length Agout de Baux, finding the place untenable, proposed to his companions to capitulate, and notice of his purpose was transmitted to the Earl of Lancaster, who immediately rode to the gates of the castle, in order to speak with the governor personally in regard to the conditions. At first the English commander refused to show any lenity, and demanded an unconditional surrender; but being piqued upon his knightly courtesy, he at length suffered the garrison to depart with their arms, and the castle was delivered up to the English army.

The taking of La Réole had a personal interest

* Froissart, chap. ccxxvii.

for Sir Walter de Mauny, distinct from his feelings as one of the principal commanders of the British troops. More than twenty * years before the period of which I speak, at a tournament given in Cambray, a young knight, the son of John de Levis, Maréchal de Mirepoix, was accidentally killed by the Lord of Mauny, father to the gallant knight so long attached to England. Peter de Levis, uncle of the dead cavalier, then held the episcopal see of Cambray †; and although such events were common at all military games, and in this case the occurrence was purely accidental, he vowed to avenge the death of his nephew, and was only pacified by the Lord of Mauny undertaking a pilgrimage to the shrine of St. James in Galicia. The pilgrimage being accomplished in the year 1324‡, De Mauny, on his journey homeward, passed by the town of Réole, then besieged by Charles of Valois, and presented himself in the camp of that Prince, bearing letters from the Count of Hainault. Charles received him with kindness, and entertained him at supper; but as he was returning to his own tent at night, accompanied by several of his suite, he was waylaid by John de Levis, as it would appear, and slain, with all who accompanied him.

The supposed offender was immediately arrested by order of the king, and his property was seized: but the house of Mirepoix was too powerful in Gascony for justice to be executed with vigour

* Froissart, chap. ccxl. † Hist. de Cambray, tom. i. p. 365.
‡ Hist. de Languedoc, tom. iv. p. 199.

against its chief; and, at the end of a year, the maréchal was not only set at liberty, but his estates were restored without any judicial investigation. The bodies of the Lord of Mauny and of his followers were buried in a small chapel then without the walls of La Réole; and Sir Walter de Mauny, as soon as the town had fallen on the present occasion, offered a high reward to any one who would show him the place of his father's sepulture. An old inhabitant of the town was soon found who brought him to the chapel, which, since the murder, had been enclosed within the city walls, and pointed out to him a small tomb of marble, on which he said would be found an inscription to justify the assertion that there lay the ashes of the Lord of Mauny.* Sir Walter stooped down, and amidst the dust of many years, perceived some Latin words; the import of which a knight of that age was little capable of comprehending; but sending for a man whose trade was more in letters than in arms, Sir Walter soon heard the meaning of the inscription; and by it the assurance of his old guide was confirmed. The remains of the father were transported to Valenciennes by the pious care of his son, and the minor canons of that city reaped the benefit in an annual sum expended on masses for the soul of the murdered noble.

A number of towns† upon the Lot and Garonne

* Froissart, chap. ccxli.

† No sources of information exist, as far as I have been able to discover, which might serve to rectify the account of Froissart in re-

were taken within a very short space of time after the fall of La Réole: Montpesat, Castel Moran, Ville Franche, Miremont, Tonneins, Damasens*, and several other places, were captured either by stratagem or force; and having reduced a great part of the Bazadois and Agenois to submission, the Earl marched boldly across the country, and laid siege to Angoulême. The terrors of his name were sufficient to induce the burghers to treat, and giving twenty-four hostages for their good faith, they agreed to deliver the town at the end of a month if not relieved by a French army. To extend his conquests as far as possible before that army could be assembled was the policy of the Earl of Lancaster; and he was now the more desirous of gaining every strong place as easily as he could, a general summons having been issued for the nobility of the neighbouring provinces to meet the Duke of Normandy in arms at Toulouse on the 3d of

---

gard to the order in which these places were captured. Any one who compares his statement with a good map will see at once, that without supposing the course of the Earl of Lancaster to be the most erratic that ever was known, there must be some inaccuracy; and as his chronology in regard to the Earl's campaigns is proved to be false throughout, it is not difficult to imagine that he inverted the order of events, though the events themselves really happened. The siege of Angoulême did not take place before the 7th of November; as on that day, just a fortnight after the battle of Auberoche, John Duke of Normandy signed charters in that city. Before the 6th of January, 1346, however, he had retired as far as Loches, in Touraine; and it is therefore probable that between those two periods the conquest of Angoulême, Poitiers, St. Jean d'Angely, and all the neighbouring country, was made by the Earl of Lancaster. See Dom Vaissette, tom. iv. p. 258.; and proofs, p. 200.; and note at the end of this chapter.

* Froissart, chaps. ccxliii. ccxliv.

February *, which was now not far distant. Accepting therefore the terms proposed by the citizens of Angoulême, which were honourably fulfilled, he instantly proceeded to fresh conquests; and, after subjugating a very large tract of country, including the towns of Poitiers and St. Jean d'Angely, he turned his arms against Blaye. But that city contained a resolute garrison, by whom the defence was protracted till, the winter setting in with great severity, the Earl was compelled to raise the siege and retire to Bordeaux.†

The preparations of France however had not escaped his attention; and as he had no farther opportunity of acting vigorously in the field, he detached large bodies of his troops to reinforce the garrisons of the various towns he had taken; and then waited calmly at Bordeaux, to observe the movements which his enemy showed a disposition to make as soon as possible in the spring. The French muster was held at Toulouse early in February; and the Duke of Normandy, who took the command in person‡, found himself at the head of more than a hundred thousand men; with which he immediately reduced Miremont and Ville Franche in Agenois. At the same time a considerable French force laid siege to Angoulême; but John of Norwich, who commanded in that city, made a brave defence; and after attempting to storm the walls more than once, the French commander for-

* Vaissette, Hist de Languedoc, tom. iv. p. 259.

† Froissart, chap. ccxlv.

‡ Idem, chap. ccli.

bade any farther efforts to take the place by assault, and reduced the siege to a blockade.*

The number of his troops however soon exhausted the provisions in the immediate neighbourhood; and the Seneschal of Beaucaire, one of the most enterprising leaders in the French army, proposed to sweep the lands in the neighbourhood of St. Jean d'Angely. He set out, accordingly, with a thousand men-at-arms, and approached that city; but, finding that the English garrison had driven out eight hundred head of cattle to graze in the neighbouring meadows, the seneschal determined if possible not only to make himself master of the oxen, but of the fortress also. Placing the great body of his troops in ambush in a valley, he boldly approached the walls with sixty men-at-arms; and, having collected the cattle, drove them off in the gray twilight of the morning, before the eyes of the English sentinels. The warders speedily aroused their sleeping comrades, and the whole garrison was soon in motion to pursue the handful of marauders who had performed so daring a feat. According to his preconcerted plan, the

* I have not thought proper to reject the whole account which Froissart gives of the siege of Angoulême by the French, though I have many doubts in regard to it. One part of his statement, however, is certainly false, as he states that the Duke of Normandy commanded at the siege, which ended, according to his own account, either on the 25th of March, the latest of the two dates, which he himself gives, or on the 2d of February, the earliest. Now, the Duke did not assemble his army till the 3d of February, and, according to Vaissette, did not take the field till the end of March. However, it is certain that the Duke signed letters at Montauban on the 22d of March; and, being then 150 miles from Angoulême, could not have marched thither, and reduced that city by blockade, before the 25th.

seneschal suffered himself to be overtaken in the valley where his friends were stationed; but no sooner had the English soldiers entered it, than they found themselves assailed on all sides by an immensely superior force, and were ultimately all either killed or taken. St. Jean d'Angely surrendered immediately; and having furnished it with a French garrison, the Seneschal of Beaucaire returned to Angoulême with honour and success.

In the meanwhile a scarcity of provisions had made itself felt in Angoulême; the people of the town were attached to the interests of France; and John of Norwich had no small cause to fear that they would open their gates to the enemy, whose determination of reducing the garrison by hunger was sufficiently evident. In this dilemma, the English commander, finding it impossible to hold out, resolved at least to save himself and his comrades from death or imprisonment; and as there was no reason to believe that the French would grant any terms but those of absolute surrender, he determined to accomplish by stratagem what could not be otherwise effected.

On the day before what is called in England Lady-day * —which was then held by all parties as a solemn festival of the Roman church, — the English

* Froissart says in the first instance that it was on the day of the Purification of the Virgin (2d February). This, however, is proved to be incorrect, as the French army was not called to assemble before the 3d of that month. He, however, declares afterwards that it was the *Jour Notre Dame*, which undoubtedly referred to Lady-day, or the 25th of March.

commander presented himself on the battlements, and by signs demanded to speak with some of the besiegers. On their approach he informed them, that he wished to hold a parley with the French commander himself, or with one of his marshals; and this request being communicated to the principal officer, he immediately mounted his horse and proceeded to the spot himself. The leader of the besieging force naturally concluded that the garrison wished to treat for a surrender, and asked if such were the case?*

"Far from it," replied the English officer; "I merely wished, my Lord, to beg you, out of reverence for our Lady's day, which falls to-morrow, to grant us a truce for that day alone, so that it may pass over in peace on both sides."

The French commander immediately acceded; the cessation of hostilities was granted, and by daylight on the following morning John of Norwich threw open the gates, and marched out with all his garrison. The French army instantly flew to arms; but the English captain rode forward, exclaiming, "Have a care, Lords, and harm us not, for we have truce for this whole day, as you well know, and we will ride whithersoever we please."

* It is not impossible that the personage whom Froissart names Duke of Normandy, and who commanded the French at the siege of Angoulême, was the Duke of Bourbon, as he was busily engaged in collecting troops during the early part of 1346; and we lose sight of him from the 4th of March, when he was at Lanzerte, on his march in some direction, we know not whither, till the 2d of April, when he had returned to Agen. This is merely conjecture, however. It is only certain that it was not the Duke of Normandy.

The tidings flew rapidly to the French commander, who kept his word, saying, "Let them go, let them go, in the name of God!" and the English garrison, delivered from their perilous situation, made the best of their way, we are told, to the strong town of Aiguillon, which was shortly after besieged by the Duke of Normandy himself, with the powerful army which he had collected at Toulouse.

It would seem that the Earl of Lancaster had anticipated this movement; for we find that he had despatched thither a reinforcement of forty men at arms and 300 horse archers, led by several of the most renowned knights of his army, whose names must not be omitted in this place. The Earl of Pembroke, Sir Walter de Mauny, Sir Frank Von Halle, Sir Thomas Cook, Sir John de Lille, Sir Robert Neville, Sir Thomas Bisset, Sir John de la Zouche, Sir Philip of Beauvais, and Sir Richard Roehcliff, were the leaders of the reinforcement sent to Aiguillon; and we have reason to believe that, after their arrival, the garrison amounted to about 1200 men, consisting of 400 men at arms and 800 archers.* Provisions of every kind, warlike stores, and skilful workmen, had been collected in the city; and when the Duke of Normandy at length sat down before it†, the eyes of the whole country were turned towards the siege and

* Villani, p. 870.

† Between the 10th and the 19th of April. On the first of those days the Duke signed papers at Agen, and on the latter was before Aiguillon. Vaissette, ubi supra.

the defence, anticipating the long and vigorous resistance which the place was destined to offer. The immense force of the French, stated by most accounts at 100,000 men, and by none at less than 56,000 *, promised, if properly employed, to wear out the garrison by mere fatigue; but a variety of preliminary steps were to be taken, in regard to which numerical superiority was little advantageous. The fortress being situated on a narrow tongue of land, between the Lot and the Garonne, it appeared necessary to cast a bridge over the latter river, in order to approach the walls on the weakest side. This operation was immediately undertaken by the engineers of the French army, who, with 300 carpenters, working day and night, soon made considerable progress; but when the bridge was about half finished, the garrison, whose position on the river enabled them to keep several vessels in readiness, embarked a body of men at arms in three small ships; and the workmen, with those who defended them, being put to flight, the half-constructed bridge was totally destroyed. The attempt to build was immediately renewed; and though day after day, Sir Walter de Mauny and his companions, in continual sallies, slew the workmen and impeded their labours, yet at length the bridge was finished, and the French army passed the river.

An immediate assault was made on the fortress from the land side; but, after continuing their efforts till night, the assailants were obliged to retreat. Day after day the attempt to storm was renewed, some-

* Villani, lib. xii. cap. xl.

times the whole army mounting to the walls at once, sometimes divided into parties, which continually relieved each other, and poured fresh tides of warfare upon the gallant defenders of the place. Whether, on the one hand, the immense means of communication afforded to the garrison by the two rivers, or want of foresight, or want of inclination, on the other, prevented the Duke of Normandy from attempting to blockade the place, I cannot tell; but it is evident that the French army in no degree surrounded Aiguillon, and encamped, it would seem, only on the side of the land. It is possible that the Duke of Normandy, according to the chivalrous notions of the day, imagined that more honour was to be gained in taking the city by force than in reducing it by famine; and it is clear that foraging parties daily issued forth from Aiguillon without any obstruction being offered to their exit, though they were frequently encountered by adverse detachments on their return. On one of these occasions, Sir Walter de Mauny had nearly fallen a victim to his boldness. Having sallied out, as he frequently did, with 100 or 120 companions, while returning embarrassed with booty, which he had swept from the neighbouring country, he was met by the Lord Charles of Montmorency, loaded also with provisions for the army, but accompanied by at least 500 men. De Mauny, notwithstanding the inferiority of his force, did not avoid the encounter; and a fierce struggle ensued, in which the English were upon the point of defeat, when, news of the skirmish having reached

Aiguillon, the Earl of Pembroke issued forth to the aid of his companion in arms. The battle was now renewed with greater fury than before; and Sir Walter de Mauny, who was found dismounted and fighting on foot, surrounded by the enemy, was freed from his perilous situation. The French were ultimately dispersed, after a long and gallant resistance, and Charles of Montmorency returned to the camp with the mortification of defeat.

In the meantime the active measures of the siege were not relaxed. Engines of immense power had been brought from Toulouse, and others were fabricated on the spot, which night and day continued to shower into the town vast quantities of missiles of all kinds*; but the defences of the place were so strong that little damage was done, except to the roofs of the houses immediately adjoining the walls. A great effort was made by the assailants to force the gate; and after a tremendous struggle—in which the common soldiers pressed forward furiously, in hopes of obtaining 100 crowns, which the Duke had promised to any one who should first win the drawbridge—the chains were at length broken by a multitude of armed men in the boats below, and towards night the bridge was gained. The gate, however, resisted all the efforts of the French soldiers; and a number were killed or wounded by blocks of stone, beams of wood, pots of quicklime, and flights of arrows poured down from above, so

* There is every reason to believe that several cannon were here employed, as they were certainly provided for the army of the Duke of Normandy.

that at nightfall the attempt was abandoned; and before the next morning the bridge had not only been recovered by the garrison, but had been rendered even more capable of defence than it was before.

At length four large moveable towers, called cats, were constructed, capable of containing in each of the stages with which they were furnished a considerable number of men at arms; and, according to a very common custom, where the place attacked was defended on one or more sides by water, these machines were placed on board ships, and brought by that means against the walls of the town.* The preparation of the engines, which was tedious and laborious, had long been perceived by the besieged; and on the only points against which they could act, there had been erected four large martinets†, a sort of machine for

* These towers which were brought against Aiguillon have been named beffroys, and it has been asserted by a modern writer that this was the first time that they were ever used upon the water. A glance into James of Vitry will show that they were employed on the water a century before. The difference between the cattus and the beffroy originally was, that the cattus was merely a covered gallery, by means of which the besieged approached the foot of the wall; while the beffroy or belfragium was a high tower, which generally overtopped the ramparts The two, however, were afterwards combined under the name of a chat-chateil, the full description of which, with an explanation of the very passage of Froissart which mentions the use of that machine at the siege of Aiguillon, may be found in Ducange's Observations upon Joinville, page 68. folio ed.

† The martinet, the catapult, the balista, the mangonel, the warwolf, the trebushet, the espringal, the petrary, and several others were all instruments intended to effect the same purpose, though they accomplished it by different means and with greater or less power. That purpose was to cast immense blocks of stone or quantities of darts either against a particular point, or at random into a besieged town. — See Grose's Military Antiquities.

casting blocks of stone, which soon disabled the whole of the towers on which the enemy had bestowed so much pains, and sunk one of the ships that bore them, drowning the soldiers on board. Such repeated rebuffs would, doubtless, have induced the Duke of Normandy to raise the siege, had he not bound himself, we are told, by oath not to rise from before the walls of Aiguillon till that fortress was in his power.* He persevered, however, for more than four months in his resolution, till other circumstances compelled him, by the call of superior duties, to break his rash vow.†

In the meanwhile, the Earl of Lancaster had not been forgetful of the situation of his friends; and, occupying the strong post of La Reole with all the troops he could collect, he exerted himself to harass the besieging force, and cut off all its detached parties which ventured beyond the immediate vicinity of the camp.‡ At the same time he called on all the English partisans in Gascony to take arms and join him at Bergerac, and engaged a number of mer-

* Villani, p. 856.

† D. Vaissette, Hist. de Languedoc. tom. iv. p. 261.

‡ Villani, lib. xii. cap. 61., and several other authors, copying his statements, declare that the Seneschal of Guyenne for the King of France, with a large detachment from the besieging army, was defeated in an attempt upon a fortress on the Dordogne, and that the leader himself was taken. I have not, however, given this circumstance a place in the text; because, after very long search, I have not been able to find that Philip had at this time any officer bearing the title of Seneschal of Guyenne. Perhaps Villani meant the Seneschal of Beaucaire, who was undoubtedly with the army which besieged Aiguillon. In regard to the dates of the war in Guyenne, it is singular to remark that Villani is much more correct than Froissart.

cenary auxiliaries from the small states in the neighbourhood; by these means he collected a force sufficient to justify him in taking the field in the beginning of August, although still infinitely inferior in number to that of his adversary. Before this time, however, he had received intelligence that the King of England had landed with a mighty power in Normandy; and counting on his sovereign's skill and fortune, he calculated truly that, ere long, events would happen in the north of France which would compel the retreat of a great part, if not the whole, of the French army from Guyenne. Towards the 17th of August, then, he began his march for Bergerac, where he was met by all the troops which could be withdrawn from the garrisons of the strong towns throughout Gascony. Scarcely had he arrived there, when envoys from the Duke of Normandy reached him, desiring a truce on the part of their master, who, beyond all doubt, had before this time received intelligence of the invasion of Normandy, and the first successes of the English king. The Earl of Lancaster rejected the proposal without hesitation; and the messenger's return was the signal for the breaking up of the French camp before Aiguillon.* So rapid, indeed, was the departure of the Duke of Normandy from the vicinity of that fortress, that a great part of his baggage was left behind; and it would appear† that even his troops suffered severely

* August 20. 1346. Robert of Avesbury, p. 142. Froissart, chap. ccxcviii.

† See the letter of the Earl of Lancaster.

from the confusion and disarray of his hasty retreat.* Little time was allowed him to take any measures for the protection of the cities he had regained in his short campaign, ere news of the fatal field of Cressy †, and a peremptory order from his father to hasten his steps towards Paris, called him at once from the spot, and the whole country was left open to the efforts of the Earl of Lancaster.

A detachment from the garrison of Aiguillon hung upon the rear of the French army; and during a long retreat a number of prisoners were

* Knighton says (col. 2583.) that the Duke of Normandy quitted his camp secretly, leaving his army to make their retreat as they could; but there appears not to have been the slightest foundation for such a rumour.

† It has been generally stated, though quite erroneously, that the news of the battle of Cressy caused the Duke of Normandy to raise the siege of Aiguillon. This is proved beyond all doubt to be false by the letter of the Earl of Lancaster himself, who states that the French raised the siege on the Sunday before the day of St. Batholomew, which Sunday occurred in the year 1346, on the 20th August; while the victory at Cressy was won by the English monarch on the 26th of that month. It is therefore more than probable that intelligence of the rapid approach of Edward towards Paris caused the Duke to retire from before Aiguillon; though very likely ere he absolutely quitted Gascony, the news of Cressy fight and the annihilation of his father's forces, as well as the peremptory command which we know that Philip sent him to return, hurried his retreat. It will be perceived that, through the whole of this account of the proceedings in Guyenne, I have called the commander-in-chief of the English troops the Earl of Lancaster, instead of giving him the title of the Earl of Derby, which has been copied from Froissart by most of the English historians. His father, however, died in 1344, according to some accounts; in 1345, according to others; but, at all events, the nobleman of whom I speak had certainly become Earl of Lancaster before any of the events above recorded took place, as the very first order addressed by Edward III. to that nobleman, as his vicegerent in Gascony, bears the title of Earl of Lancaster.

taken*, from one of whom it would appear the first news of the battle of Cressy was communicated to the English in Guyenne.† Sir Walter de Mauny, anxious to be present at the great events passing in the north, now acquitted one of the knights whom he had captured of all ransom, on condition that he would procure him a safe conduct from the Duke of Normandy, to enable him to traverse France in safety. This was easily obtained; and while the Earl of Lancaster proceeded to reduce all the small towns and forts

* Froissart, ccxcviii.

† Froissart distinctly states that a prisoner taken by Sir Walter de Mauny gave the first intelligence; but, as he declares that this knight was captured at the raising of the siege, and we know that the siege was raised before the battle; as he says too that the prisoner then went to Paris and returned, and we know that Sir Walter de Mauny was at St. Jean d'Angely before such a journey could have been performed, I should have rejected the whole account as false, had not the letter of the Earl of Lancaster confirmed the facts, though it altered the details. By comparing the two accounts we find that the following circumstance had occurred, beyond doubt, within thirty days after the siege had been raised: — Sir Walter de Mauny had obtained a safe conduct from the Duke of Normandy to proceed to join the King of England by land; he had gone as far as St. Jean d'Angely, his followers had been there arrested, he himself had made his escape, and the tidings had reached the Earl of Lancaster on the banks of the Charente. These events could not have happened had the Duke of Normandy gone to Paris immediately after quitting Aiguillon, and had Sir Walter's messenger followed him thither and returned with the safe conduct. I am therefore inclined to think that the Duke retreated upon Toulouse and Languedoc, remaining in the south till after the news of the battle of Cressy had reached him.

It is to be remarked, however, that one difficulty exists in regard to the precise day on which the siege was raised. It will be seen in the Earl of Lancaster's letter, that he states it to have been on the Sunday before *St. Barthu*, which has been rendered, I think correctly, St. Bartholomew. Others, however, believe that he meant the decollation of St. John Baptist, or the 29th. Nevertheless the tidings of Cressy could not have reached Aiguillon on either day.

which had surrendered to the French Prince in the Bazadois and Agenois, Sir Walter pursued his way towards Calais. At St. Jean d'Angely, however, his safe conduct proved of no avail; and though he himself, with two companions, made their escape and reached Orleans, the rest of his attendants were seized and cast into prison. At Orleans the gallant knight was not more fortunate himself, being arrested in despite of all remonstrances, and carried thence to Paris, where he was placed in the châtelet. Philip of Valois, with the insane fury which characterised the latter years of his life, not only countenanced his arrest; but, mindful alone of the exploits which the knight had performed against him, threatened loudly to put him to death.*

His situation, however, was no sooner known to the Duke of Normandy, than, flying to his father, he demanded the instant liberation of the man who had only trusted himself within the land upon the assurance of his honour. Philip refused to perform the act of justice that his son required, and again menaced the prisoner with death. High and bitter words ensued between the King and the Prince; and John is said to have then first used that magnificent maxim which is so honourably associated with his name: "If justice and truth," he said, "were to be banished from the rest of the earth, they ought to find a refuge in the bosom of kings." He then

* It is probable that the French King excused this act of violence, on the pretence of feudal rights over Hainault, the country of De Mauny's birth.

quitted his father, declaring that he would never arm again in his cause, nor cross the threshold of his palace, till Sir Walter de Mauny was set at liberty.*

Philip adhered to his determination for some time; but at length changed to the opposite extreme, set the prisoner free, invited him to his table, and endeavoured to wipe out the memory of the indignity he had offered him by extravagant and costly presents. These Sir Walter de Mauny received at the time; but after having joined his royal master at Calais, he returned them under Edward's direction to the King of France, and had no reason to complain that he had been deprived of a benefit.

In the meantime† the Earl of Lancaster, dividing his forces into three bodies, left one in the neighbourhood of Bazas, under the command of the Lord of Albret; another, under the Count de Duras, was so stationed as to protect the Agenois; and with the third the Earl himself advanced towards Saintonge. On his march he took Sauveterre and Châteauneuf sur Charente. At the latter place, hearing that the followers of Sir Walter de Mauny had been arrested in St. Jean d'Angely, he marched instantly to attack it; took it by assault, and placed an English garrison within the walls, as well as inflicted an annual subsidy upon the inhabitants. After remaining for eight days at St. Jean d'Angely, the Earl pursued his march towards Poictiers, but was repulsed in an

* Froissart, chap. ccc. † Robert of Avesbury, p. 143.

attempt upon Niort.* St. Maixent, however, was captured; and the English army then appeared before a small but well-defended town, called Montreuil Bonnin, which contained a royal mint.

The inhabitants showed themselves determined to offer a vigorous resistance; and the Earl, to encourage his soldiers to the assault, promised that whatever each man took should become absolutely his own, without being subject to those deductions which the laws of war at that period made in favour of the superior officers.† The men boldly and joyfully mounted to storm: the town was soon captured; and one of the archers, unknowing his good fortune, took possession of a house attached to the mint, in which was a quantity of gold, far exceeding his utmost dreams of wealth. When he saw the magnitude of his prize, he never supposed that the promise of the Earl would justify his appropriation of such a treasure. Securing the house, he ran to that nobleman, and telling him what he had found, besought him somewhat importunately to take it into his own possession, and place a guard over the spot. "Keep what you have got, honest archer," replied the Earl. "I am not a man to give in child's play, and take back again. No treasure you can have found is sufficient to make me forget my word."

The town and castle of Lusignan were also taken; and at length the English army appeared before

* Froissart, chap. cccii. † Barnes, p. 374.

Poitiers itself.* That city is scattered irregularly over a large space of ground, filled with gardens and vacant spaces, and containing so much within its walls that a very large garrison indeed would be requisite for any efficient defence. A number of nobles and knights from the adjacent country, however, had thrown themselves into the place; and all the wealth of the environs had been there collected for the sake of security. A vigorous resistance was made; and on the first day's assault the English forces were repulsed. On the same evening a better reconnoissance of the ground was effected; and the weaker parts of the fortifications having been discovered, a threefold attack was begun the following morning, which ended in the capture of the city.† A great number of excesses were committed by the soldiery; and many of the citizens were killed in the streets, though all the principal persons made their escape into the country by the various gates.

Several smaller towns and villages in the vicinity were subsequently captured; and after staying eight days at Poitiers, the Earl of Lancaster returned to St. Jean d'Angely, where he remained during a considerable length of time, endeavouring both to conciliate the inhabitants of the immense

* Robert of Avesbury, ubi suprà. Several accounts would seem to imply that Poitiers had been captured by the English in the preceding year, and, like St. Jean d'Angely, had been retaken by the French; but I am inclined to believe that such was not the case, and that this was the first siege of the former place by the English army. Froissart, ibidem.

† 4th of October, 1346.

tract of territory he had acquired, and to provide for its defence against the enemy. He then returned to Bordeaux, where he embarked the plunder which had been taken during his short stay in Guyenne, and returned to England, bearing with him sufficient wealth to enrich his country for many years.*

* See notes, page 522. and page 526. The order of the Earl of Lancaster's proceedings during this campaign is one of the most difficult points to determine that I have yet met with. The only certain dates which we possess give us the following facts: Before the 24th of August, 1345, he had taken Bergerac. Between that day and his victory over the Count de Lille besieging Auberoche, which took place on the 23rd of October, he must have taken and garrisoned Auberoche, Pellagrue, and Libourne, gone back to Bordeaux, and returned to deliver the garrison he had left in Auberoche.

These facts are certain; but all that follows till the raising of the siege of Aiguillon in the succeeding year is derived from inference, conjecture, or the accounts of chroniclers known to be inaccurate in their dates. The first question that suggests itself is, where did the Earl direct his steps immediately after the battle of Auberoche? whether to Angoumois and the parts of Poitou, which he certainly conquered at some time during his stay in Gascony, or towards the higher Garonne? Undoubtedly to the Garonne and the South. The army of the Count de Lille, which had defended the south, was utterly annihilated by the battle of Auberoche on the 23d of October. The higher parts of Gascony were thus left open, while Angoumois was defended by the Duke of Normandy with a considerable force; and it is probable that such was the reason which induced the Earl to turn his steps towards the Garonne, leaving a large tract of well-garrisoned country between himself and the Duke of Normandy. Such, I say, was probably his reason; but that he did so is certain, for, that he did not advance at that time upon Angoulême is proved by the fact of the Duke of Normandy having signed charters in that city on the 7th of November, 1345, fourteen days after the battle of Auberoche; and that the Earl took La Reale, Aiguillon, Montsegur, and other places on the Garonne, during the autumn of 1345, is shown by the established fact of his having repaired, garrisoned, and provisioned them before the 3d of February, 1346, at which time the Duke of Normandy made his first movements to recover them. When, then, was it that the Earl captured Angoulême, St. Jean d'Angely, Poiters, &c.? in the year 1345, or after the retreat of the Duke of Normandy in 1346? This, I acknowledge, is doubtful; for if he did take them in the former year they must have been retaken by the French, and again captured by the Earl in the latter year, as Froissart implies that they were. This, though I doubted it at first, I am now inclined to think the correct view in regard to the fate of all these towns except Poitiers. In the first place, Froissart lets fall one of those accidental statements of a minute point which confirms his general account. He states that the Earl raised the siege of Blaye, after taking Angoulême, &c., on account of the severity of the weather. Now this must have been in 1345, because the Earl was not there during the succeeding winter. In the next place, the Earl himself, in his account of his conquests in 1346, never mentions Angoulême, though we know that it was taken either in that or the foregoing year; and, in the third place, he implies that he treated St. Jean d'Angely with greater severity than other captured towns, which would scarcely have been justified by the arrest of Sir Walter de Mauny, and probably was occasioned by the citizens having yielded their city at once to the French, when the English garrison had been decoyed into an ambush, as described by Froissart. With regard to Poitiers, I am very doubtful; but do not think that it was taken till 1346.

My opinion is, that as soon as the Earl had completed his conquests on the Garonne, and found that the Duke of Normandy had quitted Angoulême, he turned his arms in that direction, and conquered a considerable portion of Angoumois. As soon as the Duke attacked Aiguillon, Lancaster gave his whole attention to frustrate the enemy's attempts in that quarter; and, in the meantime, some other French commander, perhaps the Duke of Bourbon, recaptured Angoulême, St. Jean, &c., which were again taken by the Earl in the subsequent year, after the Duke of Normandy had been foiled before Aiguillon, and his army dispersed.

APPENDIX.

No. I.

Observations on Note 1. Page 28.

My expressions in this note were inaccurate. Instead of saying that the right under which Edward claimed the crown of France "*was* technically called the right of representation," I should have said "was affected by that technically called the right of representation." The following comparison, however, of the three great law cases of those times may elucidate this point:—

The claims of Edward III. to the throne of France, those of Robert of Artois to the county of Artois, and those of John of Montford to the Duchy of Britanny, were all affected in some degree by what was called the right of representation.

Edward contended in the fullest extent that, in regard to all successions, an individual transmitted to his heir, his rights, both positive and contingent; and farther, that in rights which were barred by sex alone, as soon as the individual in whom they would otherwise have been vested could produce a representative, qualified by sex, the rights which were but latent revived in full force in the person of that representative.

Robert of Artois contended only that an individual transmitted to his heir male his rights positive and contingent.

John of Montford founded his claim exactly upon the reverse proposition; namely, that in Britanny an individual could not transmit to his heir at his death rights which were contingent; and that if he could, he would still be barred from transmitting a male fief to a female.

In all cases of fiefs, I believe the doctrine propounded by Edward was correct, except where local or customary law could be shown against it. Fiefs were universally held by military tenure, and as women could not serve in arms they were excluded by the salic law; but that law was very early modified, and by producing a representative to fulfil the tenure — during infancy a guardian, and after marriage a husband — the law was satisfied, and the fief was permitted to descend to women. That the law was equally applicable to the crown there can be no doubt; but up to the time of Edward III. no instance had taken place of the same modification of the law having been admitted where the throne was concerned, which was very general in regard to common fiefs. But putting aside all these questions, Edward was barred from the succession by a nearer heir, Charles the Bad, King of Navarre; so that his claim was idle.

Robert of Artois was deprived of the fief which would have been his father's had he lived, by a decision of the French peers in regard to the customary law of Artois.

The claim of John of Montford was rejected by the same court, upon proof that the salic law did not obtain in Britanny, and that the contingent rights of each individual descended at his death to his heir, according to the custom of that duchy.

In regard to one point connected with this question very great difficulties exist. It will be seen in the text that I have given credit to the statement that Edward the Third claimed both the regency and the throne of France after the death of Charles le Bel. The first of these claims, that of the regency during the pregnancy of Joan of Evreux, is not proved by any state paper; but it seems to me a clear inference from the proceedings of the court of peers of France that such a claim had been put in. That commissioners were appointed by the King to assert his claim to the throne after the throne proved to be vacant, there can be no doubt; but Mr. Hallam thinks that they never executed their commission, and it is very probable that his view is correct.

No. II.

"Tresch' fitz no' pensoms bien q' vo' estes desirons assavoir bones novelles de no' et coment il no' est avenuz puys n're aler Denglet're si no' vo' fesom savoir q' le joedi' ap 's ceo q'on no dep' times du Port D'orewell, no' siglames tut le iour et la nuyt suaunte, et le vendredi en tour hour de noune no venismes s' la costere de ffiaundres devant Blankebergh ou no' avioms la vewe de la fflote de nos enemys qi estoyent tut amasses ensemble en port del Swyne et p' ceo q' la Tyde, n'estoit mis adonges p' assembler a eux no 'yherbergeasmes tut cel noet, le samady le iour de seint Johan bien ap 's houre de noune, a la Tyde nous en noun de Dieu et en espoire, de n're droite querele, entrames en dit port, s'nos ditz enemys, qi avoyent assemble lours niefs en moult fort array et lesqux fesoient ml't noble defens tut cel iour et la noet ap's, mes dieu p' sa puissaunce, et miracle, no' ottroia la victorie de mesmes noz enemys de qai no' m'cioms si devoutement come no' poems. Et si vo' fesoms savour q' le nombre des niefs galeyes et g'nt barges de nos enemys amounta a IX^xx. et ditz, lesqueles estoient toutz pris sauve xxiiij. en tout, lesqueles senfuirent et les uns sont puye pris s' mier (sur mer) et le nombre des gentz darmes et atres gentz armez amounta a xxxv mill, de quele nombre p' esme cink m^l sont eschapees, et la remenaunt ensi come no' este donc (donné) a entendre p' ascuns gentz, q' sont pris en vie, si gissent les corps mortz, et (en) tut pleyn de lieux s^r la costere de fflaundres. Dautre p't totes nos niefs, cest assavoir Cristofre et les autres qi estoient p' dues a Middelburgh, sont ore regaignez, et il yount gaignez, en ceste navie trois ou quatre auxi graundes come la Cristofre: les fflemengs estoient de bone volente, davoir venuz a no' ala bataille du commencement tanqe ala fin issint dieu n're seign^r ad assez de grace monstre de qei', no' et toutz nos amys sumes tut ditz tenutz de lui rendre grace et m' ciz. N're entent est a demorer en pees en le ewe taunt, qe no' coms pris c' teyn point ove no' alliez et autres nos amys de fflandres de ceo q' soit affaire. Trescher fitz dieu soit gardeyn de vo'. Don' souz n're secree seal en n're nief Cogg. Thom', le Mescredy en la veille seint Piere et seint Paoul.

"14° R. Edw. 3^li."

No. III.

Eeuwigduerende Verbond.

In den name svader ende soens ende shelichs gheests ende in de eere der reinre maghet sinte Marien der moeder gods.

Allen den ghenen die dese jeghenwordeghe letteren sullen zien of horen lesen. Wy Jhan bi der gracien ons heeren Hertoghe van Lottrike, van Brabant, ende van Lymborgh ende marcgrave des heleghes rycx. Lodewyc Grave van Vlaendren, van Nevers, ende van Retheest, Comoengemayers, scepenen, raet, ende alt commun van den steden van Brabant, Loevene, Brucele, Andwerpen, Shertoghenbossche, Nivile, Tienen, ende Leewe, borchmeesters, voght, prooost, scepenen, raet, ende alt comun van den steden van Vlaendren, Ghend, Brucghe, Ypre, Cortrike, Audenaerde, Aelst, ende Gheroudsberghe. Saluut in onsen heere met kennessen der waerheit. Weten alle dat wy Jhan ende Lodewyc, Hertoghe ende Grave vorenghenoemt met onsen vorenghenoemde steden ende onse vorseide steden met ons bi ghemeenen consente ende rade, ziende ende maerkende dat de goede lieden van beeden landen Brabant ende Vlaendren, ondermaghet, onderhuwet, onderzeten ende ghebure zyn, zonder middel, den welken zaelghelic, ende ptofitelic es, in jonsten, in minnen, ende in eendrachticheden, te gadre te wesene, ende elc ane andren te clevene met vulmaecten wille ende ghetrower herten, ende ome dat dese vorseide twee lande vervullet zyn van groter menichte van volke, twelke niet ghesustineirt wesen mach zonder coepmanscepe, ende neringhe. Ziende oec ende maerkende dat coepmanscepe ende neringhe niet ghevoet wesen moghen, zonder in lande van payse, van rusten, ende van vryheden.....Omme te gadre ewelike te blivene, ende te zittene in payse, rusten, eendrachticheden, vryheden, coepmanscepe, ende neringhen, elc met andren, ende te scuwene vort an, ende te bevelne tusschen ons, ende onsen naercomers, alle zaken ende materien van ghescillen, van onpayse ende van bloetsturtinghe, ende in bescermenessen ende verhoetnessen van onsen live, goede, ende landen, ende onser naercomers, bi goeder deliberacien, ende ripen rade, omme de openbare profite, nutscepe ende orbore van den vorseiden tween landen, hebben wy Hertoghe ende Grave vors., over ons, onse naercomers, de edele van onsen tween landen, ruddren, knapen, manne, ende over hare naercomers, metten goeden lieden van den steden van beeden onsen landen vorenghenoemt. Ende wy comoengemayers, scepenen, raet ende alt comun van den vorseiden steden van Brabant borghmeesters, vooght, proosst, scepenen, raet, ende alt commun vanden vorseiden steden van Vlaendren, over ons ende onsen naercomers, met onsen vorseiden princhen ende in den name van al den andren steden, mayerien, landen ende castelryen vanden gheheelen van Brabant ende van Vlaenderen, gheordineirt, gheaccordeirt, overcenghedreghen, ende verbonden, in der manieren die hier naer volghet. Int eerste dat van desen daghe vort an ewelike ghedurende, so wie die enich van ons, Hertoghe ende Grave vors., van onsen naercommers, ofte van onsen landen, Brabant ofte Vlaendren, stoken, dringhen, besluten, veronrechten, ofte deren wilde, met orloghen ofte in wat anderre manieren, dat men ons ende de vorseide lande ofte enich vanden vorseiden landen, stoken, dringhe, besluten, veronrechten ofte deren wilde, in zielen, live, ofte goede, dat wy elc andren in goeden trouwen, ende zonder erghelist, bescudden, bescermen, helpen, verwaren ende ontcomeren zouden met live ende met goede, welken tiden ende alzo menichwaerven dat wys ofte enich van ons liedeu verzocht wesen zullen up ons selves cost, ende ghelyc ons selves lande. Behouden dien dat de ghene die den andren in helpen, bescudde ende succourse comen, souden moghen nemen redenlike ende tamelike in sanders land foinge te haren paerden.....Item dat wy, Hertoghe, ende Grave vors., onse naercomers, ofte enich van ons lieden, onse lande van Brabant, ende van Vlaendren, ofte enich van den tween landen nemermeer orloghe beghinnen, ofte voren anegripen, moghen up yemene, zonder den raet, wille ende tconsent van den tween landen vors. ofte het ne ware dat up ons Hertoghe ende Grave vors., up onse naercommers, ofte up enich van ons lieden, ofte enich van onsen naercomers, uppe onse vorseide twee lande ofte enich van dien landen, orloghe, quetsinghe ofte dere voren beghonnen ware, bi enighen princhе, ofte andren persoen, dat wy ons ende onse vorseide twee lande, elc tsine, zonder tconsent ende den raet van den andren verhoeden, bescudden, bescermen, ende verwaren mochten in dit stic. Ende danne ware elc andren sculdech ghehulpech te sine in der manieren dat verclaerst es int eerste point van desen verbinden. Item waert zo dat wy eneghe orloghe te gadre beghonnen, ofte ghemeene aneghegaen waren up yemene, ofte wanconst de eene ome des anders zake beiaghet ofte ghecreghen hadden, dat de een heere, ende syn land, zonder tconsent van den andren heere ende zinen lande, nemermeer vrede, bestand, pays, nocht acord maken soude. Item hebben wy ghelooft ende gheloven, elc andren, dat wy omme de vorseide twee lande te houdene in goeden payse, coepmanscepen, ende neringhen, zullen helpen beraden ende troesten, de een den andren, met al onser macht, ende in allen zaken, ende hebben ghenomen ende nemen al nu elc van ons lieden, binnen sire macht ende heerscepyen beede bi watre ende te lande de lieden ende alle de inwonnende van den andren lande ende elken zonderlinghe in onse bescaermenesse ende zeker behoed, ende int ghelike alle coeplieden, van so wat lande zy zyn, hare goet, haer coepmanscepen, ende hare messnieden, comende, wesende, ende keerende binnen den palen vanden vorseiden tween landen, betalende hare rechte tolne, costumen ende sculden, ende van haren mesdaden hare amenden naer wette ende usagen van den lande. Ende es onse ghemeene consent, ende begherte, dat de coeplieden vanden vorseiden tween landen, hem paisivelike onderlinghe gheneren, ende dat elc copen mach in sanders land alle manieren van coepmanscepen, ende die voeren, ofte doen voeren, binnen sinen lande te sinen profite zonder belet ofte verbot van yemene, betalende dat zy sculdech zyn te betaelne in der manieren dat vorseit es. Item hebben wy gheordineirt omme de coepmanscepen, ende neringhen te behoudene den vorseiden tween landen, dat men ordineren, ende slaen sal eene ghemeene munte, goet ende waerdech, die haren loop hebben sal in beeden den landen vors. de welke sal bliven staende in eenen pointe, zonder erghen ende zonder verwandelen te eweliken daghen of het ne ware by ghemeene consente ende overeendraghene van den princhen, ende beeden den gheheelen landen boven gheseit, ende daer toe sal men nemen, ende kiesen twee persone van elx heeren weghe vors. eenen persoen ute elkere van den drien goeden steden van Brabant vors. dats te wetene, Loevene, Brucele ende Andwerpen, ende eenen persoen ute elkere van den drien goeden steden van Vlaendren, dats te wetene. Ghend, Brucghe ende Ypre, die waerdeine der af wesen zullen, dats te wetene de waerdeine ute Brabant ghecoren, de vlaendersche munte waerderende, ende de waerdeine ute Vlaendren ghecoren de brabantsche munte waerderende, de welke waerdeine ute Brabant comen zullen in de stede van Ghend, ende de waerdeine ute Vlaendren, in de stede van Lovene, telken drien maenden, ofte cortre bi also dat hem orbore ende profyt dinct teweliken daghen ghedurende, ende zullen hare assaye doen loyalike, ende in goeder trouwen, ende up den eed die sy daer af doen zullen tallen tiden dat mense vermaken of verniewen sal.

Daer bi es te wetene, dat alle andre munten, zonder dese die loep hebben zullen binnen den vorseiden tween landen, ghepryst ende ghewaerdert zullen wesen naer der rechter waerde ende prise van der ghemeenre munte vorseit. ITEM wart zo dat wy ofte enich van ons lieden, ofte onse naercomers, of enich van hemlieden te eeneghen daghen, de een van den andren ons van onrechte te beclaghene hadden, ofte doleirne in zo wat manieren, in zo wat zaken ofte hoe menichwaerven het wesen mochte, waert van zaken der princhen, den landen, den steden, den castelryen, ofte singuleren personen touchierende, dat de ghene die hem te beclaghene hadden, de zake van haerre clachte ombieden souden bi boden ofte bi ghescriften, den heere, den goeden steden van den andren lande, ofte den ghenen wies lieden ende subgiten men die mesdaet ane leoghen soude ende verzouken daer af recht ende beteringhe naer der mesdaet, ende zo ware die heere, zine steden, ofte de ghene die aldus verzocht ende ghesummeirt wesen soude, dat onrecht ende die mesdaet sculdech te beterne, ofte te doen beterne, ende te doen berechtene, den ghenen wien het touchieren ende aneghaen soude binnen acht daghen naest volghende der tyt dat zys eerst verzocht wesen souden. Ende int stic dat dese zaken niet af gheleit ende ghebetert worden binnen dien acht daghen, also vorsiet es. Omme te verhoedene dat nemermeer, te eneghen daghen, risen noch spruten moghen, orloghen, gescillen, ofte discorde tusschen ons Hertoghe ende Grave vors., tusschen onsen naercomers, tusschen onsen vorseiden tween landen, noch tusschen eneghen steden, castelryen, ofte singuleren personen van den vorseiden tween landen, hebben wy gheaccordert ende verbonden al nu, dat elc van ons Hertoghe ende Grave vors., ofte van onsen naercommers ewelike ghedurende, ende tallen tiden dits te doene wesen sal, nemen sal twee goede lieden van sinen rade, elke van den drien goeden steden van Brabant, enen scepene ende elke van den drien goeden steden van Vlaendren vorseit, eenen scepene, de welke tiene persone vergadren zullen in dat land daer de ghene toe behoeren die hem beclaghende zyn ende in eene van den drien goeden steden van dien lande die naest es der stede daer dat onrecht ghedaen ofte gesprunt es, binnen achte daghe naer dien dat zys vermaent wesen zullen zonder fraude. Ende zullen doen openbaerlike haren eed, als zy vergadert wesen zullen in presentien elc van andren, up de beleghe ewangelie loyalike te ondervindene, ende te inquireirne trechte ende tware vandien clachten, geschillen ofte discorden, ende die te termineirne, te sententierne ende te accordeirne naer rechte ende redenen, zonder eneghe partye daer in te draghene, ende zullen beletten ende verhoeden alle zaken ende materien van discorde, ende ne zullen ute diere steden nemmermeer sceeden of het ne ware dat zy ofte enich van hemlieden bi zonnescine der ute voere ende binnen dien zelven daghe bi zonnescine weder der in quamen, tote der tyt dat zy alle de zaken daer zy omme vergadert wesen souden ghetermineirt, vereffent, ghepoint, ende gheaccordeirt zullen hebben, den welken tienen personen die aldus ghecoren ende ghedeputeirt wesen zullen, ende also menichwaerven als te doen wesen zal, wy ende elc van ons lieden over ons ende onsen naercomers gheven al nu vulle macht, auctoriteit, ende speciael bevelen, die zaken daer zy toe gecozen, ende ghedeputeirt wesen sullen te inquireirne, te termineirne, te sententierne, vereffenne ende te accordeirne inder manieren dat vorseit es. Ende gheloven alle ende elc van ons lieden, bi hem, over ons, ende over onse naercommers, te houdene ende te vulcomene wel ende ghestadelike al tgond dat bi dien tienen ghedeputeirden, gheinquireirt, ghetermineirt, ghewyst, vereffent, ende gheaccordeirt wesen sal in allen dien zaken ende in elke zonderlinghe, zonder nemmermeer iet te doene ofte te attempteirne in contrarien. Gheviele oec dat enich van den vorseiden tienen personen quame van den live ter doot, binnen den terminen dat zy vergadert waren omme te traitierne, eer dat zy hare last gheterminеirt souden hebben, zo es onse consent ende wille hoe menichwaerven het gheviele dat de ghene bi wien dien persoen ghecoren ende ghedeputert was, eenen andren vanden zelven rade ofte scependome kiese ende stelle in sine stede binnen derden daghe naer dien dat mens verzocht wesen sal zonder fraude, den welken wy ende elc van ons lieden, over ons, ende over onse naercommers, gheven al nu, alzulke macht, auctoriteit ende bevelen in allen zaken, als dandre hadde eer hi quam van den live ter doot, ende zullen dese ghedeputeirde ende elc van hem lieden bedwonghen ende gheconstringeirt zyn, de vorseide commissie ende lastinghe te anegane ende te doene inder vorseider manieren bi den ghenen diese kiesen, ende deputeren zullen, bi also dat daer of enich overhorech wesen wilde ofte in ghebreke. Waert oec zo dat de vors. tiene persone ofte enich van hem lieden up enich stic daer zi mede ghelast wesen souden beghaerden den raet van den ghenen daer hi bi ghecoren ware, dat zy hem beraden mochten, an de ghene die van den zelven rade, ofte scependoume wesen souden, mids dien dat zy ute diere stede daer de commissarisse vergadert wesen zullen niet sceeden zouden, zonder inder manieren dat vorseit es. Item hebben wi gheloofť ende gheloven, elcandren in goeden trouwen, dat omme zake die ghescien ofte ghevallen mach, tusschen ons of tusschen enich van ons lieden, tusschen onsen naercomers, of tusschen enich van hem lieden, wy noch onse naercomers ne zullen doen of nemen andre wrake, noch orloghe porren, noch pandinghe doen doen de een up den andren, zonder de clachten doende ende daer af recht heesschende ane de ghene die daer toe ghedeputeirt wesen zullen inder manieren dat vorseit es. Ende ne zullen eneghe zaeken doen noch ghedoghen te doene, daer coepmanscepe bi belet wesen mach, vryhelike te gane ende te keerne van den eenen lande in dandre, hare recht betalende also boven gheseit es. Item hebben wy gheaccordeirt ende verboden, omme alle de pointen die hier in ghescreven staen, ende elc point zonderlinghe ghestadelike te doen houdene te eeweliken daghen zonder breken, dat waert zo, dat wy Hertoghe ende Grave vorseit, ofte enich van ons lieden, onsen naercommers ofte enich van hem lieden te eeneghen daghen ieghen dese verbonde ofte jeghen enich point dat in dese lettren ghescreven es staken of ghinghen in zo wat manieren het ware, bi ons of bi andren persoen dat daer bi dese ordinanchen ende accorde van minder waerde ofte min gestade niet wesen zouden. Nemaer dat de ander heere ende beede de gheheele lande vors. dien here die dese zaken in enich point breken wilde constraingeren, ende bedwinghen souden met al haren vermoghene te doene houdene dese ordinanchen ende elc point zonderlinghe in der manieren dat zy gheordineirt ende hier ghescreven zyn. Ende ne zullen ghedoghen de vorseide twee lande, elc van sinen heere ende prinche die hier of rebel ofte contrarie wesen wilde, dat hi nemermeer bi hem, of bi andren persoen, eneghe renten, profite, baten, amenden ofte andre vordeele heffen zal, ontfaen, ofte in sine orbore in enegher manieren laten comen tote der tyt, dat zy alle dese verbonde, vorworden, ende accorde, ende elc point zonderlinghe wel ende ghetrouwelike houden ende vulcomen zullen. Waert oec zo, dat enich van den vorseiden landen, Brabant ofte Vlaendren, eenighe singulere steden, castelryen, mayeryen, ofte singulere persone, zo wie zy waren van den eenen vorseiden lande ofte van beeden, jeghen dese verbonde ofte jeghen enich point dat der in ghescreven es, staken of ghingen, in zo wat manieren het wesen mochte, dat daer omme dese ordinanchen ende acorde niet min bliven souden, goet vast ende ghestade. Nemaer dat beede de heeren ende princhen metgaeders den landen, steden, castelryen, mayeryen, ende communen die dese verbonde wel houden souden, de andre rebelle ende overhoreghe constraingeren, ende bedwinghen zullen, zonder enich delay met al haerre macht ende met allen manieren van constrainten die zy up hem lieden ende up hare goet doen zullen moghen, tote der tyt dat zy alle dese verbonde, voorwaerden, acorde ende elc point bi hem wel ende ghestadelike houden ende vulcomen zullen. Item omme dat alle daghe niewe zaken ende materien sprutten, risen ende vore oghen comen daer den vorseiden landen af come mochte commer ende profyt, zo zyn wy gheaccordert, elc met andren, dat de vorseide twee heeren, ende hare naercomers, ende de vorseide sesse goede steden van den vornoemden tween landen, elkes jaers ewelike ghedurende, te drien terminen, van haren lieden zenden ende vergadren zullen, dats te wetene up de viertiensten dach naer de lichtemesse onser vrouwen, binnen der steden van Ghend, up den viertiensten dach naer sente Jans dach middels zomers in de stede van Brucele, ende up den viertiensten dach, alre heleghen dach, in de stede van Aelst. Ten welken steden ende vergaderinghen, men ordineren, ende overeendraeghen sal, alle manieren van zaken, ende goeden pointen die met desen acorde ende verbonde ghaen moghen, ende die den vorseiden tween landen inbringhen moghen nutscip, orbore ende profyt. Ende omme dat wy ende elc van ons lieden willen ende begheren, dat dese payse, acorde, vorwaerden, ende verbonde die in desen lettren ghescreven staen, zyn ende bliven wel ghetrouwelike ende vaste ghehouden ende vulcomen, teeweliken daghen, zonder in enich point, ofte artikel daer tsieghen te gane, of te doene in eenegher manieren, hebben wy, Hertoghe ende Grave vors. over ons, over onse naercomers, over de edele van den vorseiden tween landen, rudders, knapen, manne, over haere naercomers ende over alle dandre steden, castelryen, mayerien, ende communen van onsen vorseiden tween landen, die hier specialike niet ghescreven zyn, ende over hare naercommers met onsen steden vorenghenoemt, ende zy met ons over hem ende hare naercomers, ende inden name van den tween gheheelen landen vors., alle dese zaken, acorde ende vorworden, ende elc point zonderlinghe, ghelooft ende verbonden, de een den andren, bi onsen rudderscepe, bi onser trouwen, zekerheden, ende bi onsen eede openbaerlike ghedaen, ende gheleit onse handen up te heleghe ewangelie, te houdene, ende te doen houdene te eweliken daghen zonder breken, ende metgaeders desen hebben wy ghelooft, ende gheloven elc andren, dat wy nemermeer zouken zullen noch ghedoghen te zoukene dispensatie, ofte verlaet van pauesse, van coninghe, van eenegben souverain, ofte van eneghen andren prelaet ofte prince, no absolutie van onsen gheloven, ofte van onsen eeden, die wy hier ghedaen hebben, ende ne zullen laten, omme verbot, ofte bevelen van eneghenoverheere, wy en zullen houden alle de zaken die hier in ghescreven zyn, ende elc point bi hem wel ende ghestadelike, ende ne zullen ons stellen daer of in eneghen blivene of vinderscepe, noch en sullen quite scelden, de een den andren van enegher saken, die vorseit es, noch en zullen laten, omme eneghe zake die herte ghepensen mach, of die ghescien mach, wy en zullen houden, de een den andren, alle de vorworden, pointe ende artiklen, ende elke zonderlinghe, die in dese lettren ghescreven staen. Ende al noch hebben wy ghelooft, de een den andren, ende gheloven, over ons, ende onsen naercomers, omme alle dese saken bet te verzekerne, dat achter tlyf van ons Hertoghe ende Grave vors., de ghene die ons lande ende heerscepyen, alse oire, ende naercomers bezitten zullen, vore den tyt dat zy ontfanghen wesen zullen ter heerscepyen alse Hertoghe ofte Grave, elc van hem lieden voren doen sal, alzulke eede, obligatien, ende ghelooften alse wy ghedaen hebben, ende boven ghescreven syn. Ende ne zullen ghedoghen van deser tyt vort an, nochte onse naercommers in haren tyt, dat enich persoen, gheroupen zy ten rade van ons, ofte van onsen naercommers, hi en sal doen voren eede bi sire trouwen, ende up de heleghe ewangelie te helpene ende te radene de payse, acorde, verbonde, ende alle de zaken, die in dese lettren ghescreven staen, te houdene met al zire macht, gheheelike ende vulcomenlike zonder nemermeer eneghe zake te secghene, te doene noch te radene in contrarien. Ende in alzulker manieren, zullen beloven ende zwaeren de scepenen, baillue, dandre rechters, ende officyers van onsen steden ende landen vors. ten beghinsele van haren officien ende staten, ende al diere ghelike alle manne ter tyt dat zy haer leen ontfaen zullen van ons Hertoghe ende Grave vors. ende van onsen naercomers. Ende es te wetene dat alle de vorseide ordinanchen, vorworden ende verbonden, ende elc point zonderlinghe, ghemaect, ghelooft, verbonden, ghezekert ende ghezworen zyn, behouden in allen andren zaken die hier niet ghescreven zyn, den vryheden, den wetten, costumen ende usagen van elker stede, castelrye, ende mayerie van den tween landen boven gheseit. IN ORCONTSCEPEN van desen dinghen hebben wy Hertoghe ende Grave boven gheseit, over ons ende onsen naercomers, metgaeders onsen steden, dats te wetene van Brabant, Loevene, Brucele, Antwerpen, Shertoghenbossche, Tienen ende Leewe, ende wy Arnoud bider gracien ons heeren, abt van Gemblours der ordine sente Benedictus van den bisscopdoume van Ludeke ter beden van den scepenen, ende al den comune vander stad van Nivele over hem lieden, ende haren naercomers, bider redenen, dat zy gheenen ghemeenen zeghel hebben, ende van Vlaendren, Ghend, Brucghe, Ypre, Cortrike, Audenaerde, Aelst ende Gheroudsberghe, ende onse vors. steden mes ons, over hem, ende haren naercomers, ende in de name van den tween gheheelen landen boven gheseit, dese lettren ghezegelt met onsen zeghelen huuthanghende. Ende omme de meerre verzekerthede van allen den zaken, vorworden, ende verbonden vernoemt, te houdene ende te doen houdene, wel ende loyalike, hebben wy ghebeden, ende verzocht, ane de edele van onsen tween landen, dats te wetene wy, Hertoghe vors. ane onse ghetrouwe Otten heere van Kuyc, Willemme heere van Huerne, ende van Gaesbeke, Thomase van Diest heere van Zelem, Willemme heere van Wesemale maerscalc van Brabant, Willemme van Duvenvoorde heere van Oesterhout, Jhanne heere van Rotselaer drussate van Brabant, Jhanne van Loen heere van Agimont, ende van Walem, Heinric Bertoud heere van Duffle, Jhanne van Levedale borghgrave van Brucele, Willemme heere van Boecstele, Jhanne heere van Sombreffen, Jhanne van Kuyc heere van Hoestraten, Lodewike heere van Diepenbeke, Diedericke van Walencourt heere van Aa, ende maerscalc van Henegouwen, Heinric van Walencourt heere van Faverchines, Lodewike van Berlaer heere van Helmont. Gillisse van Quaderebbe heere van Berge, Arnoude van Aelbeke, Jhanne Pyliser, Jhanne van Kersbeke, Hermanne van Os, Lonisse van der Borgh rentmeester van Brabant, Jhanne van Meldert, Jhanne Pulleman drussate van Brabant, Jhanne van Wineghem, Daneele van Bouchout, Heinric van Botersem Heinricke van Walem, Raese van Graven heere van Lyntre, Goesswine heere van Godsenhoven, Ywaine van Meldert, Arnoude van den Wiere, Willemme van den Bossche, Gheraerde van Vorselaer borghgrave van Gheldenake, Jhanne van Ymmersele, Goline van Vilvoorden Utenhove, Jhanne van Crayenem, Jhanne van Scoenhoven, Kaerlen vander Rivieren, ende Woutren heere van Melyn ruddren. Ende wy Grave vorseit ane onse ghetrouwe Heinricke van Vlaendren heere van Nieneve, Philipse heere van Axele, Symoene van Mirabel heere van Pereweiz, Gheraerde heere van Raesseghen ende van Lens, Rasen van Gavere heere van Heremeiz, Arnoude van Gavre heere van Scorense, Jhanne van den Gruuthuse heere van Ha, Rogiere Bryseteeste heere van Buxhem, Jhanne van Axele, Oliviere heere van Pouke, Willemme van Nevele, Goessine van den Moure, Wulfaerde van Ghistel den oem, Gheraerde van Raeseghem heere van Crayenem, Gheraerde van Outre borghgrave van Ypre, Jhanne van Belle, Justase Passcharis, Rogiere heere van Lichtervelde, Zeghere van Dronghene heere van Melle, Gheraerde van Ghistele, Daneele van Rosenbeke, Rogiere Bryseteesten, Symoen van der Maelsteden, Rogiere van Vaernewyc, Gheraerde van Mourseke, Willemme van Straten, Jhanne van Poelvoorde, Jhanne van Masseminne, Raesse van Erpe ruddren, Jhaene van Ayshove, Ghiselbrecht van Leeuwerghem, Gheraerde van Massemme, Daneele van Dronghene, Jhanne van Herseele, Jhanne van den Moure, Arnoude Bernagen, Jhanne van Huntkerke, Lonisse van Mourkerke, Hughen van Steelant ende Jhanne van Lokerne cnapen, dat zy ende elc van hem lieden de vorseide ordinanchen, accorden, overeendragheene, vorworden ende verbonden, inder vorseider manieren willen ghloven ende zweren te houdene ende te doen houdene met al haren loyalen vermoghene, ende dat zy hare zeghele hanghen willen aen dese presente lettren, metten onsen, der steden, ende sabs boven gheseit, in orcontscepen van haren wille, ende consente. Ende waert zo dat gheviele in eneghen tiden, dat wy, onse oire, ofte onse naercomers ghinghe of wilden gaen, jeghen dese verbonde, in enegher manieren, dat niet ghevallen sal, of God wille, dat de edele boven gheseit, ofte enich van hem lieden niet ghehouden souden wesen ons te helpene in enigher manieren in dat stic, nemaer dat zy houden zouden de vorseide accorde ende verbonde, te eweliken daghen, ende elc point bi hem also vorseit es. Ende int stic daer zy ofte enich van hem lieden doen zullen dat wi hem ghebeden, ende verzocht hebben, wy noch onse naercomers, en zullen hem nemmermeer daer af wanconst draghen, noch zullen hem daer omme grief ofte scade doen, noch ghedoghen te doene, nemaer in dat doende zullen wise verhoeden, en bescermen, loyalike tsieghen allen lieden. Ende waert zo dat enich van onsen rechters, officyers, ofte subgiten, of daden in enich point in contrarien van den vorseiden zaken, ende wy Hertoghe ende Grave boven ghenoemt, ofte onse naercomers waren in ghebreke, de ghene die dat doen zouden te corrigeirne, wi willen, ende verzouken, ane de edele van onsen landen dat zy, ende elc van hem lieden met onsen vorseiden steden, helpen met al haerre macht, dat de ghene die dat ghedaen zullen hebben worden ghecorrigeirt naer den mesgripe. Ende wy de edele boven gheseit, ter beden ende verzouke van onsen lieven ende verminden heeren vors., hebben ghelooft, ghezekert ende ghezworen, bi onsen eeden, openbaerlike ghedaen over ons ende over onse naercomers, te houdene ende te vulcommene, ghestadelike zonder breken, alle de zaken die in desen lettren ghescreven staen. Ende in kennessen en orcontscepen der waerheit, hebben wy ane dese presente lettren ghehanghen ons zeghelen, metten zeghelen van onsen lieven ende verminden heeren, ende haren steden, ende sabbts boven gheseit. Ende waert zo dat gheviele dat enich zeghel die vorseit es, een ofte meer ghebrake ofte achter bleve te hanghene ane dese jeghenwordeghe lettren, daer bi en willen wy niet dat dese zaken ende verbonde zyn van minderre waerde, nemaer dat zy zyn ende bliven also ghestade, ende van alzulker macht, als zy wesen zouden, of alle de zeghelen daer an vulcomenlike ghehanghen waren. ENDE al noch hebben wy Hertoghe ende Grave vorseit, over ons, ende onsen naercomers, met onsen vorseiden steden, ende onse steden met ous, over hem ende haren naercomers, ende in de name van den tween gheheelen landen boven gheseit, ghelooft ende gheloven, elc andren, dat waert zo dat dese jeghenwordeghe lettren in eeneghe tide waren ghevioleirt, gheerghert ofte ghecorrumpeirt waert van parkemente, vander scrifturen, ofte van zeghelen, dat wy wedergheven ende verzeghelen zouden, den ghenen van ons die dies ghebrec hebben zoude alzulke lettren ende alzo suffichante als dese zyn, alzo varinghe als wy dies verzocht wesen zouden zonder fraude. Dit was ghedaen, ende gheaccordeirt te Ghend up den derden dach van der maent van December, int jaer ons heeren duzentich, drie hondertich, dertich ende neghene.

No. IV.*

De Fœdere cum Johanne de Monteforti, et de Comitatu Richmundiæ sibi concesso. †

Rex, omnibus ad quos, &c., Salutem.

Sciatis quod,

Cum illustris Johannes, Dux Britanniæ, et Comes de Monte Forti, Consanguineus noster carissimus, attendens injuriam, per Dominum Philippum de Valesio, super detentione regni Franciæ, nobis factam, zelo justitiæ contra dictum Philippum nobiscum fœdus pepigerit et amicitiæ firmitatem; et propter hoc idem Philippus dictum Comitatum de Monte Forti, cum pertinentiis; tanquam sibi confiscatum, in manum suam seisiri fecerit, et illum detineat sic seisitum;

Nos,

Affectionem multam, quam idem Dux nobis gratanter ostendit, meritò ponderantes, et proindè volentes indempnitati suæ prospicere, sicut decet, concessimus ei pro nobis, et hæredibus nostris, Comitatum Richemund', habendum et tenendum, cum castris, villis, hamelettis, feodis militum, advocationibus ecclesiarum, abbatiarum, prioratuum, hospitalium, capellarum, et aliarum domorum religiosarum, wardis, maritagiis, releviis, escaetis, piscariis, parcis, boscis, warennis, feriis, mercatis, libertatibus, liberis consuetudinibus, servitiis, tam liberorum tenentium quam nativorum, et omnibus aliis ad dictum Comitatum Richemund' qualitercumque et ubicumque spectantibus sive pertinentibus, eodem modo quo claræ memoriæ

* From No. III. to No. IX., inclusive of both, refer to the wars of Brittany, detailed in Chapters X., XI., XII., and XIII.

† Rymer, Fœdera, vol. ii. part ii. p. 1176.

Johannes, nuper Dux Britanniæ, et Comes Richemund', eundem tenuit Comitatum, quousque idem Dux dictum Comitatum de Monte Forti recuperaverit, vel sibi fuerit restitutus;

Ita quod idem Dux dictum Comitatum Richemund' cum prædictus Comitatus, de Monte Forti, sic per eum recuperatus, vel ei restitutus fuerit, nobis vel hæredibus nostris dimittere teneatur, nisi uberiorem gratiam, quam, continuando cum augmento penes nos gestum laudabilem, de exuberantiâ regiæ munificentiæ sperare poterit, sibi fecerimus in hâc parte.

In cujus, &c.

Teste Rege apud Westm. xxiv. die Septembris.

Per ipsum Regem.

No. V.

De Castris et Munimentis, infra Ducatum Britanniæ, pro Receptaculo Regis concedendis. *

Rex, omnibus ad quos, &c., Salutem.

Sciatis quod,

Cum inter nos et Almaricum de Cluzon, tutorem et custodem Johannis filii et hæredis Johannis Ducis Britanniæ et Comitis de Monti Forti, inter alia sit concordatum, quod omnia villæ, burgi, castra, fortalitia, et portus maris, in Ducatu Britanniæ, nobis tradantur et liberentur, custodienda per nos et nostros, pro receptamento et securitate nostri, et hominum nostrorum, ac salvatione partium illarum, durante guerrâ in partibus illis motâ, prout in quadam indenturâ, indè inter nos et prædictum Almaricum confectâ, pleniùs continetur;

Nos,

De fidelitate dilecti et fidelis nostri, Walteri de Manny, pleniùs confidentes, assignavimus et deputavimus ipsum ad omnia villas, burgos, castra, fortalitia, et portus maris, nobis in eodem Ducatu, juxta conventiones prædictas, liberanda, quæ pro nobis et nostris oportuna et necessaria viderit, nomine nostro recipiendum, et salvò et securè custodiendum, et custodiri faciendum, quousque aliud indè duxerimus ordinandum,

In cujus, &c.

Teste Rege, apud Westm. x. die Marrii.

Per ipsum Regem.

No. VI.

Will' de Bohun, Comes Northampton', Locum tenens in Regno Franciæ constituitur.

Rex, Consanguineo suo carissimo, Willielmo de Bohun, Comiti Norhampton, Salutem.

* Rymer, Fœdera, vol. ii. part ii. p. 1189. † Ibid. p. 1204.

Sciatis quod,

Cum inclitum regnum Franciæ ad nos sit jure successorio legitimè devolutum;

Nos,

Tam de adipiscendâ plenâ possessione quam de bono regimine dicti regni, summè soliciti, ac de vestris probitate, fidelitate, et industriâ, intimè confidentes, vos in regno prædicto, resorto, et pertinentiis suis universis, locum nostrum tenentem et capitaneum facimus et præficimus per præsentes;

Concedentes et committentes vobis merum et mixtum imperium, gladii potestatem, ac jurisdictionem omnimodam altam et bassam cognitionem et decisionem omnium causarum, tam criminalium quam civilium,

Cum potestate locum tenentes, capitaneos, judices, et ministros, quoscumque, prout expedire videritis, deputandi et amovendi,

Ac jus, quod nobis in dicto regno competit, vendicandi, petendi, et prosequendi, et eidem regno vos immiscendi, ac corporalem possessionem ipsius, et pertinentiarum ejusdem, etiam in manu forti, si oporteat, apprehendendi,

Excercitum congregandi et ducendi, de guerrâ equitandi, et contrarios et rebelles expugnandi et puniendi;

Ac omnes et singulos, qui ad pacem et obedientiam nostras venire voluerint, ad hujusmodi pacem et fidelitatem nostras admittendi, et eis pardonationis et remissionis gratiam faciendi, et eos super hoc assecurandi;

Ac omnia alia et singula, faciendi, et exercendi, quæ ad officium hujusmodi locum nostrum tenentis et capitanei pertinere noscuntur, et quæ pro recuperatione et conservatione jurium nostrorum ibidem, et bono regimine dicti regni necessaria vel oportuna fuerint, etiam si mandatum exigant speciale, et quæ nos facere possemus et debemus si præsentes illuc essemus;

Promittentes nos ratum et gratum habituros quicquid, nomine nostro, feceritis in præmissis, et quolibet præmissorum.

Et ideò dilectionem et fidelitatem vestras attentè rogamus, quatinùs, onus et honorem hujusmodi magnanimiter assumentes, circa recuperationem et conservationem jurium nostrorum prædictorum, et bonum regimen dicti regni, sic prudenter et strenuè laboretis, ut vestram fidelitatem et gestum laudabilem debeamus meritò commendare, et repensiva retributionis uberis præmiare.

Mandavimus enim Archiepiscopis, Episcopis, Ducibus, Marchionibus, Comitibus, Vicecomitibus, Baronibus, et personis aliis quibuscumque, in et de dicto regno existentibus, ut vobis, et deputandis per vos, in præmissis pareant humiliter et intendant.

In cujus, &c. pro nostro beneplacito duraturas, etc.

Dat' apud Wyndesore xx. die Julii.

Et mandatum est omnibus et singulis Archiepiscopis, Episcopis, Ducibus, Marchionibus, Comitibus, Vicecomitibus, Baronibus, et personis aliis quibuscumque, in et de regno Franciæ existentibus, quod præfatum Comitem ad præmissa facienda libenter et devotè recipiant, et sibi tanquam personæ Regis pareant et intendant humiliter in præmissis, taliter se habentes quod suæ debeamus devotionis pulchritudinem meritò commendare; scituri pro certo quod est intentionis nostræ humiliare superbos, et humilibus gratiam impartiri.

Dat' ut supra.

No. VII.

De prædicto Will de Bohun, Locum tenente in Ducatu Britanniæ creato.*

Rex, Consanguineo suo carissimo, Willielmo de Bohun Comiti Norhampton', Salutem.

Sciatis quod,

Cum quædam conventiones, inter nos ex parte unâ, et nobilem virum, Almaricum de Clizon, tutorem et curatorem Johannis de Britanniâ, filii et hæredis Johannis Ducis Britanniæ et Comitis de Monte Forti, pro dicto Johanne filio, et de dicto Ducatu Britanniæ hæredato et seisito, et pro præclarâ Johannâ de Flandria, ducissâ Britanniæ et comitissâ de Monte Forti, ex alterâ;

Et postmodum aliæ conventiones, inter dictos Almaricum, nomine tutorio seu curatorio, et Johannam, ac dilectum et fidelem nostrum Walterum de Manny pro nobis, initæ sint et firmatæ,

Prout in literis indentatis, indè confectis pleniùs continetur:

Et jam dicti, Almaricus et Johanna, per literas et nuncios instanter et devotè nos requisierint ut, cum parati sint nos Regem Franciæ recognoscere, et nobis, ut Regi Franciæ, homagium facere, ac castra, villas, et loca dicti ducatûs nobis reddere, ita quod pro expensis nostris, seu illorum, quos illuc pro defensione patriæ miserimus, redditus et proventus dicti ducatûs possimus, facere colligere, et de hiis propter hoc juxta nostrum libitum ordinare,

Velimus, ut Rex Franciæ et dominus eorum superior, contra molestantes eos super possessione dicti ducatûs defendere, et propter hoc ad dictas partes armatam potentiam destinare;

Nos,

Volentes conventiones prædictas, ut convenit, observare, et vassallos nostros defendere ut debemus,

Ac de probitate et circumspectione vestrâ providâ plenariè confidentes,

Vos in dicto ducatu capitaneum et locum nostrum tenentem præficimus et creamus, dantes et committentes vobis plenam potestatem, fidelitates et homagia, ac servitia nobis, ut Regi Franciæ, in dicto ducatu, et alia, juxta conventiones prædictas, debita et promissa, necnon liberationem et possessionem castrorum, villarum, et locorum dicti ducatûs petendi et recipiendi, nanciscendi et retinendi;

* Rymer, Fœdera, vol. ii. part ii. p. 1205.

Redditus et proventus dicti ducatûs pro defensione ejusdem colligendi et recipiendi,

Fideles nostros ibidem defendendi,

Et in hostes et rebelles nostros ibidem insurgendi, jurisdictionem omnem, nobis ibi competentem, excercendi,

Tutores et curatores dandi, decreta interponendi, et omnia alia et singula faciendi et excercendi, quæ ad officium capitanei et locum nostrum tenentis ibidem pertinere noscuntur, et quæ possemus facere si illuc personaliter præsens essemus.

Promittentes, &c. *ut supra mutatis mutandis usque ibi* præmissorum, et *tunc sic ;*

Et ideò dilectionem et fidelitatem vestram attentè rogamus, quatinùs, onus et honorem hujusmodi magnanimiter assumentes, circa præmissa omnia et singula, ut præmittitur, facienda et exequenda prudenter et strenuè laboretis, ut vestram fidelitatem et gestum laudabilem debeamus meritò commendare, et repensivâ retributionis uberis præmiare.

Mandavimus enim Archiepiscopis, Episcopis, Ducibus, Marchionibus, Comitibus, Vicecomitibus, Baronibus, et personis aliis quibuscumque, in et de dicto Ducatu existentibus, ut vobis, et deputandis per vos, in præmissis pareant humiliter et intendant.

In cujus, etc.

Teste Rege apud Wyndesore, xx. die Julii.

Et mandatum est omnibus et singulis Archiepiscopis, etc. prout supra mutatis mutandis.

No. VIII.

De Excercitu ad Partes transmarinas jam transmisso, et de Passagio Regis ordinato.*

Rex, venerabili in Christo Patri, I. eâdem gratiâ, Archiepiscopo Cantuar', totius Angliæ Primati, Salutem, &c.

Teste Rege apud Turrim London' xv. die Augusti.

Per ipsum Regem.

Consimile Breve dirigitur Archiepiscopo Eborum Angliæ Primati. Vid. M. xiv. de Dat' xxx. die Sept'.

No. IX.

Pro Roberto de Artoys, (ut dicitur) defuncto.†

Rex, collectoribus custumæ lanarum, coriorum, et pellium lanutarum in portu London', Salutem.

* Rymer, Fœdera, vol. ii. part ii. p. 1209.
† Ibid. p. 1215.

Mandamus vobis quod Henrico Galeys, attornato Roberti de Artoys defuncti, ut dicitur, undecim saccos et unum quartronum lanæ, de illis centum quinquaginta et octo saccis lanæ, quos eidem Roberto pro vadiis suis, et quorumdam hominum ad arma, et sagittariorum, secum ad partes Britanniæ in obsequium nostrum profectorum, in portu prædicto carcari, et ad partes transmarinas, solutâ dimidiâ marcâ pro quolibet dictorum undecim saccorum, et pro dicto quartrono, juxta ratam dimidiæ marcæ de sacco, absque securitate, de plata argenti, de quolibet saccorum eorumdem, juxta ordinationem, indè factam in Angliâ, reportandorum, duci permittatis.

Teste custode Angliæ, apud Kenyngton, xx. die Novembris.

No. X.

Letter from Edward III. to his Son.

"Très chier et très amé filtz, nous savoms bien qe vous desires mult de savoir bones novelx de nous et de notre estat; vous faceoms assavoir qe au partier du cestes nous esteioms heités de corps, Dieux en soit loié! desirant mesme ceo de vous oier et savoir. Très chier filtz, come nous est avenuz puis notre départir d'Engleterre vous faceoms assavoir qe nous avoms chivaché un graunt pièce en la duché de Bretaigne, le quele païs est rendue à notre obeisance od plusours bones villes et forcellettes; c'est assavoir la villes de Plouremell, et le chastiel et la ville de Malatrait, et le chastiel et la ville de Rondon qe sont bones villes et bien fermés. Et sachez que le sire de Clissoun qest un des plus grauntz de Peyto et quatre autres barons, c'est assavoir le sire de Lyac, le sire de Machecoille, le sire de Reiez, le sire de Reynes et autres chivalers du dit païs et lor villes et forcelettes qi sount droitement sour le fountz de France et de notre duchée de Gascoigne sount renduz à nostre pees, quele chose homme tient un graunt esploit à notre guerre, et avaunt l'escrivere du cestes nous avoms envoiez en lez parties de Nauntes notre cosyn de Northf, le comte de Warwick, Mons. Hugh le Despenser et aultres Banretz od graunt nombre ove cccc. hommes d'armes pour faire l'esploit qu'ils poiount. Et puis lour departir avoms novels qe le sire de Gasson et les barons suisditzse fusrent mys od un bon nombre des gentz d'armes en aide de notre dit cosin et sa compagnye; mais unquore à departir du cestes n'en avoms nulles novels de lour esploit, mais nous espoiroms d'aver hastiment bones od l'aide Dieux. Très chier filtz, sachez qe par l'avis et consail de les plus sages de notre ost avoms mys notre siége à la cité de Vanes qest le meillour ville de Bretaigne après la ville dè Nauntes, et pluis poet grever et restreindre la païs à notre obéisance; qar il nous estoit avis que si nous eussoms chivaché pluis avaunt saunz estre seur de la dite ville, le païs qest renduz à nous ne purroit tenir devers nous en nulle manere. Et auxint la dite ville est sour la mear et est bien fermez, issint qe si nous la puissoms aver il serra graunt esploit à notre guerre. Et sachez, très cher filtz, que Monsr. Lowis de Peiters, counte de Valentinès est capitain de la ville, et homme dist q'ils y sount bones gentz ovesque lui; mais nous espoiroms que par la puissance de Dieux nous aucroms bone issue; qar puis notre venue en cestes parties Dieu nous ad donné bone comencement et assetz d'esploiter pour le temps, loié en soit-il, et le païs est assetz pleinteouse des blés et de char. Mais toutz foitz, cher filtz, il covient qe vous excitez notre chaunceller et tresorer de envoir devers nous deniers, qar ils conussent bien notre estat. Chier, filtz sachez qe le tierce jour que nous fusmes herbergés au dite siége viendrent à nous un abbé et un clerc de par les cardinalx ovesque lour lettre pour nous requerre de eaux envoier sauve conduit pour venir devers nous; et nous disoient qe s'ils eussent conduit ils puissent estre devers nous entour les huit jours après. Et feissoms notre consail respondre as ditz messagiers et deliverer à eux noz lettres de conduyt pour mesmes le cardinalx pour venir à la ville de Maltrait à trente leages de nous, qestoit nadgairs renduz à nous et à notre pees; qar notre entent n'est pas qu'ils deivount pluis près aproscher notre ost qe la dite ville de Malatrait, pour plusours causes. Et sachez qe en quele plit qe nous sumes, od l'aide de Dieu, notre entent ne est toutz jours decliner à reson à quele heure qe nous serra offert. Mais qe covient que les cardinalx veignent issint devers nous ne pensoms mye delaier un jour de notre parpos, qar nous poioms bien penser de delaies qe nous avoms eu einz ces heures par tretis de eaux et des aultres. Chier filtz, à pluis tost qe nous eioms nule issue de notre siége ou d'autre busoigne qe nous touche nous vous manderoms les novelx toutdiz si en avaunt qe les messagiers puissent entre aler. Chier filtz, faites monstrer cestes lettres à l'erchevesque de Cauntirbirs et à ceaux de notre consail devers vous: chier filtz, Dieu soit gardein de vous. Doné soutz notre secré seal al siége de Vanes la veille de seint Nicholas. Très chier filtz, après l'escrivere du cestes lettres nous viendrent novels qe notre cosyn de North, et le comte de Warr, monseigneur Hughe le Despenser et lez aultres banerettes et lour companye onnt assiégé la ville de Nauntes, qar ils espoiront od l'aide de Dieux de faire esploit hastivement."

No. XI.

Letter of the Duke of Lancaster.

(See Chapter XX.)

Endroit des Novels saundroit: Sachez, que devaunt le feste de l'Assumpcion Notre Dame bien trois jours nous remuasmes de la Roel devers les parties de Bruggerak, et avoms assemblé illesqes toutz lez seigneurs de Gascoigne et autres gents, q'estoient hors de establies, à l'entent de chivacher, et avoms illesque consail ove leys seigneurs sus dits, si qe avaunt notre partir d'illesqes nous veinent ascuns gents chivalers et aultres pour demander trewes de par les Fraunceys qe gesoient unqore à siége devant Aquillon. Mais puisqe nous savoms qe monsieur le roi est arivé en Normandye, nous ne vodroms mye assentir à nulle trewe; et sour ceo les enemys se levèrent du siége la dismenge proschein devaunt le feste de Seint Barthu, et s'en départirent mult ledement, qar ils perdirent graunt partie de lour biens et de lour gentz, et lessérent lour tentes et tout le pluis de lour herneis: si que sitost qe nous le savoms nous tenismes avaunt notre chemyn en Angeneys, et venismes devaunt la Villeréal, q'est une bone ville du royalme, laquelle nous estoit rendu et aultres villes et chastiels d'entour tut plain. Et quaunt avoms establé cele ville et la païs, nous chivachoms tut la pays et alasmes droit à Tonynges et Aquillon, et les feismes establer auxy et la païs environ. Et puis reparasmes ariere à la Réole, et y demurrasmes bien huit jours, et avoms illesqes consail, et avoms illesqes tout la païs, et départismes notre ost en treis, et lessames le Seigneur de la Brette, Monsieur Bérard de Bret, seneschal de Gascoyne, Monsieur Alexandre de Camont, et aultres devers les parties de Besades; le Seigneur Duracs et aultres seigneurs de Augeneys lessames celes parties et tenismes avaunt notre chemyn vers les parties de Centogne od mil hommes d'armes. Et remuasmes le douzième jour de Septembre, et geusmes en une bone ville qe nous fust mesme le jour renduz, la ville de Salveterre. Et lendemayn quaunt nous avoms pris serment de céaux de la ville, nous tenismes avaunt notre chemyn bien sept jours saunz assaillir une ville ou chastiel tanqe nous venismes au chastiel de Nau qu'est sour la rivière de Charente, et illeosqes feismes reparailler le pount q'estoit debrusé qar l'eawe estoit si perfounde qe hommes ne poet passer par ailleurs, et passames illeosqes lendemain. Et avoms cele jour novels qe les gents Monsieur Wautier de Mauny, q'avoient conduyt des Frannceis d' aler au roy par terre, furent pris et emprisonés deinz la ville de Seint John Aungelyn; et ensi fustrent, et Mounseigneur Wautier estoit eschapé soy tierce à graunt payne: si qe nous tenismes avaunt notre chemyn devers la dite ville et l'assaillames et fust gayné par force, Dieu mercy, et les gentz gettés hors du prisone et demureasmes huit jours et establioms la ville. Et ceulx de la ville nous fisrent serment et deviendrent Engleis, et deivent de lour costage demene duraunt la guerre trover CC hommes d'armes et DC à pié en garnisoun de la dite ville; et en temps du peès acrestrent lour rentes au roy pluis par an q'ils'ne soleient paier à roi de Fraunce chescun an de III. mil escutz. Et lendemayn de Seint Michel nous chivachasmes vers la cité de Peiters, et geusmes une nuyt devaunt la ville de Lysingham q'est une forte ville, si qe homme la aloit assailler, et fust gagné par assaut, et le chastiel nous fust rendu q'est un de pluis nobles chastiels et de pluis fort qe sount garres en Fraunce ou en Gascoigne; et nous establoms le chastiel et la ville, et y lessames bien C hommes d'armes et aultres gents à pié, ovesqe eux et chivachasmes devaunt la citée de Peiters et ils requeresmes. Mais ils ne voleient rien faire, qar il lour sembla lour ville assetz forte, et si estoient assetz des gentz, si qe homme l'assailla, qe fust le proschein mersgerdy après le Seint Michel ; et fust par force gayné, et toutz ceaux de la ville fusrent pris ou mortz. Et les seigneurs q'estoient dedeinz, un évesqe et bien IIII barons, quaunt ils virent la prise de la ville s'en alèrent d'autre part. Et nous demurrasmes y bien huit jours ; et estoioms à l'escrivere des gentz de cestes al ville de Seint Johan. Et avons de bones villes et chastiels qe nous sount rendus entour, et ensi avons fait un beal chivaché, le Dieux mercy, et sumes revenuz à Seint Johan, et pensoms d'illesqes tenir notre chemyn devers Burdeaux, quelle chose sera forte à faire à ceo qe les enemys sount quillez en païs ; mais espoiroms de faire bien od l'ayde de Dieux.

END OF THE FIRST VOLUME.

London :
Printed by A. Spottiswoode,
New-Street-Square.

CPSIA information can be obtained at www.ICGtesting.com
227811LV00003B/3/P

9 781144 781567